The Poetry and Poetics of

Olga Sedakova

Publication of this book has been made possible,
in part, through support from the

Foundation for Research in Logic and Philosophy, Moscow.

The Poetry and Poetics of Olga Sedakova

Origins, Philosophies, Points of Contention

Edited by

Stephanie Sandler, Maria Khotimsky, Margarita Krimmel, *and* Oleg Novikov

With translations of Olga Sedakova's Writings by

Martha M. F. Kelly

THE UNIVERSITY OF WISCONSIN PRESS

The University of Wisconsin Press
1930 Monroe Street, 3rd Floor
Madison, Wisconsin 53711-2059
uwpress.wisc.edu

Gray's Inn House, 127 Clerkenwell Road
London EC1R 5DB, United Kingdom
eurospanbookstore.com

Originally published as *Ol'ga Sedakova: Stikhi, smysly, prochteniia: Sbornik nauchnykh statei*, copyright © 2017 by Novoe Literaturnoe Obozrenie, Moscow

Printed in the United States of America

This book may be available in a digital edition.

Library of Congress Cataloging-in-Publication Data
Names: Sandler, Stephanie, 1953–, editor. | Khotimsky, Maria, editor. | Krimmel, Margarita, editor. | Novikov, Oleg, editor.
Title: The poetry and poetics of Olga Sedakova : origins, philosophies, points of contention / edited by Stephanie Sandler, Maria Khotimsky, Margarita Krimmel, and Oleg Novikov.
Other titles: Ol'ga Sedakova (Novoe literaturnoe obozrenie). English
Description: Madison, Wisconsin : The University of Wisconsin Press, [2019] | Originally published as: Ol'ga Sedakova : Stikhi, smysly, prochteniia: Sbornik nauchnykh statei, © 2017 by Novoe Literaturnoe Obozrenie, Moscow. | Includes bibliographical references and index.
Identifiers: LCCN 2018018515 | ISBN 9780299320102 (cloth : alk. paper)
Subjects: LCSH: Sedakova, Ol'ga—Criticism and interpretation. | Sedakova, Ol'ga—Influence. | Russian poetry—20th century—History and criticism.
Classification: LCC PG3486.E24 Z8313 2019 | DDC 891.71/44—dc23
LC record available at https://lccn.loc.gov/2018018515

Contents

Illustrations

Acknowledgments

This volume of essays has benefitted from many forms of assistance—logistical, financial, and editorial. At the University of Wisconsin Press, we have enjoyed splendid advice and warm support from Gwen Walker. We are grateful for the detailed comments of two anonymous readers for the University of Wisconsin Press, which improved our volume in many ways. Superb editorial assistance and work in preparing the volume for publication was provided by Jenya Mironava and Philip Redko, and we appreciate as well the careful copyediting by Marlyn Miller.

Our larger project to produce a volume of essays dedicated to the poetry of Olga Sedakova, to appear in both Russian and English, was made possible through the generous financial support of the Moscow Foundation for Research in Logic and Philosophy (Fond Logiko-filosofskikh issledovanii). A Russian version of this volume in different form appeared as *Ol'ga Sedakova: Stikhi, smysly, prochteniia; Sbornik nauchnykh statei* (Moscow: Novoe literaturnoe obozrenie, 2017), and we are grateful to the editor at NLO, Irina Prokhorova, for her quick embrace of our project. Most essays from that volume were shortened for this one. Translations of seven essays into English for this volume, from their Russian, Italian, and German originals, were well executed by a range of translators credited in each case and in our list of contributors. We acknowledge with appreciation the excellent editorial work done by Philip Redko and Maria Vassileva on two of the translated essays in this volume, by Aleksandr Kutyrkin and Vera Pozzi, in addition to the essays where they are named as translators.

Translation has played multiple roles in the creation of this book, in fact, and translation and adaptation form the subject of more than one of our essays. We also wanted our book to add to the body of available translations of Sedakova's own writings into English. Two of our authors, Benjamin Paloff and Andrew Kahn, have done their own translations, and Emily Grosholz has used a range of published translations in writing her essay. But nearly all of our essays feature the new translations by Martha M. F. Kelly. She has translated all passages from Olga Sedakova's prose and poetry that are not otherwise marked, and we feel that she has captured Sedakova's style and tone with great beauty. We are immensely grateful to her for that work, and we regard her translations here as another way in which our collection of essays tries to establish a firmer foundation for the study of Sedakova's work.

Our greatest debt is to Olga Sedakova, for the texts that have inspired these essays and for her extensive consultations with us as editors and with a number of authors who contributed to this volume. Her generosity of spirit in discussing her work have made us all the happier to be offering this first volume of essays dedicated to her writings and to her role in creating a vibrant contemporary literature in and beyond Russia.

A Note on Transliteration and Sources

We have used a modified Library of Congress transliteration system for all bibliographical matter in this volume, although in the text itself we have used further modifications to Anglicize familiar names (giving endings as "y" rather than "ii," for example). We have preserved markers of soft signs in all bibliographic matter but dropped them in most Anglicized names in the text, and thus refer to Olga (not Ol'ga) Sedakova. But strict transliteration is preserved in the reference matter, including in the chronology.

All Russian quotations from the work of Olga Sedakova, unless otherwise noted, refer to *Chetyre toma: Stikhi, perevody, poetica, moralia* (Moscow: Universitet Dmitriia Pozharskogo/Russkii fond sodeistviia obrazovaniiu, 2010). Volume and page number are given parenthetically within the text or occasionally in notes, and, because not all readers may have access to the four-volume set, we have also included the title of the quoted material as well to make it easier to find in other editions. Readers can also find nearly all of Sedakova's writings in Russian, including those published after the four-volume set appeared in 2010 as well as many translations, on the excellent website www.olgasedakova.com and in multiple other volumes published by the poet. Those volumes, as well as translations of Sedakova's work into other languages, are listed in the chronology.

The Poetry and Poetics of

Olga Sedakova

Introduction

STEPHANIE SANDLER

The Moscow poet Olga Sedakova stands out among the many exceptionally strong contemporary writers in Russia: the integrity, intellectual force, linguistic erudition, and moral courage of her writings and public statements are matched by the sheer beauty of her poetry and the brilliance of her insights. Her worldview is in the broadest sense philological, a term that may conjure up fusty libraries and old-fashioned theories but, in her writings, it is actually the foundation for a deep and abiding belief that words richly convey meanings and enable human communication and connection even in eras of compromised or restricted thought. Sedakova lives out that commitment to the philological across a very wide range of forms: she writes poems, long and short, enigmatically simple and built into spacious, extended forms; she has written dozens of essays and tales about culture, travel, and daily life in Soviet and post-Soviet Russia; and she has written extensively about Russian literature and about major European writers in scholarly as well as personal essays. She has published eloquent accounts of how one becomes a poet and how one keeps to a moral compass. Her essays address such topics as the meanings of Orthodox liturgy, the poetry of the broad European tradition, and the role of the poet in contemporary public life. She has taught at Moscow State University and as a guest lecturer or visiting professor at universities across Europe and the United States. She is a Russian poet and writer, and yet, in a number of ways, she has long reached across languages. Her work has been translated into Italian, French, Hebrew, Ukrainian, German, Albanian, Danish, and English, and she has herself translated from Italian, German, French, English, and Latin, bringing into Russian the work of poets she admires, from St. Francis to Dante Alighieri, from Ezra Pound to Rainer Maria Rilke, from Paul Claudel to Emily Dickinson. Many prizes have come to her from Germany, Italy, France, the Vatican, and from within Russia itself. Now a much-honored poet, translator, scholar, and teacher, she has increasingly brought her quiet, considered voice into civic debates and she has spoken out on behalf of those who have been treated unjustly and in defense of freedom of belief more broadly. She has an unmistakable, firm public voice, speaking persistently for the position that literary culture should take up the responsibility to create spaces for free thought in our complex, burdened contemporary world.

The historical and social context in which Olga Sedakova became a poet bears mentioning, for it was formative in her own life and in that of her contemporaries. She was born in the immediate aftermath of what is still referred to in Russia as the Great Patriotic War, known in the West as World War II, and the Russian name reminds us that Sedakova grew up with a myth of the Soviet Union's greatness in having saved the world from Nazism and Fascism. She lived within the stability and stagnation of the mid- to late Soviet period, and she has credited her grandmother, Darya Semyonovna Sedakova, in particular with teaching her from a very young age about the enduring values of culture, both that of a folk culture where everyday words could express an appreciation for the natural world and for human kindness and that of Christian culture where those same values could be connected to an enduring idea of spirituality. A quiet mode of opposition was thus transmitted to Sedakova early on. As she pursued her education in Moscow and informally in Tartu (where she participated in wide-ranging discussions with the emerging scholars of cultural semiotics), the poet developed an independence of mind and thought that has endured. She participated in Soviet unofficial culture and saw her first poems printed in Europe in the 1980s.

The first official journal publication of her poetry came in 1988, with an introduction by Viacheslav V. Ivanov.[1] Many others followed, but that sense of herself as apart from the mainstream, and as a spokesperson for ideas and values that are often forgotten in public life, has persisted. It is a position she shares with a very few peers (Lev Rubinstein, for example), and one can argue that it has been singularly influential for the next generation of poets, a few of whom have also aspired to that kind of intellectual leadership and independence of thought (one thinks of Maria Stepanova). Even in that context, however, Sedakova has a special role because of her deep connection to Christian culture and her concern to hold the Orthodox Church to its own highest moral values. In addition, because of her profound knowledge of European languages and cultures, both ancient and modern, Sedakova holds a distinctive position among those who are speaking directly about what it means to be Russian. The intellectual matrix of her thinking is as oriented toward Dante, Dickinson, and Paul Celan as toward Osip Mandelstam and Boris Pasternak, and she is as likely to refer to philosophers as to Church doctrine, to norms of Enlightenment reason as to reasons for praising foolishness. And Sedakova insists firmly on the significance of all these forms of thought and belief for reimagining and reaffirming Russian cultural identity. Now, when so much is in flux in Russia, and not just in Russia (I write these words in 2018), including the norms of free speech and the capacity of the rule of law to govern a society, the role of public intellectual and the place of poetry in public culture are far from settled topics. We hope our book can participate in these debates. In addition to creating contexts for apprehending a poet's work on her own terms, a conversation about Olga Sedakova's position in the public arena also has much to offer us all.

With this volume, then, our aim is to begin to create an intellectual framework for understanding the still evolving, vibrant contribution of Olga Sedakova to Russian and to world culture. We present a diverse set of essays focused on a single poet that also offers an accounting of the full range of cultural issues that Sedakova has addressed, including some of the pressing questions facing Russia in the Soviet and post-Soviet years. In her work, readers can take stock of where Russian culture finds itself at the start of the twenty-first century, casting many long glances back to the past and a canny sideways glance at the unfolding events and moods in adjacent countries and cultures. As Sedakova has said herself, essays of literary criticism and philosophical reflection can be very far-reaching indeed: they can be a way to figure out what it means to be alive in our historical present.[2] While not all of our essays take on this ambitious task directly, all seek to look unflinchingly at the world in which Sedakova has emerged as a writer, and to chronicle her engagement with that world and with its forms of political, religious, ethical, and cultural expression. We aim to underscore and understand her contributions as a poet and as a thinker, presenting close readings as well as accounts of the broad themes and patterns of thought across her work. Our goal is an assessment of Sedakova's contributions to ongoing aesthetic and cultural debates within and beyond Russia. We invite readers to become acquainted with the full range of her writings, and we seek to lay a foundation on which we hope readers, as well as other scholars and critics, will build.

Our book comes at a moment when Olga Sedakova's creative work has begun to reach a wider audience within Russia as well as in other countries. Although active in the unofficial culture, she was a poet barely published in the Soviet period, and largely in illicit editions in Europe; she has now published more than a dozen books in Russia, including volumes of poetry and prose, literary and theological writings, and a dictionary of Church Slavonic paronyms (words that still exist in modern Russian but with changed meanings). In 2010, a generously complete four-volume set of her published writings appeared, with a volume set aside for each of four forms (poetry, translations, literary essays, and essays on moral and ethical topics). The active and far-reaching website www.olgasedakova.com has made everything in that four-volume set and a great deal besides accessible freely. Constantly updated and well maintained, it has added her ongoing public statements, interviews, and new writings, and includes some work in German, Italian, and English translation. Our volume features a chronology of all these volumes (that is, of all of Sedakova's writings in book form, including translations into other languages). Throughout this book, authors refer to Sedakova's occasional writings and public statements, as well as to the emerging scholarship about her as a writer and public figure.

This is a good moment, then, for a substantial book about Olga Sedakova. Our aim is to show her significant contribution to Russian intellectual life and to the humanities more broadly in the modern period. We seek to clarify the literary and cultural traditions important to her poetry, and to set out a range of approaches to her work. We have collected essays from a wide range of scholars, from different generations (there are recent PhD recipients as well as more senior scholars), from different perspectives (philosophers, poets, philologists, and scholars of Russian and comparative literature), and from different backgrounds (our contributors have been trained in Russia, Ukraine, Germany, Italy, Britain, and the United States). The essays reflect their tremendously varied theoretical orientations. They are based on literary, formal, philosophical, theological, anthropological, and/or linguistic approaches. The volume is philological, then, in the same sense of the philological that marks Sedakova's own writings.

This book was not the result of a scholarly conference. Instead, its essays were commissioned. Our editorial collective reached out to poets, translators, philosophers, literary scholars, comparatists, and Slavists in the United States, Russia, and a number of European countries. Not all were able to write for the volume, as it turned out, but the resulting set of essays has the diversity of disciplinary training and intellectual orientation we sought. It also has the kind of deep scholarly engagement that Sedakova's poetry demands. To quote the poet herself, explaining why she found it appropriate that the 2014 publication of her earlier cycle of poems *Stelae and Inscriptions* (*Stely i nadpisi*, 1982) as a separate book would include a lengthy essay by the philologist and classicist Sergei Stepantsov: "I wanted for my book, with its relatively small collection of poems, to include substantive explication. And this exegesis is not just bonus material. It's absolutely crucial for giving an image of how poetry emerges, how poetry lives alongside and together with thought."[3] The work of creating an image of the mental and spiritual world in which Sedakova writes, then, is what we proposed to our authors, and it is what we hope our readers will find in these pages. The volume is divided into several sections, each of which we now detail.

The opening group of essays, "Ways of Seeing the Poet and Her Poems," sets out fundamental themes and rhetorical patterns in Sedakova's writings about herself and her world. The essays emphasize moral, political, historical, aesthetic, and psychological forces that shape her work, and they delineate the poet's characteristic modes of thought in her poetry and also in her prose. In the first essay, "If This Is Not a Garden," Benjamin Paloff discusses what he calls "the Unfinished Work of Creation." The essay is both philosophical and philological, showing how Sedakova's poems insist upon uncertainty and mystery as constitutive of the very thing we call knowledge. Her work is seen in the context of a broader Christian humanism, and the essay circles around some religious questions raised in other parts of our book. But it does so in terms of broader gestures that are meaningful beyond communities of believers. The poet's attention to what is unspoken is seen as a creative epistemological stance. Emphasizing the genre of elegy and the imagery of gardens (Eden and Gethsemane), Paloff traces the paths along which reason and faith are put into each other's service. His essay establishes several themes or approaches that are explored throughout our book: the philosophical charge of Sedakova's poetry, her position as a Christian thinker, and her relation to her sources. Paloff also describes well the profound dialogue her poems inspire, including potential parallels with American poetry.

In "The Poet and Darkness: The Politics of Artistic Form," Ksenia Golubovich takes on a question balanced between ethics and poetics. She recalls Theodor Adorno's question, whether poetry is possible after the Holocaust, to define the fundamental ethical premises of Sedakova's writings as a problem in language: how to write in a seemingly dead-end language, a language of totalitarian lies? The answer suggests an aesthetic and ethical project like that of Paul Celan, writing in German after the Holocaust, and it is one of many connections to Celan cited by authors in this volume. Golubovich also finds in Sedakova a surprisingly productive tautology, one in which the poet creates new meanings without using resources beyond those already at hand. The essay argues that Sedakova creates a new code of human intercourse: a language that not only laments the dead and fears the future but that also restores the communion of the dead and the living, of those who survived and those who perished. Golubovich demonstrates that these new post-Gulag, post-Auschwitz, and seemingly post-ideological notions inform the imagery, syntax, and sound patterning in Sedakova's poetry.

The philosopher and poet Emily Grosholz, writing in "Childhood and Vibrant Stasis in Olga Sedakova's Poetry," begins by explaining the metaphorical and cognitive function of circles in Sedakova's writings by recourse to the disciplines of philosophy and mathematics, particularly the representation of compact spaces in topology. In her view, gestures of return to places and persons from childhood always recover for the poet what has seemed irretrievably lost. She defines coordinates for Sedakova's poetic world, making strong use of the essay "In Praise of Poetry." Drawing on the legacy of Sedakova's own teacher, Sergei Averintsev (who appears in several essays in this volume), she identifies sites of reconciled harmonies and restored equilibrium in poetic and prose texts across Sedakova's career. Grosholz's essay is unusual in our volume in that it is not based on readings of Sedakova's writings in Russian. Although she has consulted with native speakers about some images or ideas, Grosholz's reading is based on translated texts (and we retain here citations to the translations she used, rather than providing the new translations offered elsewhere in our book). This essay presents an exemplary reading of Sedakova's poetry and prose based almost entirely on translations. As a practitioner of and advocate for translation, Sedakova herself, we believe, might rejoice in such a success.

Another deeply philosophical essay is by Aleksandr Kutyrkin, entitled "The Guest at the Door: The Poetry of Olga Sedakova." This essay offers a phenomenological account of Sedakova's poetry, with examples taken from across the poet's writings. Kutyrkin argues that the fundamental measures of value and being—like memory, childhood, and creative work—can be best understood from within their representation as realities in the poetic texts. Only as an abstraction, based on these personal points of departure, can one begin to recognize authorial intentions or readerly comprehension as they are enacted in Sedakova's poetic texts.

My contribution, "Constricted Freedom: On Dreams and Rhythms in the Poetry of Olga Sedakova," is built on a paradox: Sedakova requires that art create the conditions of freedom, even as she puts freedom and constraint in necessary relation to one another. This essay maps the pathways along which Sedakova seeks freedom for art, drawing on the writings of Susan Stewart, Paul Celan, Walter Benjamin, Emmanuel Levinas, and Jonathan Culler to comprehend what Sedakova means by a "history of Russian freedom." Her use of rhythm and genre in poetry is shown to be at once constraining and liberating, and the essay concludes with close readings of several poems that imagine dreams as a steep but not impassable pathway to freedom.

Taken together, then, these opening essays make the case for Sedakova as a thinker whose poetry has philosophical underpinnings; whose aesthetic philosophy engages consistently with ethical conundrums and does not shy away from taking positions on matters of broad consequence; and whose writings devise formal means to give aesthetic depth and complexity to the substantive claims they boldly advance.

The second group of essays, entitled "Theology, Philosophy, and Modes of Knowing," considers the ways in which Sedakova apprehends the world around her and how she characteristically puts those perceptions into poetic form. There is a particular focus on connections between poetics and theology, as well as poetics and philosophy. Several of the essays explore Sedakova's position as a contemporary Christian poet and thinker, asking how her poems and essays have absorbed religious models of expression. There are comparisons to other poets and thinkers, including those whom Sedakova has written about or translated. The section opens with an essay by Andrew Kahn, "Sedakova's Book of Hours and the Devotional Lyric: Reading 'Fifth Stanzas.'" To show how poetry and faith are the two pillars of Sedakova's world, this essay concentrates on a single long poem. It establishes a relationship between prayer and poetry, based on an analogy between the acts of reading the poem and reading the Orthodox Book of Hours; reference to Rilke's volume of poetry by the same title is also pertinent. In distilling this argument, Kahn explores Sedakova's use of other poetic echoes and voices, the nature of the real versus the copy, the meaning of beauty as an object of worship, and the need to embrace loss in order to gain the world.

Next, in "The Art of Change: Adaptation and the Apophatic Tradition in Sedakova's *Chinese Journey*," Martha Kelly sees the Orthodox tradition of apophatism as both a theme and mode of Sedakova's writings: the apophatic impulse—with its discourse of emptying in order to fill—shows how late and post-Soviet Russian society might creatively reconstitute national identity across the traumatic years of transition. Sedakova makes of her art a unique model of adaptation to the ongoing change of the world, Kelly argues. In Sedakova's poetry, we encounter apophatism as an aesthetic that might transform our way of perceiving and being. The essay draws on a surprising text to make its case, one that at first glance might not seem promising for an essentially theological argument, *Chinese Journey*; but Kelly's account of the poem persuasively shows otherwise. It also offers a counterpoint to the China-focused approach to this same text offered later in this volume by a comparative literature scholar, Natalia Chernysh.

Sarah Pratt, in "Disruption of Disruption: The Orthodox Christian Impulse in the Works of Nikolai Zabolotsky and Olga Sedakova," explores the shared philosophical and theological underpinnings of the two poets' writings in terms of Orthodoxy, particularly in their representations of the icon. Both Zabolotsky and Sedakova "disrupt the disruption" that Soviet culture effected in Orthodoxy by means of their persistent dialogue between art and spiritual/religious expression. Pratt identifies a process of building consciousness and knowledge by representing the icon as a concrete object pointing to the divine, and it is a process that leads both poets toward communion with greater truth. She also connects both poets to the longer tradition of Russian metaphysical poetry (Evgeny Baratynsky, Fedor Tiutchev).

A different aspect of Sedakova's philosophical poetics is taken up in our next essay. Writing about what she calls "The Topography of the Other World in Olga Sedakova's Poetics," Ketevan Megrelishvili treats the ontological category of otherness. She identifies the topographical contours of an alternative spatial world and, through delicate analysis of the phonetic and rhythmic components of the poems, she shows how journeys to find this other place produce formal tension within the verse structure. Specific recurring images constitute this other place (among them: garden, house, threshold, heart, and dream). Such images can show this other world intersecting with familiar spaces of lived experience, but the poetry exudes a kind of verbal incompleteness or reliance on broken-off statements. As a result, this other place is always just suggested, never completely described.

Henrieke Stahl, in "The Immanence of Transcendence: Poetic Reflections on the Mystical Aspects of Olga Sedakova's Lyric Poetry," takes up a slightly different form of philosophical investigation, one rooted in the transcendental experience. She concentrates on Sedakova's representation of a poetic subject, the use of sound orchestration and poetic rhythm, and the creation of symbolic imagery across poems and poetic collections. For Stahl, these formal elements bring spiritual, indeed mystical experience into the poetry; she finds points of convergence between figures of speech and figures of the divine. Stahl's endpoint in mystical experience means that her essay also complements the work on a kind of materialization of religious knowledge in Sarah Pratt's essay, the apophatic strand brought into the foreground by Martha Kelly, and the delineation of connections between poetry and prayer in Andrew Kahn's essay.

In the third group of essays, attention turns to "Contextual Readings," with an emphasis on the "Languages, Cultures, and Sources" of Sedakova's poetry. These essays study her engagement with other persons, places, and cultures, past and present, and establish her dialogues with Russian poets influential for her work; connections with European poets whom she translated; and responses to cultural traditions that seem remote from Russian culture and yet became intimately important to the poet, like that of ancient China. The first essay is by Ilya Kukulin: "Stylized Folklore as a Recollection of Europe: Olga Sedakova's *Old Songs* and Alexander Pushkin's *Songs of the Western Slavs*." Kukulin juxtaposes the cultural and political problems that Pushkin and Sedakova sought to solve. Although they were separated by more than one hundred years, the two poets have lived at moments that were similarly marked by historical and cultural crisis.

Sedakova wrote her songs at a time when tensions between the seemingly Russian and European worldviews were at an all-time high (1980); her answer to this late Cold War rhetoric of conflict is to imagine Russian culture as at once eternal and fundamentally European and, as Kukulin argues so effectively, it is only in the context of this comparison that one begins to appreciate just how European is the outlook within a cycle of poems that otherwise are deeply rooted in Russian Orthodox folk culture. The essay offers a reading of her *Old Songs* that is broadly cultural and historical and also deeply philological.

Vera Pozzi takes up what she calls "The Poetic Anthropology of Olga Sedakova" and she does so, as her subtitle puts it, "In Dialogue with Sergei Averintsev and Boris Pasternak." Pozzi foregrounds the pervasive sense of openness to the other, the repeated discoveries of possibilities for freedom, happiness, and hope in their work. Averintsev's critical writings about reason, and Pasternak's poetic views concerning the new possibility of an outlook on life, emerge as integral parts of Sedakova's artistic outlook. It is an outlook that finds its voice in poetry as an awakening of an authentic anthropological experience, anthropological not in the sense of a social-sciences discipline, but in the sense of a deeper knowledge of what it means to be human.

Maria Khotimsky, by comparison, returns us to some degree to the theological foundations of the previous group of essays, but on fundamentally linguistic terms. In "The Semantic Vertical: Church Slavonic Heritage and Olga Sedakova's Poetics of Translation," Khotimsky establishes connections between Sedakova's extensive translation practice and the creative development of her poetry. Using Old Church Slavonic language as a model for creating new semantic possibilities, Sedakova refers to translation as a way to open new possibilities for poetic expression. She often engages in active dialogue with foreign poets and literary traditions. Khotimsky reads her translations of Dickinson, Rilke, and Celan closely, and shows how those translations, in turn, are reflected in Sedakova's own poetic practice. Bringing together Sedakova's reflections on the art of translation, her work on the Church Slavonic linguistic and cultural heritage, and her poetic dialogue with mentors and cherished poets, the essay combines analysis of Sedakova's translations with studies of individual poems. It draws conclusions about the broader shape of Sedakova's growth as a poet.

In the final essay in this group of contextual readings, Natalia Chernysh provides a richly comparative analysis of "Olga Sedakova's Journey through *The Book of Changes*." She uses the monumental *Book of Changes* (the *Yi Jing*, also known as *I Ching*) as a point of departure to assess how Sedakova encounters and interprets classical Chinese culture in her writings, particularly in *Chinese Journey*. Chernysh discovers surprising and revealing points of convergence with Chinese culture in Sedakova's work, and she offers valuable insights into the meaning of classical Chinese culture for the poet. Sedakova lived in China as a young child, and Chernysh is the first scholar to provide a substantive, detailed account of how Chinese culture makes itself felt in her poetry. Her essay also opens up an underexplored aspect of Sedakova's engagement with non-Western traditions of the visual and verbal arts.

Our book concludes with an afterword from David Bethea, who writes briefly "On Olga Sedakova and Poetic Thinking." He offers a bold rereading of Sedakova's poetry and prose as a means of ensuring the survival of verbal expression in what he calls our increasingly post-literate world. In that sense, his essay highlights the philological argument that runs through this volume. Bethea argues for the possibilities of cultural survival by contrasting the evolutionary theories of Charles Darwin and Jean-Baptiste Lamarck, as they came to be theorized within the Russian philosophical tradition. Bethea draws on Osip Mandelstam's poem "Lamarck" to define Sedakova's typical poetic persona as the opposite of heroic personalities championed by other poets and thinkers, and yet hers is a persona with the inner fortitude to outlast the evolutionary battle for survival. Like so many others in this collection, he seeks to theorize the intellectual ambitions of Sedakova's writings. He, too, is not content to describe the significance of her work; rather he charts a pathway along which one can begin to see what reading and thinking about Olga Sedakova's poetry can contribute to ongoing humanistic conversations across our various cultures.

These, then, are the essays on offer here. We also present a chronology of Sedakova's published work in book form, including her translations and the translations of her work into other languages. It is our hope that readers will use both the chronology and the essays as a foundation on which to build their own interpretations of individual writings by Olga Sedakova and of the themes and forms that define her work. Our volume is but a beginning, which awaits the work of others to complete.

Notes

1. Ol'ga Sedakova, "Solovei, filomela, sud'ba . . . ," *Druzhba narodov*, no. 10 (1988): 121–25.

2. Ol'ga Sedakova, "Opyt i slovo," interview by Ksenia Golubovich, 2013, http://www.olgasedakova.com/interview/1454, accessed March 17, 2017. Sedakova's meaning here is actually still broader, as can be seen from her comments in the essay "Blagoslovenie tvorchestvu i parnasskii ateizm" (2000). There, she describes a skeptical mindset that effectively can block aesthetic innovation, but she refuses to idealize the past. In the present, she observes, one thinks, "'So much has already been said, perhaps indeed everything! What else could our denuded contemporary possibly add to that great sum?' No one

would likely deny, at this point, that the time in which we live—our artistic time—is impoverished and stingy, as though it has come a long way down. But even in epochs that did not feel so desperately poor, the relation of culture to new art was not without conflict. After all, new inspiration occasions the upheaval of all that is and was. At times the upheaval is decisive, it risks loss and may at first glance look a lot like destruction. What survives and lives on in truly new experience is not habitual forms and canons, but rather the very tradition of human inspiration" (4:334–35).

3. Ol'ga Sedakova, "Nash chitatel' ne ponimaet modernizm," interview with Evgeniia Korobkova, *Vecherniaia Moskva,* January 14, 2015, http://vm.ru/news/2015/01/14/olga-sedakova-nash-chitatel-ne-ponimaet-modernizm-275911.html, accessed March 13, 2018.

PART 1

Ways of Seeing the Poet and Her Poems

If This Is Not a Garden

Olga Sedakova and the Unfinished Work of Creation

BENJAMIN PALOFF

As Olga Sedakova garners increasing attention in the West, even provoking the occasional lyric response, readers negotiating between Russian and Anglo-American lyric traditions must confront the challenge of the poet's suggestive and, at times, almost mystical meditations on metaphysical or ecstatic experience.[1] If Sedakova's Christian humanism has, as we will see, sometimes confused her Russian readers, it is at least as likely to do so for readers of English-language poetry, which in the postwar era has demonstrated a pronounced preference for *secular* reason. The present essay argues that this Christian humanism provides the key to understanding one of the central epistemological features of Sedakova's poems, namely, her insistent embrace of uncertainty, mystery, and incompleteness not as problems to be remedied or lacunae to be filled in, but as constitutive of reality as such. Reading her career through this frame of reference affords us a better understanding of her lyric output and provides essential context for the poet's sustained engagement with both Russian and Western religious thought.

Of course, Anglo-American poetry is not devoid of religious imagery. But while our poets occasionally write on a religious image or theological question, few have created literary careers wholly integrated into and operating from within a decades-long engagement with religious practices and theological questions. The late Polish poet Czesław Miłosz, who has enjoyed as much prominence in Anglo-American letters as any foreign-language poet in the postwar era, once ranked this "incapacity of contemporary man to think in religious terms" among "the essential problems of our time."[2] In an attempt to flip this "essential problem" on its head, Harold Bloom has argued that contemporary American poems are suffused with a *secular* religiosity, one that pervades the American experience but remains outside of established religious tradition. "So implicit and universal is the American religion," Bloom writes, "that some of its poets can be unaware that they incarnate and celebrate it," and in a *reductio* that approaches *ad absurdum*

Bloom goes so far as to claim that the religion of American poetry must be secular because its Christ is as well: "Whatever religion and religious poetry is in Europe, or in Africa or Asia, in America it is Whitmanian." Bloom goes on to write that Whitman "*is* American religious poetry, and he himself is a Christ rather than a Christian."[3]

Insofar as religion and humanism are frequently counterposed in our mainstream commercial and political discourses, overt religiosity is often assumed to be antithetical to humanist inquiry. "By ignoring the *flowing* character of science and religion," Bruno Latour remarks, "we have turned the question of their relations into an opposition between 'knowledge' and 'belief,' opposition that we then deem necessary either to overcome, to politely resolve, or to widen violently."[4] Latour plows through the opposition by declaring knowledge and belief "caricatures" of science and religion, respectively, insofar as both science and religion necessarily entail a dynamic interplay of positive knowledge and leaps of faith. Or as John Paul II announced in his thirteenth encyclical, *Fides et Ratio* (Faith and Reason, 1998), issued a few weeks after presenting the Solovyov Prize to Sedakova, Christian philosophy is not an official dogma, but "seeks rather to indicate a Christian way of philosophizing, a philosophical speculation *conceived in dynamic union with faith*."[5] For her part, Sedakova expressed the same notion in a 2012 interview by paraphrasing Miłosz: "I recall that Czesław Miłosz once wrote that after he underwent theological training, thinking of any other kind seems like arithmetic compared to algebra."[6]

How Sedakova enacts this thinking in her poems has undoubtedly become more legible to her Russian audience over time, especially when she is read within the company of poets like Elena Shvarts, Viktor Krivulin, and Ivan Zhdanov, who have likewise approached theological questions from a humanistic perspective. Among her older contemporaries, however, the greatest international attention has been paid to Joseph Brodsky, whose allegorical approach to religious motifs was easily accommodated within a postwar American tradition that largely eschews the poetry of religious devotion, particularly when it is grounded in so specific a tradition of faith as Sedakova's Russian Orthodoxy.[7] Sedakova's religious allusions, by contrast, are specifically *not* allegorical. For her, the very notion of a humanism without God is—well, if not exactly unimaginable, then imaginable only as the counterpoint through which a new humanism attains its fullest expression. In her introduction to the correspondence of Thomas Mann and Károly Kerényi, Sedakova notes:

> Classical humanism sought liberation from the doctrinal-religious regulation of life and thought [. . .]. Neohumanism [. . .], departing from the secularized, de-deified realia of the twentieth century, seeks in classical mythology a means to "connect"

> contemporary man, who has fallen—or, rather, collapsed—into non-restraint, into blind utilitarianism, into inattentive haste, to turn him toward religious depth and a worthwhile fear (*metus*, sacred awe) of that which is inaccessible to consciousness, both in the world and in himself: of the *beginning*, of the uninitiated, where *everything* is *yet* possible, and where they therefore tread in fear of shattering this potential. ("Germes: Nevidimaia storona klassiki"; 4:136–37)

Sedakova rejects a humanism that focuses on what is already known about the human subject, and which inevitably "collapses" into relativism and the sophistry ascribed to Protagoras, for whom "man is the measure of all things." In its stead, she posits a humanism that "connects" the individual with the fullness of his or her own experience, with what is known *and* "that which is inaccessible to consciousness."

In this way, Sedakova describes a humanism that has somehow gone astray. Having arisen to counter dogmatism with rational inquiry, by the twentieth century—well into what Charles Taylor has dubbed "a secular age" unprecedented in Western epistemology—this humanism had smothered its sensitivity to the world's wonder in a new dogmatism, that of scientific positivism and a strictly secular rationalism.[8] C. P. Snow's infamous lecture on "the two cultures" comes immediately to mind, with scientific reason on one side and everything else on the other.[9] The neohumanism that Sedakova describes in reference to Mann and Kerényi is therefore less an innovation than a restoration. For Sedakova, religious humanism is what humanism was always meant to be, namely, a worldview that encompasses the invisible and the unknown as well as the obvious and certain and that, in so doing, restores mystery and fear (or "awe") to their rightful place in human experience.

Here we should note the proximity of Sedakova's humanism to that of the late Sergei Averintsev, the Russian philologist who served as her mentor in matters spiritual as well as scholarly. In his enduringly provocative essay "Jacques Maritain, Neo-Thomism, and the Catholic Theology of Art" ("Zhak Mariten, neotomizm, katolicheskaia teologiia iskusstva," 1981), Averintsev describes a Catholic worldview exemplified by the thought of St. Thomas Aquinas and predicated on the complementarity of the potential and the actual, but ultimately subsumed into Church dogmatism, on the one hand, and, in the guise of the Protestant Reformation, a bourgeois rejection of the visible and material on the other.[10] With neo-Thomism, Averintsev argues, complementarity can once again come to the fore.

The need to recover this complementarity helps explain why Sedakova so frequently represents human individuality as incompleteness, a composite of potential and its realization. In "A Country Churchyard" ("Sel'skoe kladbishche"), for example, she writes:

Ты, связь времён, и если ты бываешь (а разве нет?), ты сон
выздоровленья,
ты медленно течёшь и долго видишь детей перед могилами детей.
(1:251)

You, the connection of times, and if you are here (and aren't you), you're
the dream of recovery,
you're slowly flowing, and you long watch the children before the graves of
children.

The addressee in these lines is not necessarily the deity, the reader, or the companion who has arrived at the cemetery with the poet in this particular reminiscence. As is often the case in Sedakova's poems, the second person remains unspecified, though this lyric ambiguity has a very specific ontological grounding. For Sedakova, the openness of "you" mirrors that of "I"; as she concludes in the same poem, "No one knows the shores of the other" ("Nikto ne znaet berega drugogo"). Which is, in fact, another way of saying that no one knows "the shores" of the self.[11]

This openness, already implicated within the notion of complementarity, pervades every level of Sedakova's work. It is the foundation of the relation between Self and Other—what she calls, in an incisive essay on Bakhtin, "the relation of mutual complementarity" ("otnoshenie vzaimodopolnitel'nosti") ("M. M. Bakhtin—drugaia versiia"; 4:95) between the first and third person, and thus necessarily between poet and deity. But it is also the zone of contact between positive knowledge and non-knowledge, revelation and mystery, presence and absence. Here we may discern in Sedakova the same give-and-take, "one step forward, one step back," that John Paul II criticized in Miłosz's poems, to which the Polish poet allegedly responded, "Holy Father, how in the twentieth century can one write religious poetry differently?"[12] And despite the Pope's misgivings with respect to Miłosz, such complementarity reflects the former's pronouncements on art's spiritual mission, especially in his 1999 "Letter to Artists," which describes artistic creation as an echo of the Incarnation of God in Christ, "a kind of bridge to religious experience," "a kind of appeal to the mystery," that which "must make perceptible, and as far as possible attractive, the world of the spirit, of the invisible, of God."[13]

In her own meditation on the Pope's letter, Sedakova characterizes the act of artistic creation as a doubled act of "giving": the first step is described as "inspiration as a gift *to him* from above" ("vdokhnovenie kak dar *emu* svyshe")—that is, the conveyance of mystery to the artist—and the second as "the finished work that *he* now gifts to the world" ("zavershennoe proizvedenie, kotoroe uzhe *on* prineset v dar miru"; "Blagoslovenie tvorchestvu i parnasskii ateizm"; 4:335). The challenge for the artist is to convey that mystery as integral to the reality we know. Or, as the Protestant theologian Dietrich Bonhoeffer, on whom Sedakova has also written, explained in a 1943 letter from a Nazi prison, "'telling the truth' [. . .] means, in my opinion, to say how something is in reality, that is, with respect for mystery, for trust, for hiddenness."[14] What we are dealing with in Sedakova, then, is not what is sometimes termed "the God of the gaps," the simplistic notion that holes in scientific knowledge suggest the presence of deity.[15] Rather than the dialectical movement of self-abnegation, doubt, or crisis—Sedakova is no Underground Man—the interplay of certainty and innocence is itself presented as positive knowledge, since it is only by acknowledging and *reveling* in mystery that mere knowledge attains meaning. Most of the matter in the universe, after all, is *dark*.

Sedakova points to this complementarity explicitly in a programmatic essay, "The Morality of Art, or the Evils of Mediocrity" ("Moralizm iskusstva, ili o zle posredstvennosti"): "In art, insofar as it is art and not the production of objects in the form of *objets d'art* (which we observe with increasing frequency), there is knowledge of another way of life. It expresses this radically: it says that all other ways of life are not life at all [. . .]. The way of life is blissful yearning, *Selige Sehnsucht*. And a yearning not for 'another' world, but for this one, 'this one here,' we'll say after Goethe" (4:266–67). That epistemology, theology, and art should all serve consistent and complementary aims is a matter of the highest import to Sedakova, and in one of her essays on Bonhoeffer she quotes Averintsev to similar effect: "we saw [Christianity] *simply as life*; there was no other life around us" ("my uvideli ego *prosto kak zhizn'*; nikakoi drugoi zhizni vokrug ne bylo"; "Ditrikh Bonkheffer dlia nas"; 4:506). A theory of God that rejects rational thought or that otherwise sequesters itself from the experiential world leads too easily to blindness. If there is a single reason that, unlike Elena Shvarts, Sedakova holds mystical or ecstatic experience at arm's length, it is because she finds it epistemologically unreliable and aesthetically distracting, not having found there "that more important theme of the freedom of invisible things."[16] The work of understanding how our experience of the world is suffused with those "invisible things" is, for Sedakova, the highest function of the lyric word. It demands a carefully orchestrated interplay of analysis and faith.

Dark Matter

In thinking about this interplay, I have returned repeatedly to one of Sedakova's earliest and, to my mind, most emblematic poems, an untitled work from 1973:

Неужели, Мария, только рамы скрипят,
только стекла болят и трепещут?
Если это не сад—
разреши мне назад,
в тишину, где задуманы вещи.

Если это не сад, если рамы скрипят
оттого, что темней не бывает,
если это не тот заповеданный сад,
где голодные дети у яблонь сидят
и надкушенный плод забывают,

где не видно ветвей,
но дыханье темней
и надёжней лекарство ночное . . .
Я не знаю, Мария, болезни моей.
Это сад мой стоит надо мною. (1:27)

Surely, Maria, it's not just that the window frames creak,
that it's only glass panes that ache and tremble?
If this is not a garden—
let me go back,
into silence, where things have been thought through.

If this is not a garden, if the frames creak
from the fact it cannot get darker,
if this is not that preordained garden
where hungry children sit by the apple trees
and forget the nibbled fruit,

where the boughs are invisible,
but the breathing is darker
and night's medicine more hopeful . . .
I don't know, Maria, my own illness.
This garden of mine stands over me.

Like so many of Sedakova's poems, this one begins with a question, and while questions in lyric poems tend to be rhetorical, in Sedakova's work they are nearly always apostrophic, directed at an interlocutor whose silence marks presence and absence simultaneously. Or, to put it more precisely, in Sedakova the addressee's absence becomes presence through naming—literally, in this instance, as a nod toward the Virgin—where the name or description outlines the figure of the addressee, who remains "the connection of times" from "A Country Churchyard." In this way, *de*-scription, as writing *around* its object, becomes what Jean-Luc Nancy terms *exscription*: the broadcast of being to other subjects, where those other subjects must make meaning of the broadcast, since its significance is not inscribed within a preexisting sign system.[17] It is only through this outline that the lyric "I" can know there is anyone else to talk to at all, another "I" whose very subjectivity is constituted by the speaker's lack of complete knowledge about her. As in "A Country Churchyard," where the uncertainty of the addressee's presence and the very fact that "no one knows the shores of the other" frame the Other as "the dream of recovery," here we are once again in a pastoral setting "where *everything* is *yet* possible."

I have just said that absence and uncertainty "frame the Other," and while this phrasing is scholarly convention, it is also symptomatic of Sedakova's poem, in which we encounter the "creaking" and "trembling" of frames and glass panes. Whether these belong to a window, a painting, or an icon is left in productive ambiguity. In any case, the surface that separates the viewer from the object is a semipermeable membrane, since the vision allows partial access. The speaker's longing for access is innate and inscrutable in its own right—"I don't know, Maria, my own illness"—but feeling it is tantamount to the experience of Being. After all, Sedakova's use of the verb *trepetat'* ("to tremble") anticipates her later translation of *metus*, "sacred awe," as *trepet*: the trembling signals the familiar Self's encounter with the mysterious Other. Sedakova's longing for the Other is her *exscription* of her own being to herself, and it is through this exscription that she experiences Being at all.

But what if she didn't? The poem's rhetorical structure confronts us with precisely this possibility. "If this is not a garden," the poet tells us, she would just as well return to pure potential, the undifferentiated Absolute, again, "of the *beginning*, of the uninitiated"—"into silence, where things have been thought through." Coupling the proposition and its negation in this way does not dance around the truth. It *is* the truth. Only through light can she access darkness, "night's medicine"; only through the noise of frames can the poet "hear" silence, where "the breathing is darker." The logical syllogism, one of Sedakova's preferred rhetorical devices, is the grammatical expression of this complementarity. Considering one side of a potentiality leads inexorably to an examination of the other, allowing the possibility and its manifestation, or else the conditional statement and its negation, to stand together as a whole, as we also see in the opening stanza of "Song" ("Penie"), from Sedakova's cycle *The Wild Rose* (*Dikii shipovnik*, 1978):

Пение

Если воздух внести на руках, как ребёнка грудного,
в зацветающий куст, к недающимся розам, к сурово
отвечающим веткам,
        клянусь, мы увидеть должны
этот голос порфирный, глубокую кровь тишины.

Этот свет, принимающий схиму, и в образе ветхом
оживляющий кровь, и живущий по гибнущим веткам

горных роз, выбегающих из-за камней,
и, как к горю, привычных к свободе своей. (1:89)

Song

If one were to lift the air in one's arms like an infant,
into a bush bursting into bloom, toward unyielding roses, toward branches
answering severely,
        I swear we should see
that porphyry voice, the deep blood of silence.

That light, taking its vows, and in an ancient image
reviving the blood, and living along the dying branches

of the mountain roses, rushing out from the rocks,
and, as if to their grief, accustomed to their freedom.

The syllogism that introduces the poem's conceit expresses an inversion of sensory experience typical of this poet. Rather than having the roses' fragrance waft downward toward the lyric subject, Sedakova suggests that we bring the air to meet the flowers, and that we thereby invert the experience's deductive logic as well. A more conventional logical chain would have sensation leading us to source, or the invisible (here, the fragrance of roses) leading the eye upward toward the visible (the "unyielding roses" themselves). Sedakova moves in the opposite direction, proposing that we take the invisible ("lift the air in one's arms") up to meet the visible. The result, she promises ("I swear"), will be the immediate complementarity of visible and invisible, which we then draw into ourselves as fragrance. The abstract now rendered concrete—"we should see / that porphyry voice, the deep blood of silence"—what might have initially appeared as an oxymoron, that of voice described in terms of a mineral prized in ancient statuary, becomes a highly resonant demonstration of the poet's epistemology.

The syllogistic language of "Song" is not, however, the only thing it has in common with "Surely, Maria." We note the poem's pastoral setting, the dynamic interplay of aural and visual pairs (voice/silence; light/darkness), and the invocation of childhood, the air cradled in the arms "like an infant." Indeed, these motifs pervade Sedakova's writing, and with good reason. The child is the embodiment of potential in the process of its realization, just as Christ—and, especially, the child Christ, whom iconographic convention characteristically represents as a miniaturized adult—is the incarnation of God the Father.[18] In like manner, the garden that appears so frequently in Sedakova's poems is the zone of contact between possibility and realization, light and dark, as we see in the central stanza of "Flight of the Prodigal Son" ("Pobeg bludnogo syna"), also from *The Wild Rose:*

Пускай любовь по дому шарит,
и двери заперты на ключ—
мне черный сад в глаза ударит,
шатаясь, как фонарный луч.
И сад, как дух, когда горели
в огне, и землю клятвы ели,
и дух, как в древности, дремуч. (1:78)

Let love rummage through the house,
and the doors are locked—
the black garden, wavering like lamplight,
strikes my eyes.
And the garden is like the spirit when oaths were burning
in the fire and eating the earth,
and the spirit is dense, as it was in antiquity.

The garden here, though "black," behaves like light: shimmering and indistinct, yet there, striking the eyes; immaterial, "like the spirit," yet "dense, as it was in antiquity." Sedakova's darkness, in its inverse suggestion of light, becomes visible; spirit, for Sedakova, can be felt, which is why it is "dense." Materiality is always subject to destruction and decay, consumed by promises and "oaths," whereas the garden represents the dialogue between growth and disintegration, and in this way, it reveals itself as permanent, the locus of both that which is articulated and that still waiting to be said, as Sedakova also articulates in "Seven Poems" ("Sem' stikhotvorenii"):

Ты, слово мое, как сады в глубине,
ты, слава моя, как сады и ограды,
как может больной поклониться земле—
тому, чего нет, чего больше не надо. (1:225)

You, my word, like gardens in the deep,
you, my renown, like gardens and fences,
how can an ailing person bow before the earth—
before that which is not, which is no longer needed.

If Sedakova's garden is the space where potential meets manifestation, we cannot properly equate it with Eden, as Mikhail Epstein does. In defining Sedakova as a "metarealist" alongside Elena Shvarts, Ivan Zhdanov, Viktor Krivulin, and several others, Epstein gestures simultaneously toward the Platonic, suggesting that her poems "lead us into the world of a higher reality," and the strictly monistic, noting that "Metarealism emerges from the principle of *one-worldness* [*edinomirie*]; it presupposes the interpenetration of realities, and not an allusion from one, 'made-up' or 'auxiliary,' to another, 'authentic.'"[19] As much as Epstein's insights offer a productive contrast between Sedakova's art and what I have already indicated as postwar American poetry's discomfort with religious motifs *unless* they are allusive, they seem to blur the very distinction Epstein wishes to draw, that is, between the Romantic longing for a higher reality and the metarealist insistence that this is the only one we have.

Yet Epstein was not alone in grappling with the epistemological underpinnings of Sedakova's work, and early missteps in her Russian reception highlight the difficulties her work now poses to those beginning to read her in the West. Of particular note are the attacks on Sedakova published in the journal *Novyi mir* in April and October 1995 by Vladimir Slavetsky and Nikolai Slaviansky, respectively, especially insofar as the grounds for their rejection appear to be mutually exclusive. For Slavetsky, Sedakova's poems express a commanding knowledge, one that must be decoded through her dense, and sometimes obscure, extra-textual allusions. Here there is no mystery, only the reader's ignorance of what Sedakova sees: "Thus she already knew everything regarding her own poems."[20] Taking the opposite tack, Slaviansky finds Sedakova's poems unintelligible—he writes that the reader "oftentimes comes around and admits to himself that there's a great deal he does not comprehend on the simplest, most formal level, to say nothing of mystical profundities"—and ultimately asserts that the poet herself "doesn't know what she's writing about."[21] For Slavetsky, Sedakova knows too much; to Slaviansky, she knows too little and hides behind an "imponderability" or "inscrutability" (*nevniatitsa*) that is "entirely functional," serving only to obscure her own confusion.[22] Both critics latch on to only one side of a complementary pair, that of knowledge and mystery, and in so doing unwittingly enact the blindness that comes from seizing one without the other. For Epstein is correct in pointing out Sedakova's *one-worldness*, but Sedakova insists that we cannot make a claim on knowledge without seizing mystery or, for that matter, without recognizing how the two are mutually constitutive. Thus, the excellent précis provided by Viacheslav V. Ivanov: "Olga Sedakova returns a world to us that had once been gifted to us all and was forgotten for other matters."[23]

Sedakova's garden therefore cannot be Eden, for the simple reason that her garden must be inhabited by a person, preferably a child or children, those who play "before the graves of children" in "A Country Churchyard" (an arresting juxtaposition of the future that might be and the future that has already passed), or the "hungry children [who] sit by the apple trees / and forget the nibbled fruit" in "Surely, Maria." In Eden, eating the fruit abolishes both hunger and forgetting, though satiety and knowledge come at the highest price. In Sedakova's garden, longing and oblivion, the movement-toward and drifting-away, are *what it means to be in the garden*. Whereas Eden is empty of human thought, she declares that "Earthly Paradise will forever remain the place where *Adam no longer is*" ("Zemnoi rai navsegda ostaetsia mestom, gde *bol'she net Adama*"; "Dante i posle nego"; 2:191). She writes, "This garden of mine stands over me."

One more example, "A Fairy Tale" ("Skazka," also from *The Wild Rose*), will underscore how Sedakova uses the syllogism in tandem with the garden image to portray both rhetorical and conceptual complementarity. These two stanzas arrive near the poem's end:

Если это скрип и это свет,
понемногу восходящий кверху,—
сердце рождено, чтоб много лет
спать и не глядеть, как ходит свет,
и за веткой отгибает ветку.

Никому не снится этот сон:
он себе и дом, и виноградник,
и дорога, по которой всадник
скачет к ней, и этот всадник—он. (1:136–37)[24]

If this is creaking and this is light
ascending slightly higher,—

a heart birthed in order
to sleep many years and not watch how the light moves
and bends back branch upon branch.

No one has this dream:
he is unto himself both house and vineyard,
as well as the road by which the horseman
gallops toward her, and this horseman—that, too, is he.

The "garden" here is the "vineyard" ("vinogradnik"), though Sedakova clearly intends the reader to catch the literal "garden" (*sad*) within her invocation of the "horseman" ("v*sad*nik") now approaching this space of complementarity, both the domestic enclosure and its surroundings. She need not tell us that the gardener is himself (or herself) also that which the gardener cultivates. Osip Mandelstam has already done this in declaring that "I am the gardener, and I am also the flower" ("Ia i sadovnik, ia zhe i tsvetok," from "Dano mne telo," 1909), a line that Sedakova echoes aurally as well as conceptually.[25] Even without hearing the echo of Mandelstam, however, the reader can easily detect an ontology that surfaces repeatedly in the Modernist lyric, that of complementarity projected through non-differentiation. This is William Butler Yeats when he asks, "O body swayed to music, O brightening glance, / How can we know the dancer from the dance?" ("Among School Children," 1928).[26] It is also Aleksander Wat, a favorite of Miłosz, looking at a painting of ballerinas in "Facing Bonnard" ("Przed Bonnardem," 1956): "Our artist enclosed in it a ballet of possibilities / where he himself—and you—are both an observer and an author, / a corps de ballet, surely, but also a true soloist."[27] But the expression of this ethos perhaps closest to Sedakova comes from T. S. Eliot's "Ash Wednesday" (1930), which Sedakova has herself translated:

Lady of silences
Calm and distressed
Torn and most whole
Rose of memory
Rose of forgetfulness
Exhausted and life-giving
Worried reposeful
The single Rose
Is now the Garden[28]

Eliot is not, we must note, invoking "memory" and "forgetfulness" as two *different* roses. These are plainly the same rose, "The single Rose" that "Is now the Garden" and that, as such, embodies the complementarity of opposites, "Calm and distressed / Torn and most whole." Such unity of opposites suggests a congruity between that which is familiar or domesticated and that which is mysterious or alien, and this should not be surprising, since the dynamic interplay between these poles would seem to demand it. In this we can see a key difference between Sedakova's epistemology and that of Shvarts, one of her most important contemporary interlocutors. "The more inspired the poet," Shvarts asserted, "the more deeply secret thoughts take root in infinitude. For that matter, of course, in poetry 'thoughts' are not particular rational constructs, but rather musical-plastic and reasonable formations circling around an incomprehensible core like a ring of Saturn."[29] But as Maria Khotimsky has argued, Sedakova is intent on the "overcoming of the Romantic 'I,'" which is why Shvarts gives us "direct physical self-perception while stating the invisibility of God," whereas Sedakova "is filled with the ideas of sight and vision" at the same time as the lyric "I" becomes blurred.[30] Perception and assertion feed into imagination and interrogation in a continuous cycle. Thus M. E. Zvegintsova has noted that "the concept of 'garden' may manifest itself as a liminal space on the level of which a verbal and visual dialogue takes place between the worlds of the living and the dead."[31] And this may in itself help us to understand Sedakova's fondness for the elegiac mode, since presence and absence go continuously hand in hand. From Paradise to Gethsemane, what begins in one garden is renewed in another.

The Infinite Elegy

A ready example of how this interplay energizes Sedakova's poems of mourning can be found in her elegy for her friend, the pianist Vladimir Khvostin, who appears in several of her poems and essays ("Na smert' Vladimira Ivanovicha Khvostina").[32] Composed in the same period as "A Country Churchyard," the poem's second section demonstrates an insistent push and pull between assertion and questioning:

В пустыне жизни . . . Что я говорю,
в какой пустыне? [. . .]

    В саду у роз,
в гостях у всех—и всё-таки в пустыне,
в пустыне нашей жизни, в худобе

ее несчастной, никому не видной,—
Вы были больше, чем я расскажу.

Ни разум мой и ни глухой язык,
я знаю, никогда не прикоснутся
к тому, чего хотят. Не в этом дело.
Мы все, мой друг, достойны состраданья
хотя бы за попытку. Кто нас создал,
тот скажет, почему мы таковы,
и сделает, какими пожелает.

А если бы не так . . . Найти места
неслышной музыки: ее созвездья, цепи,
горящие переплетенья счастья,
в которой эта музыка сошлась,
как в разрешенье—вся большая пьеса,
доигранная. Долгая педаль. (1:258–59)

In the desert of life . . . What am I saying,
in what desert? [. . .]

In the garden by the roses,
a guest among all—and still, in the desert,
in the desert of our life,
in its unhappy
paucity, not visible to anyone,—
you were more than I will tell.

Neither my intellect, nor my deaf tongue,
I know, will ever touch
what they want. That's not the point.
We are all, my friend, worthy of compassion,
if only provisionally. Whoever created us
will say why we're this way
and will make us as he wishes.
And if not . . . Find places
of unheard music: its constellations, chains,
the blazing weaves of happiness
in which this music has coalesced,
as though in resolution—the whole great piece,
played out. Sustained pedal.

Sedakova's doubt as to the capacity of the mind ("my intellect") or language ("my deaf tongue") to "touch" the truths she gestures toward reflects a tradition that Sofya Khagi has termed "verbal skepticism," a tradition with deep roots in Russian poetry.[33] But if Sedakova remains ever aware of the limits of language relative to the world it seeks to grasp, she is not, at heart, a skeptic. There is no hint here of despair at one's own powerlessness, no disappointment at the fact that the mind and language stop short of their ostensible object. They were never supposed to reach it in the first place—"That's not the point"—because doing so would mean being blinded by that object, forever failing to see the unseen behind it, the "unheard music," the "pedal" holding the note as it decays.

Articulating this dynamic as much in her critical insights as in her poems, Sedakova has made it an especially prominent feature of her decades-long engagement with Dante. In an essay on the Italian master—who, alongside Eliot, Rainer Maria Rilke, and Paul Celan, has remained among those poets to whom she has turned most readily throughout her career—Sedakova offers what is perhaps her most explicitly Neoplatonist critique of false vision:

> Experience, as we see in Dante's examples of "mendacious vision" (optical and psychological illusions), is not the irrefutable witness of reality: he is speaking, first of all, of the condition of someone who perceives this reality. If his consciousness is cloudy and dull, if his *will* [. . .] is not free, then he sees and hears, in Dante's words, "fact." But if his consciousness is purified and tuned to the proper image, if it operates with *a free will toward a better threshold* (see the epigraph) [from Purgatorio 21:69], he sees "the form of the fact." In the conceptual language of the era, let us recall, Latin "form" corresponds to the Greek "idea." The "form of the fact" is determined by its intentional cause. And the intentional cause does not encompass [visual] obviousness and is not perceived in a simple sensual manner: one sees it with "the mind's eyes." ("Dante i posle nego"; 2:173)

In Sedakova's reading of Dante, false vision is less about seeing falsely than about seeing incompletely. It is myopia as misperception, brought about by the individual's becoming so distracted by the presentation at hand ("fact") that the concept that stands behind it ("the form of the fact") is no longer seen. The "dull" consciousness almost seems to forget to look, except "in a simple sensual manner," and therefore misses everything that one might then see with "the mind's eyes." This is why Sedakova refers to the poet's clear vision as "purified" and "tuned": free from obstruction and distraction, it is capable of receiving the broadcast from the other side of the fact at hand. Thus she declares in the poem "Strange Journey" ("Strannoe puteshestvie"): "and substance itself will swear / it had been a vision and to vision will return" ("i samo veshchestvo poklianetsia, / chto ono zreniem bylo i v zren'e vernetsia"; 1:77).

This epistemological complementarity is the basis of Sedakova's elegiac gaze, through which the lyric subject "sees" the Other by recognizing the contours of his or her absence. Like Self and Other, presence and absence are here mutually constitutive, every assertion of the "I" suggesting the "not-I," and vice-versa. This is why, in her Vatican lecture upon receiving the Vladimir Solovyov Prize from John Paul II in 1998, Sedakova states that the strongest lyric images are those that impress upon us an awe before the deeper vision that the image suggests without offering:

> The most indisputable images of poetry—and, undoubtedly, of both music and the plastic arts—carry within themselves a happy fear of depth: a fear of what this depth *is*. They (and here I would include things born in the pre-Christian era, such as Sappho's verses, let's say, or Nike of Samothrace) confront us not with some fixed "eternity": they recall the story of a strange, happier time at the very beginning of the triumph over death, of those spring weeks after Easter when the presence of Him Who Rose from the Dead, the presence of Paradise, the presence of our childhood, are like sunny flashes scattered along the earth, appearing here and there, each time all of a sudden, in various images that each time do *not* reveal themselves at first, and yet, "Did not our heart burn within us?"[34]

The quoted language (Luke 24:32) is that of Christ's disciples, for whom the inner sensation upon hearing his words is proof that they are truly spoken by their lord. Having seen him crucified, the disciples have every reason for skepticism. Their eyes can only confirm the corporeality before them. His incorporeal nature—Christ's deity—can only be detected incorporeally. Like the disciples, Sedakova suggests, we know the world before it reveals itself in its worldliness. But because this complementarity is dynamic, its inversion is also true: revelation implies its own concealment, just as presence implies future absence. The poet offers this explicitly in "Farewell" ("Proshchanie"), an early proto-elegy:

> Мне снилось, как будто настало прощанье,
> и встало над нашей смущенной водой.
> И зренье мешалось, как увещеванье,
> про большие беды над меньшей бедой,
> про то, что прощанье—еще очертанье,
> откуда-то вéдомый очерк пустой. (1:72)

I had a dream, as though time had come for farewell,
and it arose upon our confused water.
And sight got in the way, like an admonition,
about greater misfortunes over smaller misfortune,
about how farewell remains an outline,
an empty outline familiar from somewhere.

We've seen this before: the blurring of the distinction between dream and waking life; the suggestion that vision provides access to one experience while interfering with another; the sense that, if people have edges or "outlines," these boundaries are indistinct and mutable. The very act of farewell becomes the tracing of the Other's future absence.[35]

There is a clear correlation between this elegiac gaze and the kinds of ancient visual and lyric texts from which Sedakova consistently draws inspiration. Sedakova's attention to ancient Mediterranean statuary and poetry, most evident in her lyric cycle *Stelae and Inscriptions* (*Stely i nadpisi*, 1991) and in her translations of Sappho, emphasizes that which the poetic imagination must grasp *beyond* what is available visually: the absent object of a stone figure's loving gaze, the missing limbs or head of a marble statue, or else the lacunae in a scrap of papyrus that leave words forever half-spoken. We see this from the beginning of Sedakova's career, notably in her early essay "In Praise of Poetry" ("Zametki i vospominaniia o raznykh stikhotvoreniiakh, a takzhe Pokhvala poezii," 1982): "The delight or satiation that lyric poetry provides is monotonous in its essence, when compared to the variety, power and wealth of extra-poetic feelings. This is mainly the sensation of something being transformed: those same feelings, meanings, words, forms, and the human personality of the one who made this lyrical composition and of the one who is listening to it. Even the most sorrowful lyrical feeling unfurls to the music of victory. I would place a monument to lyric poetry in the form of the Winged Victory of Samothrace or the 'Victoria, Victoria' aria sung divinely by Zara Dolukhanova" (3:173–74).[36] Conventional language, to borrow Bruno Latour's formulation, informs, whereas language that can be called lyric or spiritual *transforms*: the subject who encounters such language will never be the same.[37] Nike of Samothrace and Dolukhanova's rendition of Giacomo Carissimi's seventeenth-century Italian art song befit Sedakova's monument to the lyric not only because they both express triumph—for that purpose, any number of alternatives would do—but because they are only semi-embodied, inviting the subject's participation and transformation. The statue of Winged Victory is victorious despite lacking a head or arms, which the viewer is called upon to fill in through an act of mind. Carissimi's song suffices as "monument" not *despite* being nothing more than Dolukhanova's voice, but *because* it is nothing more than a voice. That voice is no less real for being immaterial, since it connects the poet to the singer, to whom she also dedicated the poem "Song." That Dolukhanova was frequently accompanied on piano by Vladimir Khvostin reinforces the fact that for Sedakova such allusions aim not to display an erudite personal archive but to articulate the otherwise invisible community of speakers and listeners, presence and absence, in which we all play a role.

We can understand Sedakova's attraction to two of her most important twentieth-century interlocutors, Rilke and Celan, in a similar light. Celan, whose diminishing poetic line has become emblematic in twentieth-century poetics of the dynamic interplay of silence and utterance, offers what Sedakova terms "the preverbal limit of his word—not silence, but something like a moan, a cry, a lowing" ("doslovesnyi predel ego slova—ne molchanie, a chto-to vrode stona, krika, mychaniia").[38] Rilke provides an ideal of nearly absolute vision, of the preconscious immersion in reality that he terms "the Open" (*das Offene*), which is also the vision of his "Archaic Torso of Apollo" ("Archaischer Torso Apollos," 1908), lacking a head but seeing from its every surface. Yet even this vision can only be *nearly* absolute, for as Sedakova is quick to point out, we do not see *its* seeing: "Rilke described the ancient torso of Apollo as 'seeing you' with its every point. But that's how it sees in *its* world, where it is watching everything. And in fact he *is seeing himself*, as in Sappho's ode" ("Novaia lirika Rainera Mariia Ril'ke: Sem' rassuzhdenii"; 2:384). For Sedakova, there must always be an epistemological remainder, that which remains unseen or unmaterialized.[39] Creation must remain unfinished, lest it cease to be creation. The poet's task is, in this sense, not to render the invisible visible, but to enact their dynamic interaction.

Coda: The Work of Understanding

In both her poems and prose, Sedakova voices an ecumenical vision akin to another Orthodoxy, that of G. K. Chesterton. Chesterton, whom Sedakova has long admired, derides "the alternative of reason and faith," instead emphasizing their complementarity, as well as the fact that "reason is itself a matter of faith."[40] Chesterton's Christianity, and to a significant degree Sedakova's, recognizes the figure of Christ as the very incarnation of complementarity, the meeting place of God's mystery, which we access through faith, and our corporeal existence, which we experience through the physical senses and understand through our intellectual faculties. Or, to borrow Averintsev's summary of Chesterton's thought, all manifestation represents the victory of an unrealized potential over the "impossibility" that had prevented its realization: "Any thing in the world, any work of mankind worth talking about, is for him its triumph over its own impossibility."[41] One cannot pretend even to a fleeting vision of the world in its completeness without accounting for both sides of this epistemological divide, which itself may be very thin, since so much of what we spy in the world is shifting between potentiality and actuality.

The fusion of the Platonic and mystic philosophical traditions that such a worldview entails has deep roots in early and medieval Christian philosophy, most notably in Aquinas, who for Chesterton epitomized it. In teaching that only God is the complete manifestation of all potential—*ipsum esse subsistens*—Aquinas confronts us with an experiential world that consists of potentials and manifestations, and where one is no less real than the other. In this way, he reframes uncertainty or ignorance as its own form of positive knowledge, since here the truth value of an assertion is measured not only by *what is,* but also by *what could be.* This is why Chesterton characterizes Aquinas's thought as "the permanent philosophy," a rejection of the ancient tradition of Heraclitus and its notion that there is only change. "There is no doubt about the being of being," Chesterton writes, "even if it does sometimes look like becoming; that is because what we see is not the fullness of being; or (to continue a sort of colloquial slang) we never see being being as much as it can."[42]

In Sedakova's estimation—and, more importantly, in her practice—the lyric poem is an instrument by which one executes "the work of understanding" ("rabota ponimaniia").[43] Her lyric method, with its insistent return to images of potential and manifestation (*sad,* "garden"; *sozvezdie,* "constellation") and its fondness for syllogisms, places reason and faith in each other's service. An excellent illustration appears in "Apologia of the Rational" ("Apologiia ratsional'nogo"), a major essay that Sedakova penned in memory of Averintsev. Sedakova shares an anecdote in which Averintsev surprises her by declaring—and in a manner that would suggest his position is both elementary and obvious—that one's rational faculties, rather than emotional or ecstatic experience, guide us along our path toward faith: "And so Averintsev had chosen the humanities—but the kind of humanities in which the reasoning point of departure not only does not give way to the natural-scientific, but in some respect surpasses it" (4:524).

As in her commentary to Thomas Mann and Károly Kerényi, instead of completion Sedakova privileges beginnings or "departure": *nachalo,* or else *nepochatoe,* what I earlier translated as "the uninitiated," but which is more properly that which is "whole" or "untouched." The reasoning mind, in her estimation, demonstrates its reason not by reaching a conclusion, but by *not* reaching it. Averintsev's purpose, Sedakova explains, is to cultivate a correct understanding of the world as it is, which means using reason rigorously to avoid the pitfalls of self-deception, whether in the illusive certainties of dogma or the equally illusive certainties of empiricism:

> Wisdom, "the humanist spirit," is the spirit which establishes human communication, insofar as the basis of communication is *understanding*: probably Averintsev's main term. "The work of understanding": this is how he characterized philology. Seeking a term for this general object, which lies at the foundation of his various activities, he settled on *understanding. Understanding* [*Po-nimanie*], *attention* [*v-nimanie*]—these Russian words, through their very morphology, their internal form, speak of acceptance [*pri-iatie*], of seizure [*vz-iatie*]: not of repulsion, of distancing. And so Averintsev's concern is human understanding and service to it. (4:532–33)

The "work of understanding" for Sedakova is comparable to what it had been for Averintsev, though it is not entirely the same. Both the poet and the philosopher aim for "understanding." But what is *sluzhba* for Averintsev—"work," certainly, but also "duty," "office," or "service," with all the attendant connotations of spiritual calling and of a communal and codified religious practice—for Sedakova is *rabota,* "work" in the sense of "labor," that labor for which the lyric poem is itself the instrument and vehicle. Sedakova calls our attention to philological research, reflection, and insight as the means of achieving an understanding "of form, in the broadest sense."[44]

For Sedakova, philology reveals the conceptual connections not only within language, but within the reality to which language refers. In this respect, her use of philology recalls Bruno Schulz's assertion, published in his seminal 1936 essay "The Mythicization of Reality" ("Mityzacja rzeczywistości"), that philosophy "is, in fact, philology, it is the deep, creative probing of the word."[45] In a manner that only philological research can elaborate, the poetic word points simultaneously to the potential existence of its referent and to that referent's manifestation in experiential reality. That is, the word here indicates both possibility and materialization, and in this way it serves as the nexus between form—"internal form," form "in the broadest sense"—and realization.

Such a notion of form is fundamentally rooted in the Platonic *eidos.* Where Sedakova differs from the Romantic theory of forms, which necessarily privileges the ideal over the material, and where she is equally distant from proponents of *poésie pure,* with its insistence on the word's material self-sufficiency, is in her emphasis on the dynamic interplay between mystery and revelation, an interplay for which language itself serves as the meeting point between what is hidden and what is revealed. Thus Sedakova is making a point as much epistemological as aesthetic when she declares what the lyre is to the poet: "shining with the minutia of invisible things, / equipment half-divine" ("siiaia meloch'iu nevidannikh veshchei, / polubozhestvennoe snariazhen'e"; "Predpesnia"; 1:75).

Notes

I wish to thank Jamie Parsons, as well as the editors of the present volume, for their attentive reading and critique of this essay's earlier versions. Unless otherwise noted, translations of poetry in this essay, including by Sedakova, are my own.

1. See, for example, Benjamin Paloff, "Beyond the Chains of Illusion," in *And His Orchestra* (Pittsburgh: Carnegie Mellon University Press, 2015), 67–70; and G. C. Waldrep, "St. Caspar Is Missing from Your Elegy," *Parnassus: Poetry in Review* 33, nos. 1–2 (2013): 82–87. Waldrep, one of few contemporary American poets to have spent significant time living in a religious community, composed his poem in response to Sedakova's "In Memory of a Poet" ("Pamiati poeta").

2. Robert Faggen, "Czesław Miłosz: The Art of Poetry LXX," *The Paris Review* 36, no. 133 (Winter 1994): 242–73, quotation from 250.

3. Harold Bloom, Introduction to *American Religious Poems*, ed. Harold Bloom and Jesse Zuba (New York: Library of America, 2006), xxviii, xlvi–xlvii.

4. Bruno Latour, "'Thou Shalt Not Freeze-Frame,' or, How Not to Misunderstand the Science and Religion Debate," in *Science, Religion, and the Human Experience*, ed. James D. Proctor (Oxford: Oxford University Press, 2005), 27–48, quotation from 29.

5. John Paul II, "Encyclical Letter *Fides et Ratio* of the Supreme Pontiff John Paul II to the Bishops of the Catholic Church on the Relation between Faith and Reason," September 14, 1998, http://w2.vatican.va/content/john-paul-ii/en/encyclicals/documents/hf_jp-ii_enc_14091998_fides-et-ratio.html, accessed March 17, 2018. Emphasis added.

6. Ol'ga Sedakova, "Interv'iu Dmitriiu Uzlaneru dlia 'Russkogo Zhurnala,'" http://www.olgasedakova.com/interview/1075, accessed March 17, 2018.

7. For an elaboration of how Sedakova and Brodsky differ in their treatment of deity, see Benjamin Paloff, "The God Function in Joseph Brodsky and Olga Sedakova," *Slavic and East European Journal* 51, no. 4 (Winter 2007): 716–36. In a 2012 interview, Sedakova also explains her displeasure with Brodsky's poems in terms that resonate with her view on the complementarity of knowledge and mystery: "He's very much a poet of locking things down. And he doesn't have much basis for such locking-down." Ol'ga Andreeva, "Ol'ga Sedakova: 'Mozhno zhit' dal'she . . . ,'" *Russkii reporter* 13 (242), April 2, 2012, http://www.rusrep.ru/article/2012/04/02/sedakova/, accessed March 17, 2018.

8. Charles Taylor, *A Secular Age* (Cambridge, MA: Harvard University Press, 2007).

9. C. P. Snow, *The Two Cultures* (Cambridge: Cambridge University Press, 1998).

10. Sergei Averintsev, *Religiia i literatura* (Ann Arbor, MI: Hermitage, 1981), 121–38.

11. Indeed, this is arguably the most compelling debt that Sedakova's poem owes to Thomas Gray's "Elegy Written in a Country Churchyard," which, in Vasily Zhukovsky's 1802 translation, served as a kind of urtext for Russian Romanticism. Gray's poem reveals what is for the Romantics the terminal incompleteness of the elegiac utterance. The poet is unable to access the absent friend or, for that matter, to define his own limits vis-à-vis

the Other, whose presence is a function of his absence. The poet therefore produces speech that keeps looping back to the poem's speaker, since the speaker is himself the only path toward the object he elegizes.

12. Faggen, "Czesław Miłosz," 250.

13. John Paul II, "Letter of His Holiness Pope John Paul II to Artists," 1999, https://w2.vatican.va/content/john-paul-ii/en/letters/1999/documents/hf_jp-ii_let_23041999_artists.html, accessed March 17, 2018.

14. Dietrich Bonhoeffer, *Letters and Papers from Prison*, ed. John W. de Gruchy, trans. Isabel Best et al. (Minneapolis, MN: Fortress Press, 2010), 216.

15. Bonhoeffer, in fact, famously rejects the idea of "God as the stopgap" in his letter dated May 29, 1944, to Eberhard Bethge. Bonhoeffer, *Letters and Papers*, 404–8.

16. Ol'ga Sedakova, "Ob"iasnitel'naia zapiska: Predislovie k samizdatskoi knige stikhov *Vorota, okna, arki* (1979–1983)," n2, http://www.olgasedakova.com/Poetica/1534, accessed March 17, 2018. Sedakova offers this note to explain an offhand (and, for her, rare) allusion to the mysticism of Emanuel Swedenborg, whom she had just read at Shvarts's urging. Her resistance to Swedenborg distinguishes her not only from Shvarts but also from Miłosz.

17. Jean-Luc Nancy, *The Birth to Presence*, trans. Brian Holmes et al. (Stanford, CA: Stanford University Press, 1993), 319–40.

18. Averintsev points out how, in medieval aesthetics, the incarnation of God in Christ is echoed in the artistic act as such: "It would follow that art is the analogue of Christianity's principal mystery: the 'incarnation' [*vochelovechenie*] of the Absolute." Averintsev, *Religiia i literatura*, 129.

19. Mikhail Epshtein, *Paradoksy novizny: O literaturnom razvitii XIX–XX vekov* (Moscow: Sovetskii pisatel', 1988), 162–63.

20. Vl. Slavetskii, "Dorogi i tropinka," *Novyi mir* 4 (1995): 233–37; quotation from 234.

21. Nikolai Slavianskii, "Iz polnogo do dna v glubokoe do kraev: O stikhakh Ol'gi Sedakovoi," *Novyi mir* 10 (1995): 224–31; quotations from 225, 226.

22. Slavianskii, "Iz polnogo do dna," 229.

23. Viacheslav V. Ivanov, Introduction to Ol'ga Sedakova, "Solovei, filomela, sud'ba," *Druzhba narodov* 10 (1988): 121.

24. For an equally productive example from the same volume, see "Legenda sed'maia," 1:63–64.

25. Osip Mandel'shtam, *Polnoe sobranie stikhotvorenii*, ed. M. L. Gasparov and A. G. Mets (St. Petersburg: Akademicheskii proekt, 1997), 91–92.

26. W. B. Yeats, *The Collected Poems of W. B. Yeats*, 2nd ed., ed. Richard J. Finneran (New York: Scribner, 1996), 215–17.

27. Aleksander Wat, *With the Skin: Poems of Aleksander Wat*, trans. Czesław Miłosz and Leonard Nathan (New York: Ecco, 1989), 29.

28. T. S. Eliot, *Collected Poems 1909–1962* (New York: Harcourt Brace, 1963), 87–88.

29. Elena Shvarts, *Vidimaia storona zhizni* (St. Petersburg: Limbus Press, 2003), 256.

30. Maria Khotimsky, "Singing David, Dancing David: Olga Sedakova and Elena Shvarts Rewrite a Psalm," *Slavic and East European Journal* 51, no. 4 (Winter 2007): 737–52; quotations from 747.

31. M. E. Zvegintsova, "Kontsept 'sad' v lirike O. Sedakovoi," *Russkaia filologiia* [Khar'kov] 49, nos. 1–2 (2013): 73–78; quotation from 76.

32. In addition to the elegy, one of Sedakova's landmark lyric cycles, *Tristan and Isolde* (*Tristan i Izol'da*, 1978–82), is dedicated to Khvostin, as is the poem "A Small Dedication" ("Malen'koe posviashchenie") and the essay "The Teacher of Music" ("Uchitel' muzyki").

33. Sofya Khagi, *Silence and the Rest: Verbal Skepticism in Russian Poetry* (Evanston, IL: Northwestern University Press, 2013).

34. O'lga Sedakova, "Schastlivaia trevoga glubiny," http://www.olgasedakova.com/Moralia/266, accessed March 17, 2018.

35. The ethical implications of this interpenetration, particularly concerning the dialogic interval separating Self from Other, warrant their own sustained treatment. The French-born philosopher Guillaume Badoual gives us a promising starting point in an essay on ethics and Sedakova. For Badoual, Sedakova invites us to think about ethics in terms that reject both deontological moralism and, at the same time, the utilitarianism that has been the dominant rational alternative to moral doctrine since the Enlightenment. See Guillaume Badoual, "'L'éthique, elle aussi, est sans fond' (Méditation d'une remarque d'Olga Alexandrovna Sedakóva)," *Philosophie* 116 (January 2013): 78–93.

36. Translation by Caroline Clark, in Sedakova, *In Praise of Poetry* (Rochester, NY: Open Letter, 2014), 173–74.

37. Latour, "'Thou Shalt Not Freeze-Frame,'" 29.

38. Ol'ga Sedakova, "Urok Tselana: Beseda s Antonom Nesterovym," *Kontekst* 9 4 (1999): 233. A shortened redaction of the interview also exists (2:537–40).

39. Stephanie Sandler draws a similar conclusion in differentiating Sedakova's visions from those of Ivan Zhdanov: "Sedakova is more likely than is Zhdanov to use the paradoxes of Christianity to write about the mysterious power of art and her mirrors offer visibility and obscurity in the same flash of light. [. . .] Mirrors in these poems open up an aperture for revelation rather than self-admiration, and Sedakova's mirrors deflect or refract light as easily as they reflect it." Stephanie Sandler, "Mirrors and Metarealists: The Poetry of Ol'ga Sedakova and Ivan Zhdanov," *Slavonica* 12, no. 1 (April 2006): 3–23; quotation from 6.

40. Gilbert K. Chesterton, *Orthodoxy* (New York: John Lane, 1909), 56.

41. Sergei Averintsev, *Poety* (Moscow: Shkola "Iazyki russkoi kul'tury," 1996), 313.

42. G. K. Chesterton, *St. Thomas Aquinas* (New York: Sheed & Ward, 1933), 208.

43. Ol'ga Sedakova, *Dvukhtomnoe sobranie sochinenii*, vol. 1, *Stikhi* (Moscow: En Ef K'u/Tu Print, 2001), 15.

44. In this Sedakova is closely aligned with Mandelstam and Nikolai Zabolotsky, among the canonical Russian Modernists she cites most frequently. This alignment also extends from epistemology to the rhetoric by which it is expressed. Mandelstam and Zabolotsky both have frequent recourse to paregmenon, the rhetorical device by which words spin off morphological variations based on the same root—that is, the same device that Sedakova uses in her description of Averintsev's "understanding."

45. Bruno Schulz, *Opowiadanie, Wybór esejów i listów*, ed. Jerzy Jarzębski (Wrocław: Ossolineum, 1989), 368.

The Poet and Darkness

The Politics of Artistic Form

KSENIA GOLUBOVICH

Immer wieder von uns aufgerissen,
Ist der Gott die Stelle, welche heilt.
Torn open by us again and again,
God is the place that heals.

—R. M. Rilke

Poetic Form and Suicide

Olga Sedakova's poetry spans the latter half of the twentieth century and the early years of the twenty-first, and as a poet she is deeply attuned to the history of her lifetime; at the same time, her poetry explores the relationship between history and eternity. And history in Sedakova's lifetime has been marked by catastrophe in the form of wars and crises, both humanitarian and anthropological. Something in the very essence, the very self-definition of humanity has been broken. A line separating the human from the inhuman has been violated, and we would be hard-pressed to restore it.[1] The man of the old order, with his well-worn sins and errors, is a thing of the past. The new man has made adjustments in response to catastrophe, and is susceptible to experiences—to kinds of pain in particular—that were previously unknown. None of the accepted categories apply anymore, including the categories of "poet" and "reader." Even the theme of suicide, so important to the poètes maudits, neurotic poets of the nineteenth and early twentieth centuries, is no longer usable. In fact, to use it now would be unethical. When the world has known absolute evil, one suicide seems like a pointless farce, and there are worse things than losing one's biological life.

We need to recognize that nineteenth-century attitudes toward suicide informed the very principles of pure art, art for art's sake, that became so influential in prewar European culture. The form-building modernist passionate rhetoric of the poètes maudits required that death on an individual scale mark the limit of human experience, that biological death serve as a metaphor for the soul's fall from grace or the soul's liberation from the banal. Their rhetoric aestheticized death and presented art as a form of personal immortality, itself necessitating the death of the artist. If ordinary life was like drab prose, and literature (life's mirror) was the art of the possible, then pure poetry—which, as Stéphane Mallarmé claimed, reflected neither people nor things—was the art of what could never be, the unheard-of. The impossible and unheard-of were understood as the juxtaposition and fusion of dichotomies (night/day, light/darkness, love/hate) into a single incandescent, pulsating knot. William Blake (forgotten in his own time and rediscovered in the Modernist era), Charles Baudelaire, Arthur Rimbaud and Mallarmé, Yeats, and Pound later on, and all those who sprang from the movement for pure art, built their texts on these pulsating contradictions, generating vivid, hallucinatory images that burned away humanity's lowly origins. Within each dichotomy, death was the ecstatic limit of the positive term (day, light, love). But death was itself a contradiction, a union of irreconcilables (for example, flower and carrion in Baudelaire). As such, it brought forth a residue or bloom, a dazzling, ephemeral, irresistible vision—an erotic super-image—that enthralled the reader. This is what beguiled great Russians too—Alexander Blok and Nikolai Gumilev, and even early Osip Mandelstam and Marina Tsvetaeva.

It is exactly this spellbinding poetics—a poetics of extremes, graftings, and hybridizations—that no longer suffices for Olga Sedakova. Moreover, this poetics will not be politically immune to the challenges of totalitarian practices in the twentieth century. Suicide for the sake of immortality (which is precisely how the Russian intelligentsia interpreted the Russian Revolution) works no more. Art for art's sake can produce artistic tyrants, destroying human banalities for the sake of their own Gesamtkunstwerk. Juxtaposition and contradiction no longer serve to face down the challenge. The poet's frame of reference has shifted from personal suicide in the face of the banal to the unthinkable banality of the deaths of millions. The poet has to go beyond one person's death, even the poet's own death and its glorification, and to stand up to the changed vision of Death.

One for All

In Theodor Adorno and Max Horkheimer's groundbreaking book, *Dialectic of Enlightenment*,[2] the authors pose their famous question, which serves as a watershed dividing the high modern from the postmodern: can there be poetry after Auschwitz? Or after the Gulag? This question is inscribed over the Gates of Our Time, just as "know thyself" was once inscribed in the Temple of Apollo. Adorno and Horkheimer's question is open to interpretation, but its implications for poetry can be summarized as follows: if there is a liminal situation of evil whose very existence invalidates all traditional poetry, then poetry can no longer be considered a liminal situation—that boundary where humanity comes in contact with the most awful and crucial things. Poetry cannot cope with such encounters; it breaks down, shows itself false and unhelpful. But in that case what is it good for? After all, poetry has always been considered a conduit to the otherworldly, with poets being specially ordained to undertake this journey. In folklore, poets journey to the dead, teeter on the edge of insanity, and look directly upon the most dreadful. They do this not for themselves, but because poetry is marked by the same sacred rift that divides the human from the inhuman, separates man from beast and god, and determines humanity's future trajectories. Poetic skill is bound up with prophets and bards, with access to the greatest terror and the highest salvation. The poet goes where his readers, being ordinary people, cannot, but where they nevertheless must go *because* they are people. The poet goes there on behalf of all. He is a scout, a diviner, a pioneer.

At the same time, much in Sedakova's work indicates how important it is for her that poetry correspond to specific historical experience. We find evidence for this in her essays on the twentieth-century Russian humanitarian crisis and its aftermath (from the early work "Journey to Briansk" ("Puteshestvie v Briansk")[3] to "Mediocrity as a Social Danger" ("Posredstvennost' kak sotsial'naia opasnost'"); as well as in her poetry ("Elegy That Turns into a Requiem"/"Elegiia, perekhodiashchaia v Rekviem"; "Nothing"/"Nichto"). In fact, it runs through her entire poetics, which were formed in deliberate opposition to the traditions of Soviet poetry as well as high modernism.

Sedakova's willingness to take risks goes hand in hand with her resolution to be a poet in earnest, a poet above all. In our time, this means a poet who renounces forcefulness, glaring contrasts, hypnotism, hallucination, dramatic effects, and other forms of ecstatic delirium. But neither does Sedakova retreat into the quotidian, writing about its joys as many poets do now, and dismissing the challenges of pure art as totalitarian and destructive. Instead, she finds the courage to go forward, to follow where our fate leads us.

Sedakova takes up these ideas in her essay "In Praise of Poetry" ("Zametki i vospominaniia o raznykh stikhotvoreniiakh, a takzhe Pokhvala poezii," 1982), the text that addresses her early suicide attempt, and in her early poem "The Cursed Poet" ("Prokliatyi poet"), where suicide becomes only the first half of the journey and leads to a mysterious convalescence. In this poem, she dismisses the very idea of suicide as a step into the unknown, a rite of passage, and she accepts a responsibility to go further, to truly face that which is "scarier than Goethe's *Faust*" ("postrashnee *Fausta* Gete").[4] Because that is the path that lies before humanity, before Sedakova's reader, whether or not the reader admits it. We cannot run away from our dead, we cannot betray them again. We have to follow where they take us. If not, we have no forgiveness and no right for happiness. Dante went down to hell and climbed to heaven to answer his readers' questions: What is the source of true happiness, the source of salvation and punishment, and will there be happiness after death? To rephrase Adorno and Horkheimer's question in a Dantean light: How can we be happy after Auschwitz and Gulag, after what humanity has shown itself capable of? Seen this way, the question is less a verdict than a problem to be solved. Certainly it means going beyond the traditional poetics of warring oppositions, or integrating this poetics into a bigger picture, one that is still full of possibility.

Sedakova and Tolstoy: The Ethics of Caring for the Sick

Sedakova was not the first to summon us down this path. That distinction belongs to Leo Tolstoy, an artist of the highest order from Sedakova's point of view, who possessed an uncanny sense about the future. Sedakova's line, "as though it were possible to forget / that happiness wants to be / and sorrow wants not to be" ("kak budto mozhno zabyt,' / o tom, chto schast'e khochet byt,' / a gore khochet ne byt'," *Chinese Journey/Kitaiskoe puteshestvie*; 1:342) recalls the simple cadences of *Anna Karenina*'s famous first sentence: "Happy families are all alike; every unhappy family is unhappy in its own way."[5] Ludwig Wittgenstein—another of Tolstoy's great interpreters—was rapturous over the simplicity and mystical clarity of this line, which could never be mistaken for any other.[6]

For Wittgenstein, Tolstoy was an ethical authority and, along with Fyodor Dostoevsky, Europe's last religious thinker. He believed that Tolstoy had an intuitive understanding of the logical form of fact, particularly when it came to good and evil. According to Wittgenstein, good and evil cannot themselves be expressed through language, but constitute the limits of language, the place where language falls silent. And yet, with any fact, as its limits are elucidated by language, it becomes increasingly obvious whether the fact is good or evil. This is one of the paradoxes of mystical or religious thought. Tolstoy was a master of exposing the implicit ethical form of a fact. His way of looking at things made it immediately clear whether those things were good or bad, without his needing to explain it. Wittgenstein calls this ability mysticism, and in Tolstoy's works, Natasha Rostova is just such an innate mystic. She sees right away whether or not something is wrong, whether or not someone is happy, and as a result she herself arrives at happiness. This ethics of happiness relates not to the content of facts, but to their immediately evident form. Where the content seems perfectly fine, the form will reveal inherent badness or wrongness. Tolstoy's ethics of happiness closely resembles Wittgenstein's, as do Sedakova's investigations into the rigorous logic of language.

By alluding to Tolstoy in the line about happiness and grief, Sedakova turned over a new leaf for poetry. For Sedakova, unlike the decadents or Romantics, grief is simply that which wants to stop existing in us. And pain is that which wants to stop hurting, and nothing more. Pain is just pain, and it need not exist.

Pain is pain is pain. Sickness is sickness. Another, analogous example of this kind of thought: "Fate resembles fate / and nothing else" ("Sud'ba pokhozha na sud'bu / i bol'she ni na chto," *Tristan and Isolde*, "First Prelude" ["Vstuplenie pervoe"]; 1:145). "Destiny"—that weighty word—is brought down to size, divested of every metaphorical expansion of its meaning. Destiny is equal to itself and nothing else, an absolute identity, a tautology. How are we to understand such tautologies? The same way Tolstoy understood them, as that which is "the same as everyone's." Your pain is the same as everyone's, and it signifies only pain. This ethical use of a language common to all was rejected by the poètes maudits, who opted for a poetics of the eccentric gesture and jarring contrast, the crossing out (for example, Tsvetaeva's dash) that annihilates commonplace ideas. It is this poetic crossing out that Tolstoy rejected in his rebuke to the Symbolists,[7] and Sedakova rejects it as well. Words should mean what they usually do, what they mean for everyone.

At the same time, Tolstoy's ethical position is neither a rejection of contradiction, nor a retreat to the healthy simplicity of traditional morality. For all her positive traits, Natasha can also be capricious and unchaste; and Tolstoy's other great heroine-mystic is none other than Anna Karenina. Tolstoy was unable to condemn Anna, to harden his heart against a person he loved. His empathy and love for Anna, as her creator, and his reevaluation of marriage as an institution in his later years, attest to how profoundly the experience of writing *Anna Karenina* changed him. It is as though something else had come into being at the same time as Anna, and this something led Tolstoy beyond domestic comfort and warmth. His infirmity proved stronger than the available cure (marriage, children, household). Moreover, for Tolstoy, the human soul is at its most authentic not in the middle of salubrious activities like mowing, threshing, or childbearing, but sitting by the deathbed (be it Kitty nursing her husband's brother, or Ivan Ilyich, who plays two roles—he is at once a dying man and the one who sits at a bedside, offering comfort). If the soul standing before the sufferer proves righteous, it becomes a source of comfort and even of epiphany to someone on the threshold of death.[8] "That very thing" ("to samoe"), as Ivan Ilyich says, reaching his own end. "Not that!" ("ne to!"), as Anna cries out in death, still without an answer. This ability to accept the irrevocably sick, to accept the dying and become an answer to it, is itself authentic poetry. Anna could find no such answer, no answering gaze. As a true creator who must follow the same path as his protagonists and readers, Tolstoy forged ahead to ever-greater depths of suffering.

What do the dying see in the dark? Why are they suddenly overjoyed? Perhaps they have been shown another image, another world arranged according to other laws. We need only recall the entry in Tolstoy's diary where he writes that one can kill without it being a sin, but one can also eat a piece of bread and it will be a sin.[9] Recall that for Tolstoy, the content of a fact is unimportant; meaning is constituted by the form of a fact, its appearance. These new images are distinct from ordinary thought—as they were for the Decadent poets—but not antithetical to it. On the contrary, everything is left as it was. In just the same way, two unequal acts—the theft of bread and the killing of a human being—are equal before that which redeems one and damns the other. And though the same reason informs these two judgments, they may easily be reversed depending on the situation. Herein lies the logical and religious riddle of the universe: what makes the world the way it is, and what accounts for its differences? Identity precedes contrast, just as unity precedes contradiction. The driving force behind this view is the simple but vital idea that the same sun shines on righteous and unrighteous alike. Sedakova's engagement with the problem of sin is related to this idea, which is at once highly formal and deeply religious.

In the poem "Sin" ("Grekh"), that "same thing"—thought keeping its own measure—is evidently hard at work:

Можно обмануть высокое небо—
высокое небо всего не увидит.
Можно обмануть глубокую землю—
глубокая земля спит и не слышит.
Ясновидцев, гадателей и гадалок—
а себя самого не обманешь. (1:184)

You can fool the high, high sky—
the high, high sky can't see everything.
You can fool the deep, deep earth—
the deep, deep earth is asleep and can't hear.
Clairvoyants and fortunetellers, too—
but yourself you'll never fool.

Each couplet is structured around a turn: the first line of each couplet announces a theme, while the second line contains a kind of epiphany. Sedakova underscores this internal movement within each couplet by capitalizing the first word of the odd-numbered lines, but not of the even-numbered ones. The "high heavens" of line 1 is almost liturgical in register, while the explanation in line 2 uses a middle style that evens out the meaning. Heaven is "high," which is why it cannot see what happens on earth. The juxtaposition of "high" heaven and "deep" earth registers not as a contrast, but—on the contrary—as a kind of identification. These two antipodes, these abysses, turn out to be neighbors (and similar ones at that) once we have brought them to the surface. Meanwhile, the theme of vision brings forth new kinds of vision. The clairvoyants and diviners, whose ingenuity allows them to see into the heart of things from the outside, grasp their essence with other eyes. Their appearance in one of the emphatic, odd-numbered lines associates them with a high register, as do their inertia and mysteriousness. They are the same as heaven and earth in that they, too, see nothing. In the following line they are answered by a commonplace formula, a phrase everybody knows: "But yourself you'll never fool" ("a sebia samogo ne obmanesh'"). With its colloquial, prosaic intonation, this line is not dramatically contrastive, but, as it were, instantly affirming. A pricking, rather than a contrast; the perforation of a smooth surface; a blow struck against the previous construction. Moreover, the blow is struck with something completely equal to itself, which, in turn, intensifies the pricking action. The prick of conscience—a tool by which humanity uses pain to gauge ethics—works in a similar fashion. Conscience does not grant us new knowledge; it lets us see old, familiar things in a new light, as a sudden realization. The pricking is produced by the very form of a fact out of its own self, a form that says something equivalent to itself and at the same time different.

In the *Tractatus Logico-Philosophicus*,[10] Ludwig Wittgenstein treats tautologies and contradictions—our compulsion to repeat the same thing or mutually exclusive things—as illustrating the very form of the world; namely, the limits of our ability to speak. Tautology and contradiction amount to the same thing. Voicing an absolute contrast and saying two identical things both mark the limit of what can be said. Beyond this limit lies either nonsense or simple, silent clarity—the inexpressible (inexpressible because no one knows why it is thus and not otherwise). At the same time, it is still possible to *show* one's own limits, even though these limits cannot be proven, described, or articulated. Wittgenstein was fascinated by phrases in Tolstoy that marked the content of a fact as good or evil. In this sense, the task of the poet is precisely this incandescent demonstrability, this arrival at a clear vision of the limits of the world. By the light of this incandescence, we begin to see what cannot be said. By leading us to the edge, the poet opens a perspective onto something that exceeds language. And while the Decadent poets relied on contradiction, Tolstoy experimented with a more difficult, and more interesting, approach. He used tautology, that which *comes after* contradiction. At the point where the only possible words are "I am dying—I don't want to die" (a soul-shattering expression of terror), Tolstoy found a reply that inverts this very expression into a positive statement: "Yes—life!" He thereby translates a contradiction into an expression of absolute oneness. Tolstoy pursues this difficult formal turn in "The Forged Coupon" ("Fal'shivyi kupon"), "The Death of Ivan Ilyich" ("Smert' Ivana Il'icha"), "The Cossacks" ("Kazaki"), and *War and Peace* (*Voina i mir*). And it is this turn, enacted at the logical limit of the world, that Sedakova (who is in complete agreement with Tolstoy on this point) pursues in her own work. In the first stanza of "Sin," she performs a formal turn at the logical limit of her own utterance. Of all Russian poets, Sedakova is perhaps the one in whom mysticism and logic combine in equal measure, while her ethics of the turn bring her close to Tolstoy. The sickness that drove Tolstoy beyond family and habitual existence did not vanish with his death; on the contrary, it intensified and was bequeathed to his successors, those who have sought an answer to the problem of the world's Great Sickness, which Tolstoy never found.

David Sings to Saul

In order to take the measure of Sedakova's poetic thought, one need only find the fulcrum around which her poetry revolves. For one thing to turn into another, that thing must also rotate around its own axis, performing a 180-degree turn or "aspect change";[11] moreover, this change must occur at the very edge of that thing. Interestingly, the Russian word *krai* ("edge/region") invokes a similarly high-stakes play on meanings: *krai* can signify both a delimiting feature—a boundary mark—and an expanse, a region. In the poem "David Sings to Saul" ("David poet Saulu"), David's singing comforts the ailing king, Saul:

Ты знаешь, мы смерти хотим, господин,
мы все. И верней, чем другие,
я слышу: невидим и непобедим
сей внутренний ветер. Мы всё отдадим
за эту равнину, куда ни один
еще не дошел,—и, дожив до седин,
мы просим о ней, как грудные. (1:222)

You know, my lord, we all want death, all of us.
And more truly than others, I hear:
this wind that's inside us, unseen, unsubdued.
We'll give it all up for this broad place, where no one

has ever set foot,—and 'til we have gone gray,
we'll beg, as a babe for the breast.

This is the poem's culminating point, the death-wish toward which the poem as a whole has been moving, flowing from the furthest realms (*kraia*) of experience, from the realm of domesticity where "men go to war" and "women spin the fleece from Gideon's times" ("zheny priadut runo iz vremen Gedeona"). We can observe this movement clearly in the first several stanzas:

Да, мой господин, и душа для души—
не врач и не умная стража
(ты слышишь, как струны мои хороши?),
не мать, не сестра, а селенье в глуши
и долгая зимняя пряжа.

Холодное время, не видно огней,
темно и утешиться нечем.
Душа твоя плачет о множестве дней,
о тайне своей и о шуме морей.
Есть многие лучше, но пусть за моей
она проведет этот вечер.
[...]
И знаешь ли, царь? не лекарство, а труд—
душа для души, и протянется тут,
как мужи воюют, как жены прядут
руно из времен Гедеона. (1:221)

My lord, what you hear is my soul for your soul—
not some doctor or guard making good
(aren't my stings entrancing? you hear that, right?),
no mother, no sister, just a long winter yarn,
and a handful of huts in the sticks.

A cold time to be alive, not a fire in sight,
it's dark, and you won't find much solace.
Your soul weeps for the all of the many days,
for its close-held secret, for the sound of the seas.
There are better than mine, but just for tonight
let your soul pass the time with my soul.
[...]

You know, don't you, king, it's no pill, just hard work—
one soul for another, as men go to war,
as women sit spinning, there stretches before us
the fleece straight from Gideon's times.

This is the central point of pain, the razor's edge of sickness, the frontier of the native land (*krai*), and the final pricking of truth. We long for death. Let us linger here, rather than rushing after the poem's rhythm. The pain is here, in this very spot, and at the edge (*krai*) of this pain, all pain will gather.

As Sedakova says in another poetic formula, "Death is an illness of the mind" ("Smert'—bolezn' uma") ("Second Stanzas: On the Death of a Kitten"/"Stansy vtorye. Na smert' kotenka"; 1:272). Tear sickness from the mind, refute mortality, turn the intellect, and death will no longer exist. In its place will be what Tolstoy described as life's edge, the big "yes!" of life in its entirety, life in the act of passing through us and having us as its limit, its fulcrum. We are the means by which life itself sees. This "big" life begins from the moment we say yes to death, and then flies backward into our daily lives, our habits, everything we once held dear ("we've brought all of it here / from there" ["ottuda siuda / my vynesli vse"], as David sings to Saul). But our previous "small" life, given to us from the other side of our usual way of thinking about ourselves, no longer fears death. What Tolstoy, Wittgenstein, and Sedakova have called the actual life of a person is never daunted by the fear of death, because it is free to say "yes!" to anything, to give an answer to everything.

Unlike Rilke's poem on the same theme, in which David depicted various erotic tableaus in his songs, alleviating his master's suffering through a kind of anesthesia, Sedakova's David pursues the pain, intensifies it, listens to its voice, and isolates only the most painful—the most contradictory—part: the fear of death itself. Death is the horizon, the peak where they suddenly stand together, king and poet, as the avalanche starts. It seems impossible to go on. Could they go backward, into the hallucination? Or forward, into the abyss? And suddenly, David shows the king something entirely unexpected: an expanse, his native land:

вечное *да*
Такого пространства, что, царь мой, тогда
Уже ничего—ни стыда, ни суда,
Ни милости даже: оттуда сюда
Мы вынесли все. (1:222)

the eternal *yes*
of such a space that, my king, nothing is left

anymore—not shame, not judgment, nor even
mercy: we've brought all of it here
from there.

The space beyond the death-wish, the "other place," where the fear of death turns out to be a wish to live, but differently: more fully, openly, limitlessly; not limited by oneself, but radiating outward from oneself. We are frightened not of death, but of not having accepted life, of never having figured out how to live.

Here is how Sedakova describes this in her poem "Night" ("Noch'"), from the cycle *Tristan and Isolde*:

жизни не хватает,
[. . .] жизни мало жить. Она себя хватает

над самой пропастью. (1:172)

of life, there's not enough,
[. . .] there's little life to live. It clutches at itself,

hangs over the abyss.

Or in the words of Albert Schweitzer (a quotation Sedakova admires): "I am life that wants to live in the living environment of life that wants to live."[12] Here is that fulcrum, the end-point where everything starts, and before which all possibilities lie open. David shows Saul that the mountain, the sickness, the king are not the furthest limits. Everything is simple, there is always a way out, a way to turn things around and escape from the self. Elsewhere, Sedakova has described the man who leaves the self behind, St. Alexis, the Man of God. The king, who sees himself as the center of the world, has chained the world to himself, is sick with himself and cannot leave his self behind. "Turn around," says the singer. "Let go"; "leave yourself behind."

To understand how profoundly Sedakova explores this theme, we must recall the story of Saul's conflict with David, the cause of the king's sickness, the reason only David can console him, despite being his personal enemy, despite being fated to take his place on the throne, despite terrifying the king as though he were the king's own limit, his killer. If the king is the limit of the world, then there is a place "beyond you," as the singer tells him. You are not the limit. Everything could still change. And consciousness loosens its grip, and what had been restrained inside the man can flow freely. It is a great pleasure to experience such breadth, such depth, such distances. It is a complete and utter affirmation of ourselves. At the end of our suffering, meaning expands, and the question that we could not answer, that backed us into a corner, shrinks to the size of a needle's eye, of "a crumb of dry bread" ("s kroshku sukhogo khleba"; 1:330). Pain is the hook that lures something bigger than itself. And it is healed by an absolute and unexpected expansion of the very thing that we thought had reached its semantic limit, its edge. What is pain, after all? Pain is the final boundary of living things, a signal of the end. And things hurt at their limit because they do not know where to go from there; they have come up against themselves. They are merely their own boundary. Therefore, the poet's task is to carry it across this limit. In this sense, the title "David Sings to Saul" takes on a whole new meaning. The name David, with its strong contour of consonants, seems to engender sound, like the lips of a singer, while the words that follow are marked by open vowels. Indeed, the name Saul is sung, as though it were sound becoming breeze. David sings "Saul," names Saul, even as he sings *to* him.

A Vocabulary of Desire

So far in our analysis, there is one important theme we have not addressed: "sorrow wants not to be," "you know, my lord, we all want death" ("gore *khochet* ne byt'," "my smerti *khotim*, gospodin"). Pain is pain, in part, because it *wants* to not be there. This rather strange cognitive turn reflects our own search for something as well, namely desire. Pain is desire, and it also contains desire. To put it differently, the path of pain—the path through pain—leads us down the path of desire; moreover, desire is strongest where pain is most severe, where it cannot be relieved. Ultimately, as Tolstoy, too, believed, the only relief—the only consolation—is "Everything at Once" ("Vse, i srazu"; 1:416). There is an affinity between Sedakova's work and "high" psychoanalysis, the kind that rejects crude interpretations of Sigmund Freud. The idea is not to help people become socially adjusted, but to show them the true nature, and power, of their desire; in particular, their desire to understand the source of their pain by changing how they think about it. Jacques Lacan articulated a similar idea about desire, and the difference between desire and pleasure, when he wrote: "Do not renounce your desire."[13] Desire causes pain by disrupting habit and abolishing the comfort zone. Desire inflicts still greater pain when it transcends our daily routine. The greatest desire, the death wish, is also the greatest pain, as David says in Sedakova's poem. This is not a wish to die, however, since that would mean desiring the end of desire; it is, rather, a wish to live in a completely different way, to live freely and fully at all costs. Only then will the pain disappear; only then will it be transfigured into the thing it had striven to become all along: infinite well-being.

This is the kind of desire Sedakova describes in her poem "Beggars Walk Down Streets" ("Nishchie idut po dorogam"), from the cycle *Tristan and Isolde*:

А вдруг убьют?
пускай убьют:
тогда лекарство подадут
в растворе голубом.
А дом сожгут?
пускай сожгут.
Не твой же этот дом. (1:154)

And if they kill you?
let them kill:
and then they'll give you medicine,
a potion of light-blue.
And burn your house down?
let them burn it.
It's not yours, anyway.

The main theme of this section is not death but a journey. This is a journey beyond the limits of the self, a journey through the landscape of desire and revelation, across the threshold of pain, into a world that seems morbid because it accepts what human beings are loath to accept, even though it is precisely what they need. In *Three Dialogues*, Samuel Beckett—another poet of extreme tautology—describes the rules of composition in the following way: "There is nothing to express, nothing to express it with, nothing to express it from, no strength to express, no desire to express, or need to express."[14] For Beckett, these were logical conditions for the appearance of images. For Sedakova, by contrast, this same desolate landscape turns into beauty. If we were to express Sedakova's goal using Beckettian language, it might go like this: "To do the same thing, in the same one's place, in the same one's presence, with the strength and desire of the same one, and with a strong commitment to the same one." Or, as she puts it in her poem:

Хочу я Господа любить,
как нищие Его.
Хочу по городам ходить
и Божьим именем просить,
и все узнать, и все забыть,

и как немой заговорить
о красоте Его. (1:154)

I want to love the Lord my God
as much as His poor do.
I want to go around the towns
and ask for alms in God's good name,
find out all things, forget all things,
and like the mute lift up my voice,
His loveliness to tell.

In this sense, Sedakova's creative efforts are like the compiling of a comprehensive medical dictionary, a dictionary of concepts derived from pain, and of words culled with their pain, at their semantic limit. But these words also contain a secret desire for well-being, for a time when words will be free to pursue other meanings, beyond their native habitat, to look out onto something different, while bestowing hope and opening their arms to the future. It is in this spirit that Sedakova compiled a dictionary of paronyms,[15] in which she glosses common Russian words with their Church Slavonic meanings.

Sedakova's method for each pair of homonyms is not to rhyme them—rhyme would imply a discrepancy in the pair—but, quite literally, to produce an echo. The part she considers an echo is not the distant Church Slavonic term, but the close Russian one—the one that is more effaced. The Russian term is the muffled echo of a far more potent sound. This work of scholarship seems to have grown out of the poet's inability to explain why she felt compelled to pick one word over another, to transfigure the sound of everyday words by passing them through an elevated linguistic register, and, having lifted them to that height, to give them back to us, so that we can use them. It is difficult to overstate this dictionary's effect on our understanding of Russian. By drawing a distinction between a Russian word and itself, it amplifies the word's resonance, and through this accretion of meaning by repetition, we are granted a sudden, *other* vision of the underlying thing the word denotes. New ways of thinking are able to grow out of a cognitive landscape that seemed dead.

One example of this kind of semantic rereading is the fate of the word *ozloblennyi* ("embittered," in contemporary Russian). In Russian, this word denotes the influence of rancor, an aggressive and unshakeable condition. This concept signifies such a state of mind, and at the same time passes sentence on the person to whom it refers. But from the more elevated perspective of the higher register (the Church Slavonic definition), it simply indicates that a person has been embittered, not that he is inherently like that. Evil (*zlo*) has been inflicted on him, but this means it can be drawn out again, like bad blood, and understood. This semantic accretion reads as an act of mercy, a reprieve in place of a harsh sentence.

Judgment and Mercy

In Sedakova's view, mercy is not some obscure meditation on values, but a concrete linguistic act. In this sense, she is again close to Wittgenstein and Tolstoy. "Show—don't tell!" ("Ne govori—sdelai!"). Do not talk about what you want in order to bring mercy and hope into the world; just do the thing. In her essay "From Notes on Celan"—another post-catastrophic poet—Sedakova draws attention to the power of his verbs and the verb-like nature of his nouns ("Iz zametok o Tselane"; 2:537–40), observations that inform her own brilliant translations of his poetry. For Sedakova, Celan's words are effective—"take place"—because they must give hope precisely where hope is absent. The responsibility for meaning rests with the reader. Moreover, there can be no agreement on the ending because that would mean agreeing with the executioner.

Sedakova performs her linguistic acts on the sharp edges of words, and thoroughly understands each blow that the twentieth century inflicted on her native language (she has spoken of a "Soviet sound" and "Soviet thought process"). In this way, Sedakova turns her words into acts and renounces the well-intentioned and congratulatory. She is aware of writing in Russian after the Gulag, and makes this a deliberate choice on her part, just as Celan chose to write in German after Auschwitz. In Celan's case, the contrast implied by this choice is striking (he had six languages to choose from, and he chose the one of his family's killers); for Sedakova, however, the same contrast is ultimately a form of equivalence. She writes in her native language, the language of her childhood and parents, and this makes all the more forceful the demand that remains hidden in Celan's work, obscured by the dramatic nature of his fate: writing in one's own language after the fact, instead of writing as if nothing had happened. If we look at Celan's case from a biographical perspective—such as his refusal to naturalize his trauma by taking Israeli citizenship—the poet seems to have deliberately chosen an impossible, mangled, impoverished language, the "last" language. His parents were killed in this language, and in its wake his parents' languages, Yiddish and Hebrew, were out of the question. In the same way, Sedakova's Russian is the language of the murdered, a "last" language, an extreme language. People kill in this language, and this has made it completely abject; in fact, it is the language in which she, too, would have been killed. But for Sedakova, this "last" language must be made the language of mercy. It must become the language of good works, of kindness, of divine creation. Which, in this case, is the same thing as creating form, poetry, beauty.

It follows that Sedakova is not only one of the most beautiful poets in the Russian language, but also one of the most openly political. Her good works resurrect the dead. I do not mean that she portrays them as alive, but in her work, those who cannot rise again after what happened, rise again. Even after everything that happened, they stand with us and with her, all together, all alive: those who did not die and those who did not survive. This kind of unity is political.

There is value in finding meaning in the very place of its absence, and to find it, one has to widen the view, shift the focus. In that process, one pays the semantic cost demanded by pain, and then some. To see new hope for a new soul in the persistent question of pain is a gesture of medical ethics. It is that form that Tolstoy alone demanded in the decades before World War I, and that Sedakova has given in reply, as a poet after Auschwitz and the Gulag.

And now, at last, we can understand the poetic forms before us, the ladders of meaning we must climb. They are "tautologies of liminal contradictions"—the same thing, the identical utterance, which turns everything on its head, turns it into something completely different. It is the art of painting "white on white" and "black on black."[16]

In one of her most powerful poems, "Elegy That Turns into a Requiem," the politics of form is transposed onto beauty and precise imagery, onto the music of a march, a medieval atmosphere. It was written in memory of a dying general secretary of the Communist Party, the persecutor, rather than the persecuted:

О, взять бы всё—и всем и по всему,
или сосной, макнув ее в Везувий,
по небесам, как кто-то говорил,—
писать, писать единственное слово,
писать, рыдая, слово: ПОМОГИ!

огромное, чтоб ангелы глядели,
чтоб мученики видели его,
убитые по нашему согласью,
чтобы Господь поверил—ничего
не остается в ненавистном сердце,
в пустом уме, на скаредной земле—
мы *ничего* не можем. Помоги! (1:316)

Oh, to take it all—with everything, on everything,
say, with a pine dipped in Vesuvius
to write, as someone said, across the heavens,—
to write, to write one single word alone,
to sob and write this one word only: HELP!

in massive letters so that angels looked,
and so the martyrs, too, would see it,
those who were killed with our permission,
so the Lord believed that there is nothing
that remains in the abhorrent heart,
in the empty mind, or on the stingy earth—
we can do *nothing*. Help!

If there can be any meaning in abstract art, then it is the meaning one writes with pine trees across the sky. It consists of just one word: HELP. But the poem is not merely an unanswered request. As soon as she is done with her elaborate political appeal, an appeal with the power of a mourner's cry or a prayer for help, Sedakova breaks her own form. This amounts to an act of mercy, one that she performs by choosing mercy over judgment, despite everything she tells us, and by leading all those terrible things she relates toward that word. It is her answer to the riddle: What redeems everyone and breaks the curse? Or to put it another way: If the whole poem is a dictionary entry for a word, what is the word? The answer has to be precise, because everyone's salvation depends on it; getting it wrong is not an option. Tediousness must be avoided, along with excessive orthodoxy, judgment, and reproach. Guessing this word requires understanding and accepting something vital. This requiem is a sublime drama of mercy, an elaborate drama of salvation, yet God will come down to us anyway, holding to the narrowest passes, the subtlest changes in aspect, practically nothing. To a "butterfly's pollen" ("pyl'tsa babochki") as Sedakova says in another poem, "A Butterfly or Two of Them" ("Babochka ili dve ikh"; 1:349–50), drawing on Velimir Khlebnikov.

Who will take up that pine tree for everyone's sake and write with it across the sky? Whose writing reaches the sky? Who will speak for us all before the martyrs, writing in the "shorthand of the heights" ("skoropis' vysoty"; 1:350)? The poet. And what is the poet's task? Mercy, goodness, love, the same three things we find in Pushkin's "I have raised a monument to myself, not made with human hands" ("Ia pamiatnik sebe vozdvig nerukotvornyi"). These nouns resonate like verbs, like sacraments. All you have to do is guess them.

To lift one's suffering face and look up, to receive grace like the Prodigal Son, surprised that he is loved, to receive an incredible and unexpected meaning where one expects to find only meaninglessness—this is the astonishing task of the artist, the healer and creator of precious meanings, which Sedakova sets for herself at every turn, in every dark and frightening corner of her native language. Darkness will change to light. We will never again speak a language that kills. This historic task of reworking a national language is comparable to the historic task of its creation, which Dante set for himself and Pushkin achieved.

Sin

The poet accomplishes something with the very nature of language in its formation. It is in the nature of language that words, like people, exact vengeance and punishment. Mercy and hope are unknown to them. Words mean what they mean.

Since ancient times, the vengeful nature of the word has stood out. The word "category"—denoting the rubric for classifying different things and declaring them to be identical—is from the juridical lexicon of the Ancient Greeks, and literally means "accusation." Each thing is guilty of something, and is named accordingly. Our capacity for "judgment" (*suzhdenie*), our "discussions" (*obsuzhdeniia*), and our "consideration" (*rassmotrenie*) of things can all be understood in juridical terms, as though considered before a court. Under totalitarianism, which in both the Nazi and Soviet incarnations dressed itself in the clothing of classical antiquity, this technique of uncontested judgment becomes obvious. Everything falls into a category. The birch tree symbolizes the state, and this is good, but the dog-rose smacks of liberalism, and this is not so good. Everything lends itself to classification: hair and eye color, gestures and hemlines, turns of phrase. The Soviet man could distinguish between "Old Order," "Western," and entirely personal intonations. Everything had its place.

But Sedakova goes further. Like Adorno and Horkheimer, she sees that this judgment of things in the manner of a kangaroo court, their simplification and coarsening, is merely the result of a lengthy process that began in the Enlightenment. According to Sedakova, in both contemporary Russia and Europe, people have lost perspective on what is happening to us, have lost a broader *understanding* of the unbearable and impossible. "Look at my labor" ("Posmotri na trud moi"), is how Sedakova glosses the word *trud* ("labor, difficulty") in its Church Slavonic usage.[17] Not "praise me for my work," but "look how hard it is for me."

Could there be any other logic of judgment? In her engagement with Dante—the supreme poet of divine justice—Sedakova frequently takes up the possibility of a different understanding of judgment. Unlike Osip Mandelstam, she is interested not in the dynamic, sensuous flow of Dante's imagery, but rather in his scholasticism, and the mysticism of his logical forests. For Dante, things are culpable not for the reasons we think, but because they violate various forms of love, and Dante is inventive, witty, and precise in delineating his logic of violations, his logic of sins. This profound causality, this "other" justice, takes love as its reference point, and things have no other guilt than before their own love, their own happiness. The cause is always more desirable to a thing than its own guilt, and contains, moreover, the opportunity for redemption.

For Sedakova, it is precisely this causality, derived from joy and the desire to exist, that predominates in Christian (and even pre-Christian) culture before the advent of the Enlightenment. Earlier cultures were able to see the world from a height, like adults. Rather than strip a thing of its broad meaning, denouncing and exposing it in the process, they would find the cause of its unhappiness and redirect it to a higher level of meaning. Their true cause known, things have room to move once more. The cause of a thing's condemnation is so beautiful, so worthy of love, and so benign, that it immediately draws that thing to itself. Humanity is pursued by a terrible ignorance, the reason for all of its ills.[18] If it is Enlightenment, then it is enlightenment from within, motivated by an actual change of heart, rather than self-affirmation. And this gives us the right to inquire into the causes for a thing's pain. What restricts a thing to the point of hurting it? What makes a thing itself and nothing else? What is its biggest sin? Its biggest evil?

Sedakova's answer, given in the poem "Adam cried, but he was not forgiven" ("Plakal Adam, no ego ne prostili"; 1:217), is highly theological. Evil is probably an insistence on the self—that unshakable confidence gradually transforming into the "iron will" of revolutionaries and administrators. In this world (to return to those examples from the dictionary of paronyms) "changeable" will never become "irresistible"; "warm" will never become "ardent." Here, everyone is condemned. Each thing bears this evil in itself. Its sin is to be none other than itself, to be an obstacle rather than a conduit for the world, a king and the chief bearer of gifts, as Saul had wanted to be. To be its edge. It seems this is how things have always been, since Adam's fall.

In *Tristan and Isolde*, Sedakova writes about the same thing in a different vein, in the passage about the "dwarf":

Но злому, злому кто поможет,
когда он жизнь чужую гложет,
как пес—украденную кость?
[...]

А он в себя забит, как гвоздь.
Кто этакие гвозди вынимает?

Кто принесет ему лекарства
и у постели посидит?
Кто зависти или коварства
врач небрезгливый?
Разве стыд. (1:169–70)[19]

But who will help the evil man,
who gnaws away at others' lives,
a hound who gnaws a stolen bone?
[. . .]
He's beat himself in like a nail.
Who has the strength to pull it out?

Who'll bring this one a healing cup,
sit by his bedside for a while?
What doctor heals from envy, greed,
who has the stomach?
Maybe shame.

Shame is its own cure. Shame is a rejection of the self, the pain of being who you are, an agonizing exposure of the self to the outside world, the other. Shame is a pricking of conscience, because you are suddenly able to see something within yourself. Shame is unbearable in the same way that judgment is unbearable. Shame and judgment, one and the same, are Adam's punishment. Adam knew shame, and with it, judgment. At the same time, only shame and judgment can show us the way back. Sedakova calls shame the "doctor who has the stomach." How can shame, which is squeamish by definition, change its nature to its opposite? In this compressed poetic masterpiece, there is a broad range of meanings in the word "shame," as though it were written with that same pine tree across the sky. At the other end of one's journey, one's own trail, shame is something other than what we are used to thinking. Pain changes its nature; it changes from an internal state to the external stance of a being at its limit. Standing at the point of total negation, at the exact spot where it hurts, where it is difficult and shameful to be oneself, the exact spot I wish to escape more than anything, where I am subjected to judgment, or the labor of love.

The "cursed" poets are poets of shame. The semantic contradiction that delimits our world and, for the cursed poets, often has the appearance of indecency, is in fact a figure for the nakedness of man. Sin, like a wound, opens not to morality, with its urge to cover up the indecent as quickly as possible, but to love—a summons to judgment—which saves. It is a desire to love without boundaries, to love like God. In this sense, it is impossible to find a more religious, more Dantean, poet in the history of French literature than Charles Baudelaire, with his *Flowers of Evil*. It is precisely at the point where sin and shame are revealed that one can talk about love. Where else? The ordinary is nothing other than the smooth surface of concealed sins, where all that matters is that they be kept out of sight.

In a sense, Sedakova's poetry is a gripping mystery, a search for hidden guilt in order to make it visible, and the joy of vindicating those who were mixed up with evil. The dwarf's guilt comes from his fear of the world; he is banished into himself, into internal darkness, which, according to the poet, is his own self.

И вырвался он из мрака
к другим и новым небесам
из тьмы, рычащей, как собака,
и эта тьма была—он сам. (1:170)

And from the gloom he tore himself
and flew to other, newer heavens,
from darkness that howled like a dog,
the darkness that was he himself.

But this is already the end of the poem. What steps must be taken to reach this salvation, this realization—what are the steps of shame? How do we escape the tautology "I am I am I am I?" The way out is in the previous stanza:

—Я есть,
но пусть я буду создан,
Как то, чего на свете нет. (1:170)

—I am,
but go ahead and make me
like what does not exist on earth.

The phrase "I am" is turned inside-out. When all of you is there, the only thing outside you is that which is not. It continues:

и ты мученья чистый свет
прочтешь по мне, как я по звездам!—(1:170)

and torment's pure light you will read
by me, as I do by the stars!—

Two things happen when one is turned inside out: first, you suffer; you take the place of your prior self. You rebound from yourself. You become a map of suffering. At the same time, because a suffering creature repudiates itself in order to exist outside the self, where everyone else is, this creature endures its pain as purification. Because this creature wants to join everything and everyone, the pain turns into *light* and becomes a light for others. When one is in pain, one feels it not from within, but all over, and this is the pain of *being in the world* completely and defenselessly, the pain of being open. Therefore, the self in pain is always already the self that exists cosmically, as a constellation. Such is the strict and difficult logic of turning oneself inside out while standing in place. And the peak gain of this turning inside out is a meaning that has already been freed from pain and doubt, that towers over everything like true victory. Because the dwarf addresses someone outside himself, someone else, for whom he now lights the way. Some unspecified You, whom he loves, before whom it is only possible to stand in this manner. Who will read, by his light, his own life, his own truth, his sin and his freedom. Because nothing is hidden anymore, everything is true. And God loves human truths, no matter what they are, and God will read them.

Before us is a person who is loved, and who has come to love. Here we see Sedakova's turn, an absolute semantic turn. Every one of Sedakova's words is bashful and knows the shame of its own self—ordinary, two-dimensional, subdued. The poet understands these meanings like no one else. This is why she has forfeited the right to use stilted poetic language, a scrubbed linguistic register. Each of the poet's words contains the memory of its dislocation from a concealed linguistic place, the memory of its suffering and of the crunch of bones. Each of Sedakova's words knows that it contains a fracture. This is why her words never seem to lie next to each other smoothly. Sedakova's words conceal nothing; they begin their movement toward each other by pointing out how far they are from their known meanings. Their meaning emerges only in movement, only from their disquieting compatibility. We would like them to be together, and if they succeed, it is a miracle.

Translated from Russian by Philip Redko

Notes

1. See Ol'ga Sedakova, "Posredstvennost' kak sotsial'naia opasnost'," 4:376–417.

2. Max Horkheimer and Theodor W. Adorno, *Dialectic of Enlightenment: Philosophical Fragments*, ed. Gunzelin Schmid Noerr, trans. Edmund Jephcott (Stanford, CA: Stanford University Press, 2002).

3. Ol'ga Sedakova, *Dva puteshestviia* (Moscow: Logos, 2005).

4. Sedakova has repeatedly claimed that, in the debate between Alexander Solzhenitsyn and Varlam Shalamov, she sides with Shalamov. Solzhenitsyn's prisoners are unmistakably human; they are endowed with willpower and the ability to protest, and to think for themselves. For Shalamov, the defining figure of the camps is the "goner," a waste product of the camp's industry, a person "deprived of everything," humanity included. This figure is a reference point for the entire system—its ethical touchstone—just as the *Muselmann* in the Nazi camps served as evidence of Nazism. See Giorgio Agamben, *Homo Sacer: Sovereign Power and Bare Life*, trans. Daniel Heller-Roazen (Stanford, CA: Stanford University Press, 1998). The Russian original of this article used the following source: Giorgio Agamben, *Homo Sacer* (Moscow: Izdatel'stvo Evropa, 2011).

5. Leo Tolstoy, *Anna Karenina*, trans. Constance Garnett (New York: Random House, 1965), 3.

6. Here and elsewhere, my ideas have been influenced by V. V. Bibikhin, in particular his studies of Tolstoy's diaries. See V. V. Bibikhin, *Dnevniki L'va Tolstogo* (St. Petersburg: Izdatel'stvo Ivana Limbakha, 2012).

7. Lev Tolstoi, "Chto takoe iskusstvo?," in *Polnoe sobranie sochinenii*, 90 vols. (Moscow: Gosudarstvennoe izdatel'stvo khudozhestvennoi literatury, 1951), 30:23–203.

8. For more on this subject, see Mark Conliffe, "Natasha and Kitty at the Bedside: Care for the Dying in *War and Peace* and *Anna Karenina*," *Slavonica* 18, no. 1 (2012): 23–36.

9. From Tolstoy's diary entries for October 14–16, 1859: "I dreamt the following: A crime is not a known act, but a known relationship to the conditions of life. To kill one's mother may not be the most terrible crime, and to eat a piece of bread may be. How grand it was when I awoke with this thought in the middle of the night!" Quoted in Bibikhin, *Dnevniki L'va Tolstogo*, 61.

10. Ludwig Wittgenstein, *Tractatus Logico-Philosophicus*, trans. D. F. Pears and B. F. McGuinness (New York: Routledge, 1994).

11. Bibikhin sees this as a key concept in Wittgenstein's works. It is the subject of Bibikhin's study *Liudvig Witgenshtein: Smena aspekta* (Moscow: Institut filosofii, teologii i istorii sv. Fomy, 2005). We can illustrate such a shift through a concrete example from Wittgenstein: the famous drawing, which can be perceived either as a vase or as two facing profiles. Here, any one reading immediately precludes the possibility of the other. You cannot see both the vase and the profiles. However, at the moment of the perceptual shift, you feel something like a nudge, an insight, which allows you to see something else, to see the invisible, another possibility, before it has had a chance to fill up with actual content. What you see is "the same thing," but you see it differently from yourself, as pure form that dissolves as soon as you steady your gaze. This is what we have termed "pricking."

12. A. Schweitzer, quoted in Ol'ga Sedakova, "Svoboda," presentation at the conference *Religiia i politika,* University of Parma, December 1, 2011, http://www.olgasedakova.com/Moralia/1048, accessed March 13, 2018.

13. "Ne pas céder sur son désir" is Lacan's formulation, his motto, and he adhered to it throughout his lectures and seminars. Quoted in Julia Kristeva, "Psychanalyse et liberté: Un peu d'histoire, Freud et Lacan," http://www.kristeva.fr/psychanalyse-et-liberte.html, accessed March 13, 2018.

14. Samuel Beckett, *Proust and Three Dialogues with Georges Duthuit* (London: Calder, 1965). For the Russian version of this article, I consulted the following edition: "Tri dialoga," in *Kak vsegda—ob avangarde: Antologiia frantsuzskogo teatral'nogo avangarda,* ed. S. G. Isaev (Moscow: Izdatel'stvo "Gitis," 1992), 120–28.

15. Ol'ga Sedakova, *Tserkovnoslaviano-russkie paronimy: Materialy k slovariu* (Moscow: Izd. Greko-latinskii kabinet Iu. A. Shichalina, 2005).

16. There is an important resemblance between the approaches of Rilke and Sedakova in their poetry. Rilke, too, widens the scope of meaning in order to see the familiar from a new perspective. He too speaks of the translation of meaning from the world of the living to the world of the dead, of a single circulatory system of understanding, of words as pilgrims. What Rilke calls "angels" is the unity of healthy form. Rilke's idea, however, does not involve that pricking of the reader's conscience that links Sedakova's efforts to Dante's.

17. Sedakova, *Tserkovnoslaviano-russkie paronimy,* 363–64.

18. On the perverse understanding of "reasons," see Sedakova's essay "Muzhestvo i posle nego," 4:122–23. On forgotten modes of reasoning under the aegis of "hope," see "Dante i mudrost' nadezhdy," 4:31.

19. Here, and in the English translation, the italics are mine.

Childhood and Vibrant Stasis in Olga Sedakova's Poetry

EMILY R. GROSHOLZ

Some poets understand human life as a Heracleitean river, flowing ceaselessly onward, with rhythm and rhyme to mark the passing moments, like floating leaves or ripples, but not much in the way of fixed shores, towns, and bridges. Like the Surrealists, these poets run on and on—often by means of enjambment—not always making sense and refusing to end a poem in any convincing way. One feels that if such poets could write their poems on an endlessly unrolling spool they would, in a flowing horizontal script. (The OBERIU poets, the last avant-garde group to flourish in Soviet Russia, which included Daniil Kharms, Alexander Vvedensky, and Konstantin Vaginov, tended to write in this way, and of course the French Surrealists also come to mind.) Other poets see a poem as the occasion to tell a story or make an argument: in both cases, the poem drives the reader from beginning to middle to end, or from premise to premise to conclusion. Such poems are quite "vertical," and often end conclusively, with the tragic or comic endgame or the inevitable claim, driven by the many forms of "if . . . then." (Soviet-era poets who sometimes wrote this way include Vladimir Mayakovsky, Alexander Tvardovsky, and Evgeny Evtushenko; so, too, did the earlier English poets John Dryden and Alexander Pope, although in the cause of Enlightenment reason.) In the first case, we find a barely inflected torrent of temporality, pouring out like Immanuel Kant's rhapsody of intuition; in the second case, we find the direction of history and reason, sternly ushering us up the stairs of episode or inference.

However, the poet may have another strategy: to eschew flow, flood, or ascent, and construct stasis instead. Stasis? There are two obvious, and unsatisfactory, ways to invoke stasis: death and eternity. But death is inimical to poetry, because it is mute, and so is eternity, because it has left earth behind. The poet of stasis must then somehow invent something else, like Dante's earthly paradise or Hafez's garden or Yeats's Lake Isle of Innisfree, where everything is collected, named, and mutually responsive. This kind of poetry does without narrative or inference, but not without structure: its structure is slant and works by association. Neither horizontal nor vertical, it arrays itself on the page in patterns that are somehow star-like, a compound symmetry, a lattice on the page. Arriving at the end of the line, the reader must contemplate the whole; arriving at the end of the poem, the reader is invited back to the beginning. Nothing in the world of the poem is isolated: one thing refers to all the other things, by means of love or thought or repetition of sound and sense. Poets of stasis, a stasis that is not fatal or transcendent, eschew the goal of radical novelty or the promise of Hegelian progress: the meaning of life must be not only discovered but also remembered, and shared.

Some Formal Strategies of Sedakova's "Vibrant Stasis"

Olga Sedakova is such a poet. Her poems contain little that is obviously autobiographical, and little that is recognizably historical. Although she often echoes poetic elements drawn from the work of her favorite poets (Pushkin, the source; Alexander Blok, Anna Akhmatova, Boris Pasternak, Marina Tsvetaeva, and Osip Mandelstam; and her contemporaries Elena Shvarts, Leonid Aronzon, and Joseph Brodsky), they are not located historically: rather, it is as if a conversation has become a canon, a round, with the melody repeated and harmonized.

Given Sedakova's project of creating a living stasis, earthly and divine, finite and infinite, dynamic and timeless, there are a few schema from our ordinary experience (and which find expression in mathematics, that middle ground between Being and Becoming) that one would expect to serve her purposes. And indeed, we find them in her poems quite often. The first is inertial motion: a body moving in a straight line at a constant speed is subject to no forces, so transposition by inertial motion is physically equivalent to being at rest. If you are in an enclosed room in a barge on a quiet canal, you cannot tell whether you are moving down the canal at a constant speed or are tied up on the bank. So, too, for the sailor on a calm sea, who sits against the main mast and closes his eyes: maybe he has come into port. It feels the same. The standard way of representing time is as a uniform flow, so inertial motion is a useful poetic figure for "temporal stasis," whatever that might be.

Another schema is more strictly mathematical and borrows the terminology of topology. It is the way we "compactify" infinite spaces, a kind of mapping. Thus, we can set up a one-to-one correspondence between the infinite Euclidean line and the circle, and the infinite Euclidean plane and the sphere. (The reader must be patient with a few mathematical technicalities on the next page, though I hope the diagrams convey most of the meaning of the constructions directly.

Afterward, we will return to the poetic images that embody these ideas.) In the former case, we think of the circle with radius r as sitting centered at the center of the x-axis within the Euclidean plane, just where the x-axis and the z-axis meet. Then we map the line parallel to the x-axis, at a distance r "south" of it, onto the circle in the following way. We map the point $P' = (0,-r)$ on the line (directly below the meeting point of the x-axis and the z-axis) to the "south pole" of the circle. We continue by mapping each point $P' = (x,-r)$ on the line to a point P on the circle by drawing a line from each point $(x,-r)$ on that line to the circle's "north pole" N and finding the point P where it intersects the circle. This means, if we extrapolate, that the two ends of the line, at positive infinity $P' = (\infty,-r)$ (infinitely far to the right) and at negative infinity $(-\infty,-r)$ (infinitely far to the left) both ultimately get mapped to the north pole. Draw some lines for yourself on this diagram, where P' is very far out to the right or left, and you will see that P on the circle approaches closer and closer to N, the "north pole."

Here is another way of putting it, from projective geometry: the line goes off in two different directions, forever; but if we add the point at infinity at either end, and identify infinity with itself, we can consider the line a circle. Since the standard way of representing time is as a (directed) line—often a line given direction by assigning numbers to it but sometimes just a line with an arrow tip—this is another way to both assert and deny heading off into the distance of the past or future, a way to configure stasis.

In the latter case, we carry out a similar mapping with the Euclidean plane and the sphere. All the infinitely far away points at the imagined edges of the plane, in

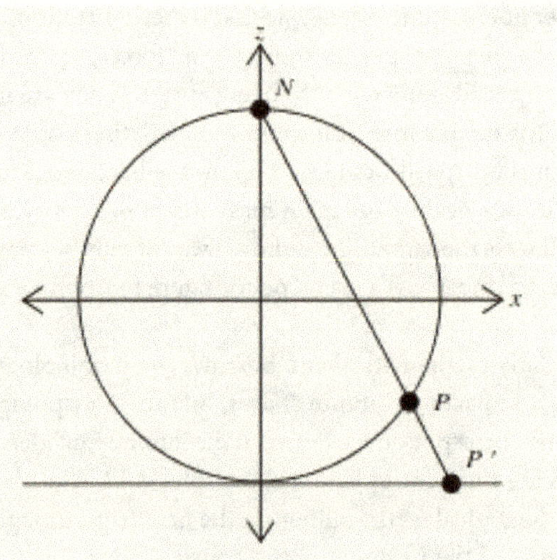

The Euclidean line mapped onto the circle.

a similar construction, map onto the "north pole." As we have just noticed, the circle and the sphere poetically often turn into the earth, so that the topmost point is the "north pole"; and in fact a version of this schema is used in making maps by stereographic projection.

These constructions are borrowed from topology and projective geometry, but (like the experience of inertial motion) they are also aspects of everyday experience. When we look up at the blue sky, we do not see it as an infinite extent, but rather as half of a sphere, a dome over our heads, because human vision compactifies. And this vision includes, at night, the Great Sphere of the fixed stars (as Aristotle and Ptolemy called it). The objects in our solar system all lie on the same plane; if you project that plane against the apparent sphere of the heavens, the intersection is the great circle called the ecliptic, on which therefore the sun and the moon and the planets appear to travel across the heavens. The constellations are clusters of stars (salient to the human eye) that appear along the ecliptic, settled "houses" in and out of which the errant planets move.

So, too, when we look out at vast distances through the windows of our house, it is as if the distances were painted on the windowpane, and so included in the house like pictures on the walls. (Pictures on the walls, in between the windows, often extend the "here" of the house far away, and its "now" far backward in time; icons do this for a Russian house in an especially striking way.) And when we look out at the ocean, limited by the curve of the earth and the finitude of sight, we see it as included in the great circle of the horizon. (Great circles are to spherical geometry what lines are to flat, Euclidean geometry.) And so we make one little room an everywhere, as John Donne once wrote, and the cosmos the house of God, where we are guests or children. This is one reason why French cathedrals

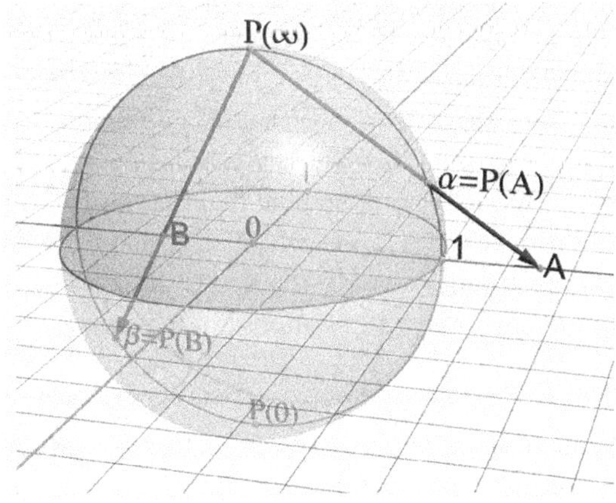

The Euclidean plane mapped onto the sphere.

have stained glass windows, and Russian Orthodox churches have golden icons and so many candles.

There is yet another visually suggestive way to compactify the plane. If you set a lattice on the two-dimensional Euclidean plane with the usual x-axis and y-axis, perhaps by inscribing parallel vertical lines at 0 and then at all the integers on the x-axis, and then by inscribing at right angles intersecting horizontal lines at 0 and at all the integers on the y-axis, you can begin the process. Impose one periodicity by identifying all the points on the x-axis that differ from each other by a unit: this turns the plane into an endless unit-width strip. Then impose a second periodicity by identifying all the points on the y-axis that differ by a unit: the unit-width strip becomes a square. The whole plane becomes a postage stamp, a square button, a seed with corners. If you carry out a version of this same operation using complex numbers instead of real numbers (the complex numbers, as Carl Friedrich Gauss showed, can be identified with the two-dimensional Euclidean plane) the folding that results from this mathematical origami becomes a torus, or ring. Poetically, we have the golden ring that is always slipping from someone's finger, lost and then miraculously recovered, or lost forever and then transformed into the secret in the depths of the garden or pond.[1]

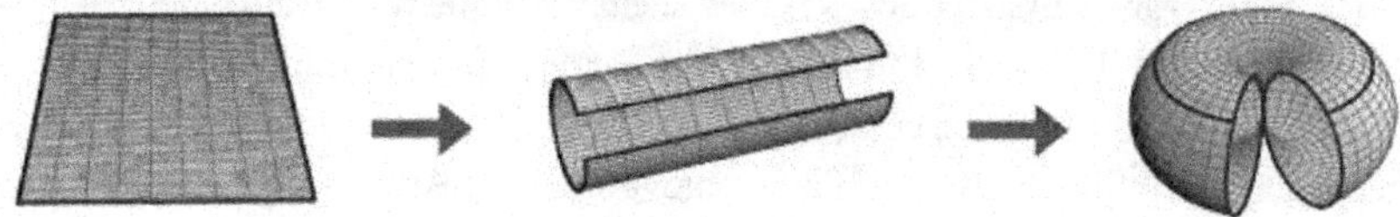

Doubly periodic functions over the complex plane are correlated with tori (rings)

The imposition and folding of the lattice is like the imposition of periodic structure on language, the special magic of the poet, which renders language memorable and lifts it out of the swift, choppy current of transience that carries all speech away: a golden ring, a golden ball. Thus, poets construct lines with the strict repetitions of rhythm, metrical structure, or the more elastic and supple rhythms of song, especially folk songs; the chime of sound—rhyme, alliteration, consonance, and assonance; the formal repetition of grammatical structure; the echoing citation of familiar and beloved texts or songs; the revival of formulaic phrases and descriptions from earlier oral traditions; the repeated invocations of a litany; and refrains.

Sedakova's Places

Some poets of poetic (and vibrant) stasis focus on a single object, which then opens up from its depths to include other dimensions; one thinks, for example, of Rilke's *Dinggedichte* ("thing-poems" that focus at a distance on an animate or inanimate object) or Ruth Fainlight's poems about worn, redolent, evocative objects, like her mother's handbag.[2] Olga Sedakova, however, typically chooses a place, and then sounds its depths. In her early essay, "In Praise of Poetry," she writes, "I don't usually remember the moment in time when I composed a particular poem, often not even the year, but I do remember the places very clearly. Because each poem is to some extent a portrait of a place. The portrait is barely discernible, remaining far beyond the threshold of the immediate content of the poem. There are only a few of these places."[3] She goes on to list a number of her poetic places, topoi or loci in a certain sense.

The first is "the surroundings of the village of Mashutino, halfway between the Holy Trinity-St. Sergius Lavra (Monastery) and Aleksandrov, which was [her] father's birthplace. There are no surroundings without a guardian spirit. And each *genius loci* loves its own style and themes. Mashutino is the setting for the 'Legends,' children's poems about Saint Alexius, and other such poems."[4] The Holy Trinity-St. Sergius Lavra is the spiritual home of the Russian Orthodox Church; it is located in Sergiev Posad, one of the most important cities of the "Golden Ring," about 40 kilometers from the town of Aleksandrov, which is in turn about 110 kilometers from Moscow. The "Legends" were a cycle of poems about the lives of the saints, among which the life of St. Alexis was one of the most popular. Mashutino, Sedakova observes, is a flat, barren, undistinguished place where the wind howls, and which has been forgotten by history; its spirit is that of endless melancholy, like the *Sehnsucht* (longing) that permeates Rilke's *Book of Hours*.

The second site was that of the family's dacha, Valentinovka; the third, Saltykovka, where friends had another dacha. The poet associated the former with spring and summer, the latter with winter. But the fourth was the most important. She writes, "But the center of all the places, the stolen cradle, is Perovo Pole, [. . . which] used to be a place of petty bourgeois life with rowan and silver fir bark between the double window frames, woodworm patterns, valances on the beds, pails in the hay and wild cucumbers on the fence. A house ruled over this place: in the house was a stove, by the stove my Grandmother. [. . .] I have never met a more Christian person; it seems it is more unusual to meet a true Christian than a genius in this world. Perovo Pole reminded me, as a whole, of a deep carved cradle, the scoop of folded palms, a basket of unlit coal."[5] And finally, she mentions Azarovka, where she has a house in the country and spends about half of each year; it lies to the south, between Moscow and Tula, the town near Tolstoy's estate Yasnaya Polyana. Notice that none of these places is the city where she grew up, Moscow.

Perovo Pole no longer exists; it has been turned into a housing development. And Sedakova's grandmother died long ago. But poetic stasis does not need to take time into account; the passages and promises of time are beside the point. Sedakova observes, "I do not need to revisit these places. I can see them without closing my eyes. And I not only see the things I remember, but can also sometimes examine or find a new knot in the floorboard at Perovo Pole, or a stand of bushes at Mashutino. These are probably gifts from the spirits of those places. Like everything in the world (even if they conceal it from themselves), they want to have their say, and are pleased if a listener comes their way." She associates these landscapes with dreams, and images—constant, recurrent images. "As if they were all various folds lying within the same depth, the last, final depth."[6]

This is, of course, the house we never leave. In his book *The Poetics of Space*, Gaston Bachelard observes that all of us carry within us, as a memory that belongs both to body and soul, the house of our childhood. This house, I think, must have a garden; that is, there must be a way in which it links us to the wild beyond, through windows and doors, the "middle terms" of the sunroom, veranda, porch, kitchen garden, and lawn. Thus, Colette remembers her mother's house in the lovely memoir *Sido*, because she grew up on the edge of a village in Burgundy, from which she was free to wander away into the woods and fields. But Simone de Beauvoir, who grew up in a Paris apartment, reverts in memory to her grandfather's manor house in Meyrignac where she went every summer.[7] Likewise, Olga Sedakova, who grew up in Moscow, returns to village or suburban houses, and in particular her grandmother's house in Perovo Pole. Bachelard also reminds us that just as the house-garden-countryside unites culture and nature, the central, lived-in floors of the house are flanked on high by the attic, where present and past are conjoined by a ladder, and below by the cellar or basement, where the conscious and unconscious are linked by those dark stairs. All there, altogether, all at once. He writes, "The house shelters day-dreaming, the house protects the dreamer, the house allows one to dream in peace. Thought and experience are not the only things that sanction human values. The values that belong to day-dreaming mark humanity in its depths."[8] And Sedakova is a poet of depths.

The Wild Rose; *Gates, Windows, Arches*; and *Stelae and Inscriptions*

So, we should look especially closely at poems by Sedakova with traces of her grandmother, children, the strain of a lullaby, the edge of a garden between a village and green hills, St. Alexis, and the shades of those who still remain. In a very early book, *The Wild Rose: Legends and Fantasies* (1978), we find "Morning in the Garden." There at the center lies the image of sky reflected in a small bowl of water, a round mirror of water that in other poems shines up from the bottom of a well. Sometimes the round mirror is the whole ocean within its horizon, the circle constructed by the eye, contained in the eye: the compactification of the infinite, by vision and by thought. The planets appear as stars, though they are planets, and they move along another circle, the great circle of the ecliptic. And we should recall that the circle is the geometric figure with infinite symmetry.

> Is it light or a bush?
>   I push it aside and stand.
> Whatever I hold, like the wind, I hold, barely looking at what I've found.
> It's just the water, it's just the wind rocking the light.
> It's a saucer of water, reading the position of the planets.
>
> No one is with me, but this light . . . at last we're alone.
> Let it be taken, drunk up, and celebrated, as is usually done.[9]

In a glass of wine, sometimes the lover who makes a toast or the worshipper who takes communion, sees himself, or herself, reflected, startled, looking back.

The burning bush, which burns not with painful heat but with light, also often appears in these poems: things shine from within, a manifestation of their earthly divinity. And so do people, even the alcoholic father who shows up in a poem, "In the Liquor Store," from *Gates, Windows, Arches* (1979–83), so like vinegar and the crown of thorns, a scourge, a sinner.

> for how long am I to burn inside the mountain?
> For how long will death howl,
> and the earth wheeze in sparks,
> flying up golden, from the blood?
> And all that was will be again. (41–42)

Or Lycinius, in "To Lycinius," from the same book, who must answer the question: "who lives / in the golden core of a candle's flame so that it can smile till the end?" (43). Or the person in "Spring," "illumined, written up and flown about" by the emerging sun of spring amidst the well of chance occurrences and the golden gypsy necklaces, who offers and retracts an invitation to come visit, who is however now "no longer there" (44). Where did she go? Nothing is ever truly lost; sin lends itself to redemption, matter to alchemical metamorphosis, silence to song.

The cycle *Stelae and Inscriptions* (1982) is dedicated to Sedakova's friend Nina Braginskaya, a classics scholar at Moscow State University: the poems meditate on antique gravestones and epitaphs, calling up those enigmatic souls. One of them, "The Figure of a Woman," invokes perhaps a grandmother beside a poplar tree: "Having turned away, / She stands in a large / and voluminous shawl. It seems there's a poplar / next to her. It seems that way. There's no poplar. / But she would be willing to turn into one / just like in the legend" (48). In one of the following poems, however, "Inscription," the poet seems to address her friend directly, and they are walking. But the progression of the walk and of the poem is diverted, turned back onto itself, because the walking is dreamed, because "hello" is identified with "goodbye" and uttered in parting, and because the earth is round: all roads are inscribed on, and by, the earth. (The line becomes a circle.)

> Nina, in a dream, or my mind—we were walking
> one time on some old-fashioned road,
> alongside, as it seemed to me, various
> white and smoothed-down flagstones.
> "Not the Appian, some other one,"—
> you said to me,—"it's not that important, the number of roads
> in their cities that crossed from one grave to another
> was legion." "Hello!"—we heard—
> "hello!" (that, as we know, is the favorite word upon parting.)
> "Hello! How clearly you look at the earth that's so dear.
> Stop: I look with the eyes of the gigantic earth.
> Only the emptiness looks. Only the unseen we see.
> So go ahead faster or I'll leave you behind." (53)

As Pushkin once wrote, "But everything has already been said, all concepts have been expressed and repeated in the course of centuries: so what? Does it follow that the human spirit no longer produces anything new? No, we will not begin to slander that spirit: the human mind is as inexhaustible in the grasping of concepts as language is inexhaustible in the linking up of words."[10] The poet of stasis scorns the illusion of novelty, the honed arrow of time whose "cutting edge" literary critics and writers of manifestos are so thrilled by. Rather, the aim of poetry is to recreate, to go to the heart of things, to find or lament the hidden ring that lies in darkness, waiting to be recovered, the lost child who is waiting under the stairs or at the edge of the field. Or to recall the banished poet from the Caucasus. Pushkin is admittedly only sometimes a poet of stasis, when he writes songs, or epigrams in his Hafez mode; his narrative and dramatic works clearly exploit the possibilities offered by time and history, though his fairy tales tend to bring narrative around back into the charmed circle.

Beginning of a Book and *Evening Song* (1996–2005)

In a recently published collection, *Beginning of a Book,* there is a poem to an old nurse (echoing one of Pushkin's), a poem to St. Alexis, and a lullaby; and in *Evening Song* (1996–2005), we find a childhood memory, and a song with a river at its heart.[11] When you start reading the first book, it is only the beginning; but by the time you arrive at the end, it is still the beginning . . . of a book. An important feature of any poem, which lends itself to Sedakova's preference for stasis, is that it can be read over and over. Likewise, a line can be seen altogether on the page, though we must run through it for its sense; however, much of its poetic meaning, as William Empson explains in *Seven Types of Ambiguity,* lies in reading the line both as a fixture and as a transition.[12] So too the whole book of poems offers itself to be reread; indeed, we could even read it backwards, last poem first, on to the first poem, read last. A poet of stasis might not mind this kind of reading, and Sedakova employs various strategies that emphasize or redouble this peculiar feature the poems can exhibit, of re-beginning at the end. Thus, memorable poems and books of poems detach themselves from time, especially when they are learned by heart. This strategy will work until all books are swept away, or, perhaps for Sedakova, until they are all gathered together and led home by the Good Shepherd, the owner of poetry, into the fold.

Thus, too, all our spatially constructed house-gardens, all the many mansions in our Father's house, resist time: we can walk from attic to cellar, from cellar to attic; from the hearth to the edge of the woods and back again. Even once we have left, provisionally or conclusively, we can come back again, to be welcomed into the kitchen, to stare reflectively and wistfully at the windows of a house where we are no longer welcome, to live under the stairs, to watch the still living go about their many tasks, aware of us and yet unaware.

Beginning of a Book opens with a set of three poems dedicated to John Paul II, of which "Rain" is the first. Sedakova met John Paul II four times between 1995 and 1998. In her encomium, "In Memory of John Paul II," she writes, "The icon he prayed to was one of Our Lady of Kazan painted in Russia (the icon was sent to him from the Fatima Monastery after the attempt on his life, and, in his own words, saved his life)—this was the icon he presented to the Russian Orthodox Church last year as a gift. We missed the wonderful opportunity of a possible first meeting after a thousand-year interruption."[13] She admired him for maintaining his compassion and active leadership despite his physical suffering, and his "humanism," despite all he had lived through during the Nazi and Soviet occupations of Poland: the seeds of redemption lie in every human soul. And she admired him for reviving the old, Aristotelian sense of politics, so dear as well to her teacher Sergei Averintsev: "politics, the 'common cohabitation,' not only in the Christian, but also in the ancient Greek, that is, in the original meaning, as it is stated in Aristotle, means something totally different: the organization of common life on the basis of mutual *philia* (the Greek word that is translated into Russian both as 'friendship' and 'love'), that very relationship about which Christ questioned St. Peter."[14] Grace is for everyone; piety does not give you the right to scorn others and cut them off.

The poem "Rain" must be quoted in full; its layout on the page is important, too.

"It's raining,
and they say there is no God!"
old Nanny Varya used to say
at our house.

Those who used to say there is no God
now light candles before icons,
order special liturgies,
and mistrust people of other faiths.

Nanny Varya lies in the churchyard now,
and the rain pours down,
magnificent, incomprehensible, abundant,
it pours and pours
without knocking on anyone's door. (54)

Rain is not a misleading figure for grace, and neither is sunlight: "magnificent, incomprehensible, abundant." And Sedakova's nanny lies in the churchyard near one of her places, a *genius loci*, hidden but named, and still grateful for the rain; a cemetery is often the garden of a church.

St. Alexis is an especially beloved figure in the traditions of the Eastern Orthodox Church. (Recall that the central figure in Fyodor Dostoevsky's *The Brothers Karamazov*, Alyosha, is also named for St. Alexis.) Syriac legends (412–35) recorded a "Man of God" who lived in Edessa, Mesopotamia as a beggar, and shared his alms with other poor people; he was found to be a native of Rome after his death. The Greek version of this legend turned Alexis into the only son of a wealthy Christian Roman of the senatorial class, who fled an arranged marriage to follow his holy vocation. Disguised as a beggar, he lived near Edessa, but later returned to Rome, so changed that his parents did not recognize him. However, as good Christians they took him in and sheltered him for seventeen years: he slept under the stairs, praying and teaching catechism to children. After his death, his family found writings on his body that revealed his identity, and his life of penance dedicated to the love of God. He returns again in "Sant Alessio, Roma," which begins by addressing the swallows of the Aventine Hill:

when you fly
who knows to or from where
past branches of orange trees and umbrella pines . . .
a fugitive returns to his parents' home,
which is deep-lying and age-old, like water in a well.

The unrecognized saint, a beggar living in the darkness under his parents' staircase, becomes a figure for the divinity at the heart of everything: "No, not everything will disappear, / not everything will vanish. / This insignificance, / this needed-by-nobodiness, / what / a mother and bride will not know / will not disappear" (56).

The next poem involves compactification. In "A Lullaby," the house itself, a pillowed bed, and a seashell compactify experience, drawing in the open ocean and then the stars; and the house is Sedakova's grandmother's house.

Candlelight casts a figure eight,
ships sail onto the open sea,
the sea stirs in a pillow:
in a pillow, in a seashell, in a distant window.
Where's the Christmas knitting needle of the star?
Where is my grandmother, my sweet sister?
We've walked together for so long
and we've talked:

look, it's such a familiar,
such an unknown doorway!
Who's missed us here?[15]

Oddly, the house is childless, and yet the children return: "here beds have been made for us / and we are taught to live in peace, / we will not part." And then the window performs its magic, airing the house and tucking in the sky:

A face flashed in the window.
We have to take off our shoes when we enter.

The evening star stretched its hands to us
like an all-seeing but blind mother. (59)

Compactification allows the circle to complete the line and make lost time return, a seashell to fold in the ocean, and the north pole to gather in the heavens.

Near the beginning of *Evening Song,* in "Trees, Strong Wind," the windy trees are mapped back into a seed, and back onto an eye:

poor trees, trees of a summer house,
trees of the wind contained inside a grain:
eyes different, translucent to the end,
and roots deeper than the depths of the eye. (57)

They seem to stand beyond the need of human beings for warmth and shelter and the conversation of friends: "dressed in silk they rise / over the undistinguished shame of fences / and they alone in this peaceful village / want nothing, nothing at all." However, when the wind rises, they speak and acknowledge a need that all creatures share. The knife-like wind

returns warmth and rustling to them,
both the blood and sound of a stolen voice:

"Father, you see that everyone needs something.
I need your grace
or I will lie like the debris of fallen leaves
from impenetrable roots." (57–58)

So the trees speak like the great thorn whose branch Dante cuts in canto 13 of the *Inferno,* from which the soul of the poet and suicide Pier delle Vigne cries out, or like the myrtle broken by Aeneas in book 3 of Virgil's *Aeneid,* which bleeds and cries with the voice of Polydorus, Priam's son: both souls driven to death by political treachery.

Sedakova also plays with the smooth inertial motion of a ship, or the stasis-motion of river-grass viewed from the perspective of the river, in "A Song":

We'll pass into the shadow and there
in the shadow, oh, quiet earth
I'll speak with you
as though in the motion of a ship

the way riverside grass speaks
kissing the river's feet,
the way a buried treasure speaks
or a forgotten man. (60)

And the ring, and St. Alexis, again. If we hope for rest in the midst of what must always remain in motion, or if we hope for circulation in what seems to be permanently at rest, then motion and rest are equated. In "A Childhood Visit to a Village," more contradictions follow, confounding the logicians who construct arguments. The garden of Pushkin's Tsar Berendey with its golden apples releases the Firebird, who is perhaps poor Maryushka in another tale, the fabled embroiderer. Devoted to her village and her art, she spurns an evil sorcerer, who turns her into a Firebird and himself into a bird of prey; high over the village he attacks her as she flies away, but before he succeeds in killing her she scatters her burning feathers like a series of blessings, gold and beautiful.

O, such misfortune that would seem
not to be misfortune, but reliable news:
nothing but sorrow is left on the earth;
the truth is a sorrow that follows another sorrow.

These are the paradisal colors of the fiery bird,
the infinite words: be silent! (62–63)

To the identification of silence and speech are added misfortune and fortune (in still other tales, the Firebird brings both), and truth and sorrow. As John Keats once wrote, "Heard melodies are sweet, but those unheard / Are sweeter; therefore, ye soft pipes, play on; / Not to the sensual ear, but more endear'd, / Pipe to the spirit ditties of no tone."[16] Thus if we listen for what must remain inaudible, silence is equated with song; and if we hope for what must remain invisible, blindness is equated with sight. And logical contradiction is the mark not of falsity but of truth.

But let us come back by a different path to the topic of childhood. In the essay "Once Again about Childhood, Poetry and Courage: Answers for Elena Stepanian," Sedakova remarks that we owe to Romanticism the recognition of "the independent value of childhood," and she adds, "The discovery of childhood as another consciousness, another connection between things, another method of communicating to the world [. . .] was very fruitful—and form-making."[17] She cites Rainer Maria Rilke, Andrei Bely, James Joyce, Velimir Khlebnikov, Boris

Pasternak, G. K. Chesterton, and Pavel Florensky as writers who owed their enlightening new ideas to the memory of childhood. Her own childhood was very happy: "The childhood that I remember, or more precisely—my early childhood to about the age of five, is undoubtedly golden. Even the early problems, illnesses, and fears are that color."[18] The good will of a small child is alchemical: it turns everything to gold. And on the whole, Sedakova was fortunate: her family was well-to-do, quiet and loving, and she had both a nanny and her grandmother to take care of her. She also had the fairy tales of Pushkin, and later all his poems.

Her grandmother seems to have been an extraordinary person. Sedakova writes, "I could say something about my grandmother Darya Semyonovna such as the following in a poem by Pasternak: 'You meant everything in my life.'" She was wise, thanks to "her profoundly enlightened faith, without the tiniest of superstitions and crudity that you can often find in the piety of common folk (she was from peasant stock)." Her prayer and thoughtfulness had a "monastic refinement." Her language was like that of the fairy tales of Pushkin, she was funny, and she had a gift for teaching. "In my childhood I could say only one thing about her: that it was *interesting* to be with her, that I was afraid to miss a moment and could not tear my eyes away from her. It was not as interesting for me to be with almost anyone else the rest of my life to this day."[19] This is an impressive claim, coming from someone who was friends with Averintsev, Shvarts, Brodsky, and Yuri Lotman, among many others. In an interview in 2012, Sedakova returns to the topic of children, and mentions Vladimir Bibikhin's study of the babble of very small children. He poses this question: when an infant, all alone, pulls itself up in its crib and starts to babble, "who is the child trying so hard to talk to?" His answer is, "the owner of language." Sedakova emends his remark: "the owner of poetry." Thus, one way for her to sound the depths of language and sources of poetry, she suggests, is to return to "the preverbal perceptions of my early childhood, traces of which still shimmered in my memory," because children have the gift "of seeing everything as it is."[20]

Averintsev and Aristotle's *Rhetoric*

Olga Sedakova often cites Sergei Averintsev as one of her most influential teachers. In his introductory essay to a selection of her essays in English translation, "Freedom in 'Post-Everything' Culture: The Religious Philosophy of Olga Sedakova," Slava Yastremski notes that her PhD dissertation (1973/1983) was on the funeral rites of the ancient Slavs, and that her knowledge of Slavic folklore was complemented by broad learning in Greek and Latin.[21] The collection includes her essay "Hermes: The Invisible Aspect of Literature" (to which I will return), where she claims Hermes, god of the crossroads, as a figure for the kind of politics and the notion of humanism that she found in the writings and lectures of Averintsev. Yastremski reminds us that Averintsev was a scholar of Byzantine culture at a time when, under Soviet rule, religion was all but banished. He wrote about early contacts between the Slavs and the Byzantine Greeks, the artistic exchanges visible in Greek and Russian icons, and religious texts, "thus placing Russian culture in the context of Mediterranean culture."[22]

It was in those days difficult to attend Averintsev's lectures in the basement of the Museum of Eastern Arts in Moscow, not only because they were unofficial and unannounced, but because everybody wanted to attend them. How to find a seat? Along with the work of the scholar Yuri Lotman, they were a breath of fresh air, reviving the traditions of the past that were, of course, still alive in Russian culture although Soviet policy tried wholly to negate them. Yastremski notes, "their views were in direct opposition to the official system and, according to Sedakova, did much more for liberating their readers and listeners than what Sedakova calls 'Bohemian opposition.' They stood against the totalitarian system not by attacking the individual expressions of its inhumanity, but by offering an image of such a human mind and such a cultural tradition that before it the official system could do nothing but turn into dust."[23] These two figures, more than anyone else at the time, restored the lost traditions of literature, philosophy, and religion, the accumulated wisdom of the past. For Sedakova, "culture was freedom. [. . . We] perceived culture as our salvation. For us culture in its broadest historical aspect was that very freedom and height of the spirit denied to us by the Soviet system."[24]

Why is Averintsev, then, pertinent to the topic of this essay? Because of the strong analogy in Sedakova's works between the poet returning to the house of childhood, the house we never leave, as well as her grandmother; and the scholar returning to the childhood of her culture, and the elders. In Averintsev's writings (and in those of Lotman), Sedakova found the source, the heart, the lost ring in the pond, the seed in the garden that only waits for warmth and rain to spring up again. It was invisible, but it was always there. And it was a well of meaning, both by offering a way to find positive significance in one's own life, through tales, myths, and lives of the saints; and also by providing a model of social interaction and productive politics, the model derived from Aristotle's *Rhetoric,* the text that links his *Nichomachean Ethics, Poetics,* and *Politics.* The important point about this lattice of texts, which Sedakova makes often, in many different ways, is that the guidance they provide is *deep.* "Depth" was a term favored by Vladimir Solovyov, a nineteenth-century philosopher dear to Dostoevsky, Lev Shestov, and Sedakova, all of whom rejected what is facile, banal, or superficial, including any kind of transparently self-consistent recipe for "progress." In fact, depth when we encounter it is usually marked by contradiction: the crossroads of Hermes, the cross of Christ, the gathering-in of space and time as we live in the midst of its dispersal and evanescence. As Sedakova puts it in her "Speech at the Bestowal of the Vladimir Solovyov Award," he sought—she seeks—"the theme of the infinite worth and nobility of the *living as living* (outside the preconceived differentiations between the 'spiritual' and 'carnal,' the 'mortal' and 'eternal')."[25]

And here we see, in another light, the moral import of Sedakova's figures of compactification throughout her poems. We don't need to storm ahead, we humans, always accelerating towards some alleged radical novelty; we need to circle back around and sink into what we already are, reflectively sounding the depths. Instead of losing ourselves in the infinite outness of things, we should gather the infinite back around, and bring it home: that is what circles are for. Against the modern, hyper-Cartesian, hyper-Humean, Nietzschean error of supposing that human beings are totally free creators, Sedakova recalls the vision of Dostoevsky and Solovyov: "For one who sees himself not through the measures of private existence but through relations to 'all of life'—especially through those relations by which Solovyov saw himself—for such a person the human will is not enough."[26]

Consider the first two stanzas of her poem, "Fifth Stanzas: On the Art of Poetry," from the cycle *Iambs* (1984–85). Here the emphasis is on calm and stasis, and on depth: the secret cistern, the fish (perhaps the magical fish who can bring up the golden ring in its mouth) in the hidden depths of the pond, like truth hidden in a book, or the ocean sounding in a shell.

A great thing is a refuge for herself,
a broad deep pond or Trappist's far-off cell,
a mythic fish that swims the hidden depths,
a righteous man, reading his Book of Hours
concerning the day that has no meaning;
a vessel holding her own beauty in.

And as the ocean swims inside a shell—
a valve in the heart of time, a trap as well,
walking on velvet paws, a marvel in a sack,
a treasure hidden in a sleeping draft,
so in my mind, inside this creaking house,
she goes, and holds her magic lantern up.[27]

And here are the final two stanzas, the last of which displays its incompleteness, sending us back to the beginning.

A great thing is a loss to end all loss;
a Mediolanian glimpse of paradise;
its hearing is attuned; on the tuned string
fear strums away; dust is an animate thing,
and like a flame-tugged butterfly, it cries,
"I will not be the thing that I will be!"

The future rolls into the spacious house,
the secret cistern, forcing its way at last . . . (79–81)

This is what it looks like, what it feels like, to be related to "all of life." Sedakova describes the experience of the artist in paradoxical terms: choiceless freedom, objectless fullness, and goes on to claim, in her exchanges with John Paul II, that the mark of artistic freedom is beauty, and its aim is the freedom of others, associations that lead on the one hand to Pushkin and his "Christianity," and on the other to Averintsev's Aristotle.

The problem with the forms of argument (premise/premise/conclusion) and of narrative (beginning/middle/end), both of which we also owe to Aristotle, is their conclusiveness. They lend themselves to misuse. Here is the argument; the premises are true, thus you must accept the conclusion as true. Here is the story; this is what happened. Iron-clad conclusiveness is typical of regimes where power reigns and is unresponsive. The Soviet era in Russia provided sheaves of ready-made arguments and the grand narrative of dialectical materialism: take it or leave it. In her memoir about attending Lotman's funeral in Estonia, "A Journey to Tartu and Back," Sedakova gently satirizes the degeneration of civility in everyday life in Russia, spawned by those habits of iron conclusiveness.[28] And she also notes elsewhere that under that regime, political virtue became mere refusal, turning one's back on the conclusions: thus, the arts of deliberation were lost.

These arts were also what Averintsev's thought and writings restored. In her essay about him, "A Discourse on Method," Sedakova finds them first of all in his syntax. "Averintsev's writing amazed us with its lengthy syntactic breathing (the liberated speech of the epoch did not go further than 'choppy' phrases), and the 'protracted' syntax by itself speaks to many things: to the gift of balance first of all (I mean mobile equilibrium, the freedom in deviations that is given by the conviction that a decisive shift in this or that direction can be quickly and precisely compensated)."[29] Here is the vibrant stasis again, discovered in the syntax of Averintsev's prose, where it acquires further moral, political, and poetic significance. Sedakova contrasts it not only with the iron reasoning of the Soviet era, but also with a certain myth of Russia related to its immense geography: "the Russian soul is expansive and knows no measure in anything, and it is proud of that expansive and unbridled nature." In between, she hopes, there is a golden mean, another place to look for the Russian soul: early church architecture and icons, the stories in *Lives of the Russian Saints*. "A flexible and mobile equilibrium is what distinguishes this order of things."[30]

We should recall here how Aristotle's *Rhetoric* bridges the *Ethics* and the *Politics*, by explaining how productive deliberation takes place. One of Averintsev's most important books is *Rhetoric and the Origins of the European Literary Tradition*, which presents a "reflective traditionalism."[31] The *Rhetoric* teaches that speakers must have good character (the central term in the *Nichomachean Ethics*) and be recognized by their audience as having good character. You cannot be virtuous if you are not effective, you cannot be effective unless you can persuade others to act with you, and you will only be persuasive if others respect you. So, then, you must present your best evidence, without deceit or bullying; and you must listen as others present their best arguments. And then you must deliberate, with care and good will, because nobody understands everything, people disagree for good reasons, and nobody can tell the future.

As Sedakova explains, this is precisely how Averintsev proceeds. "The form of address, the addressee, the reader are present in the very structure of Averintsev's phrases; a possible reaction of the interlocutor is taken into consideration before the statement is made; his objections or perplexity are allowed for, anticipated, and discussed; his opinion is valued and never taken advantage of; he is safeguarded against the danger of a hasty conclusion. And precisely this addressed nature of his speech, its 'peopleness' best of all distinguished Averintsev's statements not only from encased academic discourse, but also from the wild, unsociable attempts to overcome the general muteness by the artists of those years." What Averintsev offered was "a courteous and entrusting word, an unhurried and unforced conversation." Neither command nor incantation: Averintsev offered "amicable and orderly communication with the Other as with 'one's own.'"[32] And so too, Sedakova sought a poetry of sanity and measure, a poetry, as she says, sufficiently paradoxical. Iron conclusiveness dispels contradiction, and insists on its own strictly inferred claims, its own story, driving the opposition mad; but a vibrant stasis tolerates contradiction and brings it to fruition.

Elegies

If we are looking for an expression of these insights in Sedakova's poetry, we might read her elegies. Recall that Sedakova mentions Velimir Khlebnikov as one of the poets for whom "the discovery of childhood as another consciousness" was especially fruitful. Her elegy "A Butterfly or Two of Them" is dedicated to

Khlebnikov's memory. He began as a student of mathematics; after a period in St. Petersburg when he was associated with the Futurists, Khlebnikov spent five years between 1916 and 1921 wandering. His futurism devolved into the somewhat mad conviction that there was a law governing human history and if one could discover it, one could predict the future. He ultimately died of poverty and homelessness. In the first section, Sedakova calls on him, borrowing images from his poems as well as his habit of coining neologisms (like the word below translated as "timegrove"):

> But you also, with whom I could live, even in the earthly timegrove,
> could look at me at least with the eyes of a Scythian idol
> but, I beg you, come with me! (88)

His "butterfly's dust" becomes the poet's ink: "With a butterfly's dust, Velimir, or with something smaller, / we were decorating the litter of the world." (The tiniest grain, the dust on a butterfly's wing, is like the mustard seed of faith, which can move mountains.)[33] And in the second section, she writes with it.

> A butterfly soars and in the sky
> writes in the shorthand of the heights.
> In the tiny millstone of the azure
> and orange grain,
> someone's features will be ground into dust.
>
> Sweet desire is stronger
> than a passionate, brute force.
> Then draw quicker, quicker—I still understand—
> with delicate ink, with pointless loftiness. (89)

The poem ends in a paradoxical image of prostration, someone's face ground into dust, both in adoration and in acknowledgment: ashes to ashes, dust to dust. But the earth is heavenly.

> Inscribe three or four words somewhere,
> write to someone who is there:
> we are kneeling, and again,
> and with a hundred thousand again,
>   on the heavenly earth,
>   we lie with our face at his feet.

It is because miracles are grander than speech,
grace is better than the end,
because a butterfly soars farther in the countryside,
because a father has mercy on us all. (89)

If you had only come to my village, Sedakova seems to say, my grandmother would have taken you in; or rather, I will take you in, you survive because "a butterfly soars farther in the countryside," and we both write with the spangled dust of butterflies and the shadowy dust of the earth. Khlebnikov as a poet was in many respects just what Sedakova often objects to: mad and doctrinaire. Yet he still wrote wonderful poems; so she takes him in, honors him, and finds a way to engage him in dialogue, in this very poem.

There are elegies for Vladimir Nabokov, Anna Akhmatova, Joseph Brodsky, and Ivan Zhdanov (who is Sedakova's contemporary and indeed still living). And then we find her elegy for Sergei Averintsev himself, "Earth." It is an especially beautiful compactification, and a descent, and it is full of contradictions. The earth is a blind mother, and there is an old woman in the center, handing out candles to everyone, as if we were small children afraid of the dark—which, as W. H. Auden pointed out in his "September 1, 1939," we are.[34] (I am surprised that Auden doesn't come up in Sedakova's essays as often as Eliot.) She stands at the entrance to the Monastery of the Caves (one of the oldest monasteries in the Slavic world, in Kiev, hidden in caves carved out by the Dnieper River), which may also evoke the Church of the Holy Sepulchre in Jerusalem, as well as the Delphic oracle, posed with its raving priestess by a chasm in the rocks on the slopes of Mount Parnassus, beneath the Castalian Spring. Mount Parnassus was after all the home of the Muses; and Apollo probably inherited the site from Gaia. And there are sailboats on the ocean and birds (like dreams) sailing across it too, in straight lines at a constant speed, riding the wind and staying where they are, "where we can sail," as Pushkin wrote in "Autumn," beside the small gnats and the twittering swallows, singing and flying in place just at the end of Keats's "To Autumn."[35]

When in the east the nocturnal abyss is about to blaze,
the earth begins to shine, returning

the excess of the delicate bestowed light that it no longer needs.
The thing which answers to everything has no answer for itself.

Who will answer you in this vale of tears,
the simple greatness of the soul? The greatness of a field

which neither before an onslaught nor before the plow
conceives of defending itself: one after another,

all of them who pillaged her, trampled and plunged
a plowshare into her chest like a dream after the dream disappeared

somewhere in the distance, in the ocean where all things, like birds, resemble
  each other.
And the earth sees them without looking, and says, "Lord, forgive them!"
  after each one.

Just this way, I remember, an old woman in the Monastery of the Caves
fits a candle into the hand of everyone who descends to the elders

as though into the hand of a small child who goes to the fearful place
where God's glory dwells, and woe to those whose life is not the Bride,

where one hears how and why the sky's breathing.
"God save you," she says to the ones who do not hear her. (97)

But near the poem's end, the poet loses patience with the patient earth, the patient teacher. Why do you put up with the insult, the offense, and endlessly forgive?

. . . Perhaps to die is finally to kneel?
And I, who will be earth, look at the earth in amazement.

Purity, you are purer than primordial purity! from the field of bitterness
I ask the reason for forgiveness and refuge,

I ask: can you, raving one, really be happy
for the ages to swallow insults and to bestow rewards?

Why do you like them, in what way do they please you?
    "Because I am," she answers.
    "Because we all really *were*." (97–98)

And there is the answer, which returns us to the beginning of the poem: existence itself, the dark earth full of light, the shining earth "returning / the excess of the delicate bestowed light that it no longer needs." The poem that comes to mind immediately, as this poem circles about, is Auden's "Song for St. Cecilia's Day."[36] Benjamin Britten turned it into three songs, where the haunted children reappear to rise upon a flood of music inspired by the patron saint of musicians.

So, we see the grandmotherly figure, uniting Athens and Jerusalem as she offers candles and wisdom, at the entrance to the Holy Caves. And we return to Averintsev and his peculiar form of dialectic, so much like Sedakova's, which never rests in one or the other of the usual dichotomies: Westernizer versus Slavophile, mystic versus rationalist, romantic versus skeptic, individualist versus collectivist. His way of reconciling opposites produces a living synthesis, a discourse or vision that is not a compromise and not a machine. Sedakova writes,

> He usually does not disprove one opinion without giving its due to something opposite, and giving us a notion that these polarities are not so much opposite, because they both are equally opposite to something else—to something *healthy* that answers to the state of things both within and outside of us; opposite to the center of the mobile equilibrium as two elementary, irresponsible deviations from it; the opposite to living mobility as a convulsive thrashing—or as a petrification. [. . .] The name that stands behind such a trans-dualism should have already appeared, Aristotelianism—the golden mean, Aristotelian ethics, accepted as a cognitive method; *sophrosyne*, sanity or chastity, the world of ancient Greek wisdom and Christian asceticism.[37]

And she adds:

> Averintsev's general hermeneutic method, no matter to what it is applied, presupposes a submerging into that depth where the most elementary dichotomies occupy neither the first nor the last place. Not the first—because something earlier, a common, third thing is projected in them. Not the last—because the energy of their contrast includes their future or possible coupling, a living harmony. The notion of harmony here is extremely far from an ordinary one, which means something like a vague compromise, a discarding of extremes; instead, it means the coupling of polar elements in their pure and unyielding form, a game of the coupled but unmerged elements. Precisely because of this the "golden mean" of an accountable understanding turns out to be so variegated. [. . .] The gold of this mean is the dynamic inexhaustibility of meaning. Such inexhaustibility is answered by an understanding and not by an interpretation.[38]

So too Sedakova ushers pair after pair of horned and clawed, feathered and furred, contradictory words into the "mobile equilibrium" of her poems, an ark floating on the great floodwaters in a straight line at a constant speed, the ark to which the dove returns, and where the rainbow is visible from time to time.

Notes

1. For a useful introductory account of these constructions, see I. M. Singer and J. A. Thorpe, *Lecture Notes on Elementary Topology and Geometry* (New York: Springer, 1976).

2. Ruth Fainlight, *New and Collected Poems* (Tarset, UK: Bloodaxe Books, 2010).

3. Olga Sedakova, "In Praise of Poetry," trans. Caroline Clark, in *In Praise of Poetry*, ed. Caroline Clark, Ksenia Golubovich, and Stephanie Sandler (Rochester, NY: Open Letter, 2015), 141.

4. Ibid. St. Alexius in the quoted passage is the same St. Alexis referred to below.

5. Ibid., 143.

6. Ibid., 144.

7. Emily Grosholz, "The House We Never Leave: Childhood, Shelter, and Freedom in the Writings of Beauvoir and Colette," in *The Legacy of Simone de Beauvoir*, ed. Emily Grosholz (Oxford: Oxford University Press, 2004), 173–91.

8. Gaston Bachelard, *The Poetics of Space*, trans. Maria Jolas (Boston, MA: Beacon Press, 1994), 6.

9. Olga Sedakova, *Poems and Elegies*, trans. Catriona Kelly, Michael M. Naydan, Andrew Wachtel, and Slava I. Yastremski (Lewisburg, PA: Bucknell University Press, 2003), 40. The quoted poem here conforms to the spacing as printed in the English translation; the Russian original (1:116) is somewhat different. Hereafter, citations to *Poems and Elegies* will appear parenthetically in the text.

10. Cited in Caryl Emerson, *The First Hundred Years of Mikhail Bakhtin* (Princeton, NJ: Princeton University Press, 1997), 286–87.

11. Many of these poems were published individually, but the book as a whole did not appear separately.

12. William Empson, *Seven Types of Ambiguity* (New York: New Directions, 1966).

13. Olga Sedakova, *Freedom to Believe*, ed. and trans. Slava I. Yastremski and Michael Naydan (Lewisburg, PA: Bucknell University Press, 2010), 241.

14. Ibid., 242.

15. See Aleksandr Kutyrkin's chapter for the full text of this poem, in Martha Kelly's translation, as "Cradle Song."

16. John Keats, "Ode to a Grecian Urn," in *Complete Poems and Selected Letters of John Keats*, ed. E. Hirsch (New York: Modern Library, 2001), 238.

17. Sedakova, *Freedom to Believe*, 63.

18. Ibid., 64.

19. Ibid., 65–66.

20. Sedakova, *In Praise of Poetry*, 191–93.

21. Sedakova, *Freedom to Believe*, 9–24.

22. Ibid., 15.

23. Ibid., 16.

24. Ibid.

25. Ibid., 225.

26. Ibid., 221.

27. See Andrew Kahn's chapter for his full translation of "Fifth Stanzas."

28. Sedakova, *Freedom to Believe*, 27–60.

29. Ibid., 143.

30. Ibid., 143–44.

31. Sergei Averintsev, *Ritorika i istoki evropeiskoi literaturnoi traditsii* (Moscow: Shkola "Iazyki russkoi kul'tury," 1996).

32. Sedakova, *Freedom to Believe*, 144–45.

33. Matthew 17:20.

34. W. H. Auden, *The Collected Poetry of W. H. Auden* (New York: Random House, 1945), 57–58.

35. Keats, *Complete Poems*, 249–50.

36. Auden, *Collected Poetry*, 203–6.

37. Sedakova, *Freedom to Believe*, 147.

38. Ibid., 149.

The Guest at the Door

The Poetry of Olga Sedakova

ALEKSANDR KUTYRKIN

What follows is intended as a commentary on an observation by Cardinal Gianfranco Ravasi: "Accompanied by the changing colors of Sedakova's (iridescent) poetics, the reader journeys to the soul's innermost depths in search of an authentic self, encountering various tropes and emotions (or attachments) along the way, which contrast with the poet's unwavering resistance, incredulity, and bewilderment before the senselessness of worthless apparitions."[1]

Here is a house with many doors. As in a fairy tale, one of them is always locked. Perhaps we should say that it is always open, and thus seen by no one. Someday the poet will walk through that door, only to see that there are more guests in the house than she, their host, could ever have imagined.

In one of our conversations, Olga Sedakova acknowledged feeling uneasy with the way her readers express their gratitude: "Your poems! It's like I wrote the lines myself."[2] Surely this is difficult to hear for a poet who has taken to heart, with the utmost discipline of one who is heroically cast out, the truth that artistic mastery, as Mallarmé said, "casts a chill."[3] However, let us assume that after a moment's hesitation, Olga Sedakova *did* get past this. The poet's estrangement from the world order and repudiation of it are obvious and deliberate. It is a pained response to the lessons and currents of meaning whose source is deep within European culture. The estrangement of the world order itself is no less obvious. However, taking the step from one obvious point to another is no simple matter. There is too much risk involved, and having read too little is not the least of them. There are dangers of which only the poet herself is aware.

Olga Sedakova takes this step. One could write an entire cultural treatise about the "weather at the door," which in its hour of birth "resembled a hospital rose" ("Prokliatyi poet" ["The Cursed Poet"]; 1:40). The plague that strikes half a continent, the "birth of the clinic" in a barren social order, the crystal vessel of verse in which words are imbued with a spiritual otherness—one could easily expand this list of images. But this is not the task at hand. Rather, we should cultivate the same sense of wonder with which we gaze into the countenance of this "hospital rose" ("gospital'naia roza") growing at the world's door. Noting the freshness of this image would be like pointing out the quick-wittedness of a great philosopher. These two quiet words draw forth the entire canon of "pure poetry," while leaving behind the soft aura of grace. Though this rose, a guest at the door, casts both a visual and an acoustic spell, these spells merely prepare us for the arrival of another beauty, one that by its very nature is neither seen nor heard. This latter beauty stands defiantly before the "ailing" world; before its vernal power one can only say, with a sweeping gesture, "behold!"

Гляди: неподалеку от села
лесник проснулся. У него дела:
простукивать и слушать бор еловый.
Он вглубь уходит, и земля тепла.
И сердцевина каждого ствола
звучит и плачет: Боже, я здорова! (1:41)

Look there: beyond the village just a spell
the forester's woken. He has much to do:
he'll tap at trees and listen to the fir stand.
He'll plunge into the woods, where earth is warm.
And from its heart's core every single trunk
sounds out and sobs out: good God, I am well!

Here we can begin to understand the ingenuous praise and deep-seated gratitude in the words of a reader who says, "it's like I wrote the lines myself." In an instant, the reader discovers the chiming or tone that has lived all this time in a corner of daily existence. No one can be separated from that inner state whose song can be found everywhere—in wind and woodpile—and whose light reaches the soul so easily that a story of unprecedented love and affection is effortlessly spun:

—Я люблю тебя,—я говорю. Но мимо,
шагом при больном, задерживая дух,
он идет с лицом неоценимым,
напряженным, словно слух. (1:107)[4]

"I love you," I say. But he steps past
as though I were a patient, holding back
his spirit, his face unfathomable
and tense as hearing.

The challenge is to ascertain the aspiration of Sedakova's verse and the internal history of her creative process. The real significance of diction, rhythmic choices, increasingly complex (or, occasionally, blissfully simple) metaphors can only be understood in relation to the semantic and ontological telos of the poetic genius. That is, its concrete existence, which clearly states its aim in the language of emotion, like the rush of blood to a numbed limb. It is the feeling of reanimation in the reader, who feels as if "someone inside me is [. . .] rising up, raising a head," which elicits that gasp of joyful amazement: "like I wrote this myself!"

In other words, the immediate identification of the "poet in me" with a given poem's lyric subject can be completely free of sentimentality. Rather, poetic individuality dispels its own particularity not in order to dissolve it in some preexisting or hurriedly manufactured universal expression but to create an opening in the self for the influx of life-giving waters. These are the terms that can help us understand Olga Sedakova's poetry, and that delimit the horizon of her aspiration. The stream of life-giving water conveys poetic existence as self-perfecting and self-defining history. This history readily submits to the strict forms of poetic contemplation, and in doing so flies in the face of the emptiness of what is called the "historical process."

In her essays, Olga Sedakova often approaches the idea of form as resistance.[5] Given her biography, it is no surprise that Sedakova's notion of resistance sometimes coincides with that of the unofficial culture, what in Russia is called the "second culture," which emerged in the 1960s and 1970s in several major cities. For that young artistic milieu, the revelation of new aesthetic forms was as exciting as the "revelation of the soul" in the famous lines of Joseph Brodsky's "Great Elegy for John Donne" ("Bol'shaia elegiia Dzhonu Donnu," 1963). Essentially, they both boil down to the same revelation: Soviet reality was a proposition lacking any existential value of its own, while dogmatically asserting ownership over space and time. While this revelation offered little sociological insight, its real contribution lay in the idea that being is something entirely other than an object created by and for the collective, and deadened by formulas and clichés.

This act of breaking forth into life rejects the pathos of private experience. Love for what grows toward an unlikely blossoming always carries a risk and has nothing in common with the calmness of solitude:

> Я жизнь, которая хочет жить
> в живом окружении
> жизни, которая хочет жить.
> *А. Швейцер*

Я жизнь в порыве жить.
Из горла закипая,
побегом выбегаю
к живым в порыве жить.

Сквозняк за рукавом.
Я с верхнего регистра
качу, цепляя искры
в растущий острый ком.

Играет угольком
погоня за гоненьем.
Я жизнь. Я непрощенье
в порыве жить в живом. (1:20)

> I am life that wants to live in the living environment
> of life that wants to live.
> *A. Schweitzer*

I'm life that soars to live.
I boil up from the throat
and shoot toward the living,
the soar of life to live.

A draught tugs at the sleeve.
I sway from highest note,
catch sparks as I descend into
a flashing, growing clod.

It plays around with coal,
pursuing persecution.
I'm life. I'm unforgiveness
for soaring live to live.

This 1971 poem offers us a first glimmer of insight into the "hurtling existence" that could make someone blurt out: "it's like I wrote them myself." We do not have the time or willingness to figure out this impulse, and no amount of psychic effort can anticipate it. The twelve short lines of this poem, from the first appearance of the "I" to the last mark of punctuation, hurry to reveal their cosmic pattern and a form that seems to construct itself. The conventional order of the decrepit world is illusory or even just insolently *proposed*. This is why the I-form—the youthful "I" and the self-interrogating form—so unexpectedly speaks itself as "unforgiveness":

> Я жизнь. Я непрощенье
> в порыве жить в живом. (1:20)

> I'm life. I'm unforgiveness
> in soaring live to live.

This is a far cry from the thematic horizons of moral reprobation, and even the cold wind of Ibsenesque retribution. Consider the paradoxical character of the semantic and rhythmic emphases in the word "unforgiveness" ("neproshchen'e"), a neologism not found in any Russian dictionary (including the authoritative Russian dictionaries by Ozhegov and Dal'). At first glance, this word seems out of place in a lyric poem—after all, its deepest semantic layer is stamped with pure negation and detachment. However, the soaring quality of this line is so powerful that the enthralled reader will only superficially register this semantic layer. Incredibly, we begin to see that the whole question of forgiveness and unforgiveness has been incorrectly formulated. The youthful spirit discovers that unforgiveness is not stony detachment, but a rejection of all preconceived notions of forgiveness. It rejects every gesture of opportunistic and indiscriminate consent, which, on a precise scale of values, would register as the lowest form of duplicity (*podlost'*). Such duplicity can mean willful ignorance of the miraculous luminosity of the world, but the youthful spirit wisely guesses that counterfeit forgiveness is merely a weapon of reproach, a reproach that annihilates all creativity. For what is reproach, if not life that has forgotten itself and sunk into oblivion? It is life in reverse, anti-life (*protivozhizn'*), a longing not for death but for the narcotic point that allows the living to say: "Better never to have been born."

Olga Sedakova has always been attuned to what steals like a thief into the realm of the living, the way a worm burrows into a beating heart. And with the utmost composure, her response is, as we know—resistance (*soprotivlenie*). We can understand very little of her poetry until we come face to face with her essential aspiration—until we contemplate and look into the face of her resistance. Why is this resistance so strong, so unassailable, so tied to the striving toward form?

At first, the answer seems clear: she opposes any annihilation or annulment of form. This annihilation can take the shape of a kind of facelessness, which is always ready to impose itself in its strangely provocative manner: on one hand, it announces itself as absolute passivity, obediently absorbing and dissolving the inviolable laws of nature and so-called social progress; on the other, it declares its intention to subjugate everything else to this norm of passivity. Feigned passivity triggers a blind and unprincipled activity, setting its dragnet as a provocation to any true principle of form.

This is but one point of departure, and the question demands that we look closer. This resistance is not just the sum of reactions to negative circumstances, and not just a personal response to the challenge of a broken social order. Strangely enough, this resistance is not reactive; we might even call it proactive. There is a striking semantic dissonance at work here: is not every act of resistance an action directed against something else? And if we are able to forge a link between resistance and desire so strong that desire itself becomes a pathway for resistance, doesn't this mean that desire is in some way reactive? Common sense urges us against such a conclusion, since desire—especially when conceived as a "striving toward form"—should be a desire *for* something, a striving toward, but never a withstanding or standing against.

Yet in the face of logical analysis, the poem itself evades capture. Like any living thing, it comes up against various traps as well as the threat of oblivion. Even so, the poem succeeds so well that as it soars, it returns to its origins, the place where all living things begin their striving.

What spiritual premise allows the poem such headway in its soaring forth to live? What causes the lexical content of the word "unforgiveness" to suddenly catch fire and, like the work of an alchemist, burn down to produce something utterly new, drawing back the very curtains of creation? We turn again to the poet's words regarding resistance, which entered her soul in her youth and has, like youth itself, remained there since: "As far as resistance is concerned [...] I would now put it this way: resistance to something improbably vast and never fully comprehensible; to what, as a rule, everyone around you somehow finds acceptable; to what reason is ready to conceal by clever reinterpretation, but what plain perception recognizes right away—by its smell and sound and color."[6] Most surprising of all is the very fact of this resistance. Its insistent presence. It is surprising because it seems completely unintentional, lacking any definite object to struggle against. Of course, the poet as a person recognizes this "now," but the poetic self has known it all along. Living through desire, like all beings, the poet is unembarrassed that her resistance has no object, since she is certain that it bears no resemblance to that objectless longing so familiar to us all.

And so it is not the facts themselves that provoke resistance, no matter how ugly they are or the dangers they pose. As her journalistic essays and public statements demonstrate, Sedakova has always been true to her civic stance. This is not because she is attached to certain ideas about the so-called social order and would go to any length to defend them. Such convictions may or may not exist, changing as they do with one's experience of the world. In any case, they are not the source of her resistance. Rather, resistance is called into being by that which is also the source of negative facts (which can seem entirely innocuous) and to which these facts bear witness. This entity is a kind of social, or rather, anti-social (*protivo-sotsial'nyi*) a priori. In spite of its indefinable character and vastness, it exercises ruthless control over human destiny. But this is not its true mission. Every effort to erect a unified structure proceeds from a certain resolve. If this resolve is firm—as it has to be to warrant investing the lives of millions in an organizational structure—then this firmness must be based on a value judgment.

"Better not to have been born at all." This value judgment cannot be opposed or disputed because its rejection of all value removes it from any Thou-relationship, to use Martin Buber's terminology. It can only meet your eye with a gaze of command or interrogation. Such a systematic evasion is the essence of duplicity (*podlost'*), its innermost core, where it finds its perpetual self-justification.

The creeping threat of annihilation tirelessly reproduces its own thief-like existential state and leaves its stamp everywhere, in every corner of the social fabric. To behold and survive the metaphysical chasms of empirical thievery, the poet must possess an extremely broad field of poetic vision and breath, and the ability to give her subject compressed and precise dramatic expression, as in her "Elegy That Turns into a Requiem" ("Elegiia, perekhodiashchaia v rekviem"). It is for good reason that this poem invokes Elsinore, where the prince hesitated before committing his hand to betrayal. The opening line of the poem—"a miscreant steals cotton" ("podlets voruet khlopok"; 1:309)—takes the form of an anthropological theorem: a duplicitous creature, consumed by depravity and seeking to debase himself and others, commits a petty theft out of metaphysical necessity. Lacking anything that is genuinely its own, this creature incessantly pulls everything into itself, while dramatically and demonstratively feigning its worth. This collapse of anthropological standards—which is like a real part of the program to "educate the new man," and not an exaggerated front-page story—confuses the very coordinates by which we orient ourselves: "'Below,' which here means 'ahead'" (1:312).

All this makes up a single line of the poem, which describes the profound loss of form that comes about when, to the silent bewilderment of all, mankind seems to vanish from earth:

и тишина, как в окнах Леонардо,
куда позирующий не глядит. (1:309)

and silence, like in Leonardo's windows,
out of which the model does not gaze.

What can the poet say, standing in this apocalyptic landscape before the body of one who has lived atop the power vertical—as though jeering at the world? What the poet says will make the jeer seem disdainful, even impossible. In the face of death, the poet and the dead man are equals:

О, взять бы все—и всем по всему,
или сосной, макнув ее в Везувий,
по небесам, как кто-то говорил,—
писать, писать единственное слово,
писать, рыдая, слово: ПОМОГИ!

огромное, чтоб ангелы глядели,
чтоб мученики видели его,
убитые по нашему согласью,
чтобы Господь поверил—ничего
не остается в ненавистном сердце,
в пустом уме, на скаредной земле—
мы *ничего* не можем. Помоги! (1:316)

Oh, to take it all—with everything, on everything,
say, with a pine dipped in Vesuvius
to write, as someone said, across the heavens,—
to write, to write one single word alone,
to sob and write this one word only: HELP!

in massive letters so that angels looked,
and so the martyrs, too, would see it,
those who were killed with our permission,
so the Lord believed that there is nothing
that remains in the abhorrent heart,
in the empty mind, or on the stingy earth—
we can do *nothing*. Help!

We recognize the *nothing* in the last line—"We can do *nothing*" ("My *nichego* ne mozhem")—because it is the fabric of our being. We join the poet in contemplating, as she does in her later poems, what "creating hands have never touched" ("Nothing" ["Nichto"]; 1:400). Like each of us, the poet stands before the Throne of Judgment. The silence of the Lord is not the silence that was "reflected in the windows of Leonardo"; rather, it is the gaze that recognizes its faithful. And so, not everything within us is nothing. There is a step we can take—without knowing anything about the source of its power, its *potentia*—that makes everything out of nothing. It leaves no visible trace, no chance of turning inner wealth into an object for display that would permit observation and control.

Sedakova's attention to—and love of—composition go beyond some unconscious "will to form," arising as they do from the artless conviction that "form speaks for itself."[7] Like every poet, she puts her trust in the intuitive interplay of dynamic forces. In Osip Mandelstam's "Notre Dame," the invisible arc from cathedral to poem is a quicker way to get from Paris to Moscow: "But the more attentively, o fortress Notre Dame" ("No chem vnimatel'nei, tverdynia Notre Dame").[8] Still, Sedakova's pictorial imagination is a far cry from the semantic reifications we find in modernism. There, blood is still inscribed in semantic space, whereas in reality the "thing" itself, if one honestly tests its weight, is unthinkably heavy.

Sedakova's compositional choices express a type of obligation. They represent what we might call a "morality of form": it is less important that the poem, cycle, or book harmonize in counterpoint (this is a minimal requirement), than that the movement of meaning initiated within the reader feel *truthful*. This is no simple task. In reading Sedakova, we most often find open seams that cannot be sewn together by any dialectic or traditional lyricism. Any kind of "anti-step" (*protivoshag*), cunningly spurred on by an inclination to lower the stylistic register, is out of the question. Once read, Sedakova's poems become a threshold we cross into a changed existence. The resonance left by her verse in the refashioned chamber of the soul is the secret knowledge of each reader.

The ultimate reason for the opening of semantic seams is the rupture, that hiatus, that appeared during the Fall and relies on the incarnation of a Thou for realization. The innumerable consequences of this rupture include, for one, the ambivalence of every word employed. Here lies an existential threat to poetry no less serious than the challenge to the lyric after Auschwitz. Is the world illuminated, or is light merely a pretext for creating contact with each other and the surrounding world? And is this friction thus miraculously harmonized? This is the very subject of the prince's conversation with those "friends of his youth" that Sedakova invokes in another passage in "Elegy That Turns into a Requiem":

Мир, как бывало, держится на нас.
А соль земли, какую в ссоре с миром
вы ищете,—есть та же *Tuba mirum* . . .

—Так, Розенкранц, есть та же *Tuba mirum*,
есть тот же Призрак, оскорбленный миром,
и тот же мир. (1:314–15)

The world, it rests upon us as before.
But the salt of the earth you seek in quarrels
with the world,—it is the *Tuba mirum* . . .

"See, Rosenkrantz, it is the *Tuba mirum*,
it is the Apparition offended by the world,
and it is that same world."

This poem is part of the cycle *Iambs* (*Iamby*, 1984–85) It is followed by "The Unknown Martyr" ("Bezymiannym ostavshiisia muchenik"), which begins unexpectedly: "Renounce my faith? A laughable idea" ("Otrech'sia? Eto bylo by smeshno"; 1:317). Why "laughable"? Based on the title, we might anticipate "wretched," "ignoble," or even "petty"—almost anything but this! And why is the reader's attention immediately preoccupied with propriety? There is no answer to this question: this sense of propriety cannot be verified since it sets the standard for truth in the first place. We can, however, attempt to give some account of it. "Renounce?" This internally directed question, to employ the terminology of the philosophical empiricists, activates the idea of renunciation in me and presupposes the renunciation itself. My conscience tells me that this idea already lives inside me—as a shadow, a memory, a much-anticipated heady pleasure. But if the idea of renunciation, in all its variety and continuity, is weighed and judged according to one's conscience, then one erupts in laughter. Laughter stops it in its tracks.

This is a special kind of laughter, distinct both from our reaction to immobility or slowness, and from a focused rebuke. Let us look closely at the line. Renunciation is laughable not because the act itself is absurd, but because experiencing all of one's fleeting states of mind at once is the same thing as being engulfed by annihilation (*nichtozhenie*). In what remains of life afterwards, renunciation is just a word, an empty generality.

Metaphysical laughter is like the laughter of the sky. It is a soundless laughter. That in which this laughter resounds squeezes itself down to a single strangulated truth, which remains the same throughout time: "Better never to have been born." But the person who is able to laugh like this, and in whom this silent laughter has resounded, is already empowered to accomplish everything. With this laughter, he knows that he is born again, and therefore what is "better" seems to him clear as day. Like Lazarus, the idea that "we can do nothing" lies at the entrance. And now—not merely in his dreams, but in his own house—he becomes all-capable. For as it comes into being, the poem draws back the curtain, and man—that patient of social clinics—finally encounters the sky as an interlocutor, and addresses it as "you":

—но тебя,
все руки протянувшие ко мне,
больные руки! (1:318)

—but you,
all you who reach your hands to me,
those ailing hands.

The Catholic theologian Simon Tugwell, invoking the spiritual wisdom of St. Thérèse of Lisieux, says about one of her revelations: "Many Carmelites dreamt of offering themselves up as 'martyrs' to God's justice. Thérèse thought very differently. She believed that to fear God was a terrible mistake. Rather, it is God who fears us. He is helpless before us; having thrown Himself upon our mercy, He awaits and requests our love."[9] Here we must practice restraint: "those ailing hands" do not justify sentimental projections. And the poem will not allow them, for despite its seeming simplicity of meaning, it is most complexly intoned. This intonation is characteristic of Sedakova's mature writing and it is the core principle of her poetics.

Sedakova's verse contains a notable peculiarity quite rare in Russian poetry—a kind of secondary sounding of the verse (*vtoroe zvuchanie stikha*). This element is significant in our quest for the internal history of Sedakova's poetic world. Let us turn to one of her early poems, "Lament" ("Plach"), written in 1975:

Вот она, строгая жизнь, посмотри, на прорехе прореха,
зеркало около губ, эхо, глядящее в эхо.
И сухие глаза закрывая, волосок к волоску подбирая,
трудные швы теребит и кивает, себя обрывая . . .
Как ты уйдешь от меня, по-другому живая? (1:44)

There it is, life in its sternness, and look, there's a rip in the rip,
the mirror around the lips, the echo that watches the echo.
And shutting its dry eyes, and gathering hair to hair,
It tugs at its hard seams and nods, and tears itself apart . . .
How will you leave me now, so differently alive?

In these first five lines our eyes are drawn to a wealth of letters—a treasure trove, to be clear, of letters, not sounds. We are speaking here not about a numerical letter count or about individual *letters* that are comparatively rare in poetic acoustics (it would be useless to compete with the Futurists in this arena). We are speaking precisely about a cache of letters, as if someone were to share her impressions after gazing at a diamond mine, in which the diamonds converse amongst themselves and glimmer at the observer in greeting. After all, this glimmering speaks to something else, something related to the subject of their oblique conversation.

Let us imagine a child running a stick along the pickets of a fence. In this somewhat barbaric manner, he awakens a tune known to all children, in which each and every note rings clear, as in the image conjured in one of Sedakova's earliest poems "One day when I die through and through" ("Odnazhdy, kogda ia umru do kontsa," 1967):

И каждая нота в мотиве таком
сама по себе и к тому же с ледком,
как буквы в Клину и Коломне . . . (1:17)

And every note in this matchless motif,
each on its own, and add ice to that, too,
is like letters in Klin and Kolomna . . .

A lot of this can be explained by the poet's youth, that April ferment that lives, according to Pasternak, "in the wind testing the branch" ("v vetre, vetkoi probuiushchem"). However, in spite of the poet's assurances that each note exists in its own right, we sense that these notes, this array of letters, each have a purpose. Klin, Kolomna, the "entrance into the imperial city" ("The Linden Tree" ["Lipa," 1972]; 1:23)—these may represent a first speculative attempt at naming this purpose. Of course, we soon see that naming has no power here. Consider the poem "To the Memory of an Old Woman" ("Pamiati odnoi starukhi," 1975):

А там, говорит, темнота, и не знают глаза человечьи,
какие птенцы под окном, и зачем они бьются

и просятся в окна, и сладко так, сладко щебечут,
о лестнице шаткой, о жизни, о жизни, о блюдце. (1:45)

It's dark over there, she says; human eyes have no idea
what chicks cluster next to the window and throw themselves at it
and ask to get through, and how sweetly, how sweetly they cheep
of the rickety staircase, of life, of life, of a dish.

The poem becomes a narrative, which wants to forge ahead, but also to turn back, as if flickering.[10] It is like a passionately told story, in which the speaker believes and does not believe his own words, marveling at them while sensing that they *must* be spoken. The current of life does not symbolize other worlds but unravels into something else. Our world is a fabric that is constantly being woven and at the same time unraveling, striving melodically as if backward.

In Sedakova's poems "[the] path upward and [the] path downward" are not the same. The form that soars in testing itself is encumbered, because its destination is not peaceful completion, but the open space of a home found in poetic time. Its object is not transcendence but the "poetic dwelling place of mankind," and that makes it more problematic. One can entrust it to the treasured soul, as in "A Small Dedication" ("Malen'koe posviashchenie"):

Будто вдруг непомерные двери
растворяя у всех на глазах—
и навстречу, как розы в партере,—
время, время в бессмертных слезах. (1:236)

As though suddenly measureless doors
Open wide before everyone's eyes—
and a parterre of roses drifts toward you—
time, time in undying tears.

The problem of poetic time concerns not its existence and proximity, but the fact that the reader must be ready to experience it. It is not housed in the golden chest of memory but is the very air that memory—our ability to gather fragments into a whole—breathes. For this reason, poetic time is inseparable from us. But in order to enter this time through effort or recollection, one must heed the messenger, as Sedakova writes in the late poem "The Angel of Reims" ("Angel Reimsa"):

Нет, я не об этом обязан напомнить.
Не за этим меня посылали.
Я говорю:
ты
готов
к невероятному счастью? (1:415)

No, I'm not here to remind you about that.
That's not why I was sent.
I'm saying:
are you
ready
for unbelievable happiness?

For the strenuous movement of poetic form, the path upward is also the path forward. The soul's inexhaustible readiness to undertake this movement signifies its willingness to entrust poetic time to anyone who is open to it. The eternal within us, which asks for our love with open arms, has nothing to show for itself but this poetic time. In other words, it has everything in its possession and is willing to part with all of it the only way it knows how: everything at once, as the poem title has it ("Vse, i srazu").

[. . .] и без размышлений,
без требований благодарности или отчета:
всё, и сразу. (1:416)

[. . .] with no deliberation,
with no demand for gratitude or account:
everything at once.

The reader approaches the fullness of poetic time, taking poetic form along as his companion—onward and upward. The reader does so with an effort of recollection. But it is in the nature of recollection to anticipate a certain preordained return. From the beginning of her poetic maturity, as early as the poem "Surely, Maria, it's not just that the window frames creak" ("Neuzheli, Mariia, tol'ko ramy skripiat," 1973), Sedakova has been aware of this return movement, of its unforgettable *immediacy* and *beneficence*:

Если это не сад—
разреши мне назад,
в тишину, где задуманы вещи. (1:27)

If it isn't the garden—
then let me back in
to the silence where things are thought up.

This movement back is neither apostasy nor opportunism. There is no trace here of a weary sigh. Nor is it a rebellious refusal (*otkaz*) that prompts the strange desire to "return one's ticket" (after all, what can be returned to someone who can only bestow?).[11] The staging of this event is carried onto the transcendental plane, where it enters the realm of poetic form. It has nothing to do with empirical rejection or with any individual point of view. The conventional form of a negation—"if it isn't the garden"—reminds us that our limited knowledge of the soul and its "intrinsic faculties" determine our approach to the threshold and our momentary hesitation there. To use the language of Hegel's metaphysics, poetic time "in itself" is realized through the movement of poetic form—upward and onward; but the "for itself" points toward an eschatological horizon.[12]

This movement back is an unraveling. But it is also a return to that source thanks to which poetic time exists. Poetic time depends on a first principle (Ancient Greek *arkhe*, beginning) which structures every vision (*vídenie*). Consequently, a vision can never appear on its own, even when it hits like a flash of lightning.

This is why totality, the authentic experience of "everything in everything," "the appearance of the universal," is not the final word. It's not that the universal can only be divined or grasped in a flash of insight, based on the ontological conditions or anthropological framework of human existence. More important is how the life of the poetic word has been determined in the West: it is moved as much by a notion of encounter (*vstrecha*) as by that of separation (*razluka*).

Let us take a look at this quiet farewell, its words spoken after the lips have already closed in Sedakova's poem "Elegy to a Linden Tree" ("Elegiia lipe"):

Вся музыка повернута в родную,
неровную и чуткую разлуку,
которую мы чуем, как слепой,—
по теплоте. И я в уме целую
простую мне протянутую руку—
твой темный мир и бледно-золотой. (1:324)

All music points itself to our innate,
uneven and responsive separation
that we sense like a blind man,—
by its warmth. And in my mind I kiss
the simple hand stretched out toward me—
your dark and pale-gold world.

Healing is not the final word, either, for although revelation and the attainment of wholeness can bring healing, what can the healed man do after the sky has reached out its ailing arms to him, and he has heard the lullaby sung to the infant-universe sleeping beneath its solitary distant star? Besides the weightless, all-encompassing, bright, and brave air of memory, there is also a flame in which love's unknowable and terrible name lies hidden:

потому что это правда страшно:
сердце знает свой предел.
Подойти и взять такого брашна
сам никто не захотел!—(1:355)[13]

because to tell the truth it's frightening:
the heart knows its own limit.
To approach and claim such sustenance as this . . .
no one would dream of it!—

On this frontier, where a person loses sight of the contours of the "self," perhaps even of its memory, courage is useless and readiness hides its face. The unraveling world will, in the end, unravel until flame alone can assign resonant names to the threads:

мир, рассыпанный на вещи,
у меня в глазах теряет вид:
в пламя, в состраданье крепкое, как клещи,
сердце схвачено
и блещет,
как тот куст: горит и не сгорит. (1:356)

the world that's scattered into things
loses shape before my eyes:
the heart is seized

as though with pincers, into flame and strong compassion,
and glistens
like the bush that, though it burns, is not burned up.

We might say that in healing, people do not actually cut themselves off from illness, but choose it freely. Illness is neglected, but not with that worldly neglect in which ruin and inertia triumph, and the rising billows of the universal and incomprehensible gain momentum. The illness of the social body becomes personal. The self is given over to the empty house of its second birth, like an overwhelming feeling of acceptance, which has no proper name, sweeping over the soul. "The best thing is to have been born."

"The patient was waking." So begins Sedakova's poem "Illness" ("Bolezn'") from her first book of poetry, *The Wild Rose*. A house emerges from the mist, but at the same time remains inside it, and when the lamp within is lit, the reader will feel:

Как в доме, который однажды открыт,
где, кажется, все исчезает навеки—
но кто-то читает, и лампа горит (1:109)

As in a house that is open just once,
where everything seems to vanish forever—
but someone is reading, and the lamp is on

The person reading by lamplight is a sentinel standing watch at a door that leads to the greatest good. Someone reads inside a house that has never been locked but that will only be opened once. That person is reading this poem. As for the poem, it does not matter that at some other, happier time it was written down on a sheet of paper. All that matters is that the reader sitting by the lamp, book in hand, dares to climb the mountain that leads away from childhood, and that the reader's courage not fail.

Why? Because the poem must come into being twice: as an artistic fact and as a personal action. Sedakova's poetry is a self-renewing attempt to articulate a certain absolute judgment. However, this judgment has already been articulated. What is important is not its content or motivation. Rather, it is of singular importance that the judgment be carried out, be equal to an action.

The reader recognizes internally the energy of the action, its reality as a debt or duty directed toward what is best. This austere summons leads the reader through flickering constellations of disintegrating objects to the threshold of the house where the lamp is still lit. The reader is not a guesser of semantic riddles or a hunter of metaphors. The reader mentally creates a pathway into a growing desire, and it takes on a kind of finality, not because of some external imperative but because the reader is steeled for a decision that will lead into maturity:

Я думаю, учит болезнь, как никто,
ложиться на санки, летящие мимо,
в железную волю, в ее решето,
и дважды, и трижды исчезнуть за то,
что сердце, как золото, неисчислимо. (1:109)

I think illness teaches us better than any
to lie down in the sleigh as it goes flying past,
in its iron will, in its sturdy sieve,
and to disappear twice, and thrice: after all,
the heart, like gold, cannot be counted.

Poetry's mission is often interpreted as the restoration of man's Edenic state. Poets who subscribe to this idea approach creative work with great dignity.[14] However, Sedakova's understanding of creativity is markedly different, and this distinction is crucial. This question demands a separate, in-depth study, because it serves as a juncture of key anthropological and metaphysical principles in Sedakova's poetics. Here we will consider just a few aspects of this important subject. There is a striking suggestiveness in poetic texts constructed with the intention of restoring a paradisiacal vision. One feels the presence of a *beguiling* force in them.

There is another question to consider: could we change our reading of this paradisiacal text and see its powers as those of a beguiling reverie rather than a rapturous journey? For in this case the reader's state of mind becomes the poet's main concern. Rather than being led into a world where every step is filled with the ecstasy of enchantment, the reader is gently lulled to sleep. This drowsiness is not a product of transformations of the mind, when the mind falls under the sway of the image, but rather comes about when some of its critical functions are weakened.

Sedakova's poetry steers clear of such suggestiveness. Only the wakeful soul can speak of its own miraculous health, or about its freely chosen ailment, which opens the soul to all that moves past it. Her poetry seeks a world that matches its ambition, one that does not bear the mark of Edenic harmony. This does not mean that dissonance or rebellion are deliberately thematized in her work.

The landscape of Sedakova's poetic world is suited for moving through at a quick pace but is unsuitable for rapid decision-making. Her attention to the rationality (*umnost'*) of Pushkin's Muse,[15] like her attention to the spread of mediocrity across the social landscape,[16] does not permit us to pin down the indeterminable object of her resistance, but does help us identify a common theme among its qualities: to use a Pushkinian epithet, the skill of swift (*rezvyi*) exposition.[17]

We can characterize the globalized project that becomes an object of resistance as non-naïve naïveté (*nenaivnaia naivnost'*), which finds an outlet in a variety of political, social, and cultural practices. This is not the place to discuss its role in social life or ponder how reality unfolds in history in relation to cultural tradition. We can say, however, that this tendency in human behavior signals a new unwillingness to enter into contemplation—that is, to commit to taking a step toward thought, to answer its call. The decision to take such a step is tied to the pull, whether direct or indirect, of poetic form in its unfolding.

The turn away from thought is expressed in a multiplicity of purposes and an array of possibilities. Our living environment or what we might call a life-like world starts to resemble an amusement park, in which anything is possible, as in one of the late poems, "Civilization" ("Tsivilizatsiia"):

человек, как известно, смертен—
но из этого правила,
очень вероятно, возможны исключенья. (1:410)

people, as we know, are mortal—
but I'm very nearly certain
there are exceptions to this rule.

However, it is not clear why these possibilities hold back, why they keep us suspended in dreamless slumber. The paradox is that they hold back only because something else keeps them from our attention. If we were to notice them, we would be brought into the light of these possibilities. They remain at a distance, like something liminal outside the realm of actual experience, something not yet invested with meaning. Meaninglessness is the only thing that makes their distance from us acceptable.

Purposes and possibilities remain outside our attention because we are fixated on something else, our attention mesmerized and bewitched by it. This enchantment grows more solid and content with itself because it knows of the possibilities just beyond the periphery of the known universe. Behind a naïve exterior, there stands an enchanting and solidifying force, which separates its inferences and practical conclusions from any hint of naïveté. "Better not to have been born": this value judgment reveals itself not in a single flash of insight but slowly, by casting a spell on the gaze, and systematically luring our attention inside its domain. In this realm of the indistinct, there is no place for the concept of a limit understood as a boundary line or shield against the infinitely formless. The same goes for the concept of the center: Life itself, as the basic prerequisite for any value judgment, is forced to the far end of the spectrum of possibility, where "yes" and "no" stand on equal ground. Viewed from a distance, they are indistinguishable except as stationary points of reference on the same continuous incline:

Те, кто говорили, что Бога нет,
ставят теперь свечи,
заказывают молебны,
остерегаются иноверных. (1:399)

The people who used to say there's no God
light candles in church these days,
they order prayers for the dead
and look askance at people of other faiths.

This is the second stanza from the poem "Rain" ("Dozhd'"), the first in a short cycle dedicated to Pope John Paul II. Over the course of the poem, different existential horizons appear; they remain unnamed but a calm, thoughtful reading will discern their unmistakable presence. Each of these horizons could furnish material for a chapter in a philosophical or theological treatise on this poem. It is as if the poem can be heard in the silence after the passing of thunder, alone in the world. The pouring rain cannot disturb the still air or the clear vector of thought, as in the first stanza of this poem:

—Дождь идет,
а говорят, что Бога нет!—
говорила старуха из наших мест,
няня Варя. (1:399)

"It's raining,
and they say there's no God!"
said an old local woman,
Auntie Varya.

To what place does the phrase "and they say" refer? We know this place where anything can be said—precisely because nothing has been said. *Nothing* (*nichto*) speaks; this speech comes from a place of countless purposes and possibilities, from our inclination to nothingness.

The old woman speaks from her old age; she is local, literally "from our parts" ("iz nashikh mest"), where "we" stands for the human race, the great tribe of adopted sons and daughters, growing old without losing sight of our childhood. She tells us it is raining. She truly speaks, because through the work of the poetic persona her words become irrevocable actions, upholding our collective memory, as in the images from one of the earlier poems, "Childhood" ("Detstvo," from "Starye pesni," 1980–81):

Помню я раннее детство
и сон в золотой постели.

Кажется или правда?—
кто-то меня увидел,
быстро вошел из сада
и стоит улыбаясь. (1:183)

I remember early childhood
and my dream in the golden bed.

Was it truth, or just a dream?—
someone caught sight of me,
he rushed in from the garden
and he stands there, smiling.

Childhood is irrevocable because it once reflected the infancy of the universe. "Once I was *thus* beheld," the reader thinks. And rightly so. Nor is the reader mistaken about being the one who "wrote the lines," inasmuch as grace, which rains down on everyone indiscriminately and is possible "without expecting gratitude or account" because each person once had the ability to enter into poetic time. A poet is merely someone who has managed to hold on to that readiness. The poet was given this ability and was able to sustain it.

Childhood is irrevocable because, in the sublime calm of the poem and in its "changing colors" (recalling the quotation from Cardinal Ravasi), we see ourselves alongside the deceased, who have become our children:

Няня Варя лежит на кладбище,
а дождь идет,

великий, обильный, неоглядный,
идет, идет,
ни к кому не стучится. (1:399)

Auntie Varya is lying in the graveyard,
and it's raining,
a great, abundant, boundless rain,
the rain goes on and on
but knocks at no one's door.

In order to turn back, we have to knock loudly and firmly—once, twice, and again—on that door that is never locked. This knocking, and the limitlessness that does not knock on doors because it is already knocking in our hearts, and every step we are capable of taking—are the co-creators of Sedakova's poetic world. This world echoes with thunder and is never self-satisfied, just as a person is never content with the self alone, even if this self has been healed or saved.

Let us conclude by turning to one of Sedakova's poems in full. It comes from *Evening Song* (*Vecherniaia pesnia*, 1996–2005):

Колыбельная

Поют, бывало, убеждают,
что время спать, и на ходу
мотают шерсть, и небо убегает
в свою родную темноту.

Огонь восьмерками ложится,
уходят в море корабли,
в подушке это море шевелится:
в подушке, в раковине и в окне вдали.
И где звезды рождественская спица?
где бабушка, моя сестрица?
мы вместе долго, долго шли
и говорим:

смотри, какой знакомый,
какой неведомый порог!
Кто там соскучился? кто без детей и дома,
как в чистом поле, одинок?

Мы не пойдем, где люди злые,
куда не велено ходить,
но здесь, где нам постели застелили
и научили дружно жить,

мы не расстанемся.
В окне лицо мелькнуло.
У входа нужно обувь снять.
Звезда вечерняя нам руки протянула,
как видящая и слепая мать. (1:370–71)

Cradle Song

They sing, it once was, so you believe
it's time to sleep, and on the way
they wind their wool, and the sky runs off
to the darkness whence it came.

The fire lies down in figure eights,
the ships go off to sea,
this sea stirs in your pillow:
in your pillow, in the seashell, in the window far away.
And where is Nativity's knitting needle?
where is grandmother, my sister?
we walked together a long, long time,
and we would say:

look, how like home that doorway,
how unlike our own!
Who's missing someone there? who's all alone,
no children or home, like someone left in an open field?

We will not go where people are mean,
where we're not meant to go,
and here, where they've made up our beds
and taught us to live in harmony,

we'll never, ever part.
A face flashed in the window.
We must take off our shoes by the door.
The evening star stretches its arms toward us
like a mother who's blind and can see.

The poet returns again and again to the *pure* fabric of the world. It is pure not because the grime on its surface does not seep into it, nor because the indistinct figure that roams to and fro is powerless to harm an image that is eternal and not drawn by human hand. No, the world is pure because it stands alongside us. What does it cost for something to "merely" exist? As long as thought does not linger on the question of what it takes for something to exist, gratitude and praise will not even be directed to our own perceptiveness but just our organs of perception.

After reading such a poem, the reader returns to it again and examines individual lines, pausing before each one. This is how one learned to look at flowers—here is a flower, and there are its petals—or at a tree, gazing at it from a distance so that the soul sings softly to itself while the reader stands in silence.

Behold the luck of the reader—"We must take off our shoes by the door." It is as if a snowman is giving us a big smile. The world is the same and not the same—all at once. Might we say split in two? And why not: words recede before such a smile. We see the interior of a house, where the light is about to go out so that everyone inside can sleep and know that soon they will wake again; and there, beyond the threshold, a living dream, living as if the laws of physics had been rewritten and all references to gravity had been replaced with the rules of internal rhyme.

"We must take off our shoes by the door." Every wonderful poem contains lines in which the geometry of thought is subjected to whimsy, which is at liberty to play favorites. Newton's homogeneity and uniformity are exchanged for an Einstein ring: the closer we draw to an object and the more intently we examine it, the more distorted the space around it appears. Holding our breath as we shift our attention from word to word, we set the landscape of the phrase into motion: something suddenly stands out for us, and a profusion of meanings (as if coming out of nowhere) rushes downward like a mountain stream across the open expanse of the poem.

Usually, such lines are found at the beginning of a poem, as in Pushkin's "A nocturnal mist rests upon the Georgian hills" ("Na kholmakh Gruzii lezhit nochnaia mgla"), or Blok's "A girl sang in a church choir" ("Devushka pela v tserkovnom khore"). However, the line we have here comes at the poem's end. The two lines that follow it, and conclude all that was written and said, seem to stand outside the poem. We cannot speak about these two lines using ordinary language because they repeal the laws of earthly kinship. Not even the most wonderful poem can work its way into scripture, but a sheet of paper on which a poem is written can certainly lie alongside scripture.

So, what is it? What emerges in this guileless phrase? The necessity of an irrevocable decision, which lays the world to sleep in a crib of purity and links verbs to their actions—"they wind their wool, and the sky runs off" ("motaiut sherst' i nebo ubegaet").

"We must take off our shoes by the door." This phrase wills us to move *back*, to turn our breath.[18] When we do, existence—that testimony to holiness and salvation by which the world first makes itself known—rolls in like a benign earthquake. Rising from the poem's innermost depths, it gravitates toward everything earthly. Descent, the only means by which the divine can address itself to the earth and because of which it inexplicably places itself below all that is earthly, takes the form of an attitude declaring absolute good, inviting us into its intimacy, gesturing toward its mystery, and leading each creature to the threshold of unimaginable creation.

This attitude draws the poem in and encourages its preference for indirect speech, ensuring that all images of eternity pass above it, barely touching its surface and moving along with remarkable speed. There are traces of these points of contact all along the verbal texture of the poem, but they hardly matter. Symbolic figures are not important in and of themselves, for a poem is more than a mere collection of felicitous discoveries. All-important is that existential whirlwind that harms no one and heals all; it does not demand emphatic utterance but rather easily matches the poem's conversational, but by no means confessional, tone. And yet this succession of images is no mere literary device: any intellectual daring or aesthetic flourish is superfluous in that sea of song, where the child's cradle rhymes with the world's lullaby. It is to the infant-universe that these songs are intoned—songs about its priceless inheritance and the pirate's treasure that will soon be found, and about "time, time in undying tears."[19]

So what is this thing that reveals itself at particular moments in childhood, and stitches itself with a special thread into the fabric of song, looking so childishly serious that the caring gaze cannot leave it alone until the last instant?

Simply put, it is this poem, which begins softly and ends with an equally gentle reminder: one must remove one's shoes at the door of the sanctuary. To put it thus is not only simple but also just—not because the poem is imbued with aesthetic infinity, but because a wonderful poem, containing the whole of human fate, is itself the simple radiant object. But the longer we inhabit the poem, the more we sense its vulnerability, its ultimate unfoundedness. Here it lies before us, fixed in writing, on the open page of a book or transcribed by someone's hand. Let us try closing the book and setting the page aside. Has the world changed? Has anything been displaced, repaired, or undone? And have our own hopes, motivations, and commitments changed?

The more perfect the poem, the more confidently we can answer these questions in the negative. But this does not mean that the poem has no meaning. The poem is complete, its composition balanced, its intonation perfect, but it departs from itself because it rejects the poetic effort of continuity, and exists in an absolute state, in a form that is hard to define. The poem becomes a finite object, now forever in kinship with man.

Translated from Russian by Bethany Braley

Notes

1. Cardinal Gianfranco Ravasi, "Kazhdoe khudozhestvennoe vyrazhenie . . . ," trans. Ol'ga Sedakova in *Kniga pozdravitel'nykh poslanii Ol'ge Sedakovoi* (Moscow and Azarovka, 2010), 8.

2. Conversations between Aleksandr Kutyrkin and the poet, May–June 2014, Moscow.

3. Cited from Stéphane Mallarmé, "Berthe Morisot," in *Divagations*, trans. Barbara Johnson (Cambridge, MA: Harvard University Press, 2009), 101. The French original is "Toute maîtrise jette le froid."

4. The poem cited is "Gde-nibud' v uglu zapushchennoi bolezni."

5. "Opposition's main highway," writes Olga Sedakova in the introduction to her collection *Journey of the Magi* (*Puteshestvie volkhvov*), "is the 'striving towards form.'" Ol'ga Sedakova, *Puteshestvie volkhvov* (Moscow: Itaka, Logos, 2005), 15.

6. Sedakova, *Puteshestvie volkhvov*, 16.

7. Sedakova, "Iosif Brodskii: Volia k forme," 3:490–503.

8. "But the more attentively, O fortress Notre Dame / I studied your monstrous ribs." Osip Mandelstam, "Notre Dame," translation cited from Clare Cavanagh, *Osip Mandelstam and the Modernist Creation of Tradition* (Princeton, NJ: Princeton University Press, 1995), 70.

9. S. Taguell [Simon Tugwell], "S. Tereza iz Liz'e," *Stranitsy: Zhurnal Bibleisko-Bogoslovskogo instituta sv. apostola Andreia* 4 (1996): 141.

10. Compare the following statement by V. Iu. Faibyshenko: "The urge to impose form can be viewed from its own future, from the perspective of unseeing vision and of anticipation—not of a completed object in which this urge will come to rest, but of that which calls it into being and in which it embodies itself, so that each newly attained form itself becomes an urge, an experiment, a flicker or a flash of lightning." Faibyshenko, "Chtenie chtenii: O germenevtike Ol'gi Sedakovoi," in *Dva venka: Posviashchenie Ol'ge Sedakovoi* (Moscow: Universitet Dmitriia Pozharskogo, 2013), 67.

11. Translator's note: this is a reference to Ivan Karamazov's rebellion, as well as to Marina Tsvetaeva's allusion to this line in her poem "O tears in my eyes!"

12. Compare: "Form is not a waystation on the road to a final, incarnate state, but a momentary opening of the veils behind which all things stand. Vision is the creation of forms—not their simple production, but the flickering penetration of the universal." Faibyshenko, "Chtenie chtenii," 67.

13. The quoted poem is "Hildegarde" ("Khil'degarda").

14. See, for example, Sedakova, "Leonid Aronzon—poet kul'minatsii," 3:515–28.

15. Ol'ga Sedakova, "'Ne smertnye tainstvennye chuvstva': O khristianstve Pushkina," in *Muzyka: Stikhi i proza* (Moscow: Russkii mir, 2006), 416–33.

16. Sedakova, "Posredstvennost' kak sotsial'naia opasnost'," 4:376–416.

17. In Pushkin's line, "And your tripod shakes with a childlike friskiness," Sedakova sees a characterization of night thickening above human poetic time: "True, this is simple stupidity, 'childlike friskiness,' but the games these adult children play are frightful and take place in inappropriate settings" ("'Ne smertnye tainstvennye chuvstva,'" 418). "Stupidity" and "childlike friskiness" emblematize a spreading social disinclination *toward* silence and contemplation. These essential human characteristics are being replaced by a stock market, where a constant reassessment—that is, the practice of turning things inside out—occurs within a universal field of reversal.

18. Editors' note: this image is a reference to Paul Celan's 1967 volume *Atemwende,* usually translated into English as *Breathturn.*

19. The quotation comes from Sedakova, "Malen'koe posviashchenie," 1:236, partly cited above.

Constricted Freedom

On Dreams and Rhythms in the Poetry of Olga Sedakova

STEPHANIE SANDLER

> Freedom is only possible under the conditions of human finitude and with concern for boundaries.
>
> —Svetlana Boym, *Another Freedom*

In "The Meridian," Paul Celan expresses an idea about art, identity, and distance that is uncannily consonant with the worldview of Olga Sedakova: "Art makes for distance from the I. Art requires that we travel a certain space in a certain direction, on a certain road."[1] Sedakova's lyric poems and the personae they create well exemplify the "distance from the I" that Celan observes as inherent in all art, but he also suggests that art, in its power to affect us, is constraining. Art pulls us out of our movements and sets us on its own path.

Olga Sedakova similarly directs the reader's imagined movements down a "certain road," and a fundamental paradox results: in this constraint, the poet seeks to set her readers free. Sedakova tasks art with the responsibility to create the conditions of freedom, and in her own poems and essays she encourages readers to meditate on the foundational, phenomenological freedom inherent in the creative process.[2]

To set free by means of constraint is for Sedakova herself to follow a certain path, associated with motifs of walking, of being directed, as articulated by Celan but also by others. This essay's title phrase, constricted freedom ("stesnennaia svoboda"), comes in fact from a late poem by Osip Mandelstam, "Limping unwittingly toward the empty earth" ("K pustoi zemle nevol'no pripadaia," 1937), with its metaphor of walking with an uneven gait. Sedakova wrote a long, meditative essay about this poem in 2014. It draws together many strands of her thinking—on poetics, on Petrarch and Dante, on the aesthetics and ethics of beauty, and above all on freedom. Near its end, Sedakova calls attention to the phrase "stesnennaia svoboda," and reads it in connection with the limping gait and imperfect beauty of the poem's subjects: "We could never imagine Petrarch's or Dante's fairest ladies as cripples. Each is wondrously flawless, as these poets constantly remind us. It goes without saying that they could not possibly walk with a limp—and if they did, we would never describe the sight as 'sweet,' dolce. In Mandelstam's stanzas, we find a new notion of beauty—what I would describe as an 'energetic' beauty, impelled by an animating flaw, a constrained freedom."[3] Sedakova will pursue the paradoxical contrast between physical imperfection and a determination of beauty, but in Mandelstam's eyes, as she notes, there was only perfection. Reflecting on the stroll that occasioned this poem, Mandelstam is said to have told its addressee, Natasha Shtempel, that she had a perfectly fine way of walking ("u vas prekrasnaia pokhodka").[4] But the poem's opening reiterates the challenge of a beautifully unbalanced stride:

К пустой земле невольно припадая,
Неравномерной сладкою походкой
Она идет—чуть-чуть опережая
Подругу быструю и юношу-погодка.
Ее влечет стесненная свобода
Одушевляющего недостатка

Limping unwittingly toward the empty earth,
With a gently uneven gait
She walks, keeping a little ahead
Of her quick-footed friend and young man about her age.
She is drawn forward by the constrained freedom
Of an animating defect

I offer a simple, literal version of the quoted lines, but a more expressive condensation of the poem has been created by the poet Christian Wiman. It catches the poem's tragic, loving tone beautifully. Here are those same opening lines:

As if to limp earth empty and to lift it up
With every hobbled heavened step;
As if to piece and place some delicate wreckage
Freely and fully in the space by which it's bound;
As if the halt in her were a halt of mind.[5]

Wiman, too, juxtaposes freedom with constraint: that "delicate wreckage" is another metaphor for the work of making art, a metaphor that, to a Russian ear, has taken Akhmatova's "rubbish" ("sor") in a direction Walter Benjamin would recognize. Wiman suggests the rubble of history's chaos, from which Benjamin's angel of history, his *angelus novus,* can only recede.[6] Sedakova assembles her texts from that same wreckage, and like Wiman she does so by working "freely and fully in the space" framed by her blocks of poetic texts.

Sedakova connects the kind of freedom she is seeking to an understanding of history, another reason to keep Benjamin's angel in mind. In her essay "Our Teachers" ("Nashi uchitelia," 2006–9), Sedakova invokes the reckoning with past crimes that occurred in Germany, a reckoning that required citizens to acknowledge that these crimes were part of their collective heritage. Such a reckoning has not happened in the Soviet Union, she says, where citizens have failed "to admit that they are heirs to the very people who, according to official versions, chopped down this forest with the frenzy of a mob."[7] The forest of stumps and splinters is another metaphor of that wreckage of history.

Sedakova feels, however, that she and her fellow citizens are still more harmfully deprived of the stories of those who set examples by their freedom and dignity. This is for her the "history of Russian freedom." The exemplars of free behavior and free thinking include persons of faith, but also a range of writers, musicians, artists, and teachers: "[The voice] of communion of creative, reflective culture. Here, too, we find another remnant of the 'unseen,' those founders of our invisible history of freedom. We might call them apologists for human dignity (perhaps even nobility): for the reflective human, the eloquent human, the gifted human, the human who has sought after beauty and meaning, in Pushkin's words the self-reliant human—in short, the cultured human, *Homo sapiens sapiens, Homo humanus*" (4:713). Her examples quickly appear after this passage of description, and as she names them, she exposes still another failure: each generation has seemed unable to pass along its discoveries of these liberated, liberating heroes: "these flashes of freedom were not part of an ongoing chain of events, there was no development and continuation, as is usually the case with histories" (4:714). In effect, each generation is failing to teach its successors, which threatens to make "Our Teachers" a sadly ironic title. Yet the essay also names teachers as a source of wisdom; some—at university, in school, in private lessons—were themselves manifestations of freedom even in the darkest periods of Soviet history. Others found the lessons in written texts, for example, the poet Ivan Zhdanov, who discovered this freedom by reading Tolstoy. In Sedakova's writings, it is Pushkin who often opens a gateway to freer thinking, as in the passage from her essay on Mandelstam.[8]

Art's lessons are not only thematic, of course, as borne out by Pushkin's example and that of Sedakova's teachers. Freedom can be expressed in the way in which ideas are conveyed. This is why teachers of astronomy or phonetics or music could be conduits to freedom for their students. For a whole host of reasons, the Russian language itself is understood as a place to find freedom; conversely, its impoverishment during the Soviet period was experienced as a stunning—stunning in the sense of silencing—site of the lack of freedom. To regain the capacity to use language in a rich, expressive manner was a prized, ambitious goal. Sedakova cherished this linguistic freedom in the writings of Sergei Averintsev, also named in "Our Teachers" and treated in her work on a number of occasions following his death in 2004. Sedakova wrote that his own use of language modeled free expression brilliantly: "Averintsev's early publications struck the reader first and foremost as a linguistic event. What was striking was the forgotten wealth of Russian vocabulary that they contained (easily integrating even academic barbarities) and the assured ease with which they addressed him, their verbal force and precision, their careful and beautiful design, at once sober and poetic—everything that up to that moment seemed impossible in our country."[9] In a footnote, Sedakova gave more examples of Soviet Russia's urgent attempts at free speech, ranging from the stuttering speech act, "I can speak" ("Ia mogu govorit'") at the start of Andrei Tarkovsky's film *The Mirror* (*Zerkalo*, 1975), to the recovered language of Varlam Shalamov's prose. The staggering effort to move from stunted, groping expression to full and rich acts of speech, Sedakova adds, leaves its effects on the traumatized speech act, so that a speaker often tries, but does not get to the point of speaking freely. The challenge now, in the post-Soviet period, is to find pathways to genuine linguistic and cognitive freedom.

The freedom under discussion here is thus a form of inner freedom. People born before the revolution often had it deep within themselves, Sedakova notes in "Our Teachers," citing the fictional characters in Andrei Bitov's novel *Pushkin House* (*Pushkinskii dom*, 1978, published in Russia in 1987).[10] It struck Sedakova deeply, as a "skill in conversing with oneself, knowledge of oneself. In their thoughts and deeds, they could turn to something within themselves, which those who had been re-educated did not do" (4:716). It might be practiced by someone who stood in Red Square in protest, as Natalya Gorbanevskaya did when Soviet tanks rolled into Prague, holding a sign "for your freedom and ours" ("za vashu i nashu svobodu"), or by someone on trial for anti-Soviet acts who had the courage, as Andrei Sinyavsky and Yuli Daniel did, to refuse to beg for mercy from the state. This inner freedom was also exemplified by Mikhail Panov, whose integrity Sedakova praises in the final sentence of this essay; her university professor, he unfailingly remained true to himself. Everyone who met him, Sedakova concludes, would always recall him as someone "who had opened a vista for you onto freedom" (4:718).

To open up a vista onto freedom is something quite different from making a speech about freedom or telling someone to stop moving through life as if shackled or blinkered. Sedakova describes Panov as putting before his students and other interlocutors a view, an opening, a possibility, which must be chosen and embraced. In a sense, Sedakova is making a virtue of the fact that no history of secret freedom was passed down among the generations: the moment of discovering that secret for oneself is also the moment of taking on the responsibilities and joys of freedom itself.

As Sedakova explained in an interview with Alexander Kyrlezhev, "For me the success of an artwork betokens the success of freedom, the personal freedom of the artist, a freedom that bears forth the source of liberation for others" ("Razgovor o svobode s A. I. Kyrlezhevym"; 4:55). She emphasizes the importance of this moment of transmission: "The creative task and the ideational task are complete when, together, they bring freedom to the human being. The very possibility of granting freedom is in and of itself a gift" (4:54). Here, too, Sedakova names Pushkin as the supreme exemplar of this freedom and this gift: he can leave things unfinished, as if cleansed by the refusal to adorn or to extend. That readiness to leave work incomplete is more complex than it might seem: Sedakova says that this is the main goal of the freedom she seeks to create in her work—a purity that has to be created by not giving in to the temptation to load up the text with more words, more terms. Or, we might say, returning to Celan's metaphors, more pathways for thought: there is a path down which the poet wishes us to travel. Her restraint in diction or imagery, in rhythm or in rhyme, is itself the gesture that leads to freedom.

Lyric Freedom and Lyric Constraint

Sedakova has now for nearly twenty years been writing extensively about the pathways of freedom in her prose essays. Those essays speak of broadly philosophical issues pertinent to everyone living through the aftermath of the demise of the Soviet Union, indeed to all of us living in a world marked by global financial crises, poverty, and violence. Many were written for occasions, in response to the awarding of a prize or as inaugural lectures and keynote addresses, and thus first delivered to audiences who listened to the poet's voice as she enunciated her words, whether speaking in her native Russian or in other languages. That quality of live speech is also found in essays intended for publication. Sedakova speaks to her audience, whether in a lecture hall or on the page, as if to equals, never condescending but also never letting us off the hook. We are held to the poet's rigorous standards in thought and ethical perception: we are asked to think about complex social and philosophical issues, in a language formed into conversational, harmonious, and unfettered sentences. The free-flowing ideas of the essays are their own inspiration to free thinking.

Olga Sedakova's essays are as potent a cultural force as her poetry. Just as she stands out among poets of her generation for her capacity to fundamentally rethink the possibilities of lyric poetry, so she has made a landmark contribution to the genre of the essay in Russian letters, both because of the range of her essayistic writing—across *moralia* and *poetica,* as the four-volume edition of her writings has it—and across the genres of philosophical argument, theological investigation, philological investigation, and memoir. I want, for the remainder of this essay, to focus on the poetry and see how the pathways of freedom set forth in her prose are followed.

To turn to poems is to be reminded of poetry's linguistic and intonational resources, of its capacities for melody and articulated rhythms, for rhymes and strophes that punctuate our thinking into much shorter bursts of ideas than do the paragraphs of expository or narrative prose that enliven the essays. Sedakova's restraint in form, image, and genre in the poetry slows readers down, signaling the need to absorb the elements of the text one at a time, to appreciate every word, every choice of italics, every decision to put white space around the text to visually set it off. In teaching patience, the poet is also directing attention away from tempting distractions in the social or natural world, and in the discourses of poetry itself.

One of those distractions is a kind of verbal excess, a rush to offer more and more words to say something that is elusive or difficult. Sedakova, it should be said, is not without her resources in exploring a very wide range of lexical possibilities: her wide knowledge of languages, ancient and modern, has made her a brilliant translator; and her linguistic skill is evidenced by her remarkable dictionary of difficult words, as she was eventually to name her dictionary of Old Church Slavonic paronyms.[11] One suspects that, if she wished to, she could outdo Nabokov in his verbal flourishes and multi-linguistic puns. But her poetry largely swerves away from any such ornamentalism—and toward elegantly melodic lines made out of the plainest, simplest words.[12] It is not that the poetry is minimalist, but rather that its restricted lexicon and frequent recourse to repetition redirect us back onto the poem's own few words, teaching us that what looks like paucity is in fact a source of wonder.

The repetitions come to have their own rhythms, and the quality of rhythmic expression both sets Sedakova's poetry off from that of her peers and separates her poems from her prose. Of all the features and characteristics of lyric poetry, rhythm is perhaps the most compelling, at once expected and potentially uncanny. As Jonathan Culler writes, "Rhythm is one of the major forces through which poems haunt us, just as poems themselves are haunted by rhythms of other poems."[13] Culler draws on the work of Amittai Aviram, asking what makes a rhythm "work" on us. Aviram, Culler notes, "stresses that by physically engaging us and distracting us from the semantic dimension of language, rhythm 'confers upon us a momentary feeling of freedom from any particular finite construction of the world.' In focusing on the rhythm we increase the possibility that the poetic use of language will renew perception, through its new orderings, 'undermining the distinctions and definitions of reality as we ordinarily live them.'"[14] Renewing perception, as Culler puts it, is a secular language for what is in Sedakova more often the work of spiritual renewal, but she is also enough of a post-Romantic poet to share the view that renewing the freshness of sense perception is itself a kind of spiritual work. To free us from finite constructions of the world is to free the mind from the world's fetters on our imagination, to draw on another term prized by the Romantics. The rhythms and diction of Sedakova's poetry seek to unfetter the imagination.

Amittai Aviram's core argument has to do with rhythm's ability to seize the imaginations of poetry readers. Rhythm communicates, but not by semantically meaningful actions, he insists.[15] It is a beat, a pulse (although with a more complex periodicity than a heartbeat),[16] and as such, rhythm operates by the same paradoxical methods as do the constraining freedoms that Sedakova's poetry pursues: rhythm takes hold of us, we "succumb" to rhythm that is "coursing through us," in Susan Stewart's phrases, which she in turn has drawn from the work of Paul Valéry.[17] For Stewart, reactions to rhythm are embodied: we physically sense the beat of a poem, and in the regular repetitions of alternating stressed and unstressed syllables our minds are freed.

That contrast between body and imagination is also meaningful in the narrative structure that most often appears in Sedakova's poems about freedom, the dream. With our bodies stilled in sleep, our minds move us across spaces and times with a freedom far exceeding the physical reality of daily life. The limitations inherent in a sleeping state produce fantastic forms of unboundedness.

Sedakova has written several poems that are presented wholly as dreams, including "Death comes to me often in dreams" ("Mne chasto snitsia smert' i predlagaet," which appeared in *The Wild Rose*, dated 1976–78; 1:99); "The Dreamer" ("Snovidets," also in *The Wild Rose*, 1976–78; 1:138–39); and "Dream" ("Son," in *Old Songs*, 1980–81; 1:200). One of these, "The Dreamer," is written in a ternary meter and in quatrains, but the other two use free verse or broken iambic lines to build a unified, short lyric. There is great diversity in the handling of dreams in these poems: one ("Dream") relies on the Prodigal Son's dream; another ("Death comes to me often in dreams") is written in the first person and oriented around a metaphor, a double ladder, that recalls Jacob's dream in the book of Genesis. The longest and most complex is "The Dreamer," which begins with the darkness in which dreams might appear; there the multitudes quicken to the possibility that a dream is about to descend ("is it about me?" / "ne obo mne li?" the poem asks, l. 7, 1:138). But as the poem picks up momentum, a first-person speaker thinks that instead an immortal gesture of mercy may be impending ("tak pervogo vzgliada / ia ispolniaiu bessmertnuiu zhalost'?" ll. 15–16, 1:138). Then the physical action of the dream is more directly evoked, concluding the poem:

Тайный магнит, сердцевина преданья,
волны влеченья, горящие в мире,
камни, и странствия, и предсказанья
подняты до неба в темном потире!

Падает воля, и тело не хочет,
и не увидит. Но скажет, кончая:
нет ничего, чего жизнь не пророчит,
только тебя в глубине означая! (1:138–39)

The secret magnet, the heart of a legend,
waves of attraction that burn in the world,
stones and meanderings and prophesies
raised to the heavens in a dark chalice!

The will collapses, the body refuses,
won't see it. But at its end it will say,
"There's not a thing that life does not foretell,
telling of you, only you, down deep."[18]

Sedakova says here directly that the sense of will or agency recedes in dreams when bodily capacity for desire or for independent vision is also most fully absent. At such a moment, the capacity of dreaming to offer revelation swells to fill all available imaginative space. There is nothing that cannot be foretold, and nothing that cannot be drawn back into signifying the dreamer.

The poem presents dreaming as a form of imaginative creation and revelation. Other poems speak more directly to the possibility of divine revelation, some of them cast as legends and tales—which "The Dreamer" suggests in its image of the secret magnet (l. 19). I turn now to poems that present themselves explicitly as legends and tales. Even with their rules and limits as fixed genres, Sedakova's legends and tales permit great imaginative freedom.

Tales, Legends, and the Stuff of Dreams

Genre conventions play a major role in the narrative twists and turns, realized personae, and the specific rhythms of Sedakova's dream poems. Those genres often appear in the poems' titles, which sometimes offer only the signal of genre and some minimal notion of sequencing: "Second Legend," "Singing," "First Stanzas," "Old Songs" ("Legenda vtoraia," "Penie," "Stansy pervye," "Starye pesni"). Sedakova has poems with more evocative titles, but this pattern, using a genre designation with some modest occasional epithet, is common in her work, and in effect one of her signatures.[19] When the legends, songs, and stanzas come in numbered sequences, readers are reminded that each will be part of a larger whole, and that the borders around a particular poem are not entirely secure. Sedakova writes in a Mandelstamian tradition in this and other senses, where the poems talk to one another and engage in forms of repetition—or, as Ksenia Golubovich calls it elsewhere in this volume, forms of tautology—that send us down a familiar and yet always slightly changing pathway.

Once again, we confront the paradox of constraint, for even as the poet takes us on strange journeys, we experience the poems as nimbly moving through the rigors of fixed forms.[20] The dream poems thematize these paradoxical expressions of freedom; they cluster around two genres or poetic modes: the tale or fairy tale (*skazka*) and the legend (*legenda*). Both genres introduce logically impossible worlds into seemingly realist narrative frameworks. They are sites for exploring worlds of fantasy. Similar explorations have been undertaken by other important contemporary Russian poets, with quite different results: compare the science-fiction fantasies of Fyodor Svarovsky and the narrative poetry and ballads of Maria Stepanova.[21] What makes the ghosts, revenants, and vampires of Stepanova and the robots, cosmonauts, and time-travelers of Svarovsky similar are the poets' reasons for turning to events and persons that do not conform to the norms of reason or objective reality: Stepanova and Svarovsky seek to introduce psychic realms that are spiritually and psychologically compelling, that make a kind of alternative sense to the reader. Sedakova to some degree works with a similar motivation, but she instead offers the speaking objects or telekinesis of the folktale to suggest animacy where only inertness should exist. And she offers the capacity for divine vision and bodily miracle in the lives of saints, prophets, and biblical figures. In effect, Sedakova will take her readers toward the miraculous rather than the supernatural.

Consider the genre of the legend, a term that suggests a whole host of narrative possibilities, both a tale about a person of note (and an archaic meaning in English is saint's life, a meaning that Sedakova's poems invoke) as well as a tale handed down from one generation to the next. The root of the word is the verb meaning to read, *legere,* but it is a gerund, a noun connoting things read. In choosing to title a poem a legend, Sedakova is reminding us to hear the etymological source, and thus to recognize that the poem we read is itself a reading, a compilation of previous legible sources. Sedakova's "Tenth Legend: Jacob" ("Legenda desiataia. Iakov"), for example, draws on a biblical story.[22] Jacob is celebrated in a number of Sedakova's poems, which recount his wooing of Rachel and his dream of God at the place he was to name Bethel. Although Jacob's is an Old Testament story, it resembles well the saints' lives and New Testament parables often favored by the poet for her legends. It offers precisely the kind of dream that Sedakova's poems often narrate as a means of creating a sense of freedom.

The genre of the folktale or fairy tale (*skazka*), however, sits at the very core of poetic creation, in Sedakova's view. Her essay "The Power of Happiness" ("Vlast' schast'ia," 2000) opens by making that claim:

> The protagonist of "The Golden Cockerel," Stargazer, appears in the work's prologue—a sign that everything we are about to witness takes place in another world:
>
> Somewhere in the thrice-ninth kingdom,
> In the thrice-tenth realm—
>
> in a fairy tale. In other words, somewhere near the very heart of poetry, near art "as it should be." As Novalis writes, "A fairy tale serves as the model for poetry. Everything poetic should be like a fairy tale."
>
> And in fact, the fairy-tale element illumines even those works that seem bleakest, even the most dramatic and troubling—for they, too, belong to art. The very essence of art—sound, color, gesture, the free word—resembles the magic objects in fairy tales: the golden apples, the magic flutes, the talking trees. (4:271)

Sedakova emphasizes two things here that are important for her own tales: first, a text that conveys action in a remote, separately imagined world is drawn closer to the essence of poetic creation by that very distance; second, the magical elements and objects in a tale are themselves emblematic of the aesthetic properties of the text—its texture, its intonations, and above all its free-ranging discourse (its *svobodnoe slovo*). It is the otherness of the imagined world that liberates.

In her essay in this volume, Henrieke Stahl treats one of these poems, "The Fairy Tale" ("Skazka"); she notes that the unnamed feminine persona (called only "ona"/"she") exists in a threshold space that allows movement between worlds. These forms of movement—between house and garden, between wakefulness and dream—are allegories for one another, all forms of quest that travel across the many spaces of Sedakova's poems. One has to wonder, why are we ever at a threshold? To better experience freedom, the poet seems to answer.[23] The vantage point at the brink of a cognitively separate space is like the god Janus's ability to look both forward and backward in time, or Tiresias's knowledge of female and male embodiment. For Sedakova, this spatial and epistemological metaphor opens pathways that free us from choosing. Tales and legends—those narrative structures where multiple realities coexist comfortably—become ideal envelopes for her dream poems.

Sedakova's longest poem in this form is ironically named as having practically no plot, although it is filled with quests, adventures, and biblical and literary allusions. "A Fairy Tale in Which Almost Nothing Happens" ("Skazka, v kotoroi pochti nichego ne proiskhodit," the final poem in the volume *Gates, Windows, Arches*, 1979–83), consists of 14 parts and 146 lines, in trochaic tetrameter (the quasi-exception is the breaking of one line as two, in trochaic dimeter). The trochaic meter, a traditional folkloric rhythm, creates a useful semantic aureole for unreal, imagined events and for the blurry transformations of characters, objects, and events.[24] The driving force of trochaic meter can be strong and musical, and each line potentially begins with a realized stressed syllable. Some of Sedakova's poems where meter is most intensely felt are in ternary meters, with their still more lilting music, but she gets a similar kind of rhythmic charge from these trochees. They show the kind of "reversed intentionality" invoked by Susan Stewart and drawn from the work of Emmanuel Levinas. Here is an extract from the Levinas essay "Reality and Its Shadow," one that is slightly longer than the passage quoted by Stewart, which has a helpful bearing on our poem:

> Rhythm represents a unique situation where we cannot speak of consent, assumption, initiative or freedom, because the subject is caught up and carried away by it. The subject is part of its own representation. It is so not even despite itself, for in rhythm there is no longer a oneself, but rather a sort of passage from oneself to anonymity. This is the captivation or incantation of poetry and music. It is a mode of being to which applies neither the form of consciousness, since the I is stripped of its prerogative to assume, its power, nor the form of unconsciousness, since the whole situation and all its articulations are in a dark light, *present.* Such is a waking dream.[25]

Levinas takes us from rhythms and their impositions on our freedom to the image of a dark dream, and remarkably he does so by the precise pathways along which Sedakova travels so often, including in this poem: by means of renouncing the specificity of the self, the I.

The Freudian approach has emphasized idiosyncratic, repressed desires as the underlying work of dreams. Sedakova is pushing back against the Freudian model, not because she resists an idea of dream work as revealing unconscious desires, but because she is suspicious of Freud's foundational notion of a bounded, individuated, autonomous subject. Levinas, remarkably, not only tells us explicitly that we must move along the pathways of anonymity in order to understand this form of rhythmic impact on the psyche, but he also writes of a "subject" who is at once poet and reader, carried along by the created rhythms. The subject in our poem has shed all traces of individual specificity. Indeed, another reason that Sedakova turns to legends and dreams is for their conventional personae who can also seem strangely like familiar but non-specified human subjects.

"A Fairy Tale in Which Almost Nothing Happens," then, has a dreamer and a dream. It takes us to a far distant land, and it evolves according to the transformative logic of both dreams and fairy tales. In the beginning, we encounter a sleeping man, very like the beloved dreamer of dreams, Jacob:

Засыпающему снится
жаркий полдень, плоский камень
и заваленный колодец.
Камень нужно отложить. (1:266)

Someone falls asleep and dreams of
midday heat, a flat, smooth stone
and of a well that has been sealed.
Someone needs to move the stone.

Sedakova here telescopes several moments from the story of Jacob (Genesis 28:10–22, 29:1–3), for when the dreamer falls asleep, he lays his head on the smooth stone that he will, after God comes to him as a vision in his dream, erect as a marker of God's presence at Bethel. But when he sets off on his journey from that place, he comes to three flocks of sheep and a well upon which a stone lies. The shepherds cannot go home until they water the flocks, and they cannot water the flocks until the stone is moved. In that pause of understanding the obstacles to motion, Jacob sees Rachel, and the Bible tells the famous story of his toiling for her for seven years. At this moment of understanding, though, he rolls the stone from the mouth of the well so that the sheep may be watered. The stone's movement seems to facilitate the dream, a dream that seems familiar as if, he will note half-jokingly, from the book of Genesis.[26] Elsewhere in her poetry, Sedakova recreates Jacob's dream in rich detail, but here the content of the dream—the vision of God—is elided.[27] Or, perhaps, not elided, but transferred into a different dream, a different vision.

To move toward that vision, the poet will turn her dreamer's thoughts toward art-making or, as it is called in the poem, "pesnopen'e," the singing of hymns. We read in part 5 of the poem:

Страшно дело песнопенья
для того, чей разум зорок,
зренье трезво, слово твердо
и над сердцем страх Господень.

Нужно петь, как слабоумный,
быстро, пестро, бесприютно,
нужно бить, как погремушка,
отгоняющая змей: (1:268)

Singing songs is fearsome work
if your mind is sharp and keen,
sight is sober, word is firm,
heart is moved by fear of God.

Sing more like the feeble-minded,
quickly, colorfully, unguarded,
beat more like a rattle shaken
just to scare the snake away:

In these mysterious lines, the fear of God is mixed in with the miracle that enables song (and that line, "Singing songs is fearsome work," will be repeated at the end of the poem, l. 132, reiterating its importance).[28] The one who experiences song-making as awe-inspiring has a sharp mind, sober vision, firm language, and a heart involved in the making of song. The singing of praise here is meant to be loud, rattling, as we find in the Psalms.[29] Singing must be done as if without too much intervention of reason: the connotations of the Russian for "feeble-minded" ("slaboumnyi") might be understood almost etymologically, as if the strength of the word—"word is firm" ("slovo tverdo")—is inversely proportional to the willed diminishing of the mind's powers. Its work is all devoted to strengthening the heart and spirit.

Lessons of mind and heart are what this fairy tale will have to offer, as its intrepid dreamer moves through imagined spaces as if through an enchanted land, holding up the lantern of dreams ("fonar' snovidenii"; 1:268) to penetrate the blackest darkness, illuminating at last the same three words that had come to our dreamer in the first part: "the sheep, the sun, the maiden fair" ("ovtsy, solntse i devitsa," first heard in l. 16, 1:267):

Но что же:
все исчезло, превратилось,
овцы, солнце и девица,
и шумит снотворный мак,
перетряхивая зерна,
рассыпая *чудный сон.* (1:269)

All right then:
everything has vanished, changed,
the sheep, the sun, the maiden fair,
the soporific poppy sounds,
shaking out its poppy seeds,
scattering a *wondrous dream.*

The miracle-dream is in italics, beckoning our attention. Sedakova does that sometimes to signal a quotation from other poets, and here it seems likely that she has in mind Pushkin's several usages of the phrase ("chudnyi son").[30] But the miracle of the dream affects the poet's images in this passage as well, indeed it seems almost to emerge from the images and from the sounds—literally in the case of the strangely noisy poppy seeds that induce sleep and thus make dreams possible, but also in the sounds of the words themselves. In the Russian original the repetition of the words "ovtsy, solntse i devitsa," a paronomastically potent phrase, literalizes the promise of transformation in the preceding line in its recombination of the "v," "s," "ts," and "d/t" sounds. The power of these words to be connected to one another binds them together in this phrase and then seems to free them to appear as separate presences in the dream that is now recounted.

We are at about the halfway point of the poem;[31] a dream with many parts now unfolds. It opens with a fairy-tale lexicon and obstacle-strewn travel to a shepherd's hut, a wondrous place perched precisely at the juncture between nature and culture. The speaker will pause as she comes across the hut's threshold. It is a crossing into the inner spaces of her dream.

В бедной хижине альпийской
жил да был один знакомый

мне пастух. Пройдя тернистый
узкий склон, перебредя
ключ студеный—я у двери
постучала и вошла. (1:269)

Once upon a time there lived
a shepherd in a poor Alpine hut,
a friend of mine. I picked my way
across the thorny slope, I crossed
an ice-cold brook—and at his door
I knocked, and let myself inside.

These lines retrace the dreamer's difficult path to the shepherd's hut, which had already been recounted, so in that retracing, the poet has steadied our gaze on the transit itself, reminding us that all fairy tales travel a treacherous path: we arrive at the scene of treasured revelation only when we expose ourselves to some risk.

The treasure is imaged as gold, as treasure often is, a thread spun from golden lambs, golden light over a golden hearth (ll. 81–92). The epithet is repeated so many times that it is as if the dreamer is trying to assure herself that the gold is truly there, indeed as if the alchemy of the word could make the gold real. Her insistence is so determined that when the shepherd begins to speak, she interrupts him to make space for her own reiterations (ll. 95–106). In a poem where almost nothing is said to happen, surely the discovery of the hut of gleaming light and objects is as important as the meaning of its golden presence, and surely the shepherd's words of wisdom and his parting gift can wait.

если кто-нибудь поверит,
я клянусь, что много счастья
я видала—но такого
невозможно увидать:

ходит золото в рубахе,
на полу лежит соломой,
испаряется из чаши
и встречается с собой

в золотых глазах ягненка,
наблюдающего пламя,
и в глазах других ягнят,
на закат в окно глядящих . . . (1:270)

if there's any who'll believe it
I can swear that I have seen
great happiness—but this kind you
will never ever lay your eyes on:

gold that walks around in clothes,
lies like straw strewn on the floor,
rises, steaming, from a cup
and comes upon itself in golden

eyes of lambs, who gaze entranced
by flames that dance and sway before them,
and in eyes of other lambs
who watch the sunset through the window . . .

The sound repetitions of these lines as well as words and images assert again and again the splendor of what is seen. They create powerful tautologies of vision. The poet sees gold materialized out of air and steam, as if all substance could absorb the radiance. And she sees it doubled in the reflecting eyes of the lambs: her own act of looking is repeated by their eyes, and as lamb looks at flame, the poet observes the eyes of other lambs who look beyond the hut, to the golden rays of a setting sun. Little wonder that the poet claims to have seen the happiness of good fortune and of something like joy.

The tale will go on, giving the shepherd a chance to speak, to offer the protecting gift of felt boots ("valenki") for the visitor to wear as she trudges off into a landscape now fully described as snowy, emblematic of Russia's wintry weather, perhaps. The ending also gives the poet a chance to evoke yet again the multiplying forms of gold, in objects both tiny (golden flecks ground by an enchanted mortar) and vast (oceans and heavens). Before these beautiful images conclude the poem (ll. 135–46), however, the poet reflects on her own thought processes, and once again she slows things down. The lines repeat an observation heard earlier in the poem:

Страшно дело песнопенья,
но оно мне тихо служит
или я ему служу: (1:272)

Singing songs is fearsome work,
but it's work that serves me meekly
or it's me that does the serving:

The making of songs invokes fear perhaps because the song is an act of praise, born in humility and uncertainty.[32] The devotional lexicon here is unmistakable, in a word as ordinary, as plain as "serve" (*sluzhit*). When the poet says that she serves singing as much as it serves her, she echoes such meanings as a service in the sense of a call to prayer, but also to serve in reverence, to give obedience to one's God.

To end with song-making as a kind of servitude returns us full circle to the forms of constricted freedom with which we began. The rhetorical nuances of these three lines suggest perhaps more constraint than we might expect: there is the repetition of "singing songs is fearsome work," as if the poet were drawn by some outside force to repeating the line's assertion of wonder and awe; there is the circular logic of servitude, for it cannot be known who is agent, who is master. And there is the very idea of service, which suggests obedience and duty. Yet the poet's pivoting motion between agency and servitude creates a remarkably interesting opening for the freedoms of art. The syntax of open choice is as powerful as the semantics of service. In that larger realm of possibility, in that way of creating two pathways of possibility along both of which the poet invites us to travel, rests the freedom that makes all song possible.

The praise inherent in song-making grounds all of these constraints in a deeper form of freedom. Susan Stewart has written that the "noncontingent nature" of praise is emphasized again and again in the Psalms, and we might extend her insight toward the song-making celebrated by Sedakova. Stewart adds, "The volitional nature of praise lies in its being freely, liberally, and continually offered and drawn from the energies of the person who praises."[33] We sense not only the expense of energy noted by Stewart but also the creation of a kind of kinetic energy that pulses outward from the poems. That energy can be expressed as physical motion, originated in my own essay with the beautiful, uneven gait of Natasha Shtempel celebrated in Sedakova's essay on Mandelstam (and in turn we recall Mandelstam's own association of walking with poetic creation: how many pairs of shoes did Dante wear out, wondered Mandelstam in his "Conversation about Dante"). Sedakova's poet-speaker strides through multiple landscapes. In "A Fairy Tale in Which Almost Nothing Happens," when the poet arrives at the mountain hut, her discovery comes as the shepherd goes out and tells her to go on her way ("idi"; 1:271). Movement marks the advent of knowledge, not because one can then move with certainty—indeed knowledge is as likely to be transmitted as a set of questions or of enigmatic images, as it is by this shepherd—but because the discoveries one makes as one moves through space are themselves the rewards of lived experience. As Sedakova has written elsewhere: "There is always a step, there is always a move, there is always a path" ("Vsegda est' shag, vsegda est' khod, vsegda est' put'"; "Seven Poems"/"Sem' stikhotvorenii"; 1:228). We also recall Celan's words in the Meridian speech, cited at the start of this essay: "Art requires that we travel a certain space in a certain direction, on a certain road." Celan has art set us into motion as well, proceeding through the stages of a journey that may have its moments of pause and reflection but seems destined never to end.

In "A Fairy Tale in Which Almost Nothing Happens," the fourteenth and final section of the poem, takes up that sense of fate (which is to say, constraint). Here is the section in full, including the three lines cited above:

Страшно дело песнопенья,
но оно мне тихо служит
или я ему служу:

чудной мельнички верчу
золотую рукоятку—
вылетает снег и ветер,
вылетает океан.

Но оно, подобно шлюпке,
настигает, исчезая,
карим золотом сверкая
над безглазой глубиной.

Что не нами начиналось,
что закончится не нами,
перемелют в чистой ступке
золотые небеса. (1:272)

Singing songs is fearsome work,
but it's work that serves me meekly
or it's me that does the serving:

it's I who turn the golden handle
that makes the wondrous windmill turn—
snow and wind come flying out,
and an ocean comes flying out.

But the song, a bobbing boat,
catches up and disappears,
flashing golden brown, a tiny
gleam above the eyeless depth.

What is not begun by us,
what comes to an end without us,
is ground down in an empty mortar
washed by the golden heavens.

This is deceptively simple syntax. Those "golden heavens" are plausibly either object or agent of the act of grinding in the final line: grammatically, they make the most sense as agent, as translated here, yet the poem has for dozens of lines now been giving us images of the gold that might emerge from a mill. The first two lines of the last stanza also work to challenge all possible assertions of agency. We are as if left out of the equation even as the sentence confirms our overwhelming perception that we must be present at the moment of utterance: the beginning is the beginning of Creation, and the created world will extend far beyond our lifetimes, but theology has its say only as if through us, by means of our words.

As the poem suggests in its penultimate stanza, theology also speaks through our visions and dreams. They too are not in our control: we cannot even say for sure that vision inheres in animate beings: the poet compares the milled grain of snow, wind, and ocean as it moves through space to a small boat. All have their own special golden glow, one described as brown ("karii"). This epithet is normally used only to describe the color of a person's eyes or, less commonly, the color of a horse's coat. Either eyes or horses would be interesting enrichments of the swiftly changing figurative environment of these lines: horses would metonymically connect to the examples of motion, and, as animals, to the lambs a few stanzas earlier; the eyes would also remind us of those lambs, with their golden eyes.[34]

The haunting of these last lines by a set of eyes creates the fleeting illusion that all of these references to gold are also meant to create the aura of an icon. Its scene or face is not described fully, but we come to feel as if the poem, like an icon, has its eyes trained on a viewer, gazing with uncanny comprehension and with love. The poet has absorbed into her own act of verbal creation the spiritual mission of icon painting. As we know, "the icon is also a microcosm, which links together the divine and created worlds. The world of matter is represented in various forms, including animal, plant, mineral and water" (another reason why, in the final stanzas, matter is represented as snow, wind, and ocean); as a result, "the icon painter 'frees' matter as he offers it back to God in his reverent creation of an image."[35] We arrive in the end at a rigidly codified and spiritually liberating art form, the painting of icons, one final point of comparison to Sedakova's many ways of creating an art of freedom.

Notes

1. Paul Celan, "The Meridian" (1960), trans. Rosemarie Waldrop, in *Selections*, ed. Pierre Joris (Berkeley: University of California Press, 2005), 154–69; quotation from 160.

2. Compare the views of poet and theorist Susan Stewart, who finds in all art-making "a set of abandoned alternatives" because any work of art might "have been left unfinished" or might be "destroyed." Stewart, *The Poet's Freedom: A Notebook on Making* (Chicago: University of Chicago Press, 2011), 13.

3. Translated from Sedakova, "Proshchal'nye stikhi Mandel'shtama: 'Klassika v neklassicheskoe vremia,'" 2014, http://www.olgasedakova.com/Poetica/1584, accessed March 17, 2018.

4. O. Mandel'shtam, *Polnoe sobranie stikhotvorenii*, ed. A. G. Mets (St. Petersburg: Gumanitarnoe agenstvo "Akademicheskii proekt," 1995), 635. For the poem, as cited here, see 287–88. Colloquially accurate as a gesture of simple approval, his epithet *prekrasnyi* is also notable as the term for the beautiful in philosophical discourse, and Sedakova has taken her cue from his diction.

5. Wiman's translation gives the dedication as the poem's title: "To Natasha Schtempel." See *Stolen Air: Selected Poems of Osip Mandelstam*, trans. Christian Wiman (New York: Ecco Press, 2012), 69.

6. Walter Benjamin, "On the Concept of History," trans. Harry Zohn, in *Selected Writings*, vol. 4, *1938–1940* (Cambridge, MA: Belknap Press of Harvard University Press, 2003), 392.

7. Sedakova, "Nashi uchitelia: Mikhail Viktorovich Panov. K istorii rossiiskoi svobody," in *Moralia*, 4:709–18, cited from 4:709–10.

8. Sedakova follows a long line of Russian writers who read Pushkin as emblematic of free thought. As Maria Khotimsky reminded me, a very large digression could be opened here on the topic of Pushkin and freedom (and I take this occasion to thank her for her many insightful and helpful suggestions as I was writing this essay; they are incorporated throughout).

9. Ol'ga Sedakova, "Sergei Sergeevich Averintsev: K tvorcheskomu portretu uchenogo," in *Sergei Sergeevich Averintsev 1937–2004*, ed. N. P. Averintsev, N. B. Poliakova, and V. B. Cherkasskii (Moscow: Nauka, 2005), 8.

10. I write about Bitov's embodiment of this remembered freedom in *Commemorating Pushkin: Russia's Myth of a National Poet* (Stanford: Stanford University Press, 2004), 266–99. Some of the observations here about the liberating effect of Pushkin's writings on Silver Age poets and a host of others are also pursued at greater length there in chapters on Akhmatova and Tsvetaeva.

11. The dictionary appeared first as *Tserkovnoslaviano-russkie paronimy: Materialy k slovariu* (Moscow: Greko-latinskii kabinet Iu. A. Shichalina, 2005), and then, from the same publisher in 2008, as *Slovar' trudnykh slov iz bogosluzheniia: Tserkovnoslaviano-russkie paronimy*.

12. Here I cannot resist an autobiographical digression, based on my work translating *Old Songs* (*Starye pesni*), when I showed Sedakova my work in progress. She ruefully pointed out to me that the verb that was giving me the most trouble in some poems was a form of the verb "to be," "byvat'." The verb itself is supremely ordinary in its stylistic

register, and its semantics—a state of being that is habitual, repeated, entirely possible on a regular basis—thematizes the ordinary language that I am pointing to here.

13. Jonathan Culler, *Theory of the Lyric* (Cambridge, MA: Harvard University Press, 2015), 140.

14. Ibid., 167. The internal quotations are from Amittai Aviram, *Telling Rhythm: Body and Meaning in Poetry* (Ann Arbor: University of Michigan Press, 1994), 232–34 and 21.

15. Aviram does not have in mind what in Russia has been formidably studied as metrical semantics, but rather a claim that rhythm communicates something but not by means of referential language.

16. That distinction was emphasized to me by Emily Grosholz, who kindly read an earlier version of this essay.

17. Stewart, *The Poet's Freedom*, 57. Stewart cites Valéry's essay "Poetry and Abstract Thought," in *The Art of Poetry*, ed. Jackson Mathews (Princeton, NJ: Princeton University Press, 1989), quoting in 230n9 a passage that is imagistically very strong: "I was suddenly *gripped* by a rhythm which took possession of me and soon gave me the impression of some force outside myself. It was as though someone else were making use of my *living-machine*. Then another rhythm overtook and combined with the first, and certain stronger *transverse* relations were set up between two principles" (Valéry, 61). Culler (136) cites a later passage from the same essay, with the metaphor of the "living-machine" (*machine-à-vivre*), from Valéry's French original, "Poésie et pensée abstraite," in *Oeuvres*, ed. J. Hytier (Paris: Gallimard, 1957), 1:1322. I do not find the striking metaphor of the "*living-machine*" particularly congenial to Sedakova's work, but the directionality of being seized by a rhythm, and the intriguing added detail of a second rhythm overtaking the first, is pertinent and well worth keeping in mind.

18. For a different version of these lines, and a complete translation of the poem, see Sedakova, *The Wild Rose and Selected Poems*, trans. Richard McKane (London: Approach Publishing, 1997), 166–67.

19. Another signature is that of music, which acts as a structuring principle in *The Wild Rose*; there and elsewhere in her work, many poems have musical themes or musical terms in their titles.

20. I treat the theme of travel and movement in Sedakova's poetry in "Questions of Travel: Joseph Brodsky and Olga Sedakova," in *Russian Literature and the West*, part 2, ed. Alexander Dolinin, Lazar Fleishman, and Leonid Livak (Berkeley, CA: Berkeley Slavic Specialties, 2008), 261–81. A poem featured there that merits much further consideration is "The Strange Journey" ("Strannoe puteshestvie"; 1:76–77), and also pertinent are the poet's remarkable prose journeys: "Journey to Briansk" ("Puteshestvie v Briansk") and "Journey to Tartu and Back" ("Puteshestvie v Tartu i obratno"), in *2 Puteshestviia*, by Ol'ga Sedakova (Moscow: Logos, 2005). See also the excellent introduction to that volume, "Puteshestvuia v puteshestviia," by Kseniia Golubovich, 7–12.

21. See, for example, Fedor Svarovskii, *Vse khotiat byt' robotami* (Moscow: ARGO-RISK, 2007) and *Puteshestvenniki vo vremeni* (Moscow: Novoe literaturnoe obozrenie, 2009); Mariia Stepanova, "Nevesta" and "Letchik" in *Stikhi i proza v odnom tome* (Moscow: Novoe literaturnoe obozrenie, 2010), 14–22, and *Proza Ivana Sidorova* (Moscow: Novoe izdatel'stvo, 2008). Both write largely narrative poetry, however, and there are fewer examples like Sedakova's that explore these imaginative categories in the lyric.

Another apt comparison would be the mysteries, dreams, indeed the "works and days" explored by Elena Shvarts. See for example her "Trudy i dni Lavinii," in *Sochineniia*, 5 vols. (St. Petersburg: Pushkinskii fond, 2002–13), 2:168–221.

22. Note especially the poem's mysterious rendering of a good man's life (in "Legenda sed'maia. Smert' Aleksiia, Rimskogo Ugodnika"), or indeed in the other poems named in this way. The mystery of each poem is accentuated by the legends' being spread across the book *The Wild Rose*, rather than grouped together. They punctuate and separate other groupings of poem in the elaborate orchestration of the volume. Also curious, however, are the gaps in the numbering of the legend poems: why, we wonder, do we eventually read legends number 2, 6, 7, 9, 10, 11, and 12, but in no publication of the poet's work do we find numbers 3, 4, 5, 8, or indeed anything after 12? The first legend is included in the poet's early work, different in multiple ways from later poem-legends and dated 1975: "The First Legend. St. Julian Hunts" ("Pervaia legenda. Sviatoi Iulian na okhote"; 1:55).

23. In explaining her idea of "freedom as cocreation," Svetlana Boym has pointed to multiple forms of adventure as foundational: it "opens up porous spaces of border zones, thresholds, bridges, and doors." See Svetlana Boym, *Another Freedom: The Alternative History of an Idea* (Chicago: University of Chicago Press, 2012), 6. The epigraph in my essay is from the same source, page 4. I take this occasion to thank and remember this brilliant scholar and fearless thinker, with whom I was lucky to have many conversations on freedom, poetry, and much else.

24. In writing about trochaic tetrameter, Mikhail Gasparov points to its much wider range of meanings in Pushkin's texts. He reminds us of the meter's tendencies toward narrative, and he suggests a range of semantic aureoles and thematic tasks for the meter. A narrower argument about the meter was made by Yuri Lotman based on a single Pushkin poem, "Zoriu b'iut . . . iz ruk moikh": he finds essential its transition from a realist disposition of events toward grammatical and cognitive forms of the unreal. See M. L. Gasparov, *Metr i smysl* (Moscow: RGGU, 1999), 194–202, and Iu. M. Lotman, "Analiz poeticheskogo teksta," in *O poetakh i poezii* (St. Petersburg: Iskusstvo-SPB, 1996), 155–63, especially 163.

25. Emmanuel Levinas, "Reality and Its Shadow," in *The Levinas Reader*, ed. Seán Hand (Malden, MA: Blackwell Publishing Group, 1989), 132–33. The passage cited by Stewart goes on to include the following: "We have really an exteriority of the inward. It is surprising that phenomenological analysis never tried to apply this fundamental paradox of rhythm and dream, which describes a sphere situated outside the conscious and the unconscious, a sphere whose role in its ecstatic rites has been shown by ethnography." Stewart's quotation appears in *The Poet's Freedom*, 57.

26. Biblical allusions continue in the poem, mostly without the names (Laban will be named in part 7). Thus, in the second part, a certain king, sick in spirit, beckons the bringing of musicians, very much like King Saul, seeking the songs of David. Compare Sedakova's poem on these two, "David Sings to Saul" ("David poet Saulu"; 1:221–23). In writing about this poem, Elena Aizenshtein has suggested that Akhmatova's ("Rachel" ["Rakhil'"]; 1922) is an important subtext; it is true that the motifs of dust, well, stone, and water that appear in Sedakova's poem are also found there (they also appear in the Bible). But Akhmatova's poem focuses on Jacob's love for Rachel, just as she focuses in "Lot's Wife" ("Lotova zhena," 1922–24) on the loyal love felt for home and family by Lot's wife. Sedakova, by comparison, has her gaze much more steadily fixed on the nature of a dreamed

vision, and on its revelation of the nature of poetic truth. See Elena Aizenshtein, "'Vdol' ostrovov vysokikh i veselykh': O poezii Ol'gi Sedakovoi," *Neva* 12 (2014), http://magazines.russ.ru/neva/2014/12/9a.html, accessed March 13, 2018.

27. See, for example, a poem in which Jacob's ladder to heaven and its vision of angels ascending and descending are vividly shown: "Death comes to me often in dreams" ("Mne chasto snitsia smert' i predlagaet," in *Dikii shipovnik*, 1976–78; 1:99). The dream also appears fleetingly in the end of the late poem "Nachalo" ("The Beginning," in *Elegii*, 1987–2004; 1:386–87). Also pertinent is the remarkable "Legenda desiataia. Iakov" ("Tenth Legend. Jacob," in *Dikii shipovnik*, 1:130), with its distinctive, insistent, repetitive intoning of the simple claim that Jacob slept.

28. The word "strashno" is translated here as "fearsome," as awe-inspiring, but it could as easily have been wondrous, astonishing. Very likely, Sedakova is also invoking archaic usage, as she often does; see the definitions of Church Slavonic *strashno* (страшно) offered in Sedakova, *Tserkovnoslaviano-russkie paronimy*, 343. In discussing this passage, Liudmila Lutsevich suggests that the epithet be translated as "miraculous"; see her *Pamiat' o psalme: Sacrum/profanum v sovremennoi russkoi poezii* (Warsaw: Wydawnictwa Uniwersytetu Warszawskiego, 2009), 245.

29. In the words of Susan Stewart, "As we know from the Hebrew psalms, what is surrendered in praise is sound—praise is sounded by speech and singing, by the 'joyful noises' of lyres, timbals, and drums, and by the human drums of clapping and rhythmic shouting" (*The Poet's Freedom*, 35).

30. Including the mention of Liudmila's dream in *Ruslan i Liudmila*, Tatiana's dream in *Evgenii Onegin*, and the opening of the late poem "Rodrig" ("Chudnyi son mne Bog poslal"). Although the phrase appears in other poems (e.g., Baratynsky's "Novinskoe"), the rich Pushkinian context seems more likely, reinforcing the connections of freedom with Pushkin's legacy in Russian literature. Here it is both a freedom to dream and the possibilities of freedom opened up by the dreamed journey.

31. Part 8 begins at l. 75, so when the "chudnyi son" is announced, parts 8–14 are still to come.

32. In defining Church Slavonic *pěnie* (пѣние) the poet has set forth its second meaning as praise: "voskhvalenie, khvala, predmet khvaly": see Sedakova, *Tserkovnoslaviano-russkie paronimy*, 292.

33. Stewart, *The Poet's Freedom*, 36.

34. There is more to say on the subject of eyes in this poem. The enigmatic image of the "many-eyed hands" in the poem's second section ("mnogookie ruki"; 1:267) comes in a passage that describes (in all likelihood) King Saul's call for music in 1 Samuel 16:15–23; compare Sedakova's poem "David Sings to Saul," also discussed in note 26 above. On that poem, see Maria Khotimsky, "'Singing David, Dancing David': Olga Sedakova and Elena Shvarts Rewrite a Psalm," *Slavic and East European Journal* 51, no. 4 (Winter 2007): 737–52; and Lutsevich, *Pamiat' o psalme*, 245–55.

35. Mariamna Fortounatto and Mary B. Cunningham, "Theology of the Icon," in *The Cambridge Companion to Orthodox Christian Theology*, ed. Mary B. Cunningham and Elizabeth Theokritoff (Cambridge: Cambridge University Press, 2008), 136–49, quotation from 136. I cite this source because its phrasing is perfectly appropriate to my point; it draws on the authoritative studies of icons by Ouspensky, Lossky, Pelikan, and others.

PART 2

Theology, Philosophy, and Modes of Knowing

Sedakova's Book of Hours and the Devotional Lyric

Reading "Fifth Stanzas"

ANDREW KAHN

> The voice of poetry, the voice of a human in right relation with purity, profundity, and mystery—is the voice of astonishing, inexplicable certitude.
>
> —Olga Sedakova

Пятые стансы. De arte poetica

1
Большая вещь—сама себе приют.
Глубокий скит или широкий пруд,
таинственная рыба в глубине
и праведник, о невечернем дне
читающий урочные Часы.
Она сама—сосуд своей красы.

2
Как в раковине ходит океан—
сердечный клапан времени, капкан
на мягких лапах, чудище в мешке,
сокровище в снотворном порошке,—
так в разум мой, в его скрипучий дом
она идет с волшебным фонарем . . .

3
Не правда ли, минувшая строфа
как будто перегружена? Лафа
тому, кто наяву бывал влеком

всех образов сребристым косяком,
несущим нас на острых плавниках
туда, где мы и всё, что с нами,—прах.

4
Я только в скобках замечаю: свет—
достаточно таинственный предмет,
чтоб говорить Бог ведает о чем,
чтоб речь, как пыль, пронзенная лучом,
крутилась мелко, путано, едва . . .
Но значила—прозрачность вещества.

5
Большая вещь—сама себе приют.
Там скачут звери и птенцы клюют
свой музыкальный корм. Но по пятам
за днем приходит ночь. И тот, кто там,
откладывает труд: он видит рост
магнитящих и слезотворных звезд.

6
Но странно: как состарились глаза!
Им видно то, чего глядеть нельзя,
и прочее не видно. Так из рук,
бывает, чашка выпадет. Мой друг,
что мы как жизнь хранили, пропадет—
и незнакомое звездой взойдет . . .

7
Поэзия, мне кажется, для всех
тебя растят, как в Сербии орех
у монастырских стен, где ковш и мед,
колодец и небесный ледоход,—
и хоть на миг, а видит мирянин
свой ветхий век, как шорох вешних льдин . . .

8
—О, это всё: и что я пропадал,
и что мой разум ныл и голодал,
как мышь в холодном погребе, болел,

что никого никто не пожалел—
всё двинулось, от счастья очумев,
как «всё пройдет», Горациев припев . . .

9
Минуту, жизнь, зачем тебе спешить?
Еще успеешь ты мне рот зашить
железной ниткой. Смилуйся, позволь
раз или два испробовать пароль:
«Большая вещь—сама себе приют».
Она споет, когда нас отпоют,—

10
и, говорят, прекрасней. Но теперь
полуденной красы ночная дверь
раскрыта настежь; глубоко в горах
огонь созвездий, ангел и монах,
при собственной свече из глубины
вычитывает образы вины . . .

11
Большая вещь—утрата из утрат.
Скажу ли? взгляд в медиоланский сад:
приструнен слух; на опытных струнах
играет страх; одушевленный прах,
как бабочка, глядит свою свечу:
—Я не хочу быть тем, что я хочу!

12
И будущее катится с трудом
в огромный дом, секретный водоем . . . (1:305–8)

Fifth Stanzas: On the Art of Poetry

1
A great thing is a haven for herself.
a broad deep pond or hermit's cell,
a mysterious fish hidden in the deep,
a righteous person, reading his Book of Hours
about the day that has no evening.
She is herself the vessel of her own beauty.

2
As the ocean swims inside a shell—
the heart-valve of time, a trap
on soft paws, a marvel in a sack,
a treasure in a sleeping potion,—
so into my reason, into its creaking house,
she penetrates with her magic lantern . . .

3
Don't you think the stanza just above
is perhaps overloaded? Well, it's just fine
for someone who in reality is usually hauled
along by the silvery slanting ray of all images,
carrying us on sharp fins to where
we and all we have known are dust, no more.

4
I note only in parentheses: light
is a sufficiently mysterious object,
in order to talk about God knows what,
while speech, like motes suffused by a ray,
span round in particles, scrambled, scarcely . . .
But she signified—the transparency of matter.

5
A great thing is a haven for herself.
Beasts leap there and birds peck
music for food. But on the heels
of day comes night. And he who is there
lays down his labor: he sees the rise of
the stars, magnetic and tear-inducing.

6
It's strange how one's eyes have aged!
Visible to them is what cannot be seen,
and nothing else is visible. Even thus from one's hands
sometimes a cup falls out. My friend,
what we have saved, like life, will disappear—
and the unknown will rise up like a star . . .

7
Poetry, it seems to me, you are grown
for all, as in Serbia nut-trees
grow along monastery walls, where a ladle and honey,
a well and a celestial ice floe,—
even if only for a moment, but a layman watches
his fragile age, like the rustling of spring glaciers . . .

8
—O, that is all: I knew that I was doomed,
and that my reason was starved and pined,
ailed like a mouse in a cold cellar,
since nobody took pity on anyone—
everything is in motion, drunk from joy,
since "everything passes," the Horatian refrain . . .

9
Wait a minute, what point is there, life, in rushing?
You'll still have time to sew my mouth shut
with an iron thread. Have pity, give me a chance
once or twice to try out my shibboleth:
"A great thing is a haven for herself."
She will sing as our burial service is sung—

10
and so much more beautifully, they will say. But now
the night-time door opens to a half-day of beauty
let fully in; deep in the hills
the fire of constellations, the angel and the monk,
out of the depths to the light of its own candle
reads exemplary lives of guilt . . .

11
A great thing is the loss of losses.
Shall I call it a glimpse into a Mediolanian garden?
Hearing has been tuned up; on the tested strings
plays fear; dust made animate
like a butterfly sees its candle:
—I do not wish to be that which I will!

12
And with effort the future rolls
into the huge house, a secret cistern . . .[1]

Olga Sedakova's poetry is oriented to a range of spiritual, literary, and aesthetic concerns, and her instinct is always to relate the small and the large, the human and the metaphysical, the personal and divine. Her search for expressive and poetic fulfilment is unified. In this she follows the admired examples of poets, such as the avowed Catholics Paul Claudel and Charles Péguy, who have "perfectly fulfilled the laws of free art and also spoken about the truths of belief."[2] Despite her lofty vision, Sedakova's poetic art prefers unspoken implication to dogmatic assertion. The intimate drama of slow revelation attracts her rather than the posture of Romantic visionary genius.

In "Fifth Stanzas" ("Piatye stansy," 1992), and in many other works, her logical and poetic use of analogy and metaphor exemplify her belief that lyric poetry connotes more than it should wish to spell out. This is one conclusion about her literary work that readers of her essays as well as many of her lyric poems will know for themselves. Her observations about the bond between art and spirit in writers such as Pasternak, Eliot, Rilke, and Pavel Florensky further support her conviction that the "epiphany of beauty" ("epifaniia krasy") through the sensitive use of the poetic word can become the "embodiment of worship" ("voploshchennym bogosluzheniem"; 3:130). No less is to be expected from a writer steeped in medieval religion and poetics, who is avidly aware of the historic connections among poetry, vision, and especially Christian belief.[3] Her poetry is also alert to the unconscious power of song and rhythm. Her idiom flourishes on image-making and enjoyable paradox, with clusters of gnomic meaning situated in stretches of more expansive evocation. Infused with a strong religious strain yet unencumbered by dogma, her poems can combine winning address and restrained confession. These features come together movingly in "Fifth Stanzas."

References to time include the diurnal clock (ll. 5, 24, 47), aging (ll. 26, 36–40), the present (l. 34), experiential time and lifespan (ll. 40–45), and ecclesiastical/New Testament time (ll. 4, 52). The Book of Hours prescribes units of time in the form of a ritual schedule for the divine office read by monks, and also contains that other eternal, ahistorical time incarnated by Jesus Christ and embodied by the Christian faith (*illo tempore*) as an endless realm into which one enters through prayer and liturgy. Line 4 identifies the moment in the day when the act of reading takes place, a pointed reminder that one of the time zones of the poem is the day divided into canonical hours of prayer. In Orthodoxy as in Catholicism, daytime prayers are held at midmorning (Terce), midday (Sext), mid-afternoon (None), and Vespers before the night prayer (Compline).

Contriving riddles is part of how the text involves the reader, encouraging us to view chains of relations, whether stanzas or images, as objects deserving scrutiny in their own right. Paradoxical expression is a regular feature of the Slavonic hymnography. Reading as described in "Fifth Stanzas" occurs both in the world but also outside it, framed temporally by the "eveningless day." This idiom recalls the well-known liturgical phrase "undimming light" (*nevechernii svet*), used to define God and Christ as sources of inextinguishable light ("nevechernii svet"). This association is to be expected given that Sedakova's spiritual roots are known to lie very deep in the Orthodox liturgy, hymnography, and Psalter, all rich in metaphors of light. For instance, the phrase "by the Sun of truth and from the East on high" ("Solntsem pravdy i Vostokom s vysoty") names the Christ child in the Troparion of the Nativity.[4] The phrase "evening light" ("svet vechernii") names the God of love and giver of life in the prayer "O Gentle Light" ("Svete Tikhii"), which likens the God of love and giver of life to the evening light and the inextinguishable light to Christ; and the combination used here of "light without evening" ("svet nevechernii") names the Creator and Eternal Ruler of the universe.[5] These considerations lead back to the title. Sedakova wrote first, second, third, and fourth stanzas before writing this poem, and she created formal similarities among these sets of stanzas. On this occasion, however, Sedakova has chosen to publish the poem not as the fifth in the sequence "Verses in the Manner of Alexander Pope" ("Stikhi v manere Aleksandra Popa," 1979–80), but as the beginning of a new cycle, "Iambs."[6] While the stanzas fall short of the scale, gravity, and ritual composition of the book of hours, I would suggest that the poem itself forms a breviary composed for the fifth of the seven canonical hours. No longer in liturgical use, and therefore without its own designated set of prayers, a missing theoretical Fifth Hour provides a slot for a poem-cum-prayer conceived as a moment of supplication and spiritual searching. The poem encompasses the chronological time of everyday life and the privileged moment of epiphany when the monk communes with the deity.[7] The artistic alter ego is empowered to find in this moment what looks like Dantesque New Life.

"Fifth Stanzas" draw pointedly on these phrases from the Book of Hours (*Chasoslov*) as illuminating linkages on a path toward enlightenment. By transcribing these words and giving rhetorical life to a vision of their recitation, the poem seeks as much to be a book of hours as a literary utterance. Spiritual beauty ("krasa"), another name for grace, rhymes in its usage here with hours as a matter of design. Knowing Sedakova's erudite penchant for religious poetry, we can feel confident that the growing importance of beauty during the course of the lyric carries forward into visual language a movement toward a final state of amazement. Reflection expressed as religious lyric creates a supplementary liturgical hour in which poetry as faith, and faith in poetry, focus the mind. The act of reading the poem, just like reading the breviary (as a version of the book of hours), takes reader and worshipper across the boundary separating human and Christian time.[8]

We are listening to a contemplation of religious meditation, affording a glimpse onto the devotional reading of the "righteous person" ("pravednik"), raising questions about the status of poetry as religious act. Suggestions of spiritual content abound. Stanzas composed for a fifth hour would represent their own office, extending to the art of poetry a place in the service that seems appropriate, if to be religious also means to be religious about poems and religious in poems. The subtitle *De arte poetica* confirms this prospect in suggesting that poetic and religious language can be coextensive and augment one another.

At the heart of the poem's existential and spiritual reckoning, and threading its stanzas together, is the notion of the "great thing" as both definable and indefinable. Sedakova has written eloquently on her belief in poetic words as a type of substance. The following passage offers in miniature a theory of the poetic word as its own thing, and while elsewhere she quotes from Heidegger and demonstrates an ease with his philosophical vocabulary, this definition is very much her own synthesis:

> This is a poetry, in which one could only crudely distinguish between *natura naturata*[9]—reified in ready objects, verses—and *natura naturans*[10]—a generative prelingual source, for in its "objects" poetry exists precisely as such a source: as a "ray of force," in Pasternak's words, as "what is not," like Rilke's Unicorn, and as what, even while emerging, "has no need to be." The poets of the twentieth century sensed this revealed, revealing substance of poetry more sharply than ever before. As a rule, everything else—themes, feelings, narratives, everything that clothes and grounds this substance, whose nature is not so much to *be* as to *appear and to emerge,*—interested them much less than the poets of other ages, who were judicious, measured, "prosaic."[11]

The question of the ratio of part to whole organizes the comparisons made in the first stanza overtly and by implication. When we recall that the Book of Hours distills the poetry of the Psalter, and is itself a smaller part of that larger whole, the use of analogy looks organic.[12] Qualities predicated of "the thing" are size, depth, width, obscurity (motif of safety), and also the moral quality of righteousness linked to the idea of either a religious sect or a spiritual retreat.[13] Nouns to which "the thing" can be likened initially include a vessel, refuge, pond, fish, a shell, the ocean, a mitral valve (and synecdoche for the heart).[14] There is nothing that cannot contain something else, whether a mote of dust trapped in a ray of light (l. 22) or perhaps the vowel "a" held in the word "kapkan," and then further the mind itself. These chains of analogy are a form of word-weaving (*pletenie sloves*), a tradition readily available to the learned Sedakova.[15] The use of circumlocution and metaphor to fix the mind on the ineffable, a deity that can be conceived as an Other but not defined spatially, represents a reflex known from her religious poetry.[16] Hence small things containing big things are in a way miraculous because they must have a special property. The final comparison in the sequence is "she" in l. 12, which must be the "great thing" that fits into "reason" and goes with a "magic lantern." The poem does not name this cognitive faculty, but given the powers of visual illumination, we might surmise that the feminine pronoun looks ahead to poetry as named in stanza 7.[17] Whatever it means, the treasure turns out to be much larger than reason, yet contained by reason, and, although a container and therefore closed, nonetheless illuminated by a magic lantern. In the course of the poem, a visionary redefinition of the "great thing" emerges as an entity that gains a world by embracing loss.

In the very invocation of the book of hours, Sedakova draws strength from the example of Rilke, starting with the idea that joy is a vessel (*der Gefäß*) into which poets gather time.[18] His own poem, like a book of hours, plays with two types of time: the chronological time of everyday life and the privileged moment of epiphany. Rilke represents himself in the persona of the icon-painting monk (and the pictorial quality of Sedakova's stanzas is vibrant precisely owing to its verbal icons); his moment of communion stands for the artist empowered to create what Rilke himself calls a "second, time-wide life" by translating the divine into human language.[19] Sedakova's dialogue with Rilke, conducted in her essays, poems, and translations, is its own separate topic.[20] Here, his influence is all the more appropriate because his version of the *Book of Hours* (published in 1899, 1901, and 1903) emanated from his experience of Russia in 1902 and his perspective on Orthodoxy and religious art.[21] Ben Hutchinson, one of Rilke's English translators, notes that prayer is for him a "largely aesthetic process" nurtured by a belief that the majesty of God is not revealed but slowly unfolded in order to allow man to grasp and appreciate the divinity properly. Illumination is painted in meticulously applied layers and small emblems rather than in a flash of bright light. In crafting a verbal equivalent for this pictorial metaphor, the poetry of both Rilke and Sedakova adopts repetitive cadences that push at edges of consciousness through images of darkness even more than light.[22] As the poem strives to enunciate an apophatic recognition of inner religiosity, it uses poetic language for an abstract yet heartfelt purpose. Yet there is a crucial difference between the two poets. While Sedakova understands Rilke's conviction that consciousness gives access to transcendence, she does not adopt his faith.[23] His *Book of Hours* was inspired by the spirituality Rilke found in Russia, but it adopts a religion of art over an art of religion in which "God becomes a metaphor, not for the creative act, but for the art object."[24]

Sedakova does not give an outright definition of the greater substance. Instead, she requires the reader to work inductively and to think visually about types of entities. A series of images (a "hermit's cell," a "broad deep pond," a "mysterious fish," a "secret cistern") provide examples of something that thanks to its size can serve as its own shelter. The reader is invited to visualize the bigness of the great "thing" as a dimension that remains unnamed but conceivable and embodied through analogy.[25] This allows us to make sense relationally of what may be beyond definition, an example of what Susan Stewart has called the "invocatory act."[26] It would certainly not be hard to convert all of the objects and statements given in the first two stanzas into a riddle: "What is its own haven, a hermit's cell, and a broad deep pond?" to which the answer could be nothing more precise than a "great thing." Is that a concession to the ineffable quality of this feeling or entity, or an acceptance of apophatic representation? These listing stanzas have religious echoes. Their common mystery reinforces their collective purpose as objects formulated in relation to some greater mystery (*tainstvennost'*). The images of the sect, pond, and fish are linked through metonymies of depth and breadth as metaphors for the unknown and profound, here articulated as mystery. By definition, a "sect" is religious, and deep because physically and spiritually removed from the world like a monastic or hermetic body. By association, a fish found in the deep that is also like a righteous man (and transitively also as deep as a sect and wide as a pond) would be like the whale that swallowed the prophet Jonah and saved him from evildoers, finally spewing him back into the world to perform righteous acts. The "mystery of the fish" obviously refers to the mystery of Christianity (*taina* being a liturgical word, with the fish as a verbal and iconographic emblem also conveying multiple Christian meanings). It bears a further link to the image of the hermit's cave, anticipating the reference to the monastery in stanza 7 and the monk in stanza 8. One medieval definition of the deity, whether formulated in Aristotelian terms as the prime mover or theologically as the Holy Father, is as an entity that is perfect in itself and entirely self-sufficient. The image of the righteous man reading the Book of Hours takes us full circle to the idea of the divine element in the human as the self-contained and perfect subject as well as object of devotion.

Devotional lyric nurtured on the quest for spiritual illumination cannot gain authenticity by celebrating creative epiphany. If the poem describes a process, and this reading will suggest that it does, then it is about a concentric movement outward to the next set of encompassing wholes. "Fifth Stanzas" is hardly alone in Sedakova's oeuvre in aligning spiritual and visual movement. Stars, sacred texts, visions, and angels all inhabit a realm to which the eyes of her lyric speakers are naturally drawn, and often. The poet carries "two books" that light her way from above ("In the Spirit of Leopardi"). Yet light and dark are antinomies that cannot be sundered any more easily than body and soul: the vision illuminated is of a "darkness of predeterminism opened" ("otkryta t'ma prednaznachen'ia").[27] No less exuberant in its association of spiritual enlightenment and height is the "Portrait of an Artist in his Own Painting" ("Portret khudozhnika na ego kartine," 1976–78), which pictorially flirts with Mannerist conventions by surrounding the speaker with angels dancing on the rooftop, emblems of a laughing heaven in which beauty abides.[28] Yet even here optimism cannot be sustained, and the poem descends into darkness and a valley of sin (evoked by the biblical story of Lot and Sodom). Another lyric, "The Dreamer" ("Snovidets," 1978), opens on an image of invincible darkness that snuffs out a candle, but once the mind lapses into a state of complete darkness, relinquishing all awareness, then there is a path toward a deeper self that resides within the self and defies articulation. A striking vista opens in the "Mountain Ode" ("Gornaia oda"), which moves in sharp vertical contrasts. The first stanza alone juxtaposes height ("vysota"), emblematized in heavenly azure (a favorite color of the Symbolists, of course) and a valley of earthly astonishment only to soar up again in the image of the Gothic as the embodiment of the "vector of verticality" (1:231–35). These contrasts recur strikingly in the tenth stanza of that poem where the gift of perceiving the supernal realm hides in the buried depths of a tree. For Sedakova the two planes cannot be separated, since the heavenly and earthly nurture one another: the speaker of "Night Embroidery" ("Nochnoe shit'e") is mesmerized by the sight of constellations but retreats from her own metamorphosis, like a figure of myth: "What then shall I do with my earthly dust / until a better sun has arisen?" ("Tak chto zhe ia sdelaiu s perst'iu zemnoiu, / poka eshche luchshee solntse ne vyidet?" 1:241–42). Whether it comes in the form of chiaroscuro or height or color, contradiction is a generative principle in Sedakova's image systems. Not all forms of contradiction are paradox, but insofar as "Night Embroidery" aims to reconcile life and death, dark and light, near and far, contained and limitless, it does lay a Pascalian wager on the force of belief.

In "Fifth Stanzas," the prayerful self is both the smallest focal point in that arrangement and its absolute center. The third stanza rescues the notion of the over-freighted or saturated stanzas as a problem by transforming them into the vehicle for imaginative progress. Yet there is a sting in the tail. While the combination of "silver rivulet" and "magic lantern" might suggest equivalence among sincerity, plenitude, and spiritual reward, the poet interjects a blunt reminder of mortality. Logical overload, as spoken of here, acknowledges the limits of reason to fix the "great thing," whether Christ, religion, faith, prayer, or beauty. The possibility of predicating such a list suggests the openness of a form praised for its capacity to contain. Yet a poem written in strict stanzaic form implicitly wishes to control overflow, curbing the risk of overstatement and trusting repetition and refrain to contain the uncontainable. If at this point the poem professes to pull back from its analogy-making, exercising humility but also a suspicion of too much eloquence as delusive, it shifts to other forms of signification that are no less rich in connotation. Like the church that shelters both worshipper and sacraments, a stanza can contain a mystery. Furnished with riddling objects and images, each beautifully shaped stanza is like a room, and surely Sedakova hears the Italian word for "room" (*stanza*) here.[29] The recurrence of the idea of mystery extends to Christian emblems represented in the "mysterious fish" and the "silver stream," phrases linked by the implied combination *rybnyi kosiak* to mean a school of fish.[30] Surplus will be much to the point at the end of the poem: spiritual perception overwhelms stanza 12 by generating two more lines that are either a supplement or an incomplete new beginning. It is part of the duality of a poem that oscillates between obscurity and perception, puzzlement and enlightenment, colloquialism and formality, that it closes with an eye to the future, introducing the image of a container that is secret—an open secret that takes us back to the opening idea that the "great thing" is only a shelter, not a final destination.

"Fifth Stanzas" gently dispels hesitation through escapism in metaphorical and imagistic chains. At the beginning of stanza 4 a second rhetorical intrusion occurs in which the poet speaks in a self-conscious aside. Mystery (*tainstvennost'*) cannot stand too much directness, just as devotion requires the special circumstances of a service sheltered from day. Despite the protest about its over-wrought style, with stanza 4 the poem once again funnels understanding through images and refuses direct definitional statement. The stanza speaks of matter as translucent and light as a mysterious object, a paradox of transubstantiation that is religious in nature. Light as the antithesis of darkness may stand for understanding against the incomprehension of a benighted state. Even light turns out to be its own mystery ("dostatochno tainstvennyi predmet"), and contains its own element of impenetrability, defined as either particle (speck of dust) or as beam (a ray of light). Speech is by analogy more like the ray. Illumination must be indirect.

And speech, and perhaps above all poetic speech, oscillates between signification and connotation, and syntax between assertion and connotation. The poem claims transparency for what is penetrated by light. But can we visualize a speck of dust, said to be solid matter, penetrated by light? Can we imagine speech or language of that degree of transparency? There seems to be no denying that figurative language brings us closer to something essential. Even the meaning of the colloquial phrase "God knows" seems to oscillate between "God knows what this mysterious object *tainstvennost'* is about" and, when glossed more expansively as the definite object of the predicative clause, "light is a sufficiently mysterious object that it knows what God is talking about." Sedakova has manipulated the syntax so as to encourage these alternative paraphrases.

The aphorism "A great thing is its own shelter" recurs in four variations in stanzas 1, 5, 9, and 11. Repetition makes it an article of faith for the reader that the meaning of the poem and the meaning of the assertion move together. Stanzas constitute their own container, holding the content of the Book of Hours (*urochnye chasy*) and serving as a blank page on which emblems, the birds and beasts as typical zoomorphic figures of the missal, are illuminated.

In the fifth stanza, gnomic pithiness yields to imagistic vibrancy, populating the imagined page of the Breviary, and the actual page of the poem, with a roster of leaping beasts, pecking birds, musical notation. "There" ("tam") is both the book of hours and the more perfect world represented in it that offers artistic and spiritual sustenance. Beauty is aural, visual, and also verbal. The reference to the natural diurnal order and sequence affords an indirect reminder of the paradox that a Book of Hours, when used regularly, serves the reader as a precious escape from time through prayer and beauty. In addition, the fifth stanza in a poem entitled "Fifth Stanzas" itself occupies an iconic slot in the sequence, and the pun on "po piatam" underscores the idea that in an ordered series like day and night, or within the artistic system of the prayer book, entities follow on the heels of one another. At the end, the laborer or tiller, an omnipresent figure in Western illuminated books, views the light, seen earlier as a lantern, a beam, and then later as fire, as stars. Prayer is a form of spiritual labor ("trud") that lays up future grace, even as the worker lays aside his momentary work to contemplate the reward. This is the reciprocity between spirituality and grace promised by the star.

What the figure in the landscape forgets, however, is that the diurnal clock ("za dnem prikhodit noch'") portends mortal limits, and that the impulse to veneration and a life beyond derives from awareness of death. Growth comes at the expense of loss. This hidden contradiction embraces the irreconcilable antinomy of life and death as a creative principle, nowhere better seen than in the very epithet coined to describe the lachrymose star. "Tear-inducing" is the type of compound epithet common to word-weaving. The adjective makes the star an agent both of hope and sadness, implying the recognition that gaining heaven entails losing life. The star is a new form of light, relating back to the lamp at the end of stanza 2. In fact, light turns out to be the poem's most deconstructive emblem. Suffused by dust in stanza 4, it is both ray and speck, endless and confined, a perfect formal container for this poem about the representation of belief as forms of open containment. Infused with tears, light as a star radiates a path that inevitably contains the darkness of night, anticipating the reduced vision and compromised sense of life in stanza 6, the insomniac intimations of death in stanza 8, and the night thoughts of stanza 9 ending in both the silence of death and the song of lament, a further perfect contradiction. Language here is literal through possible gestures; allegorical through its moral implications of recognition; and perhaps most importantly anagogical because each visible thing points beyond to some invisible and mystical reality.[31]

Yet the light of reason is insecurely housed in the speaker's aging brain; her eyes, those windows into the soul, no longer see the divine light; and perhaps it is for that reason she drops the goblet. The harder we look, the less tangible things become in a poem in which substances are a "what" ("chto" is even less solid than a "bol'shaia veshch'"), "unknown" ("neznakomoe") and "invisible" ("ne vidno"). Yet the unknown can still remain a beacon in the image of the star in line 36 and in the beauty and musicality of line 48 with its perfect balancing of vowels and consonants. Faith enables an inner vision that sees constancy where the biological eye detects loss. And it is not for nothing that the cup, possibly both the cup of life made famous at the end of Pushkin's *Eugene Onegin* and the cup signifying the unbroken continuity of Christian faith when passed in the Garden of Gethsemane, here falls and betokens human frailty. Is this a loss of faith? Hardly, but it might be an ironic riposte to Pushkin since the phrasing and word choice here recalls his 1820 poem "Daybreak tolls . . . from my hands" ("Zor'iu b'iut . . . iz ruk moikh," 1829).[32] What falls (the verb in both poems is *vypadat'*) from Pushkin's hand, however, is an "old" copy of Dante. Does the speaker awaken into the new life or has he fallen asleep over Dante? It is impossible to know, given Pushkin's playful blasphemy, whether the spirit is abroad ("dukh daleche uletaet") because his mind is elsewhere; or whether the spirit has been transported to some higher realm of spirituality that Dante opens up. Poetry remains half-spoken and unspoken. While Sedakova's poem appreciates gradations of expression, Pushkin's sleepy doubt is not shared, hence the affectionate irony of the allusion and momentary dialogue. Physical grip and spiritual grip are not the same: in her lyric the hands loosen in astonishment at the inner vision extended in the second half of the poem. There is a momentary discomfort and uncertainty in the transition from an attachment to forms of earthly knowledge to the search for the unknown and immaterial as the new "great thing."

The reader, therefore, might expect the second half of the poem to turn from quest to reward. With stanza 7 the address to poetry branches out to a connection between religion and art. Promised by the subtitle, made visible and even inextricable through the image of the devotional book, the relation of the art of poetry to religious art is now centrally placed. Liturgical works express dogma as the sacraments of ritual, guiding the worshiper on the right words in the expression of faith.[33] What about poetry? Different kinds of propositions are channeled through the rhetorical structure. Poetry appears to be the sum total of statements produced in stanzas 7 to 12. One statement finally ties this work to its purpose as an *ars poetica* by predicating two attributes of poetry as a matter of definition: namely, that poetry can be cultivated (l. 32 tells us it grows) and that it grows for all. Is this a variation on Horace's dictum in his *Ars poetica* that "poets are born, not made"? Or is it a democratic dismantling of the distance Pushkin advocated in his "Poet and the Mob" ("Poet i tolpa," 1828) between the visionary genius and the crowd? The association with monasticism seems to rule out such inclusivity, suggesting that poetry is grown for a self-elect band of acolyte-monks such as the layman ("mirianin"). We might surmise that Serbia here stands for Slavia Orthodoxa generally, an association that is pertinent within the devotional and monastic theme. But the reference to Serbia also paronomastically extends the silver thread ("serebro") as a beautiful continuity moving heavenward to the music of the stars. The contrasting "iron thread," however, seals earthly existence in the silence of death.

The concern of poetry proves to be with the struggle of mind and spirit to find a language sufficient for apprehension as both understanding one's mortal and cognitive limits and the fear engendered by such negative capability. The dramatic opening interjection of stanza eight summarizes the sense of ebbing powers and loss. Despairing and hungry ("moi razum nyl i golodal"), must the mind lead one to the brink of despair or dumb silence, aporia rather than apophatic worship, cliché ("vse proidet") rather than poetry? By characterizing the Book of Hours as a source of beauty and piety, and of piety as beauty, the poem spatializes their closeness through the motif of the container. From the start, the reader has been invited to see this surrounding of faith as a form of wholeness: the shell as the container of sound; a dream as the container of fantasy; the skull as the container of reason; parentheses as the container of modified meaning. All the monastic artifacts listed in stanza 7 illustrate the basic architecture of part for whole as an organic ratio linking the moment and eternity, a well (l. 40) and vessel (l. 39), water and ice (ll. 40, 42) and through linguistic play, if our ears move our minds associatively from "med" to the Great Bear (in Russian *medveditsa*) and then logically to "constellations" (l. 58). Accordingly, it is not difficult to make a small leap of interpretation and to conclude that the poet herself serves as a vessel of inspiration. Repetition of the motif of the vessel recurs with delicate persistence up to a turning point at stanza 8, when the poet pleads mental fatigue.

Searching for equilibrium between loss and gain proves to be a constant now, balancing regret and joy, past and present, sleep and waking, and life and death. Mortality has grown as a theme across these three stanzas, vacating the promise that the mind as a magic lantern might generate diverting pictures. Images of the mouse and time, and of fatigue, invariably remind one of Pushkin's 1830 poem on insomnia ("Mne ne spitsia, net ognia").[34] The Horatian refrain of *tempus fugit* distills the anxieties of a stanza replete with an echo and image from Pushkin's nocturnal meditations. Like Sedakova's speaker who hovers between prayer and poetry, silent communion and speech, Pushkin explores the liminal moment between sleep and waking when existential thoughts invade a disturbed mind that magnifies the tiny into the cosmic, conflating the scampering of a mouse and the sound of the clock. Sedakova's ninth stanza expands on the feeling of desolation and follows Pushkin's own boldness by interrogating life for its meaning and providing an answer from the poem itself to the question about life's ephemerality. Through allusion, Sedakova demonstrates that lyric dialogue proves one form of continuity even within the recognition of life-sapping discontinuity. But here she goes one step further, putting the anthem of the poem in quotation marks as a line that can be pronounced as a lamentation for the dead. Self-quotation is a form of self-preservation, but is death the "great thing" and therefore itself a shelter? Or does the self shelter from it in life? There is perfect sense in the way lines relate the acknowledgments that "everything passes" (l. 48) and "everything will be lost" (l. 35). Toleration of loss and the Orthodox virtue of *smirenie* (resignation) (perhaps to be heard faintly in the word *mirianin*) might be achieved through the posture of prayer.

The first half of the poem ends with a new awareness that blindness to the physical world opens a new perspective. Reason, unfed and miserable, is no longer the container for a "magic lantern." The preceding stanza had images of sustenance in the nut and honey, now supplanted by a mind likened to a "hungry and despairing mouse." That hitting bottom, when spirit and imagination seem exhausted, turns out to be a moment of rebirth. Once again, humility is the key since the speaker can only achieve a new energy not by claiming immortality but rather by conceding and beseeching (l. 51). The art of poetry provides words of consolation, drawn from Horace and Pushkin, but also serves as a shibboleth ("parol'," l. 52) that unlocks a vision of salvation. At line 43 there is a plea that poetry might be allowed to serve as an incantation to ward off death. But the repetition of the organizing aphorism in the next line seems to accept the notion that rather than save us from death, the "great thing" will raise its voice in burying and mourning us all. Can poetry and death each be the "great thing"? On the surface these would be, at least in the Horatian and Pushkinian view, opposites. Yet they are also complementary because without death that essential motivation to create vehicles of survival would disappear. Such a joining together of these two forces in the cipher of the "great thing" affirms the poem's acceptance of paradox as the state of mind in which to grasp the antinomies of light and dark, enlightenment and searching, despair and hope, life and death that encompass the speaker.

Various boundary states define action and identity throughout the poem, bringing together, and setting off, prayer and art, inner and outer, individual and collective, private faith and sect, the words of others and one's own words. Formal boundaries also fluctuate between final end-stopping (stanzas 1, 3, 4, 5). One formal feature of the second half is the use of interstanzaic enjambment, relaxing boundaries as the mind oscillates between states and the poem unfolds a vision of joyous terror, immaterial death, and unwilling acquiescence.

Despite the motif of closure and silence of the previous stanza, stanza 9 is the only unit that runs over, and the two stanzas together generally explode barriers, including the barrier between Sedakova's own words and those of other poets, since the quotations here intensify (the figures of the angel and the monk are quintessential Rilke). Life and death, life after death, night and day, height and depth ("gluboko"/"iz glubiny"), permission and assertion go together. Punning on singing and lamenting, the speaker notes the step from life to death, from singing to mourning, and from praying to silence, moving to the threshold of a new world. The paradoxical quality of the poem as a whole, the result of its unsettling but steady ability to join contrasts and move on, culminates in the juxtaposition of two extreme visions in stanzas 9 and 10. The hint of death as a portal into openness and beauty confirms the sense of expansion that is a feature from stanza 5. The light of the candle and the fire of the celestial constellation are part and whole, investing a near theological certainty in the power of images to create a vision of the transcendent.

Yet this radiance does nothing more than counter the previous evocation of death as a mouth sewn shut into silence. Is the psychological purpose of this hideous and visceral suggestion to bring the mind back to an image of openness and exaltation? Here the poem repeats as a mantra or charm the opening line. Through self-quotation the speaker makes the poem's opening line a key to its own meaning. The term used to signify this shibboleth is "parol'," introducing the possibility of a passing allusion to Saussurean linguistics and the opposition of language as a system and the poet's own language or vocal capacity, which has been forcibly closed down. Sedakova never grandstands or makes capital out of the traditional view that the fate of the true Russian poet is suffering. Yet this image in passing at least seems to hint at the silence of coercion and to evoke two precedents. The first is Mandelstam, who famously suggested in "On the Interlocutor" ("O sobesednike") that poems never really age because their content continues to evolve as the meanings of words change. This is a view that owes much to the Saussurean interrelation of individual creation and poetry as a system. Sorely tested and never fully surrendered, that philosophy of poetic language underlies the image of lips that, buried and detached like shards of pottery, will continue to utter independently of the poet.[35] The second precedent is Brodsky's "Instead of a wild beast I entered the cage" ("Ia vkhodil vmesto dikogo zveria v kletku," 1980), a moving *apologia pro vita sua* that wards off future troubles by reviewing a litany of travail and survival with great machismo and self-assertion (shot through with its own echoes from late Mandelstam). The climax of self-assertion comes in Brodsky's closing pledge that "out of his mouth only gratitude will resound / Until his mouth has been stuffed with clay" ("No poka mne rot ne zabili glinoi, / Iz nego razdavat'sia budet lish' blagodarnost'").[36] The defiance that works for Brodsky translates into Sedakova's quiet belief that the shibboleth will release further song. If the "great thing" is poetry itself, then the poem attributes agency to language itself as a principle of continuity. Despite the shared image of the closed mouth, the specific image of sewing remains Sedakova's own. Within the Orthodox and monastic context built up over the stanzas, the motifs of needlework and death suggest the shroud in which Byzantine and Russian monks were wrapped for burial and all sewn up.[37]

The prospect of death does anything but silence the poet. Sedakova can recuperate from the "greatest loss of all losses," and Christian and Greek images of survival prompt hopeful intimations of an infinity. With stanza 11, the speaker swerves away from a definitive declaration by wanting and not wanting to confide a truth. Instead of an answer to the rhetorical question of line 52, we find a minute digression into beautiful images, flecks of connotation against ignorance just like the candle positions within the darkness. Psyche, the butterfly of Greek mythology, is the soul drawn to a symbolic flame, the new light of reawakening and possibly a resurrection into a harmonious afterlife. At least two possible glosses of the Milanese garden confirm this sense. The phrase points to the famous scene in Book 8 of St. Augustine's *Confessions*. In his garden, he heard a child's voice saying, in Latin, "*tolle, lege*," which means "take and read." Augustine was reading the letters of St. Paul, and he let the book fall open on its own. He was astonished to read the thirteenth verse of the thirteenth chapter of the Letter to the Romans, where Paul exhorts his readers to give up the way of the senses and walk the path of Christ. Augustine chose to heed Paul's advice, but it does not follow that Sedakova herself endorses Augustinian theology or strictures on celibacy. He had finally learned to make his own life an allegory, where the lessons taught by the Neoplatonists, of emphasizing the soul over the body, became an actual reality. Here the image of the open door in stanza 10 alludes to the very end of Keats's "Ode to Psyche" and the ecstatic declaration that "shadowy thought can win / [. . .] a casement ope at night, / To let the warm Love in!"[38] Rather than Augustine as the theorist of original sin, it is his narrative of religious rebirth and revelation through prayer that is germane to Sedakova. In certain monastic sects, such as the Benedictines, it is the observation of the order's rule through private reading and devotion, as well as manual labor, that teaches Love.[39] No specific identification of religious order is needed to convey how reading, an activity common to all Christian creeds and monastic sects, can transform experience through engagement with the divine office. Nor is this layer of meaning at all incompatible with a second gloss that recognizes an allusion to Leonardo's Last Supper and the story of the Passion. The central narrative of the sacrament is both fundamental to the liturgy and also, we can now see, central to the poet's own imagining of her life and death-in-life.

Whether aspiring to transcendence or fearing the afterlife, the speaker is on the horns of a dilemma: she cannot divest herself of a belief in the self and the soul as innately bodily. This is the meaning of "animate dust," an image and concept associated with natural philosophy more than with religion. Without implying any single one of numerous theories of animate matter, the phrase brings together the proverbial message of mortality, the image of "from dust to dust" central to the book of Ecclesiastes, and a belief that a divine soul inhabits the flesh.[40] But the description of death at the end captures the all too human, psychological conflict felt at the thought of a sundering of body and soul and reluctance to leave the mortal vessel. Analogy that has served the poet so well this far now finally runs out and into a dead end of indefinite neuter particles "to" and "chto," recapitulating from stanza 6 previous neuter substantives for the unknown and invisible.[41]

In a poem that begins with riddles, the obscurity of the images gradually gives way to forms of enlightenment.[42] With stanza 12, fragmentation of vision and aposiopesis delimit the moment when the mystery of faith, the starting principle of mystery that has fixed the mind on attaining through prayer, image, and analogy a sacral sense of awe, breaks off into the recognition of a new state that remains, finally and impenetrably, a secret. In "Fifth Stanzas," arriving at the totality of the parts is an open-ended mental adventure, grounded in language and images that always press outward with their symbolic dimension. Spatially and temporally, this is poetry at heaven's edge also grounded in the practice of art as the essential medium of spiritual expression.[43] So the poem comes full circle and is itself a circle as it reaffirms its openness to a secret that can be disclosed but never closed. The poem is therefore true to Sedakova's own personal vision of how poetry unites the aesthetic, worldly and unworldly. Poetic meaning lies not in absolute revelation, but in the subtle ebb and flow of glimpsed significance, preserving the essence of *tainstvennost'*. Art, both verbal and visual, coalesces into its own "great thing," while preferring the humility of openness to the certainty of dogma.

Not all of Sedakova's poems have, in fact, represented such equilibrium between two realms. In "The Ninth Legend. Lamentation for a Nun" ("Legenda deviataia. Otpevanie monakhini"; 1:80), the vision of happiness is exclusively spiritual to the exclusion of bodily joy: everything in the poem, from the iconic self-portrait to anagrammatic language, signifies entities beyond direct representation. And at the end of the marvelous "Music" ("Muzyka"; 1:388–90), a pantheistic vision worthy of Fyodor Tiutchev floods in as nature, in the sublime power of the volcano and the sea, carries a universal music, "heavenly great plains" ("nebesnaia step'"), that seem to exclude the merely mortal and an earthly in-between. Marked throughout by multiple forms of hesitation in stanzas that contain and overflow, images that recur and self-contradict, visions that materialize and dematerialize, "Fifth Stanzas" in their entirety take us to the threshold of the vision that should name, pin down, and describe the goal of prayer. And in fact, perhaps this is what the stanzas do precisely by ending on fragmentation and silence. It is sufficient to have the final confidence that we have been trusted with the knowledge that there *is* a secret. But the content of that knowledge remains undisclosed.

As a verse treatise on poetry, the "Fifth Stanzas" instantiate the special ability of poetry as aesthetic language to connote through sound structures. It is part of the unspoken but heard lesson of the poem to show that lyric can encompass entire worlds visible and invisible, heard and imagined, borrowed through other poets' words and invested with new meaning—and that is perhaps a demonstration of the sacrament of art. The end of the poem intimates a faith that individual vision can be achieved through the work of poetry. This article of faith in poetry, and in the poetry of faith, has much to offer by way of consolation and inspiration. All readers attuned to the marvelous synthesis of voices and techniques will take pleasure in the capacity of poetry to raise the dead. Voices once raised eloquently and in terror about mortality—Pushkin, Mandelstam, and Brodsky have left their audible trace—continue to be heard, absorbed into a poetic text for their phrasing, wit, feeling, and also for their wisdom (a separate study could be devoted to exfoliating even more allusions, including images that invoke Khlebnikov). Poetry does not only look to religion for its wisdom literature. In the right hands—and Sedakova is for this reason a poet's poet—poetry can compose from within its own canon a liturgy that speaks to the vital questions of life and death. Alongside this—and one hesitates to say "beyond this" since this quality is its own good—there is the prospect that the contemplation of the poem as a verbal artifact, much like the contemplation of an icon, can create a sense of what the stillness that will prepare the mind for the leap into the future of time should be. Sedakova's visual icons can only give us analogies for the shapes of spiritual being that the beholder of an icon can contemplate individually. The miracle of the poem is its capacity to suggest the infinite through the finite, to enrich lines of verse strictly limited by rules of prosody through intertextual polyphony, and to trust the power of the small to suggest the large—and the reader to carry all those worlds within.

Notes

1. "Fifth Stanzas" is translated by Andrew Kahn. The source for the epigraph is Sedakova, "'V tselomudrennoi bezdne stikha': O smysle poeticheskom i smysle doktrinal'nom," 3:139.

2. Sedakova, "'V tselomudrennoi bezdne stikha,'" 3:130.

3. See Barbara Newman, *Gods and the Goddesses: Vision, Poetry, and Belief in the Middle Ages* (Philadelphia: University of Pennsylvania Press, 2003).

4. *Mineia. Dekabr'*, ch. 2 (Moscow: Izdatel'skii Sovet Russkoi Pravoslavnoi Tserkvi, 2002), 344.

5. *Chasoslov* (Moscow: Sibirskaia Blagozvonnitsa, 2007), 178.

6. On the structure of this cycle, see N. G. Medvedeva, *"Tainye stikhi" Ol'gi Sedakovoi* (Izhevsk: Udmurtskii universitet, 2013), 151–69.

7. On monastic prayer, see Jean Leclercq's classic *The Love of Learning and the Desire for God: A Study of Monastic Culture*, trans. C. Misrahi (New York: Fordham University Press, 1961).

8. On amazement as a characteristic and cherished type of awareness in Sedakova, see Sergei Averintsev, "Metafizicheskaia poeziia kak poeziia izumleniia," *Kontinent* 120 (2004): 397–99.

9. Begotten nature (Latin).

10. Begetting nature (Latin).

11. Olga Sedakova, "Poeziia za predelami stikhotvorstva," http://www.olgasedakova.com/Poetica/161, accessed March 13, 2018. On the technique, see L. A. Dmitriev, "Nereshennye voprosy proiskhozhdeniia i istorii ekspressivno-emotsional'nogo stilia XV v.," *Trudy otdela drevnerusskoi literatury* 20 (1964): 72–89; and on the relation of apophatic silence, contemplation, and epiphany, see Jostein Børtnes, "Hesychast Doctrine in

Epiphanius' *Life of Stephen, Bishop of Perm,*" *International Journal of Slavic Linguistics and Poetics* 31–32 (1985): 83–88.

12. See Maria Khotimsky, "Singing David, Dancing David: Olga Sedakova and Elena Shvarts Rewrite a Psalm," *Slavic and East European Journal* 51, no. 4 (2007): 737–52.

13. The association of art and morality pulls Sedakova strongly toward Mandelstam, a persistent and adored presence in her work, arguably more in the essays than even the poetry. In that regard, the moments of cosmic vision in poems like "Gornaia oda" and "Piatye stansy" that seem to descend from "Slate Ode" ("Grifel'naia oda," 1923/1937) bring a latent reminder of the plumb line, Mandelstam's secular emblem for the alignment of culture and ethics as well-made systems. In Sedakova's case, her view of religion is so thoroughly humanist as well as aesthetic that it feels non-sectarian despite its Christian foundations.

14. Sedakova seems to share the aspiration found in modernism (and exemplified by Kazimir Malevich, Pablo Picasso, and Martin Heidegger) for an art that represents the interiority of things without engaging in conventional mimesis. On this point, and for a survey of expressions of the wish to get inside things, see Bill Brown, "Thing Theory," *Critical Inquiry* 28, no. 1 (Autumn, 2001): 1–22.

15. Sedakova's prose contains numerous references to this trope, whether as a verbal ornamental style ("Vizantiiskoe pletenie smyslov i ottenkov") or a verbal object ("izvitie sloves, pletenie venka, kotoryi vsegda okazyvaetsia nadgrobnym"), "Puteshestvie v Tartu i obratno," *Znamia* 4 (1999), http://magazines.russ.ru/znamia/1999/4/sedak.html, accessed March 13, 2018. See, for instance, her commentaries on religious poetry such as her essay "K poetike liturgicheskoi poezii: *Sovet prevechnyi; Stikhira Blagoveshcheniiu Presviatoi Bogoroditsy,*" http://www.olgasedakova.com/Poetica/1190, accessed March 13, 2018.

16. A point made by Benjamin Paloff, "The God Function in Joseph Brodsky and Olga Sedakova," *The Slavic and East European Journal* 51, no. 4 (2007): 730.

17. For a reading that emphasizes the grammatically feminine gender of "thing" (*veshch'*), see Catriona Kelly's chapter on Sedakova in *A History of Russian Women's Writing, 1820–1992* (Oxford: Clarendon Press, 1994), esp. 430–32.

18. "Die Dichter haben dich verstreut / (es ging ein Sturm durch alles Stammeln), / Ich aber will dich wieder sammeln /in dem Gefäß, das dich erfreut" ("The poets have scattered you / [a storm went through all stammering], / But I will gather you up / in a vessel pleasing to you"). For the poems from *Das Stunden-Buch vom Mönchischen Leben,* see Rainer Maria Rilke, *Werke: Kommentierte Ausgabe,* ed. Manfred Engel, Ulrich Fülleborn, Horst Nalewski, and August Stahl, 4 vols. (Frankfurt am Main: Insel Verlag, 1996), 1:158; for "Ich liebe meines Wesens Dunkelstunden" and "Du Dunkelheit, aus der ich stamme," see 1:161.

19. See "I cherish my mind's hours of the dark," the second poem in the sequence.

20. Perhaps the truest measure of Rilke's influence can be seen in her essay "Novaia lirika R. M. Ril'ke: Sem' rassuzhdenii" (1979), which begins with a comparison of Rilke and Tolstoy (the latter's views powerfully refuted) and widens out to consider her engagement through Rilke with essential questions of the function of art structured as dichotomies between the inner and outer, modern and medieval, emotional and intellectual. In this essay, as in "Piatye stansy," Sedakova is one with Rilke in holding that the artist must

be a "cosmic anachorite." For the texts of her translations and the essay, see the section "Rainer Mariia Ril'ke," 2:347–97.

21. On Rilke's two trips and his Russian-themed poems, see Anna Tavis, *Rilke's Russia: A Cultural Encounter* (Evanston, IL: Northwestern University Press, 1994), 35–46, with some attention to "thingness" in his cycle (46); and the now definitive Konstantin Azadovskii, *Ril'ke i Rossiia: Stat'i i publikatsii* (Moscow: Novoe literaturnoe obozrenie, 2011), esp. 7–131.

22. See especially "Ich liebe meines Wesens Dunkelstunden," which celebrates the darkness of the mind, and "Du Dunkelheit, aus der ich stamme," which cherishes the night "by lending gleam . . . to an orbit's circle / beyond whose bounds we come up against the unknown," a non-opposition that clearly matters in Sedakova's lines.

23. On this aspect of Rilke, see Jennifer Gosetti-Ferencei, "Immanent Transcendence in Rilke and Stevens," *The German Quarterly* 83, no. 3 (2010): 275–96.

24. Judith Ryan, *Rilke, Modernism and Poetic Tradition* (Cambridge: Cambridge University Press, 1999), 28.

25. On this connection as a trope of medieval poetics, see Suzannah Biernoff, *Sight and Embodiment in the Middle Ages* (New York: Palgrave Macmillan, 2002).

26. Susan Stewart, *Poetry and the Fate of the Senses* (Chicago: University of Chicago Press, 2002), 67.

27. "V dukhe Leopardi," 1:97.

28. "Portret khudozhnika na ego kartine," 1:126. The parallel between the play of light and dark as a metaphor for knowledge and chiaroscuro as a visual technique reminds us of Sedakova's fondness for Rembrandt, whose settings of biblical scenes dramatize revelation through this contrast. In her "Pis'ma o Rembrandte," Sedakova associates the aging of his eyes (she sees him as having been born old emotionally) with the discovery of a new vision; see http://magazines.russ.ru/continent/2006/130/se30.html, accessed March 13, 2018. The essay, as it happens, also draws in passing a comparison between Rembrandt and Rilke.

29. For her own play on the Russian and Italian, see her remarks in "Proshchal'nye stikhi Mandel'shtama: 'Klassika v neklassicheskoe vremia,'" http://www.olgasedakova.com/Poetica/1584, accessed March 13, 2018.

30. In "The Church as Ritual as a Synthesis of Arts" and "Celestial Signs," Florensky argued that visual signs could be symbols of transcendent wholes. See P. A. Florenskii, "Khramovoe deistvo kak sintez iskusstv," in his *Izbrannye trudy po iskusstvu* (Moscow: Izobrazitel'noe iskusstvo, 1996), 199–215. For some discussion, see Avril Pyman, *Pavel Florensky: A Quiet Genius* (New York: Continuum, 2010), ch. 5, 72–78.

31. See Gordon Teskey, "Allegory," in *The Princeton Encyclopedia of Poetry and Poetics*, 4th ed., ed. Roland Greene et al. (Princeton, NJ: Princeton University Press, 2012), 37–40.

32. A. S. Pushkin, *Polnoe sobranie sochinenii*, ed. M. A. Tsiavlovskii, B. Tomashevskii et al., 17 vols. (Leningrad: Akademiia nauk, 1937–54), 3:1:170.

33. Although not in the Marian tradition, the attention to language, poetry (especially the Psalms), and devotion has a tradition that is specifically female. See Georgiana Donavin, *Scribit Mater: Mary and the Language Arts in the Literature of Medieval England* (Washington, DC: Catholic University of America Press, 2012), ch. 3, 115–62.

34. A. S. Pushkin, "Stikhi, sochinennye noch'iu vo vremia bessonnitsy," in *Polnoe sobranie sochinenii*, 3:1:250.

35. For Sedakova, the mouths and lips are inevitably Mandelstamian. See her discussion in "Proshchal'nye stikhi Mandel'shtama."

36. Iosif Brodskii, *Chast' rechi: Izbrannye stikhi, 1962–1989* (Moscow: Khudozhestvennaia literatura, 1990), 373.

37. For examples of embroidered burial cloths (*epitaphios*) sewn shut over the cowl, see "Liturgical Textiles," in *Byzantium: Faith and Power (1261–1557)*, ed. Sarah T. Brooks (New Haven, CT: The Metropolitan Museum of Art and Yale University Press, 2004), 300–323.

38. John Keats, *Selected Poems*, ed. John Barnard (London: Penguin Classics, 2007), 188.

39. On this process and spiritual goal, see Amy Hollywood, "Song, Experience, and the Book in Benedictine Monasticism," in *The Cambridge Companion to Christian Mysticism*, ed. Amy Hollywood and Patricia Z. Beckman (Cambridge: Cambridge University Press, 2012), 71.

40. The phrase may also derive from the words "iako zemlia esi i v zemliu otydeshi" ("you are earth and return to the ground") of a burial prayer as well as echoing lines from Psalm 90.

41. On a parallel unwillingness in Tolstoy to name death and the use of indefinite articles in the neuter gender, see Irina Reyfman, "Turgenev's 'Death' and Tolstoy's 'Three Deaths,'" in *Words, Music, History: A Festschrift for Caryl Emerson*, Stanford Slavic Studies 29, part 1 (2005): 312–26.

42. See Daniel Tiffany, "Lyric Substance: On Riddles, Materialism, and Poetic Obscurity," *Critical Inquiry* 28, no. 1 (2001): 72–98.

43. For this image, see Stephanie Sandler, "Poetry at Heaven's Edge," *Slavic and East European Journal* 51, no. 4 (2007): 668–74.

The Art of Change

Adaptation and the Apophatic Tradition in Sedakova's Chinese Journey

MARTHA M. F. KELLY

> It makes little sense to speak of privileging nature or art [*tvorchestvo*] in those many places where Pasternak brings them together as one: they are linked as brother and sister. One can say more: art is life, and in life it won't do to pick and choose.
>
> —Olga Sedakova

Poetry is life itself, writes Olga Sedakova in the sentences that form an epigraph for this essay. They come from an essay on Pasternak, "'The Vacancy of the Poet': Toward a Poetology of Pasternak" (3:352–53), but throughout her essays and verse the thought resounds that poetry has no higher subject than the "birth of form" (3:512).[1] In the larger context of her writing, Sedakova means by "form," however, far more than the shape of a literary work ("its rhythm, syntax, sound structure"; 3:512). In her essay "Poetry and Anthropology," she writes of the "experience of *form* as the deepest human activity" and poetry as witness to this phenomenon. Humans display, she writes, "a need for form, a capacity for form, a delight in form and a horror of formlessness" (3:102, 103). In another essay, she proposes that the most basic human desire is the desire for form, and, moreover, that poetry is "what makes the person" ("'V tselomudrennoi bezdne stikha': O smysle poeticheskom i smysle doktrinal'nom"; 3:131, 135).

What Sedakova means precisely by form is difficult to say, especially because she seems to speak just as often of an impulse to cast off form. For her the life that poetry realizes depends on acts of a certain kind of self-denial, on a "pure agreement to disappear" (3:112). Poetry, and therefore life, happens as a thing is wiping off its face; is stepping into an unmoored boat; is looking for the tenth time in the same murky place for a pure spring; is falling toward nothingness. Pictured in all these images from Sedakova's poetic cycle *Chinese Journey* (*Kitaiskoe puteshestvie*), poetry, as she writes elsewhere, traces form as it obliterates and remakes and obliterates itself again—without cease (1:325–45). Poetry demonstrates that each phenomenon—poem, person, nature—must aspire to vanish, to open itself radically to the unknown, in order to become itself.

These seemingly paradoxical impulses of constructing and divesting form shape her poetry. Sedakova builds stanza, line, and sound; deploys rhetorical tropes; puts shapes made of words on a page; puts shapes made of sounds, of music, in the air, in the breath, in the mind's echo chambers. And yet she constructs her verse so that it works formally to empty itself, to yield, to efface itself in order to point to a stability that lies beyond it.[2] Sedakova has said that today's poetry—in Russia, at least—needs to push beyond the limits poetry has previously established because it must explore new ground. It needs to "remove the inert, sclerotic, dead fabric that obscures its Source," to push past familiar literary forms, risking protest that it is too hard to understand (3:511–12).[3] It needs to lead into nothingness, but always in the imperfective.

How do we parse what Sedakova means by "form" and understand the paradox of her call for its unmaking? And how do we understand her discussion of form in both aesthetic and anthropological terms? One solution lies in her frequent appeals, direct and indirect, to apophatic tradition—or, "theology by way of negation."[4] In Russia it is Vladimir Lossky who has discussed this tradition most prominently, in his *The Mystical Theology of the Eastern Church*, where he distinguishes Eastern Christian from Western Christian spirituality by its emphasis on apophasis.[5] For Lossky, however, apophasis comprises not mere negation, but rather a path into unmediated contact with the source of life. "When we proceed by the way of negation," he writes, "we ascend from the lowest steps of being to its summit, gradually laying aside all that can be known, so that in the gloom of full unknowing we might approach the Unknowable."[6] This same tradition underlies much of Sedakova's work, but she speaks of it at length in "The Light of Life," an essay she penned in English in 2005 to introduce Russian spiritual practices to a non-Russian audience (4:677–705). In concert with Lossky she remarks, "Those who think of [the] apophatic approach as something purely negative are very far from the Orthodox idea of it. Apophatic intention is not only to negate all positive humanly perceived qualities attributed to the Divine reality but to indirectly lead a human to the [*sic*] direct contact with it" (4:693).[7]

In Russia, apophatic theology manifests most fully in concrete spiritual practices: an influential early proponent, Evagrius Ponticus (ca. 345–99), left behind writings that would shape Eastern Orthodox monastic life and spiritual discipline.[8] The writings of Evagrius advocate both an ascetic approach to life—that is, one based on curbing earthly passions—and a form of prayer that uses neither words nor images. His works, along with those of Dionysius the Areopagite, influenced the development of hesychasm (from Gr. *hesychia*, "silence"), the primary spiritual tradition in Eastern Orthodoxy, worked out above all in monastic settings.[9] More than one famous account of Russian spirituality speaks of the Russian soul as a peculiarly kenotic one, borrowing a Greek word that means "emptying out," a word that Christian scriptures use for Jesus' self-sacrifice.[10] In the tradition that Sedakova represents, apophasis manifests as ongoing disciplines that open the human person increasingly to unmediated light.

Sedakova presents the apophatic path as the central Russian spiritual tradition, and she often speaks of the role of aesthetic forms in these spiritual disciplines. She explains in one essay, "What church art established and built in the human was not the *content* of faith so much as its *image*" ("Russkaia poeziia posle Brodskogo"; 3:131). That is, these disciplines of negation paradoxically find representation in human creations. Such vessels of faith's "image" include the paterica—lives of the fathers (sing. patericon)—with their stories of model Christians and counter-models. They also include icons. As Sedakova explains in "The Light of Life," icons facilitate the upward journey because they provide images that point beyond themselves. An icon is a "representation of the unrepresentable" and the "presence of the absent." What they show comprises but a direction—in place of "no" an "as if" (4:693, 692). And although the Greek term *apophasis* means "without words," words, too, can apparently bear an apophatic quality: in another essay Sedakova speaks of the genre of the liturgical hymn as "an icon in words" ("slovesnaia ikona") ("Vechnaia pamiat': Liturgicheskoe bogoslovie smerti"; 4:663).

Sedakova discusses apophasis as aesthetic practice found in non-church art, as well, with special emphasis on poetry. See, for instance, her discussion of the "artistic apophasis" that Mandelstam adapts from Dante (3:110). And in an essay on her recently deceased contemporary Gennady Aigi, she speaks of the poet's "extraconfessional apophasis. An invitation to meditation without figures" ("Aigi: Ot"ezd"; 3:565).

As Sedakova's prose helps clarify, we might see in her own poetry a model offered to late Soviet Russian society, an aesthetic and anthropological model. In Sedakova, the apophatic impulse—with its discourse of emptying in order to fill—seems to offer, or at least echo, one way that late and post-Soviet Russian society might creatively reconstitute national identity in the transition through perestroika, the collapse of the Soviet Union, and subsequent developments. In her well-known essay from 1984, "On a Lost Literary Generation," she describes the Soviet period as bringing about the "annihilation of form," the destruction of an organic cultural order and its replacement with symbols not corresponding to reality.[11] In a characteristic turn, she associates this loss of an authentic cultural order with the productive self-emptying of Jesus—his kenosis—in his incarnation into a slop trough, in his crucifixion. She speaks especially of those who lived through the Era of Stagnation as suffering a humiliation and hopelessness that she compares to Christ's passion. Christmas leads through death to Easter. The cataclysmic emptying out of the old order thus makes way for a new order, preparing artists to engage in the "construction of personality" ("postroenie lichnosti"). But such a "personality" bears the kenotic mark: for Sedakova the "art of personality" comprises "a personal desire to go beyond one's own limits," to discover one's own "endlessness" ("beskonechnost'"). This "endlessness" directly recalls the never-ending path of apophasis, described by Lossky and others, into the endlessness of God. The "formlessness" of the Soviet period therefore prepares the ground for the discovery of one's identity in, and with, boundlessness, fostering apophatic experience.

In keeping with the spiritual journey of apophasis, Sedakova offers a way of moving forward through and even via the disintegration of identity, on a personal and national scale. In *Chinese Journey*, a cycle I will examine here, she transposes the apophatic mode onto a landscape—perhaps an unexpected landscape—that comes to comprise, at least in part, a resistance to stable constructs. This landscape beckons the reader down the apophatic path while also pointing toward what remains ever just out of reach.

This landscape resembles an icon in the ways it projects and transforms space. Consider the oft-described "inverse perspective" by which an icon seems to flatten out dimension in order visually to draw the viewer into a divine perspective, rather than presenting the world from a human standpoint, as Renaissance perspective aims to do.[12] But the paterica, too, highlight the components of assimilation and imitation native to the apophatic way. Icons and paterica model the very act of imitation as a method of moving beyond our customary selves to find what is more essential. Sedakova underscores this capacity through her imaginary landscapes, and in this sense especially she undermines the notion of linear progression, so native to Soviet rhetoric, but also to the Enlightenment culture Peter I sought to foster in Russia. Where imitation appears most prominently as a theme in modern Russian culture, it refers to Russia's adaptation of Western culture. We will find in Sedakova's work, however, a picture of creative imitation by which one realizes identity by adapting forms that already exist.[13] From the standpoint of poetics, what the poet adapts most prominently from traditional religious works is the apophatic impulse to relinquish expectations and certainties. In this sense, imitating apophatic models produces a process or mentality rather than a fixed form. It is a way of doing things, a mode, a way of being. Thus, Sedakova proposes, at the onset of the perestroika period, an engagement with ancient religious tradition, including Russian Orthodoxy, by which one might negotiate a new, dynamic, adaptive identity, based on the apophatic mode.

Art as Vector: Icons and Paterica

In "The Light of Life," Sedakova positions icons as key conveyors of the apophatic tradition, and thereby of human identity. Icons, she says, point to the human's inmost image, the image of God. "As some Orthodox theologians put it, the image of God in the human being is its simple existence, its *being not nothing*" (4:685). Identity lies in existence itself. Thus the human's essential image that the icon makes manifest is endlessly expansive and adaptable. Sedakova speaks of the "open, dynamic and inexhaustible presence of an image" (4:686).

The work of contemporary French philosopher Marie-José Mondzain brings spatial and geographic language to bear on her study of the icon. Addressing the Byzantine icon and its legacy in *Image, Icon, Economy*, Mondzain discusses the icon as the imperial image that extends itself across space and time.[14] In Byzantium, the "symphony" of powers identified the emperor with divine power, so that the icon's dissemination throughout the empire signified the extension of central control. Thus, both the rendering and reading of the icon constituted the material realization of divine power and the aesthetic re-presentation of the powers of a physically absent figure. The very act of copying icons (imitating prototypes) works to extend and invoke power from beyond, to realize divine power in a local way. The process is necessarily adaptive, and in this sense icons picture a constant process rather than a fixed image. Mondzain writes that icons "aim at no 'resemblance' other than assimilation."[15] They are "vectors," she says, pointing beyond themselves even as they represent divine (or imperial) power in far corners of the world. They give a glimpse of the divine shimmering but embody an absence. These acts of imitation, then, bear an apophatic character—a willed relinquishment of what is familiar and local, a privileging of the icon's economy over our personal (or regional, or national) economies. Icons also occasion relinquishment in presenting the divine center as it moves beyond our grasp. Mondzain emphasizes the icon's imitative process as a dynamic approach, an adaptive attitude. An icon propels us forward on a journey.

The language that Mondzain uses resonates strongly with Sedakova's writings—with the way she writes not only about apophatism but even about the fundaments of her creative vision. In her essay "In Praise of Poetry"—Sedakova's "poetic credo," as Stephanie Sandler describes it—the poet recounts an experience she had at age fifteen, an experience that changed her life as it clarified her calling ("Zametki i vospominaniia o raznykh stikhotvoreniiakh, a takzhe Pokhvala poezii"; 3:13–95).[16] Sedakova recalls New Year's folk divination rituals that culminated in her seeing a stove she was huddled by suddenly appear as "the center of the world, and this center was hurtling forward, or everything was hurtling past on either side" (3:37). After this moment, she felt removed from the usual order of things, a state she identifies with the fateful chosenness that distinguishes "the poet and the mob" (*poet i tolpa*)—a favorite theme of Russian poets, not least Pushkin. Sedakova goes on to describe the experience in terms that echo Mondzain's appeal to landscape and also discussions of the icon. She writes: "It was something from the realm of geometry, and not a stage play, and each time it emerged from a geometric, space-bound image: a road in a ravine, or a room at once round and cubed, or the verticals of a park of pine trees. I am mathematically illiterate, and so I do not know whether there is really such a thing as vectoral geometry, defined by directionality and attraction. This was vectoral" (3:39). Interestingly this "vectoral" image recalls a snatch of a sermon that Sedakova quotes to illustrate Russian teachings on saintly perception, as pictured by icons: "Saints [. . .] and nobody else, see our world as it is. And what do they see? They see our Earth—and all our world—flying towards the Lord. Flying like a bird, staring at one point, her wings outstretched" (4:678). Sedakova's visions go hand in hand with the geometrical forms Emily Grosholz describes in this volume. I would like to emphasize the vector itself—the extension, the flight forward, toward an ever-receding point.

We can find a very similar "vectoral geometry" in Russian paterica. These texts form another direct point of comparison for us, not only because they are verbal, but also because early on in her career, Sedakova translated select patericon stories into modern Russian. The collection from which she draws, the *Spiritual Meadow* (*Lug Dukhovnyi*), is ancient—tales translated into Slavonic in the eleventh century from John Moschus's *Pratum Spirituale*, a Byzantine text that dates at least to the seventh century (2:69).[17] Her translations circulated through religious samizdat. Some were eventually published in 1981 and 1982 in an émigré journal in Paris, *The Herald of the Russian Christian Movement*.[18] The compact stories relate events in the life of someone who is holy, who wants to be holy, or who does not care to be holy but who comes to be nevertheless. They tend to tell of monks and nuns, but the stories made their way into the world as popular religious reading. Paterica offer models—or dynamic images—of how to live a holy life, how to be like God. And in a distinctly apophatic key, they indicate that the way to be like God is to relinquish one's own ways and ideas and efforts. Indeed, many of these tales describe figures who do not observe rites properly, they do not necessarily work hard or suffer for their faith, they often do not hold places of honor in their religious communities. They frequently stray from the sanctioned paths to holiness and yet stumble upon it—precisely because of their willingness to forego familiar ways. The paterica hint that we resemble God—and therefore discover our inmost image—by what we let go, by the ways we yield.

This theme runs through the patericon accounts that Sedakova has translated. One story in particular, "The Imitator of Books" ("Podrazhatel' knigam"), embodies this mode (2:86–87). A monk tells of an elder who came to visit his monastery. The visiting elder loved to read from the patericon, and his example encouraged the other monks to read with him. Together they read about a man so holy that when thieves had robbed him, he ran after them with the items they had missed. Deeply moved, the robbers returned all the goods they had stolen. The elder then tells how he followed this example, freely offering his goods to robbers. But, a listener wants to know, did the robbers return the goods? "No," he replies, "God did not will it" (2:87).

This tale's title advertises the notion of imitation. And imitation is woven into the tale's narrative structure in multiplying layers: monks imitate a visiting elder who reads the patericon, reading with him; the visiting elder imitates an elder described in holy books; the monk telling the visiting elder's tale presents him as one to imitate. This structure implies, furthermore, that we, the reader, like the visiting elder, should also become imitators—of monks and of books.

And yet the tale presents imitation as a complicated phenomenon. The visiting elder describes his admiration for an elder he read about, and how he prayed to God for a chance to copy that example. In answer, God sends thieves to the elder, who eagerly gives them everything. The visiting elder, in other words, tells a straightforward tale of imitating a model he encounters in a holy book—directly copying the actions recorded. But someone listening to the visiting elder tell his tale misunderstands the nature of his imitation and therefore the nature of his resemblance to his model. At the end of the narrative we read a line of unattributed speech: an unnamed listener wants to know whether the results of the elder's actions also resembled the results of the actions recorded in the holy book—did the elder get his possessions back? The visiting elder answers in the negative, with perfect equanimity. God did not will it. This unattributed question, which seems to anticipate the reader's response, highlights an element apparently missing from the narrative: results. We might equally ask, "So *then* what happened?" This narrative subverts our expectations in depriving us of an outcome and raises an important distinction: one can imitate to achieve certain results, or one can imitate for the sake of imitation.

If you imitate for the sake of imitation, your resemblance has more to do with effort, or approach, than with results. The very structure of this story suggests an endless series of imitative acts, an infinite regress of models. We find not one but four narrative frames: the entry itself, the story told by "a certain monk," the story the elder tells of his own life, and the story the elder retells from his reading in the holy fathers. The central story's apparent lack of results and the layered pursuit of holiness make resemblance seem a trajectory rather than an endpoint. The structure recalls Mondzain's description of the icon as "a vector, always active," as well as Sedakova's "vectoral geometry."[19] But it also recalls Sedakova's didactic discussion of icons, where she remarks, "Paradoxically, the icon which is visible gives us an impression of looking at the invisible. How is it possible? We can suggest that it is because the images depicted on it are themselves plunged into the contemplation of the invisible. They are shown in a state of prayer. Through contemplating *them* we follow the contemplation which is *in* them, while they contemplate something that can not [*sic*] be seen on the icon. It is a depiction of a prayer that gives birth to prayer" (4:692).

Sedakova's Word Icons

Like the patericon stories she has translated, apophatism marks the very mode of Sedakova's poems, their vector. Her poetry points beyond itself to a stable ground of being in the constant change of the world. And so, like paterica, her poems model the ongoing adaptation of old traditions as well as the quality of adaptability. In a sense, her poems work to inculcate the power of letting go—that she and her reader alike might come upon their most stable identity, their being.

In speaking of Sedakova's poems as "icons in words" or as a kind of patericon, I have in mind a body of works that model a way of being in the world, in an apophatic key. In the remainder of this essay I will deal with only one cycle of poems—*Chinese Journey*. It is not a cycle that may immediately strike the reader as especially "Christian." One interpreter describes it as presenting the world from a Buddhist viewpoint.[20] This description, while not inaccurate, somewhat limits the cycle's resonance. As Natalia Chernysh writes in this volume, the cycle incorporates Christian elements even while conversing with Chinese philosophy. (Chernysh analyzes connections to the Book of Changes.) Taken as a whole, and in the context of her larger body of work, *Chinese Journey* exemplifies Sedakova's apophatic aesthetic, even in conversation with other philosophical and religious traditions. In fact, adaptability and acceptance of change or loss are elements often most associated with "Eastern" (meaning East Asian) philosophy. In the *Dao de jing*, writings from the third century BCE attributed to Laozi, we read of a spiritual "Way" (*Dao*) that depends on the discarding of stable categories. "If a *Dao* can be spoken of, / It will not be a constant *Dao*; / If a name can be named, / It will not be a constant name."[21] In such a view, only in letting go of familiar categories does one experience unmediated contact with a greater reality.[22] In these connections we glimpse the broadness of Sedakova's project—her engagement with multiple religious and cultural traditions, even as she highlights less-recognized strands from the Christian tradition.[23] Furthermore, her use of Eastern themes and images (as from the poetry of Li Bo)[24] emblematizes the adaptive impulse of apophasis and the icon—the assimilation of the putative periphery as the essential image.

Sedakova wrote *Chinese Journey* in 1986, when she was already an established poet—if not yet published in her own country. China plays a part in the poet's own story. Her father was a military engineer whose work took him and his family to China when Sedakova was young. The family lived in Beijing for a memorable year and then returned to Moscow.[25] Through her cycle the poet imaginatively links Russia and the East, conflating China and Russia as her "homeland" ("rodina"). But far from asserting a Eurasianist philosophy, Sedakova turns China into a myth, a periphery that becomes a sought-after center. Like the icon, China pictures an ever-receding vision of wholeness. The cycle, then, is no ordinary travelogue: it describes a journey of imagination that ranges into a mythical beyond—maybe death, maybe eternity, certainly the possibility of encountering and assimilating change. China, as the child's homeland, comes to stand for this destination that lies always over the edge of now. But small elements of the speaker's everyday world and images she beholds momentarily draw this place close. In the icon of her landscape, trees, water, hills, animals, art itself become models for how the poet and the reader might live into the myth, capaciously and expansively.

Chinese Journey contains eighteen poems and an epigraph from Laozi that reads, "If you dulled its sharpness, freed it from chaotic ways, tempered its luster, made it resemble a speck of dust, then it would seem to exist clearly" (1:326). With the words of this sixth-century Chinese sage, the poet introduces a world where things know how "to exist clearly"—that is, both to let light shine through and to assert their own being. She also introduces in these lines a process for attaining such clarity—a paring down or tempering that looks apophatic. Each subsequent poem pictures different examples of the process at work. We move across outdoor scenes, from a boat on a river to a pond and a tree reaching down into water, to a mountain topped in clouds, a traveler on a road, a sapphire-blue sky, the lines of a roof, an ocean, the starry expanse—and across these spaces the poetic voice also speaks out her deepest questions and experiences, often to an unnamed companion. The first and shortest poem—only nine lines—sets us up to wonder with the poet at the world she beholds.

1
И меня удивило:
как спокойны воды,
как знакомо небо,
как медленно плывет джонка в каменных берегах.

Родина! вскрикнуло сердце при виде ивы:
такие ивы в Китае,
смывающие свой овал с великой охотой,
ибо только наша щедрость
встретит нас за гробом. (1:327)

And I was surprised:
how calm the waters,
how familiar the sky,
how slowly the junk floats between the stone banks.

Motherland! cried the heart at the sight of the willow:
there are such willows in China,
they wash off their oval with great eagerness,
for only our generosity
will meet us beyond the grave.

In the world we enter with the poet, willows do not simply droop: like the monks in the paterica they efface themselves; yet precisely by working to disappear they establish the ground of their being. As readers, we, too, go through a kind of apophatic process. We begin our journey with the overturning of expectations: the first line ("And I was surprised:") ends with an anticipatory colon. The speaker cues us to give ourselves over to wonder. Such an attitude accords with key texts in the Christian apophatic tradition that view "pure wonder" as a powerful descriptive tool.[26] And indeed, Sedakova's contemporary, the late Byzantinist and prominent intellectual Sergei Averintsev, has called astonishment (*izumlenie*) a defining feature of her poetry.[27]

Certainly, we can read this first line as a prelude to the entire cycle. As we open ourselves to wonder with the speaker, the following lines, with their anaphoric "how," load impression upon impression, insistently directing the attention of the lyrical self, and so our attention, too, outward. We follow the simple and repetitive syntax of the first stanza as it seems to build from sight to insight; yet the second stanza complicates our progress. To reach the truism of the final lines—

"only our generosity / will meet us beyond the grave"—we must wade through a dense, multi-clause sentence where multiple and diverse subjects—the heart, willows, generosity—open up within one another in unpredictable sequence. The connection between impression and insight remains elusive. We discover that our "Chinese" journey is a journey "beyond the grave"—not just into death, but toward eternity, toward the endless extension of being. But the path from the world of material forms into endlessness seems hidden, as does the poetic speaker's inner logic. The pursuit begins.

Some of the cycle's poems demonstrate apophatic values in more explicitly Christian terms and others use images common to many spiritual traditions: boats, rivers, paths, stars, journeys. All of the poems, though, bear an elusive quality that draws the reader in pursuit of an image or insight—a pursuit of kenotic dimensions. While shapes and scapes shift constantly, movement never ceases. Poem 6 overtly pictures the soul's journey as a pilgrim's pursuit: "As soon as I see / a wayfarer in light, white clothes— / what should we do, where should we go? // [. . .] As soon as I see / what happens to a person— / I'd walk behind him, crying" (1:330). But even poems where a wanderer does not wander, where a boat does not float downstream or a stone sink into depths, even poems about landscapes and trees never stand still.

Poem 3 paints a portrait of trees that resemble roads along which the heart travels:

3
Падая, не падают,
окунаются в воду и не мокнут
        длинные рукава деревьев.
Деревья мои старые—
пагоды, дороги!
Сколько раз мы виделись,
а каждый раз, как первый,
задыхается, бегом бежит сердце
с совершенно пустой котомкой
по стволу, по холмам и оврагам веток
в длинные, в широкие глаза храмов,
к зеркалу в алтаре,
на зеленый пол.
Не довольно ли мы бродили,
чтобы наконец свернуть

на единственно милый,
    никому не обидный,
        не видный
            путь?

Шапка-невидимка,
одежда божества, одежда из глаз,
падая, не падает, окунается в воду и не мокнет.
Деревья, слово *люблю* только вам подходит. (1:329)

Falling, they do not fall,
they dip into the water and don't get wet,
        the long sleeves of the trees.
My old trees—
pagodas, roads!
How many times we've seen each other,
and every time is like the first,
a gasp, and the heart runs off
with a perfectly empty knapsack
along the trunk, along the hills and ravines of the branches
to the long, to the broad eyes of the temples,
toward the mirror in the altar,
to the green floor.
Have we not wandered enough now
that we can turn off at long last
onto the uniquely dear,
    uniquely inoffensive,
        invisible
            path?

The magical invisibility hat,
clothing of the gods, clothing made from eyes,
falling, does not fall, dips into the water and doesn't get wet.
Trees, the words *I love*, suit only you.

This poem describes a tree and so a static point on the horizon; yet there is nothing static here. The eye catches the tree in motion, endlessly falling toward the water. The tree catches the gaze, as it has "how many times." The eye runs along the tree's swells and grooves like a lover's hand, it enters its cathedrals and approaches its sacred recesses. The tree is a road, contours along which one may travel infinitely. It is a way to God, or spirit, or that other place China represents. With its clothing of the gods that leaves it falling without falling down, dipping into the water but not getting wet, the tree resembles the burning bush—the bush that burned but did not burn up—where God revealed his name to Moses: *I am*—the name of the heart of being. And so the tree resembles, too, the Mother of God, who is called in the liturgy *Neopalimaia Kupina* (burning bush)—the human through whom the infinite God came in human form.[28] (Certain icons associate Mary with this image.) And thus the beheld tree resembles the icon, with its "vectoral geometry." In the stillness there is movement, movement with the power to annihilate from within. Even the graphic layout of the poem suggests this dynamism, with its stanzas that trail off to the right then circle back around.[29] The poem sets in motion and restrains the power that is life and death at once. "Have we not wandered enough now?" the speaker inquires. But even dying is turning off onto another path; even relinquishing is an act. The poem moves but does not move, in the "vibrant stasis" that Grosholz describes.

This dynamism also brings to mind Mondzain's ideas. In speaking of the key components of an icon, Mondzain highlights the *épigraphè*—the inscription naming the subject.[30] As Mondzain explains, the *épigraphè* invokes the voice that bears witness to the identity of the image with its prototype. This voice makes present the divine gaze that imparts to the image its radiance. The voice, therefore, lights up the image by tracing its connection to the beloved, absent figure.[31] We see Sedakova's tree, too, lit up by a loving gaze whose voice sounds out in ecstatic verse. This voice points us along the tree's bodily contours to boundlessness. Mondzain writes that "the iconic line, as much as the Virgin's womb, is therefore a threshold always overflowing with the existence of the Word, for a gaze that resigns itself to doing without circumscription."[32] The image in this poem, as with others in the cycle, never settles into a final frame. And at the same time its essence shimmers: "Falling, they do not fall . . ." ends in an act of identifying the tree—but with a statement—"the words *I love*"—and thus an intent, a propensity, no fixed image—just a spoken word that sparks a transfiguring gaze. That this word comprises a declaration of love speaks to the divine gaze that transforms the picture into a pursuit. Alexander Zholkovsky has written of how this cycle presents love, centrally, as something that endures only by great effort, only by struggling against inertia.[33] These radiant moments, then, seem like marvelous appeals to continue down the demanding path—and so the apophatic path appears as the way of love—in keeping with Evagrius and his legacy.[34]

The apophatic path is, for Sedakova, also the path of art. Zholkovsky finds the cycle full of literary references that magnify its hermetic quality.[35] In *Chinese Journey* Sedakova makes art about art itself in a way that extends the vector along

Icon of the Mother of God of the Burning Bush (*Neopalimaia Kupina*), Russia, ca. 1750. (Courtesy of the Museum of Russian Icons, Clinton, Massachusetts)

which the reader must travel. The cycle represents a series of landscapes; but the further one reads, the more one suspects that the speaker is encountering at least some of these landscapes not in nature but in, for instance, a book of ancient Chinese prints. This meta-aesthetic position would explain some of the curious features of the first poem. The speaker launches out with a cry of surprise when she recognizes a familiar landscape: "there are such willows in China." But what are we looking at if not a Chinese scene, with its junk slowly floating between stone banks? If we were to read the poems as semi-autobiographical, we could suggest that the speaker comes across a print that evokes her childhood years in China—"how familiar the sky." One particular printing of this cycle, from 2001, supports this scenario: pasted onto the cover—as though in an old book or journal—is a reproduction of a Chinese print depicting bamboo stalks, with Chinese calligraphy running down their length on the left.[36] Entering the book through this portal, we may then read the poems as a set of prints. A light-grey emblem of bamboo leaves marks the outside bottom corner of each page, often running under the text, as though to reinforce a connection between visual and verbal representation. In a reversal of or bringing together of text and image in the calligrapher's brush, these emblems may also recall the *épigraphè* of the icon, the inscription invoking the voice and its gaze—in this feature, too, making of each poem and of each witnessed print an icon, further extending the adaptive quality of the iconic vector.

Like the first poem, the eighth poem bears images that seem transcribed from a traditional Chinese print. We espy in the first line "roofs, with your raised edges, / like astonished eyebrows"; and as we move further we catch sight of "dry banks, yellowish silver rivers, / the uneven writing of bushes—a love letter"; and we see how "two passersby bow / low to each other on the pontoon bridge" (1:334). The collection of images in these lines erases any doubt that we are seeing a distant and imagined landscape here: swallows, rivers, passersby bowing one to another. When the poet casts the bushes as a form of writing, she means it literally: the only bushes we can see are the calligraphic strokes of the artist. We take this "Chinese journey," then, via art. It is a journey nonetheless. And we are going places unseen. In the final lines of the poem the speaker remarks, "But then, no one in China is ever ill: / the sky knows / how to strike in time / with its long needle." China, then, merely signals someplace else, a kind of not-here; and in the end it, too, empties of its own content in order to point beyond. When we read, "No one in China is ever ill," we stumble once more upon that place encountered in companion poems: a place "beyond the grave" and "toward the window in the altar." So the speaker speaks to us not of China and not of Chinese prints but of worlds the very journey to and through which defines us, a journey on which she leads us through the frame of poetry. In these glimpses of an ever-receding world, then, Sedakova reclaims the paradoxically positive ontology of apophasis: its journey of loss that draws one on into greater fullness by way of beauty and desire.[37]

Poems 9 and 10 amplify this endless arc of mediation by turning to the artist herself as she creates ever-new forms. They present her art-making as a process and a mode of discovery, rather than the production of finished objects. Art-making itself succumbs in these verses to pure relinquishment, and what is left is

Front cover, Olga Sedakova, *Kitaiskoe puteshestvie* (*Chinese Journey*).

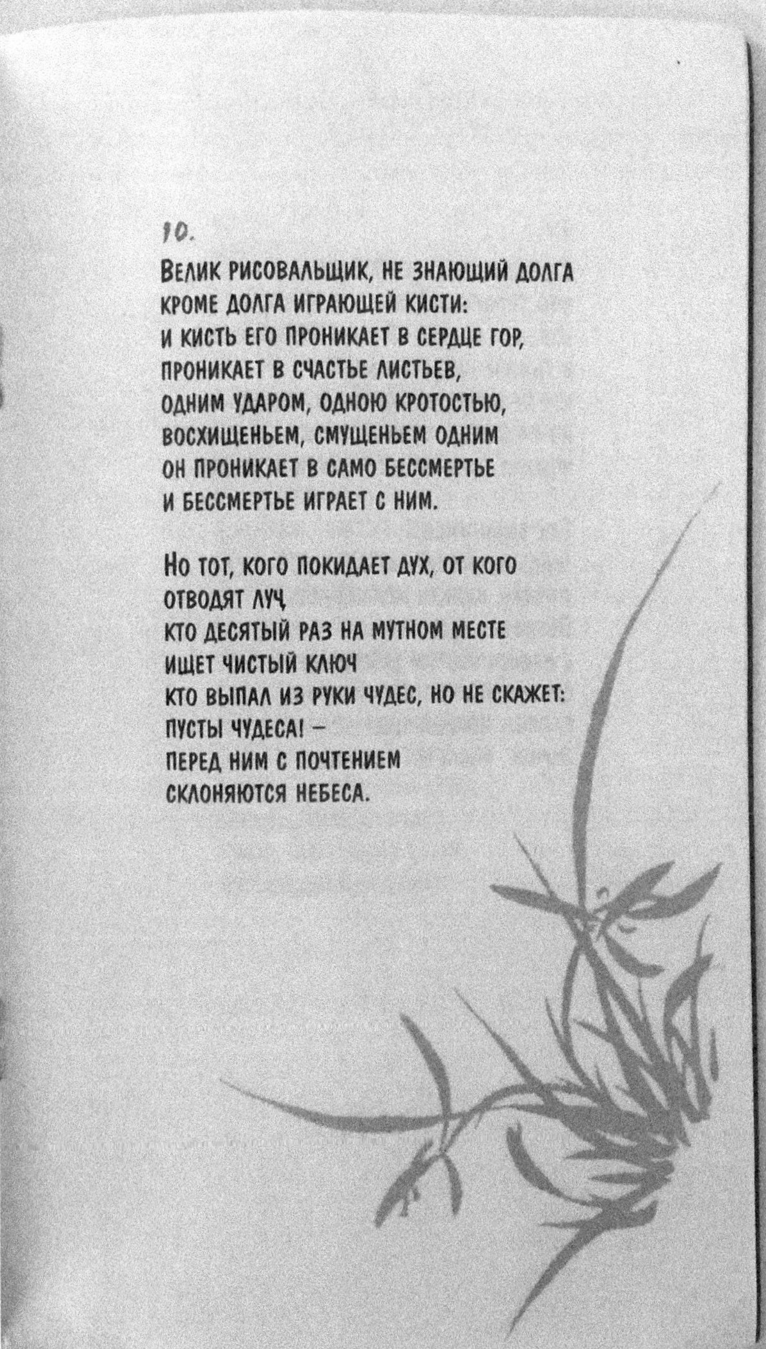

10.

Велик рисовальщик, не знающий долга
кроме долга играющей кисти:
и кисть его проникает в сердце гор,
проникает в счастье листьев,
одним ударом, одною кротостью,
восхищеньем, смущеньем одним
он проникает в само бессмертье
и бессмертье играет с ним.

Но тот, кого покидает дух, от кого
отводят луч,
кто десятый раз на мутном месте
ищет чистый ключ
кто выпал из руки чудес, но не скажет:
пусты чудеса! –
перед ним с почтением
склоняются небеса.

Poem 10, Olga Sedakova, *Kitaiskoe puteshestvie* (*Chinese Journey*).

an apophatic practice with no fixed means of expression. Poem 9 uses the image of an artist, among an array of other images, to illustrate a broader point that the first lines introduce: "Unhappy / is he who speaks with a guest while thinking of tomorrow's doings" (1:335). The following lines take up this theme—resonant with Daoist philosophy—of working with and responding to the constant change of the world. The artist appears in the poem's center as one whose brush is guided by "air and light." The artist who responds to the world's changes appears in poem 10, as well. "Great is the artist who knows no duty / beyond that of the playing brush," we read. His brush "pierces immortality itself— / and immortality plays with him" (1:336). The great artist is the one who plays; and in play we can act only by interacting. His actions—or let us say *her* actions—always answer something outside of herself, over which she has no control. By relinquishing control she breaks open windows onto the heart of things—even onto immortality itself.

But in a surprising and characteristic move, Sedakova's speaker undercuts the artist,[38] too, continuing,

Но тот, кого покидает дух, от кого
    отводят луч,
кто десятый раз, на мутном месте
    ищет чистый ключ,
кто выпал из руки чудес, но не скажет:
    пусты чудеса!—
перед ним с почтением
    склоняются небеса. (1:336)

But he whom the spirit abandons, from whom
    light's rays are removed,
who for the tenth time in the same murky place
    seeks a pure spring,
who has fallen out of wonders' hands, but will not say:
    wonders are empty!—
before him with reverence
    the heavens will bow down.

The artist, after all, still shows us material and cultural forms—hills, leaves, virtues—and so she binds us to things of the world, to which we would cling in the face of change. These phenomena, too, must dissolve if we pursue real likeness to what lies beyond—to the negation that is death, the negation of our own finite, material forms. It is only when we lose the spirit, the light, the pure spring that we can embark on a truly apophatic path. As ancient Christian theologian Gregory of Nyssa writes, "It is a fact that every body is composite, and that what is composite exists by the joining of its different elements. [. . .] And what decomposes cannot be incorruptible."[39] That is, all we make can be unmade, and so it can only point to what is not made, and to its own madeness. Sedakova's model will surrender to the emptying of all things, including herself; and still she "will not say: / wonders are empty!" Wonders are all she has left—phenomena that arise out of nothing. Only what nothing produces is not empty. When the heavens bow to this figure, we witness not merely a sign of their honor but the collapse of the entire cosmos in the face of such likeness to the unknown. The universe itself gives up its form, and only in this way survives.

Chinese Journey transports us through landscapes and natural scenery in its first half, then through cosmic panoramas in the second. Further on, our guide uses magnitude to emphasize how the path of relinquishment cuts through all dimensions. Humans are compared to oceans (poem 12, 1:338); human relationships are compared to the pull the "magnet of the star" exerts on the tides (poem 13, 1:339); Li Bo's glass of yellow wine to the moon (poem 13); a flute to the mountain crevices through which winds blow (poem 14, 1:340); the human heart inflaming with longing to the stars appearing in the night sky (poem 14); a human voice tracing a melody to the spiral of the Milky Way (poem 15, 1:341). The shifting scale of magnitude suggests on the one hand the importance of the human element, but on the other hand its tininess within the panorama of the universe. These comparisons of scale also set in play the quality of the mise en abîme that we find in the icon, its capacity as a vector pointing beyond its particular aesthetic forms. The folding of these phenomena of diverse magnitude one into the other reminds us of the paterica that point endlessly from one model to another to another.

The comparisons culminate in the litany of the final and eighteenth poem, which begins,

Похвалим нашу землю,
  похвалим луну на воде,
то, что ни с кем и со всеми,
  что нигде и везде—
величиной с око ласточки,
  с крошку сухого хлеба,
с лестницу на крыльях бабочки,
  с лестницу, кинутую с неба. (1:345)

Let us praise our earth,
    the moon on the water,
that which is with no one and with all,
    that is nowhere and everywhere—
the size of a swallow's eye,
    of a crumb of dry bread,
of a ladder on the wings of a butterfly,
    of a ladder thrown down from the sky.

Even as the speaker praises the earth, she glimpses something else through its frames, a beyond glorified in the things of the world—from the pattern on a butterfly's wing to the sky's depth. What is "with no one and with all, / that is nowhere and everywhere" is something we encounter precisely through concrete, observable forms—moons and crumbs and swallow's eyes—and poems. This one ends by giving praise "that, as the gardener has his garden, / the earth has its praise." In the end, we are praising the earth for the praise it evokes, in pursuit down another infinite regress. One scholar, Ekaterina Kudriavtseva, describes the cycle as a "hall of mirrors, where nothing disappears without a trace"—and therefore as an invocation of immortality.[40]

With so many gestures Sedakova urges us into the unknown. Her penultimate poem pictures this path most overtly, as we see in its first stanza:

Когда мы решаемся ступить,
    не зная, что нас ждет,
на вдохновенья пустой корабль,
    на плохо связанный плот,
на чешуйчатое крыло, на лодку без гребцов,
воображая и самый лучший,
    и худший из концов
и ничего не ища внутри:
    там всему взамен
выбрасывают гадальные кости на книгу перемен. (1:343)

When we decide to step,
    not knowing what awaits us,
onto the empty boat of inspiration,
    onto the poorly bound raft,
onto the scaly wing, onto the boat with no one to row it,

imagining the very best
and worst of endings
and seeking nothing within:
there in exchange for everything
they cast the bones of fortunetelling onto the book of changes.

But if she sends us out into uncharted waters, it is not for nothing. Our pursuit through and beyond what we see traces the trajectory of desire. Again we hear echoes of Gregory of Nyssa, who asserts, "Hope always draws the soul from the beauty which is seen to what is beyond, always kindles the desire for the hidden through what is constantly perceived."[41] We glimpse something in nature and art that draws us in—death and eternity at once, the loss of ourselves and yet our own endurance. We glimpse the unknown, the "nothing within" but something without to which apophasis points. We glimpse the other. For this reason, the more cosmic the poem in *Chinese Journey*, the more interpersonal; the more we are taken out of ourselves, the closer we come to glimpsing what, or who, is beyond us. Poem 13 asks in confoundment, "We won't part like all the rest, / like all the rest / will we?" (1:339). In poem 14 the speaker's heart ignites "in myriad requests for one and the same thing: / wake up, / look at me, my inspired friend" (1:340). In poem 15 the speaker laments, "No one looks for me, no one gets upset / or pleads: 'Stay with me!'" (1:341). It is poem 16, though, that most clearly links the apophatic practice of unknowing to love. In its second half we read,

Ты знаешь, я так люблю тебя,
что от этого не отличу
вздох ветра, шум веток, жизнь дождя,
путь, похожий на свечу,
и что бормочет мрак чужой,
что ум, как спичка зажгло,
и даже бабочки сухой
несчастный стук в стекло. (1:342)

You know, I love you so much
that I can't tell the difference between
the sigh of the wind, the noise of branches, the life of rain,
the path that looks like a candle
and what the alien gloom murmurs,
what lit up the mind like a match,

and even the unhappy knock
of a dry butterfly on the glass.

Love fires this speaker's imagination, allowing her to connect all manner of things—or maybe more to the point, love keeps her from relying on her usual ways of knowing. Or, to follow Zholkovsky's explanation, this speaker manifests an extraordinary love that overcomes the inertia of the straightforward, that perseveres through the "unconstrained fickleness" of the poetic imagination.[42] In the light of these verses the poet's comparisons across orders of magnitude betoken love, specifically the kind of love that takes us out of ourselves—to cosmic lengths—in order to establish our inmost being.

Just as the patericon accounts assert human potential to resemble a God we cannot possibly see, Sedakova's poems assert our potential to bear the look of the eternal, in all its incomprehensibility. Poem 11 tells a tale in its first stanza of recognition that reminds us of patericon visions of holiness:

С нежностью и глубиной—
ибо только нежность глубока,
только глубина обладает нежностью,—
в тысяче лиц я узнаю,
кто ее видел, на кого поглядела и
из каменных вещей, как из стеклянных
нежная глубина и глубокая нежность. (1:337)

With tenderness and depth—
for only tenderness is deep,
only depth bears tenderness,—
in a thousand faces I recognize
who has seen it, who has been seen—
from stone things and glass things alike—
by tender depth and deep tenderness.

For this speaker the experience of tenderness—of "tender depth and deep tenderness"—leaves a visible mark. What is more, tenderness and depth are visible. People see it, things of stone and glass see it—and are seen by it. Our *Chinese Journey* teaches us, in fact, to "see" depth and tenderness—not through ordinary acts of vision, but through acts of surrender. We forgo our usual ways of reading and looking. We seek the path from impression to insight. We look for the tenth time in the same place for the pure spring. And wonders happen, radiant shimmerings from the edge of eternity that forever recedes before us.

Averintsev has seen in Sedakova's poetry, hand in hand with "astonishment," an impulse to remember death, an impulse he describes as ascetic in nature.[43] In a 1998 acceptance speech for the "Christian Roots of Europe" Prize, awarded by the Vatican in honor of Vladimir Solovyov, Sedakova speaks of participating in a "new Christian art"—a project she identifies in modern Russian literature, "in Akhmatova, Mandelstam, Tsvetaeva, Pasternak, Brodsky . . . For me, most of all—in Pushkin."[44] In this renewed body of literature, she perceives a "new asceticism," one premised less on fleshly abstinence than on "abstinence from what has died and what brings death" ("vozderzhanie ot omertvevshego i omertvliaiushchego"). These words may seem to contradict Averintsev's description of her poetry, not least given her apparent preoccupation with death in *Chinese Journey*. But Sedakova distinguishes between death or deathliness and death that brings life. In her essay on a "liturgical theology of death," she contends that a human lives in fullness via an innate "image of praise" ("obraz slavy"; 4:675). That is, a person's inmost being or divine "image" survives through human acts of remembering and praising. For Sedakova the remembrance of death—giving death a word, a shape—constitutes the victory of life over death, precisely "abstinence" from death's obliterating force. This new ascetic mode would enable one—a poet, a reader, a human heart—to let go of old ways, adapt to loss, and shed stultifying constructs for new words. It might feel like death, like a passage into nothingness, but it would hold out a lone hope for survival in the constant change of the world.

In one of her best-known essays, "The Morality of Art, or the Evils of Mediocrity," Sedakova touches on the relevance of art and aesthetic forms for human life ("Moralizm iskusstva, ili o zle posredstvennosti"; 4:254–70). She responds to notions of artists as amoral or immoral bohemians, and suggests, rather, that the artist can be seen as a model of asceticism—one who lets in life in all its fullness—one who lets in, therefore, what is "unpredictable, uncontrollable" (4:270, 264). Such language well befits post-Soviet realities, with all their change and uncertainty. And yet for Sedakova such circumstances give us access to the heart of life itself. "Art's moral recipe," she writes, "is expressed not so much in words [. . .] as in the work's *form*, in the liminality of this form" (4:267). For Sedakova the deathliest of dangers lie in the blissful middle. The force of life, however, draws us along the peripheries, on the way to China, on the way into the unknown, along the painful and vertiginous edge of the image, where what we know falls away into what we are becoming.

Notes

1. Sedakova addresses this idea at many points in her writing; this particular phrase appears in her introduction to her 2007 Stanford lectures, "Russkaia poeziia posle Brodskogo: Vstuplenie k 'Stenfordskim lektsiiam,'" 3:504–14.

2. Benjamin Paloff finds in Sedakova's poetry—especially in its formal aspects—an "incompletion," an emphasis on "openness and mutability" that she views as indispensable in establishing a "broader intersubjective dialogue." Benjamin Paloff, "The God Function in Joseph Brodsky and Olga Sedakova," *Slavic and East European Journal* 51, no. 4 (2007): 716–36; here, 730, 729, 727.

3. This quote comes from "Russkaia poeziia posle Brodskogo." She expresses a similar thought in "'V tselomudrennoi bezdne stikha,'" 3:128–29.

4. *The Concise Oxford Dictionary of World Religions Online*, by John Bowker, s.v. "Apophatic Theology," http://www.oxfordreference.com/view/10.1093/acref/9780192800947.001.0001/acref-9780192800947-e-583, accessed March 17, 2018.

5. V. N Losskii, *Ocherk misticheskogo bogosloviia vostochnoi tserkvi: Dogmaticheskoe bogoslovie* (Moscow: Tsentr "SEI," 1991). This work exists in English translation as *The Mystical Theology of the Eastern Church* (Crestwood, NY: St. Vladimir's Seminary Press, 1976). Translations here are my own.

6. Losskii, *Ocherk misticheskogo bogosloviia*, 22.

7. This thought is basic to Sedakova's discussion of Russian Orthodoxy throughout the essay, but she discusses apophatic theology most directly on 4:692–94.

8. For a seminal modern account of Evagrius and his teachings, see G. V. Florovskii, *Vizantiiskie Ottsy V–VIII: Iz Chtenii v Pravoslavnom bogoslovskom institute v Parizhe* (Paris, 1933), 163–65. This work exists in English translation, though split into two volumes: *The Collected Works of Georges Florovsky*, vol. 8, *The Byzantine Fathers of the Fifth Century* and vol. 9, *The Byzantine Fathers of the Sixth to Eighth Centuries* (Belmont, MA: Nordland, 1987).

9. A key account of hesychasm in Russia can be found in Lossky, *The Mystical Theology of the Eastern Church.* (As Lossky emphasizes, it was Dionysius who made the fundamental distinction in Christian tradition between "the way of affirmation [cataphatic or positive theology]" and "the way of negation [apophatic or negative theology]"; 21.) While Sedakova does not name hesychasm in the body of her essay ("The Light of Life") itself, referring to it only in a footnote (4:681), she does refer to important elements, such as the "prayer of the heart" (4:682). She also refers to the *Celestial Hierarchies* of Dionysius the Areopagite, who developed some of the language used by hesychasts in their quest to partake in the Divine Light (4:692).

10. George P. Fedotov, *The Russian Religious Mind: Kievan Christianity, the Tenth to the Thirteenth Centuries* (New York: Harper, 1960). For a well-known discussion of conceptions of kenosis in Russian philosophy, see Nadejda Gorodetzky, *The Humiliated Christ in Modern Russian Thought* (New York: Macmillan, 1938).

11. "O pogibshem literaturnom pokolenii: Pamiati Leni Gubanova," http://olgasedakova.com/Poetica/1101, accessed March 20, 2018.

12. For classic discussions of this feature, see Pavel Florenskii, *Ikonostas* (Moscow: Iskusstvo, 1994), especially 100–101, 135–36, 138–41; and Boris A. Uspenskii, "Semiotika ikony," in *Semiotika iskusstva* (Moscow: Shkola "Iazyki russkoi kul'tury," 1995), 221–94.

13. For a set of discussions on the notion of creative or adaptive imitation in the Russian literary tradition, see the special issue of *Slavic Review*, "Copies: The Mimetic Component of Remembering," 68, no. 4 (2009), and especially the introduction by Monika Greenleaf and Luba Golburt (743–57).

14. Marie-José Mondzain, *Image, Icon, Economy: The Byzantine Origins of the Contemporary Imaginary* (Stanford, CA: Stanford University Press, 2005).

15. Ibid., 70.

16. Stephanie Sandler, Introduction, Olga Sedakova, *In Praise of Poetry*, ed. and trans. Caroline Clark, Ksenia Golubovich, and Stephanie Sandler (Rochester, NY: Open Letter, 2014), 5–16; here, 5.

17. For a brief account of paterica, their origins and outlines, see Viktor M. Zhivov, "Paterik," in *Sviatost': Kratkii slovar' agiograficheskikh terminov* (Moscow: Gnozis, 1994), 72–74.

18. For Sedakova's translation see "Iz 'Sinaiskogo Paterika,'" 2:69–91. Originally published in *Vestnik russkogo khristianskogo dvizheniia* 135, nos. 3–4 (1981): 5–19; 136, nos. 1–2 (1982): 11–40.

19. Mondzain, *Image, Icon, Economy*, 98.

20. Ekaterina Kudriavtseva, "Analiz i interpretatsiia poeticheskogo tsikla: Sedakova, Ol'ga Aleksandrovna 'Kitaiskoe puteshestvie,'" in *Bildschirmtexte zur 5: Tagung des jungen Forums slavistische Literaturwissenschaft in Muenster* (Münster: JFSL, 2002), 1–5.

21. Quoted in Bryan W. Van Norden, "Method in the Madness of the Laozi," in *Religious and Philosophical Aspects of the Laozi*, ed. Mark Csikszentmihalyi and Philip J. Ivanhoe (Albany: State University of New York Press, 1999), 187–210; here, 195.

22. For a discussion of apophasis in the Laozi writings, with a helpful review of the ongoing critical discussion, see Mark Csikszentmihalyi, "Mysticism and Apophatic Discourse in the *Laozi*," in Csikszentmihalyi and Ivanhoe, *Religious and Philosophical Aspects*, 33–58.

23. This emphasis on constant change of the created universe can be found in seminal figures such as Gregory of Nyssa, who remarks in his *Life of Moses*, "In mutable nature nothing can be observed which is always the same" (Gregory of Nyssa, *Life of Moses*, trans. Abraham J. Malherbe and Everett Ferguson [New York: Paulist Press, 1978]). For Gregory, mutability comprises an important spiritual quality for it allows the one who seeks after God to be transformed into one who can participate in the infinite divine mystery.

24. For the delineation of many apparent references in *Chinese Journey* to the works of this eighth-century Chinese poet, see Aleksandr Zholkovskii, "Neuzheli . . . ? Ol'ga Sedakova, 'Kitaiskoe puteshestvie,' 13," *Zvezda* 11 (2007): 180–90.

25. "About the Author," http://www.olgasedakova.com/eng/about_the_author, accessed March 20, 2018.

26. This phrase comes from Maximus the Confessor. Roman Catholic scholar Hans Urs von Balthasar quotes this phrase in his book on Maximus (*Cosmic Liturgy: The Universe According to Maximus the Confessor* [San Francisco: Ignatius Press, 2003]), specifically in a passage where he is describing Maximus's articulation of the apophatic path: "Distance grows with increasing nearness. Fear, hesitation, and adoration grow with love. Silence increases with the progress of revelation. [. . .] The silence that lies above the

inarticulateness of concepts becomes the only appropriate form of praise, 'pure wonder, which alone describes the indescribable majesty'" (92).

27. Sergei Averintsev, "Metafizicheskaia poeziia kak poeziia izumleniia," *Kontinent* 120 (2004), http://magazines.russ.ru/continent/2004/120/av26-pr.html, accessed March 20, 2018.

28. The liturgy also calls Mary "the Container of the Uncontainable God" (Boga nevměstimagō vměstilishte) (Eighth Ikos of the Akathist, *Trīōd' postnaę* [Moscow: Izdatel'stvo Moskovskoi Patriarkhii, 1992], 326v).

29. I am grateful to Maria Khotimsky for helping me make this connection.

30. Mondzain, *Image, Icon, Economy*, 101–7.

31. See in particular Mondzain, *Image, Icon, Economy*, 106.

32. Ibid., 92.

33. Zholkovksii, "Neuzheli . . . ?" This is a basic thought that undergirds the whole article.

34. Florovsky writes that for Evagrius, "Love is the beginning of the gnostic ascent, the beginning of 'real' [*estestvennoi*] life" (*Vizantiiskie ottsy*, 164).

35. Zholkovksii, "Neuzheli . . . ?," esp. 184–88.

36. Ol'ga Sedakova, *Kitaiskoe puteshestvie* (Moscow: Graal', 2001).

37. Sedakova is not alone in this project to reemphasize the ways apophasis moves beyond sheer negation. In his far-ranging theological aesthetics, twentieth-century Roman Catholic scholar Hans Urs von Balthasar asserts, in terms that echo both Sedakova and Mondzain, "The appearance of the form, as revelation of the depths, is an indissoluble union of two things. It is the real presence of the depths, of the whole of reality, *and* it is a real pointing beyond itself to these depths." Hans Urs von Balthasar, *The Glory of the Lord: A Theological Aesthetics*, vol 1, *Seeing the Form*, trans. Erasmo Levia-Merikakis, ed. Joseph Fessio S. J. and John Riches (1982; repr., San Francisco: Ignatius Press, 2009), 118.

38. In "The Light of Life," Sedakova identifies the icon's vision—or the clarity of apophatic perception—to "the great artist's vision of reality." She goes on to add, however, "And it is even closer to the perception of a child, of an infant" (4:687).

39. Gregory of Nyssa, *The Life of Moses*, 112.

40. Kudriavtseva, "Analiz i interpretatsiia poeticheskogo tsikla." Kudriavtseva has in mind specifically the way the cycle turns back on itself, repeating images and themes in ever new settings.

41. Gregory of Nyssa, *The Life of Moses*, 114.

42. Zholkovskii, "Neuzheli . . . ?," 183.

43. Averintsev, "'Ne soobrazuites' veku semu,'" *Krug chteniia* 5 (1995): 100–101.

44. Ol'ga Sedakova, "Schastlivaia trevoga glubiny: Rech' pri vruchenii premii 'Khristianskie korni Evropy' imeni Vladimira Solov'eva, Vatikan, 1 iulia 1998 goda," http://olgasedakova.com/Moralia/266, accessed March 20, 2018.

Disruption of Disruption

The Orthodox Christian Impulse in the Works of Nikolai Zabolotsky and Olga Sedakova

SARAH PRATT

To the Memory of Nikita Zabolotsky

The Soviet authorities sought to disrupt the hold of Orthodox Christianity on Russian culture with their fervent embrace of militant atheism. As poets who came of age during the Soviet period, Nikolai Zabolotsky (1903–58) and Olga Sedakova (b. 1949) were expected to produce poetry devoid of religious impulse: true Soviet poets focused on the secular sacrifice and heroism of the people. Zabolotsky's early affiliation with the Modernist avant-garde would presumably have strengthened his anti-religious impetus. The fact that much of Sedakova's career corresponds to a period dominated by postmodernism strengthens the expectation of an anti-religious stance, although the poet herself forcefully and compellingly denies such affiliation.[1]

In spite of these anti-religious pressures, religious principles and patterns of thought lie like an aquifer beneath the surface of the works of each poet. The religious elements sometimes bubble up to the surface, creating a broad floodplain of religious meaning, and sometimes remain hidden below. Either way, the Orthodox impulse disrupts the avant-garde, postmodernist, and Soviet disruptions of traditional Russian culture, and brings Zabolotsky and Sedakova together in a diachronic common cause. The bedrock of Russian Orthodox thought establishes a seemingly paradoxical set of principles that lies at the base of the poets' works. It denies the possibility of romantic genius, while it affirms the moral power of the word, of Logos, and the moral duty of the poet to use this power. It undercuts the figure of the poet as a prophet who "owns" a prophetic gift linked to self-expression, while supporting the role of poetry itself as prophecy and a vision of truth. And finally, it supports the poets' acceptance of given, concrete reality, as well as their commitment to help others see the greater truth inherent in that reality. This stance distinguishes the two poets from their peers and predecessors and unites them in a metaphysical relationship that asserts both the freedom and moral obligation inherent in the calling of the poet.

Each poet maintains that both the word and the world need to be cleansed of the detritus of cultural pretensions and cleansed as well of dogma in whatever form it might take—constraints imposed by political ideology, religion, or by artistic movements. Such cleansing, achieved through an artistic act of purity and chasteness, allows the true nature of the word and the world to be revealed. On the one hand, this sense of unfettered exploration creates seeming affiliations with modernism and postmodernism, and serves as the source of the supposed absurdity and inscrutability that mark a number of Zabolotsky's and Sedakova's poems. On the other hand, the same absurdity and inscrutability can be seen as aspects of an apophatic effort to reach divinity, an understanding that human reason ultimately cannot grasp the greatness of God and God's works. And it can be seen as an act of kenosis, an anti-romantic emptying of self that allows the poet to see the world with the eyes of a holy fool, or perhaps to function something like a Greek chorus, to portray and comment on a reality that is at one and the same time grotesquely distorted and profoundly true.

Zabolotsky first articulates this substrate of theological thinking, especially the theology of the icon, in the OBERIU Declaration of 1928, which he wrote together with Daniil Kharms.[2] A short-lived group of artistic rebels including Zabolotsky, Kharms, Alexander Vvedensky, Konstantin Vaginov, and others, the OBERIU, or Union for Real Art (Ob"edinenie real'nogo iskusstva), represented the last gasp of the avant-garde before Stalinist culture made such experimentation impossible. Even as the tenor of Zabolotsky's poetry and manifestos change over time, a consistent vision provides the foundation for his works to the very end of his career and is stated again in two essays and a major poem written just a year before his death. Sedakova expresses her worldview in countless interviews and essays available online and in print. Her scholarly masterwork, *Church Slavonic-Russian Paronyms: Materials for a Dictionary* (*Tserkovnoslaviano-russkie paronimy: Materialy k slovariu*, 2005), exemplifies and reinforces her commitment to religious endeavor and simultaneously demonstrates the difficulty of establishing meaning and acknowledges the autonomy of language.[3]

While Sedakova occasionally mentions Zabolotsky with admiration, she does not allude to him nearly as often as to Pushkin, Khlebnikov, Mandelstam, and Pasternak. Her poem "The Golden Trumpet. Zabolotsky's Rhythm" ("Zolotaia truba. Ritm Zabolotskogo," 1979–83), mimics the rhythm of Zabolotsky's poem "In This Birch Grove" ("V etoi roshche berezovoi," 1946), but as noted by Sedakova herself, this is a form of metric acknowledgment, and not much more.[4] Ultimately, Sedakova's bond with Zabolotsky manifests itself not so much in the form of her poetry as in its philosophical underpinnings. She signals this connection in a speech accepting an honorary doctor of theology degree from the European Humanities University, which uses a line of Zabolotsky's verse in its title, and leads from Zabolotsky back to Tiutchev's poem "Poetry" ("Poeziia," no later than 1850) and, perhaps surprisingly, to Kornei Chukovsky's verse tale for children, "Theodora's Woe" ("Fedorino gore," 1926). Before engaging with the poets' texts, though, we will take a brief look at the biographies of the two poets.

The *samouchka* and the *intelligent*

The starting points of the two poets are decidedly different. Zabolotsky, who once described himself as a "coarse, unpleasant half-peasant" ("grubyi, nesimpatichnyi polumuzhik"), was born on a farm near Kazan in 1903 but was raised primarily in the remote village of Sernur, where his father worked as an agronomist and guided family life based on the "qualities of an Old Testament patriarch" ("cherty starozavetnoi patriarkhal'nosti").[5] He studied religion (*zakon Bozhii*) in the parish school, where each day began with prayers, and served as an altar boy in church. As a result, the young Zabolotsky was imbued with a sense of religion that would stay with him in one form or another for the rest of his life. At the age of six he decided he wanted to "be a poet," and stayed true the goal of "being a poet" for the rest of his life. In this combination of a "half-peasant" background and yearning for knowledge, Zabolotsky typifies what in Russian is called a *samouchka*, a self-taught, spottily educated person. While American tradition lauds a person who gains an education and "pulls himself up by his bootstraps," Russian tradition regards the *samouchka* with a certain skepticism and even amusement. As Zabolotsky's friend Nikolai Chukovsky, the son of the author Kornei Chukovsky, puts it: "[Zabolotsky] was born and grew up in a little town out in the sticks [*v malen'kom glukhom gorodke*], and everything that he knew, he had learned as a self-taught person [*samouchka*]—all the conclusions he reached, he reached on his own, and he frequently learned much later in life the things that people who grew up in a more cultured environment knew as children."[6] The kind of purposefully naïve curiosity that motivated much of Zabolotsky's poetry and drove some critics to a state of frenzy was, in the early years, partly an act of avant-garde provocation. But it was also part of the genuine, open-ended intellectual quest of a provincial autodidact.

When Zabolotsky made his way to Petrograd (subsequently renamed Leningrad, formerly and currently St. Petersburg) in the 1920s, he enrolled at the Herzen Pedagogical Institute. Had he studied at the more elite Petrograd University or the Institute for the History of the Arts, he would have come into contact with a number of leading literary scholars. But for whatever reason—perhaps a lack of qualifications because he had studied at a *real'noe uchilishche* rather than a more exclusive *gimnaziia*, or the vagaries of some bureaucratic process related to admissions or student ration cards—he found himself at the pedagogical institute, even though he flatly stated that he had no intention of becoming a teacher.[7]

Sedakova, by contrast, was a child of cultural and educational privilege. Born in Moscow to the family of a successful military engineer, she was destined to be a member of the Soviet intelligentsia. While Zabolotsky traveled abroad only once very late in life, Sedakova began her intellectual life in an international arena, gaining a perception of the world as a child when her father was stationed in Beijing. She studied at Moscow State University, finding her way around the constraints of Soviet dogma with the help of some of the finest minds of the time.[8]

Like Zabolotsky, Sedakova started writing poetry at an early age and decided that she wanted to "be a poet." But while Zabolotsky's poetry appeared to dovetail with the revolutionary ferment for a short period in the 1920s and, at least to some degree, with the demands of the Soviet state in the 1940s and 1950s, Sedakova's worldview, chosen themes, and manner of writing meant that official publication during the Soviet period was not an option.

Russian Orthodoxy in Practice

As different as Zabolotsky and Sedakova are in terms of historical period, gender, education, and cultural expectations, the fact remains that engagement with similar religious concepts marks their works throughout their respective careers. It has been argued that Sedakova's religious impulse stems from the Russian religious renaissance of the last part of the nineteenth century and the first part of the twentieth, and to the influence of the pianist Mikhail Erokhin, whom she credits with awakening her interest in painting, poetry, and philosophy, as well as music. In addition, her dissertation at Moscow State University allowed her to delve into religious issues in the context of the funeral rites of the Eastern and Southern Slavs.[9]

Beyond this, Sedakova's own particular biography creates a path to Orthodoxy with some unusual twists and turns. She was born to parents whom she describes as "Soviet people," which is to say, atheists. But at the same time, she had a close relationship with her grandmother, who was an actively practicing Orthodox Christian. Even though, according to one report, Sedakova's parents had her briefly institutionalized in a psychiatric hospital because they considered her religious beliefs a form of mental illness, her grandmother fostered and nourished her religious impulses.[10] She writes, "My grandmother was a person of true faith—she had a deep, quiet faith. She didn't get into arguments with her own children—who were Soviet people and atheists. Her world just appealed to me, and I was drawn to her. [. . .] She taught me to read Church Slavonic when I was still a child. [. . .] She used to ask me to read psalms and prayers to her out loud, and the words stuck in my head."[11] In another instance, Sedakova states, "I learned [about Orthodoxy] not from books, but from my grandmother. [. . .] From my childhood I saw what a person who prays is all about and what a person who understands and reads the scriptures is like. And I liked it very much."[12]

For all that Sedakova comes to us as a thoroughgoing *intelligent*—an intellectual poet, a public intellectual on the Russian and international stage—the origins of her Orthodoxy are not unlike those of the "half-peasant" Zabolotsky. Her first religious impulse stems from the aural, visual, tactile, and emotional experience of basic Orthodox practice. In each case, the directness and palpability of religious experience lead to an approach to the poetic word as an object with its own moral and artistic mission, an object worthy of respect, not to be trifled with for the sake of dogma—religious, political, or otherwise.

Many of Sedakova's poems have biblical or liturgical resonance, and it can be argued that her ultimate poetic interlocutor is God. And yet she rejects the terms "religious poet" and "Orthodox poet." She writes:

> I am Orthodox by conviction, but I would never want, nor would I dare, to make that a literary profession of faith. If I were to call myself an Orthodox poet, [. . .] I would have to vouch for my conformity to canon law. [. . .] There is no way I can do that. [. . .] For me poetry is unthinkable without openness of meaning, whilst religion in art, according to the common view, involves a prescriptive, engaged approach of one's knowing how the thing is going to end.[13]

Elaborating on this idea of openness, and insisting on both the integrity of literature and the integrity of faith, she writes: "Religion in art [. . .] is a wider concept, one that cannot be simply determined by content. I know quite a few 'Christian' poets whose pious intentions do not save them from sinning [. . .] against literature. What it adds up to is nothing more nor less than the breaking of one of the Ten Commandments: 'Though shalt not take the name of the Lord thy God in vain.'"[14] Second-rate religious art—art without "openness of meaning," art that purports to know "how the thing is going to end"—sins against literature, and as it does so, it takes the name of the Lord in vain. There is a set of moral imperatives involving the unforced reception of God's word and God's world that make the closed system of "Christian literature," in the narrow sense, untenable as either literature or as a manifestation of faith.

Perhaps the most striking and nuanced expression of Sedakova's Christian worldview, including her uncompromising insistence on the openness of art, occurs in connection with the honorary degree of doctor of theology awarded to her by the European Humanities University in Minsk (2003). Her acceptance speech is entitled "'In the Chaste Abyss of a Line of Verse': On Poetic Meaning and Doctrinal Meaning" ("'V tselomudrennoi bezdne stikha': O smysle poeticheskom i smysle doktrinal'nom"; 3:127–40). The first part of the title comes from Zabolotsky's poem "Night Festival" ("Nochnoe gulian'e," 1953), which in turn creates a conversation connecting Sedakova and Zabolotsky with their nineteenth-century precursor Tiutchev, and then loops back to the twentieth century to their slightly older contemporary, Kornei Chukovsky. The substance of this time-traveling conversation revolves around metapoetic concerns—how poetry comes into being, and the nature of the moral imperatives that lie at its base.

Even as the speech conveys deep respect for religious vocation, it also rejects any doctrinal limitation on art. It is here that Zabolotsky's "Night Festival" comes into play. The poem, describing a nighttime Soviet festival with fireworks, was written in 1953 and is one of the late works in which Zabolotsky gradually comes to terms with his own career as a poet. As the poem develops through its three quatrains, fireworks serve as a metaphor for writers with more successful, "flashier" literary careers, whom the poet implicitly envies. The writers with flashier careers would, of course, be those who wrote politically acceptable works reflecting an untroubled vision consistent with Soviet dogma.

The first stanza describes the setting on a city square. The second and third stanzas cited below get to the heart of the matter. The second instructs the addressee, who is a poet (very likely Zabolotsky speaking to himself), not to put too much faith in these shining silver streaks in the night, and the third reveals the basis of the metaphor, as the persona concludes that the only thing that shines eternally is the heart of a poet—not artificial fireworks—in the chaste abyss of a line of verse.

Но когда пиротехник из рощи
Бросит в небо серебряный свет,
Фантастическим выстрелам ночи
Не вполне доверяйся, поэт.

Улетит и погаснет ракета,
Потускнеют огней вороха . . .
Вечно светит лишь сердце поэта
В целомудренной бездне стиха.[15]

But when the pyrotechnician
Casts a silvery light into the sky from the grove,
Don't put too much faith in the amazing rockets
Shot in the night, poet.

The rocket will fly away and burn out,
The clusters of fire will grow dim . . .
The only thing that shines eternally is the heart of a poet
In the chaste abyss of a line of verse.

As Sedakova puts it, the last line of Zabolotsky's poem provides the "vector" for the main theme of her speech. It is indeed the last line of the poem that moves into the spiritual realm and elevates the poem beyond the standard Soviet celebratory lyrics of the time. Sedakova notes that the three words—*stikh*, which represents something very small, a line of verse; *bezdna*, which represents something immense and incomprehensible, an abyss; and *tselomudrennyi*, which carries the notion of chasteness and purity—are not natural companions. They can be connected with each other only by means of paradox and mystery. Both Zabolotsky and Sedakova charge the poet with connecting the small thing that is a line of verse to the immense and mysterious universe while remaining chaste, remaining unsullied by the easy path of dogma that knows "how the thing will end," or by the temptation of flashiness. By invoking Zabolotsky, who was sent to a labor camp for his artistic exploration, Sedakova rejects not only the constraints potentially imposed by official "religious" poetry, but the constraints of Soviet dogma as well. She proclaims that "The categorical imperative of free art makes the possibility of creativity [*tvorchestvo*] limited by religion or dogma unthinkable" (3:135, 130, 127, 128).

In Tiutchev's "Poetry," poetry is lightly personified as a female figure who descends from the heavens amid the boiling passions of fiery elemental strife. She does not partake of the flashiness—she casts no lightning bolts of inspiration. Rather, she pours the chrism, or holy oil, of reconciliation (*primiritel'nyi elei*) upon the waters, calming the stormy sea of life and freeing the sons of man from their passions. Sedakova uses Tiutchev's poem in "In Praise of Poetry" ("Zametki i vospominaniia o raznykh stikhotvoreniiakh, a takzhe Pokhvala poezii") to emphasize the integrated intellectual function of poetry: "It is pointless to think that poetry gathers or generalizes or elevates an idea that exists in a 'reality' outside of poetry. It works the other way around: 'And pours the chrism of reconciliation onto the stormy waters.' The world is a given, [. . .] it is bestowed as a gift. Poetry bestows its chrism as a gift, as something that presents itself as a lack, an object of longing and entreaty."[16]

In the thinking of all three poets, the standard concept of the burning flame of inspiration is denied in favor of a movement away from passions and heat, and toward calmness, chasteness, and purity. While Tiutchev does not directly address the issue of dogma, so important to Sedakova and Zabolotsky, he nonetheless renders dogma moot. Dogma must be enforced by human authorities in order to function, but the poetic persona in the poem is a passive receiver of poetry from a generous universe. "The sons of man" simply exist, but take no action as poetry pours the chrism of reconciliation onto troubled waters.

In her speech, Sedakova embraces the paradox of religious belief combined with the rejection of dogmatic constraint. She implicitly draws a distinction between "dogma," defined as set of rigid principles to be accepted without examination, and "theology" (*bogoslovie*) as a less defined but nonetheless constant source of vision and light for both life and art. She states: "I have always been sure that both thought and image can be fully realized only when the light of theology illuminates their depths, their distances. In this regard, art and thought are in no way different from any other human experience, which comes into being in the presence of this light, even if this light remains invisible to us" (3:127). This same vision, this same understanding of the world illuminated—but not constrained—by Russian Orthodoxy informs virtually every poem Sedakova writes. The divine is present in the world. The task of human beings is to recognize the divine presence, to participate in it. With this vision, Sedakova provides the key to her deep connection with Zabolotsky.

Well before he wrote "Night Festival," Zabolotsky had a long history of concern for the chasteness or purity of art, of art unconstrained by dogma. It begins with the OBERIU Declaration, which takes up the issue of ideological constraint in clear and specific terms. The declaration complains that the Filonov School has been forced out of the Academy, that Kazimir Malevich has not been allowed to develop his architecture in the USSR, and that leftist art has been categorized as charlatanism. Raising the issues of chasteness and purity, it states further that, thanks to the methods of OBERIU, "the world, currently beslobbered by the tongues of a pack of fools [...] is now being reborn in the full purity [*vo vsei chistote*] of its concrete courageous forms."[17]

Like Sedakova, Zabolotsky kept his eye firmly on the moral link between art, freedom, and truth. This characteristic was noted time and time again by friends and acquaintances. One acquaintance points out that Zabolotsky related to his work "as a Higher Duty, a sacred obligation, in whose name he was always ready to sacrifice any kind of convenience or material advantage." Another notes: "Whatever happened to him, around him, with his involvement or independent of him—everything was invariably, unalterably connected with his consciousness of the fact that he was a poet. This was the trait by which he ethically and morally tested everything he thought about and everything he did. [. . .] He was honest because he was a poet. He didn't lie because he was a poet. He didn't betray his friends because he was a poet. All the norms of his existence, his behavior, and his relations with people were determined by the fact that, as a poet, he could not at the same time be a deceiver, a traitor, a flatterer, or a careerist."[18]

Zabolotsky's religious sensibility had its roots firmly planted in the Orthodoxy of the peasantry before the revolution. Unlike Sedakova, whose contacts within the intelligentsia allowed her to develop a certain theological depth and sophistication, Zabolotsky had little or no connection with the Russian religious renaissance, and his religious sensibility seemed to become dormant after the revolution. But in an act highly unusual for a Soviet author, Zabolotsky wrote memoirs in which he describes his religious upbringing at length, and with a dynamism that suggests a continuing engagement with this aspect of his past. Even after the lessons of his term in camp, he neither forgot his religious training, nor did he edit it out of his memoirs for the sake of political expedience.

If, as Zabolotsky reports, his father "had many of the characteristics of the old patriarchal system" and was "moderately religious," the family most likely said daily prayers and attended church with some regularity. More than forty years later, he still remembered the short religious service with which every school day began: the auditorium with the huge gold-framed portrait of the tsar; the choir standing in front of the pupils on the left; the singing of the prayer "O Heavenly King" ("Tsariu nebesnyi"); the priest reciting the daily chapter from the Gospels; and the closing singing of "God Save the Tsar." With some amusement, he also reminisces about serving as an altar boy in the cathedral, taking gulps of communion wine on the sly, and carrying notes between the boys and the girls. The most profound expression of Zabolotsky's boyhood religious experience comes in his description of the vespers service in a passage marked by sweet nostalgia for his younger self and a deep sense of faith and potential: "the quiet vespers service in the half-dark church glimmering with candles inclined one involuntarily to pensiveness and a feeling of sweet sorrow. The choir was excellent, and when the treble voices sang 'Glory to God in the highest' ['Slava v vyshnikh Bogu'] or 'O gentle light' ['Svete tikhii'] my throat tightened and I, in my childlike way, believed in something lofty and merciful that soared high above us and would surely help me achieve true human happiness."[19]

Zabolotsky's memoirs run only to the beginning of World War I, and there is, understandably, no written discussion of his religious experience during the postrevolutionary period. We do know, however, that Zabolotsky kept a Bible on his bookshelf along with other books that he considered "vital to his work," these being editions of Pushkin, Tiutchev, Baratynsky, and others, and that the Bible was one of the books confiscated when the poet was arrested in 1938. In addition, the impact of Zabolotsky's early religious training is evident in the handful of poems he wrote or planned on religious themes. In fact, at the time of his death, Zabolotsky was working on a trilogy entitled "The Adoration of the Magi" ("Poklonenie volkhvov").[20] The sheet of paper left on his desk showed the beginning of a plan:

1. Shepherds, animals, angels
2. ______________________________

The second point remained blank. The projected poem brought Zabolotsky full circle from his earlier belief in "something lofty and merciful that soared high above us," in spite of the ravages of time and the Stalinist policy of militant atheism.

The Logic of Art, the Thingness of Things, and the Theology of the Icon

Although dogma was repugnant to Sedakova and Zabolotsky, each poet built a vision of the world on a central tenet of Russian Orthodox theology—respect for given reality. This is the reality given by God, which is often obscured by civilization, culture, or dogma. Respect for given reality includes respect for the material world and the independence of things, including words. These precepts are evident in much of Zabolotsky's poetry, especially the 1929 collection *Columns* (*Stolbtsy*), and in many of the theoretical writings of members of the OBERIU. Daniil Kharms, for example, offers a hyperbolic statement about the "thingness" of words in a letter to K. V. Pugacheva, when he asserts: "It seems that you can take this poem, which has turned into a thing [*eti stikhi, stavshie veshch'iu*], right off the paper and throw it at the window—and the window will break."[21] These elements link Zabolotsky and Sedakova to the theology of the icon, and all lead back to their conviction of the metaphysical veracity and necessary morality of independent art.

The OBERIU Declaration vehemently addresses an imagined interlocutor on the issues of the concreteness of poetry, on realism and logic, and on the issue of purity or cleansing denoted by the root *chist-*, *chishch-*: "So maybe you'll begin to protest, saying that this isn't the object you see in life? Come closer and touch it with your fingers. Look at the object with your naked eyes and you will see it for the first time cleansed [*ochishchennym*] of its decrepit literary gilding. Maybe you're going to claim that our plots are 'unreal' and 'illogical?' But who said that 'everyday' logic was obligatory for art? [. . .] Art has its own logic and it does not destroy the object, but helps one perceive it."[22]

According to OBERIU, the logic of art rests in the "collision of verbal meanings" ("stolknovenie slovesnykh smyslov"), a type of reductio ad absurdum in the realm of semantic logic, and it is the word itself, the word as an object (*predmet*) that creates the collision. The element of the grotesque in Zabolotsky's *Columns* collection comes from such "collisions," and even Zabolotsky's later verse retains traces of the same. In keeping with this principle of concreteness, the OBERIU Declaration describes Zabolotsky as the author of poetry that is a visible, tangible object waiting to be touched and held by the reader: "N. Zabolotsky—a poet of naked concrete figures, pushed right up to the eyes of the viewer. You need to listen to him and read him more with your eyes and fingers than with your ears. The object is not fragmented, but on the contrary—it is put together and solidified to the utmost degree, as if prepared to meet the groping hand of the viewer."[23]

It is through this insistence on the word as a concrete object that the OBERIU in general, and Zabolotsky in particular, take a major step toward the concept of Christ as Logos, Christ as the embodied Word of God, and from that premise toward the theology of the icon. Rooted in the Gospel according to John ("In the beginning was the Word") and the writings of John of Damascus, Theodore the Studite, and others, the theology of the icon holds that the material and spiritual worlds are inextricably interrelated but distinct. Each aspect or hypostasis is valid and valued. It is through Christ's incarnation, his existence as matter, his sacrifice in the flesh, that man achieves salvation and that the deification of the universe is assured. John of Damascus writes with passionate conviction, "I worship the Creator of matter who became matter for my sake, who worked out my salvation through matter. Never will I cease honoring the matter which wrought my salvation!"[24] Icons, as material objects, represent the dual nature of Christ and, like Christ, simultaneously provide a medium that allows human understanding of and communion with the divine. From the central concept of the word as a fleshly being or concrete object, both Orthodox theology and OBERIU ideology move toward the same conclusion: matter has the power to transform human perception to accord with "real" reality and, as it does this, it paves the way to salvation and the transformation of the world. As stated succinctly by Leonid Ouspensky, one of the leading scholars of the icon, "Orthodox doctrine about the deification of man *was* the 'theory of art.'"[25]

OBERIU ideology and Orthodox theology of the icon are also bound together by a perceived "primitivism" stemming from respect each has for the independence of the object. Kharms's brief manifesto "Objects and Figures Discovered by Daniil Ivanovich Kharms" ("Predmety i figury, otkrytye Daniilom Ivanovichem

Kharmsom," 1927), serves as a precursor of the OBERIU Declaration, and offers an idiosyncratic but in some sense clearer articulation of this point. Kharms asserts that every object has four "working definitions" that reflect the object's relation to human beings in various ways. In addition, the object has a "fifth quintessential definition" ("piatoe sushchee znachenie") that relates only to the object itself: "The fifth meaning is determined by the very fact of the existence of the object. It exists outside the connection between the object and human beings and it serves the object itself. The fifth meaning is the free will of the object [*svobodnaia volia predmeta*].... The object possesses its quintessential meaning only outside of man... The fifth meaning of a cupboard is a cupboard. The fifth meaning of running is running."[26]

In the icon, this sense of the object's identity independent of human intervention is conveyed by what has been called "isometric perspective," meaning that the object imposes its own visual logic on its own portrayal. Each object may be allotted its own perspective, its own spatial orientation, because, as noted by the Byzantinist André Grabar, "the artist looks at the image as if he were himself in the represented object's place so as to draw it in its true dimensions."[27] A further sense of "primitive distortion" in the icon and OBERIU art stems from what is called "inverse perspective," which settles into a harmonious coexistence with isometric perspective in both Orthodox icons and the OBERIU analog. Inverse perspective posits a vanishing point in front of the painted surface, rather than behind it.[28] As the icon scholar John Baggley puts it, the use of inverse perspective means that "one is left feeling that the beholder is essential to the completion of the icon. The essence of the exercise has been to establish a communion between the event or persons represented in the icon and those who stand before it, to 'make present' to another person what is presented in the icon."[29] In OBERIU ideology, this inverse perspective, this movement toward the viewer and insistence on the beholder's participation becomes evident, for example, in the statement that Zabolotsky's poetry seems to be "prepared to meet the groping hand of the viewer" and creates figures "pushed right up to the eyes of the viewer."[30]

What are we to make, then, of the disjunction between the obvious avant-garde bravado of the OBERIU Declaration and the generally acknowledged "classicism" of Zabolotsky's later verse? If we look at Zabolotsky's whole career, what we see is that the key concepts articulated in the OBERIU Declaration of 1928 continue to serve his poetry in various ways. They are then voiced again in two short essays and a poem, all written in 1957, the year before his death: "Thought—Image—Music" ("Mysl'—obraz—muzyka"), "Why I Am Not a Pessimist" ("Pochemu ia ne pessimist"), and "Evening on the Oka River" ("Vecher na Oke"). In the closing passage of "Why I Am Not a Pessimist," Zabolotsky adds the notion of "the film of everydayness" ("plenka povsednevnosti") to his store of metaphors for impediments to the perception of greater reality, along with the "literary husk" and "decrepit literary gilding" from the OBERIU Declaration. In an echo of the declaration's admonition to look at the world "with naked eyes," he writes that he, as an artist, removes the film from his reader's eyes. He conveys an unflinching commitment to given reality, to the object, and "things and phenomena," as well as a joyful, down-to-earth relation to his own calling as a poet and revealer of truth: "The genuine artist removes the film of everydayness from things and phenomena [*s veshchei i iavlenii*], and says to his reader: 'What you are accustomed to seeing every day, what you skim over with an indifferent and accustomed gaze—is in actuality not commonplace, not mundane, but full of ineffable fascination, greater intrinsic meaning, and in this sense it is mysterious. Here, I will remove the film from your eyes [*Vot, ia snimaiu plenku s tvoikh glaz*]: Look upon the world, work together with us and rejoice that you are a human being!' This is why I am not a pessimist."[31] In the essay "Thought—Image—Music," Zabolotsky uses the notion of a mask as a barrier to perception, rather than the film of everydayness, but the basic sense is the same, and the notion of purity or virginity comes into play as well. "Being an artist," he writes, "a poet is obliged to remove the accustomed, commonplace masks from things and phenomena [*s veshchei i iavlenii*], and to demonstrate the virginity [*devstvennost'*] of the world and its significance, full of mysteries."[32]

Finally, the closing segment of Zabolotsky's poem "Evening on the Oka River" picks up the notion of everydayness and moves even further toward the concepts of revelation, transfiguration, and deification of the universe. On one level, the poem describes the poet's observation of the daily phenomenon of the sun setting beyond the river. But the fact that Zabolotsky returns to the single most metaphysically fraught word in the OBERIU Declaration, *predmet* (object), emphasizing it by means of enjambment, suggests that more is at stake here. Within the setting of the watery landscape his persona gains a clearer vision of the "objects" situated around him. He uses language reminiscent of descriptions of the Transfiguration of Christ to portray the event, as he states that "the whole world burns, transparent and spiritual."

И чем ясней становятся детали
Предметов, расположенных вокруг,
Тем необъятней делаются дали
Речных лугов, затонов и излук.
Горит весь мир, прозрачен и духовен,
Теперь-то он поистине хорош,

И ты, ликуя, множество диковин
В его живых чертах распознаешь.[33]

And the clearer become the details
of objects situated all around,
the more boundless become the distances,
flood plains, back-waters, and bends.
The whole world burns, transparent and spiritual;
now it is truly beautiful, and you, rejoicing,
come to discern a myriad wonders in its living features.

Through this transfiguration, the world becomes more rather than less real. As the persona turns to himself using the biblical and celebratory verb *likovat'* ("I ty, likuia . . ."), he acknowledges that he grasps this greater reality not because he possesses exceptional human powers of individual human genius or reason. He grasps it because he himself becomes a part of the transfigured universe.

Sedakova, for her part, rarely provides the kind of full-scale manifesto supplied by the OBERIU Declaration. Her literary approach must be garnered piecemeal from a wide selection of her writings, lectures, web postings, and interviews. But the accumulated statements create an approach to art, and to poetry in particular, that is closely related to the positions of the OBERIU and to the theology of the icon, something that has generally been glossed over or missed in other studies of the religious element in Sedakova's poetics.[34] Sedakova's goal is to use the word to change our ability to see the greater meaning of given reality, and ultimately, to assure our integration into this spiritually fraught reality. In the end, it is the same message of Logos, transfiguration, and deification; the message of the theology of the icon, but expressed in Sedakova's own language. Like Zabolotsky emphasizing the revelation of given reality, she writes: "The poetic gift [. . .] is not a talent for *expressing* the inexpressible, but for keeping what has been expressed untouched and unscathed, from being robbed: to carry it into the world, to allow it to be before our eyes (which is a miracle in itself), to be and not to end" (3:136).

As Mikhail Epstein puts it with reference to Sedakova's poem "The Wild Rose" ("Dikii shipovnik"), Sedakova's work is religious not in the sense that it expresses the Orthodox creed, "but in the intensity of the act of belief itself, whose every manifestation reveals the limit of oversignification and the miracle of transfiguration."[35]

In her relation to the concrete object, Sedakova does what the OBERIU could not or would not do: she addresses the question of the icon directly. In her essay "The Light of Life," published in English, she draws a distinction between concepts, which remain as abstractions in the realm of the mind, and icons or "images," as they are called in Russian, which foster direct experience. She writes, "One needs to let images speak 'from the first person,' so to say. [. . .] Any notion estranged from the concrete experience [. . .] has no real worth here" (4:690–91).[36] And further: "One can think of whatever he likes—but one can't contemplate whatever he likes: first he needs a thing to contemplate. He needs something to be present." That "something" is, of course, an icon, in either the traditional religious sense or in the broader sense of the object (*predmet*) as defined by the OBERIU. A similar line of reasoning causes Sedakova to prefer images over symbols because symbols are less immediate. As she puts it, the intellectual activity required to decipher symbols "destroys in the observer his immediate, face-to-face contact with the image. The symbolic language bars the fundamental language of the icon—the incarnation of God and the new task of human beings to become god [deified]" (4:690–91).

Perhaps echoing Kharms's assertion that the fifth, quintessential meaning is "the free will" of the object, Sedakova stakes a claim for "the eternal freedom of the most important things in the world (which extends even to their names)."[37] Thus she suggests both the primacy of the word, or "name" in her terminology, and the potential play with meaning suggested by the OBERIU's "collision of verbal meanings." When asked in an interview, "What is your poetic dominant?" she responds: "First and foremost it is the word, the word *per se*, the word as a name. [. . .] A poem, in my opinion, serves the word." Then she elaborates a process related to the collision of verbal meanings, noting that the important thing is "the way in which many words come together so that each individual word realizes the full range of its potential, its phonetic potential, its potential for ambivalence of meaning."[38] This "ambivalence of meaning" is surely one of the things that make Sedakova's poetry such a challenge, even as it makes the poems richer. Sedakova justifies the challenge in "The Art of Translation" ("Iskusstvo perevoda"; 2:16–27) when she criticizes poetic thought that is too easily conveyed and therefore fails both to transmit the genuine meaning of the word and to establish genuine contact between author and reader. As Slava Yastremski puts it, in Sedakova's view, "The poetic composition sets the words free, liberates them from a single meaning lying on the surface, and thus allows the reader to communicate with the true meaning of the poetic word."[39]

Sedakova's grandmother makes another appearance as a formative influence in this arena as well, here for her respectful relation to the word. Sedakova describes her grandmother's almost childlike exploration of language along with her precise attention to its purity, again conveyed by the root *chist-*. The grandmother evinces respect for the word as something to be seen, heard, touched, and cleansed, a respect very close to the OBERIU's relation to the word as object.

> Behind babushka's speech in every instance there was a kind of watchfulness [*prigliadyvanie*], a kind of active listening [*prislushivanie*], of touching and feeling [*nashchupyvanie*], the habit of thinking and getting to know things piece by piece—and the habit of remaining silent when there was nothing to say (while "literary" language does nothing but swell up in those places where there is nothing to say). These were not just words, but names: unique and singular as names [. . .] elicited from things with difficulty, but for all that reflecting enjoyment of them—just for the sake of playing with them, washing them, cleansing them [*chtoby s nimi igrat', umyt' ikh, ochistit'*], just like the dishes at the end of "Theodora's Woe."[40]

The sense of words as tangible objects, as something to be encountered by reaching out, touching, and feeling ("nashchupyvanie"), and the sense of words as something to be cleansed ("umyt' ikh, ochistit'") correspond to concepts and even etymological roots in the description of Zabolotsky's poetry in the OBERIU Declaration as "prepared to meet the groping hand of the viewer." The same applies when the declaration asks rhetorically, "To feel [*oshchushchat'*] the world with the gesture of a worker's hand, to cleanse [*ochishchat'*] the object of the trash of ancient, rotting cultures—is not this the real demand of our time?" In another passage, the OBERIU reflects a suspicion of "'literary' language" similar to that of Sedakova and, presumably, her grandmother, asserting that, "the concrete object, cleansed of its literary and everyday husk, becomes the property of art."[41]

For all that Chukovsky's "Theodora's Woe" is just a children's tale or *skazka*, Sedakova's reference is particularly apt because the tale centers on the notions of concreteness and cleansing that are so important to both Sedakova and the OBERIU. Like the words covered with decrepit literary gilding scorned in the OBERIU Declaration and the unnecessary, swollen literary words decried by Sedakova, Theodora's objects, in this case her household utensils and objects, are covered with "dirt" and out of control. And just as Sedakova's grandmother and the OBERIU see a chaste truth in art, which allows them to cleanse the word, Theodora sees that she needs to clean, love, and respect her objects. She goes after her utensils, promising a similar type of rebirth as she asserts that she will make them shine like the sun:

> "Ой вы, бедные сиротки мои,
> Утюги и сковородки мои!
> Вы подите-ка, немытые, домой,
> Я водою вас умою ключевой.

Я почищу вас песочком,
Окачу вас кипяточком,
И вы будете опять,
Словно солнышко, сиять . . ."

Долго, долго целовала
И ласкала их она,
Поливала, умывала,
Полоскала их она.
"Уж не буду, уж не буду
Я посуду обижать.
Буду, буду я посуду
И любить и уважать!"[42]

"Oh you, my poor little orphans,
my flatirons and frying pans!
Come home, my unwashed ones;
I will cleanse you with spring water,
I will scour you with sand,
I will rinse you with boiling water,
and you will again
shine just like the little sun . . ."

She kissed and caressed them
for a long, long time.
She poured water over them,
washed, rinsed them.
"I will not, will not insult
my plates, dishes, and utensils.
I will, I will
love and respect them!"

In addition to their commitment to objects as such, and metaphorical or literal principles of cleanliness and respect, Chukovsky joins Sedakova and Zabolotsky in an insistence on the openness of art, and the freedom of art to move beyond the bounds of everyday logic and dogma. According to Chukovsky, children are drawn to fairy tales precisely because of a need to test everyday logic, because of the combination of the familiar and plausible (dirt and poor housekeeping) and the unfamiliar and implausible (household objects escaping, then returning home). In addition, changes in the rhythm and rhyme scheme of Chukovsky's fairy tales keep the listener engaged with jolts and twists and turns. The ear does not always hear what it expects. Valentina Polukhina notes that Sedakova, likewise, focuses on "the development of an immediate, sensual perception of the world: improving one's sight, one's hearing, and the ability to view the world through the eyes, as Heidegger says, 'of the shepherds of being,'"[43] while the OBERIU places a similar emphasis on the use of multiple senses and unexpectedness. In all these cases, it is the word—or poetry, broadly defined to include emphasis on sight, sound, and touch—that, like the icon, establishes communion between the reader or listener—the communicant—and the greater realm of meaning.

And What of Modernism and Postmodernism?

Although, as noted at the beginning of this article, the timespan covered by Sedakova's career, along with her "disruptive" and difficult poetic method, might make it possible to assume that Sedakova functions as one of the disruptive voices of postmodernism, the poet herself provides a forceful and compelling counterargument.[44] In her essay "After Postmodernism" ("Posle postmodernizma"), she makes it clear that she considers the issues surrounding postmodernism to be not merely questions of literary approach, but questions of vision and moral stance, and hence not unrelated to the questions of "chasteness" and "purity" raised earlier. Moreover, she purposefully places the essay in the volume of her collected works entitled *Moralia,* rather than the volume entitled *Poetica,* where an essay of literary criticism or theory might logically occur. She writes: "Postmodernism is not merely a creative method (its creativity is itself extremely dubious), it is also a means of perception. [. . .] A postmodernist can read any composition as a postmodernist composition. Because of this, postmodernism slips away from any definition without any constraints. [. . . To read a text in terms of postmodernism] means to free oneself from the text, to cease to experience any uncomfortable personal feelings in relation to the text, to stop taking its premises and artistic ambitions seriously" (4:368).

Clearly, such a lack of seriousness speaks directly against Sedakova's literary and moral position. She gives postmodernism the final coup de grâce and leaves no room for a personal affiliation with it as follows: "postmodernism is consistent in one thing: in the author's relation to his own text and, in general, to the world he portrays. This relation generally does not allow for any fervor. [. . .] Postmodern alienation is absolutely unacceptable to us—and for good reason!" (4:369).

It is the sage of Russian postmodernism, Mikhail Epstein, and an American expert on contemporary Russian poetry, Stephanie Sandler, who come to the rescue here. The rescue does not involve casting the lasso of postmodernism still more widely, but rather creating and engaging a new term, "metarealism," and applying it to Sedakova's work. In his definition of metarealism, Epstein describes the same kind of thoroughgoing moral commitment to art and to life that we see in Sedakova and Zabolotsky, and also the interaction of the multiple hypostases of reality, from the everyday to the divine, that create apparent distortions in their works. He writes: "Perhaps metarealism is not just art, but also a world view. And a way of life. To be a metarealist means to experience oneself as a link in a chain of many realities, and as responsible for the integrity of that chain, consolidating it through word, thought, and action. The metarealist therefore does not belong to any one reality. Not because for him these realities are a game [. . .] but because he takes reality seriously in all its dimensions."[45]

In the introduction to the same volume, the scholar Thomas Epstein addresses the issue of fervor and of emotional connection, as opposed to the postmodern principle of alienation that evoked such a heated negative reaction from Sedakova above. He writes: "As [Mikhail] Epstein and others see it, the next stage [. . .] can be called 'the new sincerity,' which emerges on the other side of the parodic and the merely playful. Not a simple negation, this bracketing of the modernist and post-modernist projects creates the conditions for the emergence of a new, multi-dimensional discourse that promises a deeper form of communication."[46]

The concepts of "metarealism" and "new sincerity" go a long way toward a retroactive explanation of Zabolotsky's *Columns* collection, which caused a furor in the Soviet press. Critics assumed that the grotesquerie of the poems represented a purposeful political satire of Soviet life and parody of Soviet values. Yet the leading Blok scholar and insightful reader of Zabolotsky, Dmitry Maksimov, states flatly, "The concept of satire does not cover these poems." Another scholar attuned to the views of the OBERIU, Anatoly Aleksandrov, states that an assumption of satire "would miss the tragic nature of [the group's] worldview." And finally, defending himself against the attacks, Zabolotsky stated, "what I write is not parody; it is what I see."[47] Sedakova, likewise, writes what she "sees." And she sees with a vision grounded both in concrete reality and the startling "ambivalence of meaning" created by her insistence on the independence of the word, meaning created when words "do not represent a guaranteed, ready-made thing, but an event."[48]

All of this notwithstanding, it is clear that Zabolotsky and Sedakova will continue to be perceived in connection with modernism and postmodernism. The perceived affiliations are not altogether wrong in terms of the literary era and environment in which each functions, and the initial impressions created by the poet's works. Still, their works are perhaps best described by Epstein and Sandler's chosen term "metarealism." Even as Zabolotsky and Sedakova function as forward-looking iconoclasts and rule breakers, they look backward to the powerful tradition of the theology of the icon. In the end, it is this combination of metarealism, metaphysics, and theology that brings Zabolotsky and Sedakova together, and that makes Zabolotsky not so much a literary influence on Sedakova, but a lodestar, a vector, a constant point of reference for her work and life as a poet.[49]

Notes

I would like to thank Stephanie Sandler and Igor Loshchilov for their formative influence on this article.

1. Mikhail Epstein, Alexander Genis, and Slobodanka Vladiv-Glover, *Russian Postmodernism: New Perspectives on Post-Soviet Culture* (New York: Berghahn Books, 1999); Albena Lutzkanova-Vassileva, *The Testimonies of Russian and American Postmodern Poetry: Reference, Trauma, and History* (New York: Bloomsbury Academic, 2015). These titles imply that the authors consider Sedakova a postmodernist, although the discussions are more nuanced. See Ol'ga Sedakova, "Posle postmodernizma," 4:361–75.

2. Robin Milner-Gulland, "Left Art in Leningrad: The OBERIU Declaration," *Oxford Slavonic Papers*, n.s. 3 (1970): 65–75; Sarah Pratt, "The Profane Made Sacred: The Theology of the OBERIU Declaration," in *Laboratory of Dreams: The Russian Avant-Garde and Cultural Experiment*, ed. John E. Bowlt and Olga Matich (Stanford, CA: Stanford University Press, 1996), 174–89; Pratt, "Avant-Garde Poets and Imagined Icons," in *Alter Icons: The Russian Icon and Modernity*, ed. Douglas Greenfield and Jefferson J. A. Gatrall (University Park: Pennsylvania State University Press, 2010), 173–89; Pratt, *Nikolai Zabolotsky: Enigma and Cultural Paradigm* (Evanston, IL: Northwestern University Press, 2000); Graham Roberts, *The Last Soviet Avant-Garde: OBERIU—Fact, Fiction, Metafiction* (Cambridge: Cambridge University Press, 2006); Igor' Loshchilov, *Fenomen Nikolaia Zabolotskogo* (Helsinki: Institute for Russian and East European Studies, 1997); Nikita Zabolotskii, *Zhizn' N. A. Zabolotskogo* (Moscow: Soglasie, 1998), and *The Life of Zabolotsky*, ed. and trans. R. R. Milner-Gulland (Cardiff: University of Wales Press, 1994); Darra Goldstein, *Nikolai Zabolotsky: Play for Mortal Stakes* (Cambridge: Cambridge University Press, 1993).

3. O. A. Sedakova, *Tserkovnoslaviano-russkie paronimy: Materialy k slovariu* (Moscow: Greko-latinskii kabinet Iu. A. Shichalina, 2005).

4. See Sedakova's reading of "Zolotaia truba (ritm Zabolotskogo)," http://www.pravmir.ru/olga-sedakova-poeticheskij-vecher-video/, accessed March 17, 2018. Ol'ga Sedakova, "O Zabolotskom," 3:437–42; "Zametki i vospominaniia o raznykh stikhotvoreniiakh, a takzhe 'Pokhvala poezii,'" 3:13–95; and Olga Sedakova, *In Praise of Poetry*, trans. and ed. Caroline Clark, Ksenia Golubovich, and Stephanie Sandler (Rochester, NY: Open Letter Books, 2014); Mikhail Kopeliovich, "Iavlenie Sedakovoi," *Znamia* 8 (1996): 205; Mikhail Perepelkin, "Tvorchestvo Ol'gi Sedakovoi v kontekste russkoi poeticheskoi kul'tury" (dissertation, Samara State University, 2000), especially section 2.3: "Real'nost' lichnogo bessmertiia: Traditsii N. Zabolotskogo i ikh pereosmyslenie v khudozhestvennoi systeme O. Sedakovoi ('Zolotaia truba')." For the abstract, see http://www.dissercat

.com/content/tvorchestvo-olgi-sedakovoi-v-kontekste-russkoi-poeticheskoi-kultury-smert-i-bessmertie-v-par#ixzz3Aavd54Ac, accessed March 15, 2018.

5. Letter from Zabolotsky to Mikhail Kas'ianov, November 7, 1921, in *Izbrannye proizvedeniia v 2 tt*, by N. A. Zabolotskii (Moscow: Khudozhestvennaia literatura, 1972), 2:208, 231, 208. See also Igor' Loshchilov, "Mikhail Ivanovich Kas'ianov i ego arkhiv" and "Materialy o Nikolae Zabolotskom v domashnem arkhive ego druga Mikhaila Kas'ianova," unpublished manuscripts; "Nikolai Zabolotskii i Urzhum" and "Nikolai Zabolotskii na Dal'nem Vostoke," in *Zabolotskie chteniia*, ed. Igor' Loshchilov (Kirov: Gertsenka, 2013); R. A. Bushkov, *Viatskie versty Nikolaia Zabolotskogo* (Kirov: Gertsenka, 2013).

6. Nikolai Chukovskii, "Vstrechi s Zabolotskim," in *Vospominaniia o Zabolotskom*, ed. E. V. Zabolotskaia and A. V. Makedonov (Moscow: Sovetskii pisatel', 1977), 227.

7. Goldstein, *Nikolai Zabolotsky*, 17. On the Institute of the History of the Arts, see L. Ia. Ginzburg, "Vspominaia Institut istorii iskusstv," *Tynianovskii sbornik: Chetvertye Tynianovskie chteniia* (Riga: Zinatne, 1990), 278–90.

8. See Sedakova's website for a basic biography and other information: http://www.olgasedakova.com/about_the_author, accessed March 17, 2018. Olga Sedakova, "Statement," in *Third Wave: The New Russian Poetry*, ed. Kent Johnson and Stephen M. Ashby (Ann Arbor: University of Michigan Press, 1992), 129–31; Sedakova, "A Dialogue on Poetry," in *Poems and Elegies* (Lewisburg, PA: Bucknell University Press, 2003), 11–20; Slava I. Yastremski, "A Revealed Miracle: An Introduction to Olga Sedakova's Life and Work," in Sedakova, *Poems and Elegies*, 10–31; Valentina Polukhina, "Ol'ga Sedakova," in *Russian Women Writers*, ed. Christine D. Tomei (New York: Garland, 1999), 2:1445–50; Stephanie Sandler, "Introduction: Poetry at Heaven's Edge," *Slavic and East European Journal* 51, no. 4 (2007): 668–74; Sandler, "Thinking Self in the Poetry of Olga Sedakova," in *Gender and Russian Literature: New Perspectives*, ed. Rosalind Marsh (Cambridge: Cambridge University Press, 1996), 302–26.

9. Yastremski, "A Revealed Miracle," 25; Ol'ga Sedakova, "Ob avtore," http://www.olgasedakova.com/about_the_author, accessed March 17, 2018.

10. Yastremski, "A Revealed Miracle," 25.

11. Ol'ga Sedakova, "'Ne khochu uspekha i ne boius' provala': Besedu vela Anna Gal'perina, 17 fevralia 2013," http://www.pravmir.ru/olga-sedakova-ne-xochu-uspexa-i-ne-boyus-provala/, accessed March 15, 2018.

12. Sedakova, "A Dialogue on Poetry," 15–16.

13. Valentina Polukhina, "A Rare Independence: An Interview with Olga Sedakova," in *Brodsky through the Eyes of His Contemporaries*, ed. Valentina Polukhina (New York: St. Martin's Press, 1992), 239–40.

14. Ibid.

15. N. Zabolotskii, *Polnoe sobranie stikhotvorenii i poem* (St. Petersburg: Gumanitarnoe agentstvo "Akademicheskii proekt," 2002), 251.

16. Sedakova, "Pokhvala poezii," 326.

17. Milner-Gulland, "Left Art in Leningrad," 70.

18. N. Stepanov, "Iz vospominanii o N. Zabolotskom," in Zabolotskaia, *Vospominaniia o Zabolotskom*, 100; V. Kaverin, "Schast'e talanta," in Zabolotskaia, *Vospominaniia o Zabolotskom*, 108–9.

19. Zabolotskii, *Izbrannye*, 2:208, 210, 213, 220.

20. Nikita Zabolotsky, *The Life of Zabolotsky*, 138–39, 169.

21. Daniil Kharms, *Polet v nebesa: Stikhi, proza, dramy, pis'ma* (Leningrad: Sovetskii pisatel', 1988), 383–84.

22. Milner-Gulland, "Left Art in Leningrad," 70–71.

23. Ibid., 71.

24. St. John of Damascus, *On the Divine Images* (Crestwood, NY: St. Vladimir's Seminary Press, 1980), 23.

25. Leonid Ouspensky, *Theology of the Icon* (Crestwood, NY: St. Vladimir's Seminary Press, 1992), 272.

26. Daniil Kharms, "Predmety i figury, otkrytye Daniilom Ivanovichem Kharmsom," cited in Ilya Levin, "The Fifth Meaning of the Motor Car: Malevich and the OBERIUty," *Soviet Union/Union Sovietique* 5, no. 2 (1978): 299. Also http://xapmc.gorodok.net/prose/1261/default.htm, accessed March 15, 2018.

27. André Grabar, cited in Egon Sendler, *The Icon: Image of the Invisible; Elements of Theology, Aesthetics, and Technique* (Redondo Beach, CA: Oakwood Publications, 1988), 148; D. S. Likhachev, *Poetika drevnerusskoi literatury* (Moscow: Nauka, 1979), 361–62; V. D. Likhacheva, "Svoeobrazie kompozitsii drevnerusskikh ikon," in *Khudozhestvennoe nasledie drevnei Rusi i sovremennost'*, by V. D. Likhacheva and D. S. Likhachev (Leningrad: Nauka, 1971), 25.

28. Pavel Florenskii, "Obratnaia perspektiva," in *Sobranie sochinenii*, ed. N. A. Struve (Paris: YMCA Press, 1985); Likhacheva, "Svoeobrazie kompozitsii drevnerusskikh ikon"; Erwin Panofsky, *Perspective as Symbolic Form* (New York: Zone Books, 1991).

29. John Baggley, *The Doors of Perception: Icons and Their Spiritual Significance* (Crestwood, NY: St. Vladimir's Seminary Press, 1988), 80–81; Ouspensky, *Theology of the Icon*, 79, 166.

30. Milner-Gulland, "Left Art in Leningrad," 71.

31. Zabolotskii, *Izbrannye*, 2:287–88.

32. Ibid., 2:286–87.

33. Ibid., 1:333.

34. Benjamin Paloff, "The God Function in Joseph Brodsky and Olga Sedakova," *Slavic and East European Journal* 51, no. 4 (2007): 716–36; Ona Renner-Fahey, "Mythologies of Poetic Creation in Twentieth-Century Russian Verse (Osip Mandelstam, Anna Akhmatova, Joseph Brodsky, Olga Sedakova)" (PhD diss., Ohio State University, 2004); Mikhail Epshtein, *Vera i obraz: Religioznoe bessoznatel'noe v russkoi kul'ture 20-go veka* (Tenafly, NJ: Ermitazh, 1994), 26–32. For a discussion of the connections between Sedakova's poetics and the icon, see also Martha Kelly's essay in this volume.

35. Epstein, "On Olga Sedakova and Lev Rubinstein," in Epstein et al., *Russian Postmodernism*, 114.

36. See Renner-Fahey, *Mythologies*; Stephanie Sandler, "Mirrors and Metarealists: The Poetry of Ol'ga Sedakova and Ivan Zhdanov," *Slavonica* 12, no. 1 (2006): 4, 6, and 13.

37. Sedakova, "Statement," in Johnson and Ashby, *Third Wave*, 130.

38. Polukhina, "A Rare Independence," 240.

39. Yastremski, "A Revealed Miracle," 26.

40. Sedakova, "Pokhvala poezii," 322.

41. Milner-Gulland, "Left Art in Leningrad," 70.

42. Kornei Chukovskii, "Fedorino gore," http://www.planetaskazok.ru/kchukovsky sth/fedorinogoresth?start=2, accessed March 15, 2018. English translation mine.

43. Polukhina, "Olga Sedakova," in *Russian Women Writers*, 2:1449.

44. See Epstein et al., *Russian Postmodernism*; and Lutzkanova-Vassilieva, *Testimonies*.

45. Mikhail Epstein, "What Is Metarealism? Facts and Hypotheses," in Epstein et al., *Russian Postmodernism*, 123.

46. Thomas Epstein, Introduction to *Russian Postmodernism* by Mikhail Epstein et al., xi. See also Mikhail Epshtein, *Vera i obraz*, 26–32.

47. D. Maksimov, "Nikolai Zabolotskii (Ob odnoi davnei vstreche)," in Zabolotskaia, *Vospominaniia o Zabolotskom*, 131; Aleksandrov, "'V shirokikh shliapakh, dlinnykh pidzhakakh . . . ,': Poety OBERIU," in *Den' Poezii: Leningrad* (Leningrad: Sovetskii pisatel', 1988), 231; Antokol'skii, "Skol'ko zim i let," in E. V. Zabolotskaia and A. V. Makedonov, eds., *Vospominaniia o Zabolotskom* (Moscow: Sovetskii pisatel', 1977), 138.

48. Polukhina, "A Rare Independence," 240.

49. Sergei Averintsev, "'Uzhe nebo, a ne ozero': Risk i vyzov metafizicheskoi poezii," in Ol'ga Sedakova, *Dvukhtomnoe sobranie sochinenii*, vol. 1, *Stikhi* (Moscow: En Ef Kiu/Tu Print, 2001), 5–13; also http://www.vavilon.ru/texts/averintsev1.html, accessed March 15, 2018.

The Topography of the Other World in Olga Sedakova's Poetics

KETEVAN MEGRELISHVILI

> But there are flashes of this new heaven and new earth, this world where death is defeated; it is not, as we know, borne away whole into the "other world." The possibility of encountering these flashes even here is exactly what is meant by the "good news."
>
> —Olga Sedakova, "Freedom as an Eschatological Reality"

The *other world*—which refers to the realm of the afterworld as well as to the divine Beginning—is by its nature a utopia.[1] It exists, most likely, beyond spatial and temporal concepts. Is it wise then to look for topography in its traditional sense as a description of a location in the metarealist cosmos of Sedakova's poetry?[2] Particularly as the poet herself dispassionately sums up the issue in one of her later poems: "Father Alexander, no one *here* / knows about what's there" ("Otche Aleksandr, nikto ne znaet / *zdes'* o tom, chto tam"; 1:374).[3] But in this posthumous address to Father Alexander Men, human nescience is focused metonymically in the spatial adverb *here*. Yet, it is also the italicized *here* that emphasizes *ex negativo* the existence of the other place.[4]

Nevertheless, it is precisely the structure of Sedakova's poetics that intensifies the theme of the other world. Poetry is a departure from the self-sufficient "I" toward contemplation not only of the outside world, but the invisible one as well; this makes knowledge of the eternally present *other* possible, and expands the boundaries of the visible tangible world.[5] The other world is a distinct ontological entity in Sedakova's artistic universe, and awareness of that other world animates the poet's work. This brings us to our main question: how does the other world manifest itself in the fabric of the verse?[6] How does poetic language deal with what is not empirically present? To answer that, we must describe the relationship between Sedakova's poetic language and the realia of its surroundings. To start, we will look at how the world is reflected in Sedakova's poetry, and how the poet orients herself in it. Since the theme of the place "where things are thought up" ("gde zadumany veshchi," in "Neuzheli, Mariia"; 1:27) permeates the poet's work, this essay will look at Sedakova's autobiographical prose in addition to her poetry, tracing motifs and images that depict the search for, approach toward, and exploration of the other world. Sedakova's philosophical and philological essays will help us conceptualize the context of her poetic work.

Why Topography?

Topography is not just the description of a place, but also the conscious human activity of studying spatial data and overcoming existential challenges. In a sense, topography means orienting oneself in the world; thus, the absurdly catastrophic wanderings of the failed draftsman K. in Franz Kafka's eternally snowy world are a result of his inability to (spiritually) inhabit the space he is exploring.[7] The draftsman K. symbolizes the alienation and homelessness of the modern human in the world surrounding him. Sedakova calls this "a state of emptiness" and considers it "the illness of our time," and she goes on to describe it in an even more radical manner: "The emptiness we are talking about is not so much an empty space, filled with nothing: it is the complete absence of space for life. 'Look, your house is left to you desolate.' In such a house, there is nothing to live by, nothing in which to live: nothing to give oneself to."[8] Sedakova cultivates the image, rare in twentieth-century Russian poetry, of a poet-theologian, combining religious and secular questions in her work.[9] In so doing, she raises ethical expectations for poets: it is their task to oppose this emptiness.

In her essay "In Praise of Poetry" ("Zametki i vospominaniia o raznykh stikhotvoreniiakh, a takzhe Pokhvala Poezii," 1982), which details her literary origins, Sedakova clearly prioritizes the elemental force of space over that of time in the creative process: "I don't usually remember the moment in time when I composed a particular poem, often not even the year, but I do remember the places very clearly. Because each poem is to some extent a portrait of a place" (3:47).

She immediately clarifies: "The portrait is barely discernible, remaining far beyond the threshold of the immediate content of the poem" (3:47). It follows that one should not bother searching for concrete realia on the surface of the poetic work. The merging of inside and outside, which inspired the Romantic poets, is a mere starting point, and their unity becomes ever more abstract: the portrait of a place is indistinguishable, not just because "there is nothing more boring in any art form than landscape," but also because the landscape endures on the retina and in one's mind, but not at all on the nib of the quill. A great example of that is the "Azarovka" cycle (1976–78), subtitled "a landscape suite" ("siuita peizazhei"). Here, Sedakova creates an eclectic mix of meditations on the theme of various toponymic phenomena and traditional images and symbols. The choice of meter contributes to the unified nature of the cycle.[10] The poems are written in amphibrachs,[11] a meter that is sometimes seen as more conducive to a neutral tone than to outbursts of passion.[12] The restrained nature of the amphibrachs helps the poet follow one of her poetic maxims—to make room for the thing or event in the poem without the figure of the lyric subject overshadowing them. Later, in "Elegy for Autumn Water" ("Elegiia osennei vody"), Sedakova succinctly formulates this idea:

Всякую вещь можно открыть, как дверь.
В занебесный, в подземный ход потайная дверца
есть в них. (1:379)

All things open like a door.
Each thing has
a secret doorway to the passage beyond heaven, underground.

Natural phenomena become overlaid with different cultural layers, and the *genii loci* and figures from old epic folk tales (byliny) come to life. The reader experiences the coexistence of different cultural periods as well as abstract concepts of time within the same landscape. Past and future, and time's cyclical character, are all coded into the very system of nature, as in this passage from "Forest Road" ("Lesnaia doroga"):

И столько пропавшей и тайной любви
замешено здесь на подпочвенной влаге,
что это, как кровь, отзовется в крови,
дорогу покажет и крикнет в овраге. (1:124)

And there's so much love lost, and so much of it secret,
submerged in the damp of the subsoil here
that it, too, like blood, will call out in the blood,
will show us the way, will cry out in the gully.

The "Azarovka" poems also express the harmonious relationships of natural phenomena on the phonetic level by means of frequent anagrammatic and alliterative connections: "There the poison berry looks out from the bush" ("Tam *ia*goda *ia*da gl*ia*dit iz kusta").

The repetition of sound clusters like "ikh," "ykh," and "okh," which resemble interjections, contributes to the sound orchestration of the emotional portrait of the "willows" ("ivy"), the "guardian of the cloudy day" ("*khr*anitel'nits[a] *khm*urogo dnia"). In the third sketch, "In the Bushes" ("V kustakh"), one can hear in the rustling of leaves the wistful words of a soul that used to live there. "Slukh" ("hearing") is anagrammatically hidden in "lesa sukhogo" ("the dry forest"), repeating the semantic link of these words: the monologue of the soul is provoked by the rustling leaves. The sound texture of the verse reveals the divine interconnectedness of phenomena hidden in nature. The poetic material displays the harmonious secret connections in the night sky like a sky chart:

> Ныряя в глубокую ткань и потом
> сверкая над ней острием безупречным—
> над черным шитьем, говорящим о том,
> что нет никого, кто звездой не отмечен. (1:124)

> Diving deep into the fabric and then
> glistening above it in infinite sharpness—
> above the black stitches that gather to tell
> how there's not one person unmarked by a star.

Nature responds by speaking and revealing its secrets. Regardless of the twentieth-century notion that nature is "hieroglyphic" and humanity has lost the ability to read and understand it, Sedakova reintroduces the motif of "the book of nature," without reducing its inherent force.[13] She does not deny the mysterious and hermetic character of nature, but realizes it in verse, simultaneously stressing its incredible mystical power and embedded divine energy. Modern people are alienated from nature and unable (or no longer able) to uncover the language encoded in natural phenomena; however, it is nature that for Sedakova becomes the place of contemplation in search of the other.

The starting point of the sketches in the "Azarovka" cycle is the intimate moment when the poet addresses a natural phenomenon—a spring bursting out of the ground. Sedakova then turns these phenomena or locations into symbols. The poet captures the transformation of real spatial phenomena as they expand into metaphysics and at the same time acquire quite personal associations:

> I cannot put down all there is to say about surroundings and places. Besides geographical features, there are things such as forest, steppe, hill, embankment, attic, corridor—and many other modes of thought. I once dreamed of crystal spears and they were called mountains (the Urals at that), I dreamed of a corridor that was a

> stretch of steppe hills with rivers disappearing underground and reappearing. Apart from describing physical objects, the names for various types of landscape signify something else as well: certain constant images. As if they were all various folds lying within the same depth, the last, final depth. A sense of the end can, after all, just as easily latch onto the image of a steppe, forest, sea, or corridor. ("Pokhvala poezii"; 3:51)

In addition to the polyphony of the landscape in "Azarovka," another characteristic feature of the topoi and spaces of the cycle bears mention: they open up and then retreat, and they become transparent in relation to time. Different epochs in Russian and European culture are revealed and merge in the landscape; one can see through them into the past, and simultaneously see the future encoded in them. The past is in conversation with the future through the present tense of the poem in "The Prophetic Bird" ("Veshchaia ptitsa"), "The Forest Road" ("Lesnaia doroga"), and "The Ravine" ("Ovrag"); as a result, the landscape becomes dynamic and animate. The device of abstracting a particular point in time is what Dmitry Bavilsky describes as the creation of an "absence of time."[14] Specific geographic realia appear to be outside of time even as they acquire a transparency that is one of the most valuable properties of water. Poetic speech should aim to resemble this divine element in its transparency.[15] The quick movement through space induces a state similar to a mystical immersion. One of the most ordinary ways of contracting space is traveling.

A Journey to the Other World

Sedakova explores the theme of travel often in poetry as well as prose, including the poetic cycles of journeys, *Chinese Journey* (*Kitaiskoe puteshestvie*) and "Journey of the Magi" ("Puteshestvie volkhvov"). The paradigm of discovery and exploration of something new,[16] and the experience of crossing geographic and interior borders, feature prominently in her work. Journeys and wanderings are inherently transitive acts in Sedakova's poetics. Movement through space is one of the ways of approaching the other. Occasionally that can be a "journey to the sky without leaving the ground."[17] A journey is also what Sedakova calls the passage to the other state, that is, the afterlife as described in her poetry, as in this poem, "Journey" ("Puteshestvie," 1980–82):

> Путешествие
>
> Когда кончится это несчастье
> или счастье это отвернется,
> отойдет, как высокие волны,

я пойду по знакомой дороге
наконец-то, куда мне велели.

Буду тогда слушать, что услышу,
Говорить, чтобы мне говорили:

—Вот, я ждал тебя—и дождался.
Знал всегда—и теперь узнаю.
Разве я что забуду?—(1:206)

Journey

When at last this unhappiness ends
or this happiness turns away
and leaves me like the tall waves,

I'll finally go on down that road
where they told me to go.

And I'll listen then to what I hear,
and I'll speak just so they say to me,

"I've been waiting for you—and you're finally here.
I've known you always—and I know you now.
You didn't think I'd forget?"—

The speaker here does not specify the journey's route; it is more important that going "where they told me to go" ("kuda veleli") brings a great, long-awaited joy comparable to *unio mystica*, an encounter-union with the Beginning. The simplicity of this dispassionate manner of speaking, similar in style to liturgical poetry with its lexical parallelisms, liberates words from their readymade, everyday meanings. On the sensory level, the state described in the poem acquires an initial immediacy, which can be felt in the conscious refusal to use rhyme and the maximal simplification of the poetic form.[18] "Journey" stages an intimate meeting, a reunification; the other world is linked to eternal memory, but that memory is one-sided: the inhabitants of such a world remember us eternally. One can find a way into the other world through certain exercises and concerted effort to remember what is essential, which lies beyond the mundane everyday consciousness.

Sedakova often imagines that situation in her work.[19] Lines in her early poems resemble the questions of prayer: "Whom have you charged to watch over me here? / Would you care to remind me, father?" ("Komu menia zdes' poruchili? /

Pozvolish' li vspomnit', otets?"; the poem begins, "Gde teni nad mol'iu dezhuriat"; 1:33). There are also these lines from "Surely, Maria" ("Neuzheli, Mariia"):

Если это не сад—
разреши мне назад,
в тишину, где задуманы вещи. (1:27)

If it isn't the garden—
then let me back in
to the silence where things are thought up.

Sometimes a voice from outside asks or orders: "Don't forget me, Olga, / and I will forget no one" ("Ty ne zabud' menia, Ol'ga, / a ia nikogo ne zabudu"; "Detstvo"; 1:183). Human nescience is countered by the eternal memory of God, as in these lines from "Knights Ride to the Tournament" ("Rytsari edut na turnir"):

Ты помнишь эту розу,
глядящую на нас?—
мы прячем от нее глаза,
она не сводит глаз. (1:152)

Do you remember that rose
that gazed upon us then?—
No matter how we hid our eyes
it does not look away.

The lyric subjects try to overcome oblivion and enter the prelinguistic sphere of silence where "things are thought up" ("zadumany veshchi"; 1:27). The imaginary journeys into the prelinguistic sphere only partially fit into the tradition of poetic journeys in search of forgotten words. Here, in the encounter with the other, language loses its mimetic properties.[20]

Как из глубокого колодца
или со звезды далекой
смотрит бабушка из каждой вещи:

—Ничего, ничего мы не знаем.
Что видели, сказать не можем. (1:211)

From a deep well
as from a distant star,
my grandmother looks out from each thing:

"Nothing, we know nothing.
And what we've seen, we cannot say."

Sedakova's distinctive prosody creates a feeling of simplicity and trust in language through these seemingly artless and clear lines. This initial impression then turns into a sense of illusory intelligibility, which arises from two different tendencies in the poem. By using the lexically, syntactically, and stylistically simple phrasing that makes up, for example, the entire cycle *Old Songs* (*Starye pesni*, 1980–81), Sedakova creates a space for empathy. At the same time, her minimal use of description opens a space of semantic freedom. The departure from unambiguity makes the reader feel disoriented, which is typical for a first foray into an unknown space of meaning. This is how the harmony of Sedakova's poetry presents itself: the construction of the poem corresponds to the nature of the object described. By touching on themes and spheres—in our case, the theme of the other world—that are not susceptible to traditional verbal exploration, Sedakova deliberately creates a moment of unspokenness (*nedoskazannost'*).[21] An unmaterialized but significant part of the unspoken utterance remains not only in the consciousness of the poet, but also in the matter of the verse, in its illusory intelligibility.[22] In Sedakova's poetic dictionary, unspokenness as an element of the unfinished, open verse form becomes one of the highest poetic qualities of a work. In her essay "Conversation about Freedom" ("Razgovor o svobode") the poet speaks with admiration of "Pushkin's strange ability to leave things unfinished—sometimes leaving a blank space where he has not yet found the right word" (4:52).

The invitation to follow language to a place endlessly new and unknown, the dynamics of the movement toward the other—these are some of Sedakova's favorite devices. She uses them to heighten the poetic tension, which does not disperse within the immediate space of the poem. It remains there until the very end, as if hovering in the air above the words:

Холод мира
кто-нибудь согреет.

мертвое сердце
кто-нибудь поднимет.

Этих чудищ
кто-нибудь возьмет за руку,
как ошалевшего ребенка:

—Пойдем, я покажу тебе такое,
чего ты никогда не видел! (1:218)

Someone will warm
the cold of the world.

Someone will raise up
the dead heart.

Someone will take these beasts
by the hand,
like an unruly child:

"Let's go, I'll show you something
the likes of which you've never seen!"

This is the final note not only for this poem, but for the entire cycle *Old Songs*. The tension of unresolved anticipation can be felt in Sedakova's use of indefinite pronouns in parallel constructions. The triple reference to "someone" counters the speaker's certainty in what to show the interlocutor. The depersonalized lyric subjects of the poem further increase its growing tension. The role of the reader also evades definition: it is impossible to determine with certainty if the reader is the intended recipient, or if the reader is but a witness to the poet's dialogue with another voice. It often seems like the poet merely creates the environment for speech, making room for it to happen. In spite of our inability to determine the speaker, the style of speech is clear: it is an unaffected voice devoid of emotional coloring. The speaker's certainty in the truthfulness of the utterance coexists with the evasiveness of the words uttered.

It is hard not to agree with Bavilsky, who finds parallels between Sedakova's expressions, such as "ved'my-vedun'i" (witches-sorceresses), and the following lines from Heidegger's essay "The Country Path" ("Proselok"/"Der Feldweg" 1949), particularly as it was translated into Russian: "The joy of knowing is a gate to the eternal. Its door turns on hinges that were once forged from the riddles of existence by a blacksmith initiated into arcane knowledge." And so Sedakova, whose poetic language possesses "a magical demiurgical power," to quote Bavilsky, "knows and guides" ("vedaet-vedet").[23]

The Heart—the Center of Being

The inexpressibility, unspokenness, and ambiguity, as well as the simultaneous certainty that the *other* exists, lead to the exact tension that characterizes Sedakova's poetry. In spite of all its indeterminacy, or ineffability, the thought of the other world is only possible here, in earthly life. According to Sedakova, earthly life makes a person unable to fully participate in the whole, which is where the border between subject and object can be felt. Poetic language is given the task of mediating between different worlds, and the task of poetry is to be conscious of the eternal presence of the other. Nevertheless, Sedakova, a master of paradox, limits language's sphere of influence: in the place "where things are thought up" ("gde zadumany veshchi"), there is silence.[24] Poetry is allotted a liminal space. For example, in the poem "Coda" ("Koda," 1979–80), one can catch a glimpse of the other through one tell-tale turn of phrase: lines high as a doorstep "lead out from an illuminated porch / in some boundless polar region" ("vyvodit s osveshchennogo kryl'tsa / v kakom-to zapoliar'e bez kontsa"; 1:292). At the same time, the sound of those lines loses its meaning, turns out to be accidental.

Despite the rhetorical aporia, Sedakova, a poet of synthesis and cohesion, does not counterpose "there" and "here," but creates moments of contact between different worlds. Their starting point is the yearning for complete unity with the Beginning, a feeling that is an intrinsic part of human nature. The subject of the poem "Alatyr'" speaks passionately of a desire to leave this world:

—Когда мне душа, как случайный прохожий,
кивнет и уходит под ливнем—смотри:
прекрасна земля Твоя, Господи Боже,
но лучше я выйду и буду внутри (1:134)

"When my soul nods to me like some chance passerby
and walks off in the rain—hear me out:
Your earth, oh, my Lord God, is splendid, it's true,
but I'd better come out and be there inside"

There is a paradoxical movement of ascent and descent not across a border, but into the very depth of something. This unexpected, unusual sequence of movements echoes Sedakova's idea that true life is to be found beyond the borders of human existence.[25] Life after death, as the poet sees it, is another, more authentic side of life. The other world surrounds us, and it is only possible to experience the other life within ourselves, with the heart as the epicenter of that experience.

The semantic image of the heart expands in Sedakova's work: in addition to the capacity for feeling, the heart acquires spatial properties. In metaphysical terms, it becomes the domain of reason and truthful speaking. In the poem "Strange Journey" ("Strannoe puteshestvie"), a train journey moves inward, into the depths of the soul: "I will travel on lost in thought in auricular emptiness, / I'll travel and travel and weep for my unending death" ("Budu ia ekhat' i dumat' v svoei pustote predserdechnoi, / ekhat', i ekhat', i plakat' o smerti moei beskonechnoi"; 1:77). Years later, in *Old Songs*, the "auricular emptiness" ("predserdechnaia pustota") gives way to the heart as the place of wholeness where the separate realms can merge. The heart is mapped onto the other world and comes to define it. It is precisely the specific properties of the heart (it is akin to a light or a gift) that are sought "there":

Плакал Адам, но его не простили.
И не позволили вернуться
туда, где мы только и живы:

—Хочешь своего, свое и получишь.
И что тебе делать такому
там, где сердце хочет, как Бог великий:
там, где сердце—сиянье и даренье. (1:217)

Adam wept, but he wasn't forgiven.
And he wasn't allowed to return
to the only place where we're alive:

"You want what's yours, you'll get it.
And what do you plan to do in that place,
there, where the heart wants as God is great:
there, where the heart is radiance and offering."

Another paradox emerges in this parable: we are alive in a place where we do not yet live, a place where true life comes into being. The road to this lost paradise amounts to a spiritual ascent, a rebirth. In addition to endowing the heart with spatial properties, Sedakova expands its semantic image by making it the acting subject in an unspecified metaphysical space, as in this poem from *Chinese Journey*:

По белому пути, по холодному звездному облаку,
говорят, они ушли и мы уйдем когда-то:
с камня на камень перебредая воду,

с планеты на планету перебредая разлуку,
как поющий голос с ноты на ноту.
Там все, говорят, и встретятся, убеленные млечной дорогой.

Сколько раз—покаюсь—к запрещенному порогу
подходило сердце, сколько стучало,
обещая неведомо кому:
Никто меня не ищет, никто не огорчится,
не попросит: останься со мною! . . .
О, не от горя земного так чудно за дверью земною.
А потому, что не хочется, не хочется своего согрешенья,
потому что пора идти
просить за всё прощенья,
ведь никто не проживет
без этого хлеба сиянья.
Пора идти туда,
где всё из сострàданья. (1:341)

By the white way, by the cold, starry cloud
they've gone, it's said, and we'll leave, too, someday:
making our way stone by stone through water,
making our way planet by planet through separation,
as a voice note by note.
There, it's said, everyone meets, turned white by the milky way.

So many times—I'll confess—my heart's approached
the forbidden threshold, knocked so many times,
assuring who knows whom:
No one looks for me, no one gets upset
or pleads: "Stay with me! . . ."
Oh, the wonder behind earth's door is not from earth's grief.
It's because we don't want, don't want our sins,
because it's time to go
ask everyone's forgiveness,
after all, no one will survive
without this bread of radiance.
It's time to go
where everything's made of compassion.

In this sketch from *Chinese Journey*, the speaker imagines wandering along the border with the other world, picturing this journey through the Milky Way with great restraint, measuring and diminishing the distances in space with each step, as the white road passes through the starry clouds. At the same time, while stepping across entire planets, the reader overcomes not real distances, but an emotional state of separation. The real landscape is replaced by an inner landscape. The white road connects to the Milky Way in the image of the "whitened" ("ubelennye") travelers, who meet each other in the promised world. There is, however, a barely noticeable crack in this picture of blessed wanderings between worlds: twice the poet removes herself from evaluating what is described, pointing the reader to the unspecified source of this information ("govoriat", "it's said"), thus casting doubt on its truthfulness. A tension is at work here as well—in the presence of concrete images, on the one hand, and openness, unspokenness, on the other. The detailed description built on traditional images in the first stanza diminishes: its plausible scenario coexists with the description of the crossing between worlds based on personal experience in the second stanza.

The confession of the poetic subject is in contrast with the anonymous "it's said," and it reveals a personal, intimate experience to the reader. The heartbeat artfully suggests the metaphor of a knock on the door (a door that opens into the other world). The introductory odic "O" colors the final lines with an entirely new intonation. In spite of the heart's address "to the one who is unknown" ("nevedomo komu"), the portrait of the other world comes together into sharp focus: it is a landscape that consists of abstract sensory experiences and states. Universal concepts from theological dictionaries are spoken by the lyric subject.

Based on these examples, we can distinguish the following aspects of poetic re-creation: sensory perception and concepts are transformed into the building blocks of poetic landscapes; at the same time, mental states acquire spatial properties and the portrait of the other world is depicted as a landscape of feeling; finally, experiences and interior spaces expand and grow by means of rapid movement across real distances.[26]

Sedakova creates a deliberately naive, pre-Ptolemaic linear map of the world, in which the earthly and heavenly spheres are placed on a horizontal axis. Their parallel nature and the motif of transit between the two spheres are represented by images of doorways, corridors, and entryways. On this map, crossing space along the horizontal axis, on which the different worlds reside, should ideally be combined with movement along a vertical axis: the true life is reached by an ascent.

Universal, abstract concepts such as forgiveness, light, compassion, memory, and love comprise the landscape of the other world. Alongside these abstractions, elements from nature play an equal compositional role. Water appears in different variations (rain, river, underground water) as a mediator between these two axes. The synchronic movement along the horizontal and vertical axes creates the shape of a cross; the poem is the point of intersection, a surreal merging of spirit and matter that takes the form of animate landscapes.

The Parallel Worlds

> I learned that there are some things alongside which life is no different from death. The one who died had, all the same, departed, and his departure was living, and he is, in some way, still wandering.[27]

The expansion of interior space in Sedakova's poems is accompanied by a diminishing of spatial concepts based on empirical evidence. Sedakova describes new spatial experiences that are not subject to the earthly laws of physics, as well as the process of spiritually inhabiting these spaces, thereby presenting a picture of the surreal unity and transformation of separate spheres. In an episode from "The Journey to Briansk" ("Puteshestvie v Briansk," 1984), during a trip to the countryside that doubles as a journey inward, the heroine falls asleep in someone else's apartment and witnesses a small flood. "The topic of water moved from the exterior to the interior" and during the night the water engulfs the imagination of the poet. Its sound pulls her into a prophetic dream: "I dreamed that I had died. [. . .] That I was no more I knew not by my lack of a body but by a sensation of uncommon love coming at me from all directions. The living are not loved like this, or rather, the living do not realize they are loved."[28]

The transition from one state to another is described not by recounting losses, but as the acquisition of new, vivid sensations: "Love was the air, the earth of this corridor or vestibule. It was a vestibule with fur coats on hangers, but at the same time a valley, and rivers were flowing through it as on a map or as you see from an airplane. The rivers disappeared beneath the earth and reappeared."[29] The topography of this passage is determined by properties of the soul and spirit in a way that is typical for Sedakova—the landscape consists of love. The juxtaposition of banal, everyday realia with abstract concepts forms a surreal picture, in which the opposition of sacred and secular is suspended. The image of the corridor, and the entryway full of coats, acquire a transitive quality, because you can exit the visible and material world through them. In the poetic treatment of this motif, Sedakova complements it with a primeval state of innocence, which may allude to the fantasy tale *The Lion, the Witch and the Wardrobe* by C. S. Lewis, in which a young heroine enters a parallel world, Narnia, through a wardrobe. The poems "Childhood Guests" ("Gosti v detstve," 1973; 1:32) and "Where shadows keep watch over moths" ("Gde teni nad mol'iu dezhuriat," 1973; 1:33) play with the motif of the prophetic dream: the corridor, entryway, and coats are semanticized as transitional spaces, in which you can recognize and sense the presence of the other.

В двух шагах от притворенной
двери в детскую, за щель
шепчут стайкой оперенной
в крыльях высохших плащей. (1:32)

Just behind the pulled-to door
to the nursery, through the crack
they whisper in a feathered flock with
wings of raincoats hung to dry.

The whispered word cannot be caught and its meaning cannot be grasped; what remains instead is the memory of a sensation: "like the angels speaking, then / not remembering why they did" ("slovno angely skazali, / ne zapomniv, dlia chego"; "Gosti v detstve"; 1:32). The child's innocent state of "blessed trust" gives him a natural ability to be receptive to the other.[30] And in the poem quoted above, the exit of the whisperer from this world into the next is marked by his metamorphosis into a natural element: "They walk out, they shower like rain" ("vmeste vyidut, livnem budut"; 1:32).[31] Sedakova compares the torturous effort to overcome forgetfulness, which clouds over all that is important, to walking along an edge. Analogously the prophetic dream from "The Journey to Briansk" is interrupted by a collision with the mundane: "I did not get to see the end of what was perhaps the most important dream of my life. [. . .] Oh, well," the heroine concludes.[32] Eternal memory is one of the attributes of the other world; on the side of earthly life, that is expressed in the negative, as lost memory. The desire to regain lost memories is the reason why the speaker asks to enter a transitional space in the poem "Where shadows keep watch over moths" ("Gde teni nad mol'iu dezhuriat"). The poem includes an obvious allusion to Mandelstam's image of the coat ("Better to be stuffed up a sleeve like a fleece cap / in a fur coat from the steppes of Siberia") as a kind of protective cover from the threats of the surrounding world.[33]

Где тени над молью дежурят
и живы еще за дверьми,
в широкую шубу чужую
меня до утра заверни. (1:33)

Where shadows keep watch over moths,
and live safely behind the closed door,

in a stranger's capacious fur coat
wrap me up until morning has come.

Let us return to "The Journey to Briansk." The prophetic dream is described using the same device of "folding" space, also typical in Sedakova's poetry, and the landscape is perceived from a bird's-eye view. A similar contemplation of earthly life from a great height, accompanied by supernatural experiences, appears in the "initiation" of the poet in "In Praise of Poetry." There, after her failed suicide attempt, the heroine remembers losing consciousness, which becomes a mystical initiation in the tradition of hagiographic writing:

> I do not know whether it was a dream or hallucination, but it is impossible to put into words. There I was, frozen for a second time on the viewing platform, when I stepped off it and landed on an unsteady, soft, yet firm, foothold like a wing. Beneath this wing, towns and seas slipped past. There's Paris, I observed. But it did not feel as if I were flying. I was being asked to consent to something (to what, I still do not know, whether good or bad), but I refused. And having refused, I found myself on the slope once more. (3:68)

In describing these visions of the other space, Sedakova introduces the motif of sleep, which, along with illness and childhood, is a kind of transitional state.[34] As we saw in "Azarovka," Sedakova transforms natural phenomena and toponymic data into abstract symbols or concepts in her poetry. The examples from her prose show the reverse process: new experiences and sensations, which arise from a contemplation of the other, are understood in comparison with natural phenomena. In the surreal dream from "The Journey to Briansk," the heroine meets inhabitants of the other sphere, whose life is described as merging with and following the natural elements:

> And the inhabitants of the vestibule lived like these rivers: they led a flickering existence. Before me stood Marina Tsvetaeva, flashing like a piece of turquoise. [...]
>
> "We only flicker, some of us more often, some less often."
>
> There was a person in the distance who flashed like sand, though not like the sand of an hourglass. There was less of him, he was rarer than sand.[35]

Nature and the element of water are not only celebrated as means of active knowledge of God and as keepers of eternal memory; they also become integral components of the landscape of the other world.

Transparency and Insight

Sedakova creates a broad semantic field for the element of water, building on the long-standing tradition of its use in philosophy and poetry, and adding exclusively positive layers onto it. Even the flood scene in the prophetic dream from "The Journey to Briansk" is free of any apocalyptic associations. Water, in all its forms, appears as absolute proof of the divine Beginning in the empirical world, felt as a strong presence in "Rain" ("Dozhd'"):

—Дождь идет,
а говорят, что Бога нет!—
говорила старуха из наших мест,
няня Варя. (1:399)

"It's raining,
and they say there's no God!"
said an old local woman,
Auntie Varya.

Sedakova draws a parallel between the eternal circular motion of water, its purposeless existence, and that other, true life, which is independent of man's ability to understand, define, explain, and apprehend it using reason. She adds a new semantic layer to the image of water by suggesting that water provides a direct link to the divine origin—the human body is physically related to the divine element. Elsewhere in her poetry, there are many examples of a posthumous transformation into rain: "and I'll be like rain, I'll hang on like the hope / of waking to sounds of another rain" ("I budu, kak dozhd', i ostanus' nadezhdoi / prosnut'sia pod zvuki drugogo dozhdia"; "Alatyr'"; 1:135); "They walk out, they shower like rain" ("vmeste vyidut, livnem budut"; 1:32). In the poem "Death comes to me often in dreams" ("Mne chasto snitsia smert'"), the other world, a place of eternal memory, has striking meteorological conditions:

Воздух из путей кратчайших,
падающих, как вода,—
но вверх. (1:99)

Air of the very shortest paths
that fall like water,—
but upwards.

The ambiguous ending of the poem shows the speaker's bliss and her epiphanic contemplation of the watery air of the other world:

я улыбаюсь,
и рука уходит
в простую воду легкого лица. (1:99)

I smile,
and my hand disappears
into the simple water of a weightless face.

The "simple water of a weightless face" embodies the idea of the natural connection between a person and the element of water. Everything that relates to water—both actions and thoughts that are directed at it—also relates to humankind.[36]

In Sedakova's poetic universe, water becomes a mediator between the worlds, and its most important feature is transparency. Water, in all of its states, has a transitive quality, unlike the mirror, which is one of the central images of Sedakova's early work.[37] A mirror forces the person looking at it into self-reflection, whereas the transparency of water allows him to look at that which exists outside the self.[38] This mystical power of water is discussed in "Elegy for Autumn Water" ("Elegiia osennei vody"), particularly in these two parts of the poem:

10.
кажется,
что ничто быстрей туда
не ведет, чем эта, сады пустые,
            растенья
луговые, лесные, уже не пьющие,—
            чем усыпленье
обегающая бессонная вода

11.
перед тем, как сделаться льдом, сделаться сном,
стать как веки, стать как верная кожа
засыпавшего в ласке, видящего себя вдвоем
дальше во сне . . .
Вещи, в саду своем
вы похожи на любовь—или она на вас похожа? (1:379)

10.
it seems
like nothing leads there
quicker than this, empty gardens,
        plants
from meadow or woods that don't drink anymore,—
        than sleepless water
that courses 'round lullabies.

11.
just before it turns to ice, turns to dream,
becomes like eyelids, becomes like faithful skin
of someone caressed to sleep seeing himself double
further on in the dream . . .
Things, in your garden
you are like love—or is love like you?

The endless stream of water in autumn is represented graphically in the tenth stanza, its spontaneous movements reflected in the use of enjambment. The tireless, wakeful flow of water is the only sign of life in a landscape of deep winter sleep. In the context of this near-death state, the running water takes us "there." To observe the metamorphosis of water is to witness the secret unbroken link to the other life. But even frozen water does not lose its mystical qualities: ice is compared to being asleep, a state that allows one to contemplate one's dual (or the other, truer) existence.[39] The metamorphosis of water is marked by a change in the poem's structure: parallelisms mimic the rhythm of being cradled and falling asleep. The notion of a dual parallel existence is reinforced by the image of the garden. In the beginning of the poem, the reader is presented with an autumnal, desolate garden. By the end of the eleventh stanza, the same garden appears as an abstract space outside of time that is filled with love, a kind of center point of existence.

The garden, like the heart, gathers together multiple images in Sedakova's work. They are not just topoi that make harmony and wholeness possible, but also center points that represent the synthesis of spatial reality outside the subject as well as the inner space of human experience.

The Garden—the Core

The constant presence of gardens in Sedakova's work is further proof of its close link to theological and liturgical poetry. Sedakova, *poeta doctus*, is certainly aware of the allusions and associations hidden in the word "garden," and she does not overwork or overburden the semantic space of her poems with descriptive detail. The allusions to Elysium or Eden, the symbol of original happiness and lack of worry, or to the garden as a symbol of the mother of God, are embedded in the very word "garden." In minimally descriptive poems, the word is mostly used without epithets.[40]

In Sedakova's work, gardens have a double spatial life, which takes place both in the earthly sphere and beyond. The garden is a harmonious totality of different natural elements and formally repeats the heavenly act of creation; the earthly garden is an image of the Garden of Eden. The garden can also be found in the metaphysical space beyond life. One can reach it posthumously by crossing the border of life, the same way one reaches the other place.

At other times, Sedakova turns the garden into a space of supernatural convergences. In one of the *Old Songs* dedicated to the memory of her grandmother, Darya Semyonovna, Sedakova describes such a meeting. What looks like an innocuous invitation by the grandmother to walk along the garden—

—Пойдем, пойдем, моя радость,
пойдем с тобой по нашему саду,
поглядим, что сделалось на свете! (1:207)

"Let's go, let's go, my joy,
let's take a walk in our garden,
let's have a look at what's been done on earth!"

—turns out to be an imaginary encounter with the soul of the dead woman. However, this unreal situation is narrated not by the addressee, but by the soul itself. The request to hold her granddaughter's hand is followed by a shift, an awakening of consciousness:

Ничего, что я лежу в могиле,—
чего человек не забудет!
Из сада видно мелкую реку.
В реке видно каждую рыбу. (1:207)

No matter that I'm lying in the grave,—
a person forgets all kinds of things!
From the garden you can see the shallow river.
In the river you can see each fish.

The minimal description here creates a feeling of intimacy and comfort. The image suggests medieval monastery gardens, places of prayer and meditative solitude, in which the element of water was often present. The union of happiness, grace, and death described in "Ninth Legend" ("Legenda deviataia"; 1:80) also corresponds to the sacral symbolism of medieval gardens.[41]

In all these examples, the garden correlates with the motif of sleep, which stands for the expansion of consciousness in Sedakova's work. This correlation suggests that the garden exists in a space that is mainly in the interior, a place in the mind. Sedakova's gardens are paved and planted with universal concepts and experiences (light, gifts, happiness, forgiveness, remembrance), and not with real plants. Maybe the other place is a specific state of the soul that can be cultivated like a garden? If water is the biological reality of man, an elemental link to creation, then the garden is the conscious, willful act of unity with the divine origin through an analogous moment of creation. Planting a garden makes one privy to the divine Beginning: one replicates the act of creating harmony out of chaos. In Likhachev's words, the garden is "a special kind of book: it only reflects the good and idealized essence of the world."[42] The ability to cultivate the garden within oneself, within one's inner world, can be a form of "good news."

The garden allows the lyric subject to encounter the other as well as a true self,[43] and similarly, the poem becomes a site of encounter with new ideas and experiences. Garden work and poetic work, with their semiotic, semantic, and aesthetic systems, are inherently small, demiurgical gestures, an imitation of the divine act of creation.[44] In this sense, poetry can be understood as an act of serving God.

To conclude, let us turn back to the "Azarovka" cycle. In the final suite, Sedakova, elevating the real garden to the realm of abstraction, creates a unique verbal garden, in which words triumph and bloom for eternity. We can read this poem as a jubilant glorification of poetry. Having survived a thousand disasters ("they set fire to the house," "they smash the glass," "they take away the clothes"), the poetic word does not perish, but responds to danger with the leitmotif "and we talk." The notion of the eternal, timeless nature of poetic speech comes across in the anaphoric repetition of the conjunction "and" ("i"), which gives the statements a triumphant intonation. The word "garden" becomes a composite vessel of different meanings of a higher order. Through the real image, the garden at Azarovka, the complex semantic spectrum of that word comes to life: it is Eden as the prototype of all gardens; it is also a monastery garden—a place of spiritual and cultural activities, like the image of scribes copying manuscripts. Sa'di's *Gulistan*, the Rigveda, and texts in Latin are also being copied; these texts all praise the divine Beginning and describe both earthly and heavenly gardens.[45] These texts triumph over death. And in the end, the word "garden" refers to the image of the poet-gardener creating an artefact—a poem, this poem.

In Sedakova's poetic universe, different realms are not in opposition to each other. Knowing and sensing the eternal presence of the other is understood as a necessary experience on the road to spiritual growth. Poetic language, which reflects prelinguistic meanings and a will beyond that of its author, has to point to the other as the truthful side of human existence; the poem becomes a means by which the reader can experience that truth. That which is other cannot be completely captured by poetry because it is fundamentally supernatural, but it appears in the material of the verse as stylistic features that convey unfinished expression (*nedoskazannost'*) and ineffability. At the same time, the poems' harmonious sound organization reinforces the connectedness and unity of the universe. The merging of these two aspects creates the sense of a growing tension, which often remains unresolved within the poem.

Across a multiplicity of images that capture the forays into the other world, Sedakova gives material presence to an expansion of consciousness and to experiences beyond perception, which occur during an overcoming and depreciation of spatial reality. Mental states acquire spatial characteristics, which become a foundation for the landscape of the other world. In addition to the transitional spaces and images that afford glimpses into the other world, there are also images of synthesis—the heart and the garden—that become the focal points of different worlds and thematize the obvious interactions of these spheres. Working with these archetypal images, Sedakova, a poet of great erudition, enriches their deep universal meanings with new layers: images come to life and acquire particular semantic nuances. And this is precisely the true task of poetry: "And like every gift—the gift of art and the gift of faith possess the power to open up, to liberate and expand the given."[46]

Translated from Russian by Maria Vassileva

Notes

1. Some of that utopian spirit is also felt in the essay that is a source for the epigraph to this essay: Ol'ga Sedakova, "Poeziia kak eskhatologicheskaia real'nost'," 4:371.

2. On Metarealism: "Metarealists, a term coined by Mikhail Epshtein in the 1980s for an alternative poetics trend to Moscow conceptualism. [. . . The] Metarealists stayed with the language and themes of the modernist poetry pushing them toward greater self-consciousness, if not self-doubt. Metarealists explore philosophical and spiritual questions, even in a secular and ironic world; they pursue multiple realities [. . .], and they share a penchant for adventurous and dense metaphor." Stephanie Sandler, "Mirrors and Metarealists: The Poetry of Ol'ga Sedakova and Ivan Zhdanov," *Slavonica* 12, no. 1 (April 2006): 4.

3. The dichotomy "here—there" is transcended later on in the same poem, "Pamiati Ottsa Aleksandra Menia," 1:374. The uniting force of love is cloaked in a natural metaphor: it peeks out like a sun through clouds. The relationship between creative love and light, and their presence in natural phenomena, often appears in Sedakova's poems.

4. Italicization has a special semantic tenor in Sedakova's work, as it is used rarely, mostly to designate complex metaphysical terms.

5. The instances of departure from the everyday in Sedakova's work should not be understood as a repudiation of life as such. On the contrary, Sedakova systematically examines the value of worldly life, of "life as happiness" (see "Luchshii universitet"; 4:287). When discussing Dante in the essay "Mudrost' nadezhdy: Dante," Sedakova stresses the positive impulse behind art in general and poetry in particular. Poetry sui generis serves to "to extricate humankind from its current state of misery and guide it toward a state of happiness" (4:314).

6. The phrase "the matter of verse" is borrowed from Efim Etkind from his eponymous monograph; here, it is used as a designation of the means of material (in our case, linguistic) transmission of content, the formal organization of the poetic text. Etkind uses that term to emphasize the deep and unbreakable bond between meaning and form (spirit and matter), which appears in the poetic text like in a "living creature." See Efim Etkind, *Materiia stikha* (Paris: Institut d'Études Slaves, 1978), 9.

7. Following Florensky's idea that "all of culture can be interpreted as acts of organizing space." Pavel Florenskii, "Analiz prostranstvennosti (i vremeni) v khudozhestvenno-izobrazitel'nykh proizvedeniiakh," in *Stat'i i issledovaniia po istorii i filosofii iskusstva i arkheologii* (Moscow: Mysl', 2000), 112.

8. Ol'ga Sedakova, "Pustota: Krizis priamogo prodolzheniia. Konets bystrykh reshenii," 4:485.

9. Ibid., 4:478. For general overviews of Sedakova's poetics, see Valentina Polukhina, "Olga Sedakova," in *Russian Women Writers*, ed. Christine D. Tomei, 2 vols. (New York: Garland Publishing, 1999), 2:1445–50; Catriona Kelly, *A History of Russian Women's Writing 1820–1992* (Oxford: Clarendon Press, 1994), 423–33.

10. Elena Aizenshtein looks at the structure of the "Azarovka" cycle and its link to musical suites; she suggests the beauty of nature as the unifying motif of the cycle. Sedakova includes twelve poems in the cycle, which, according to Aizenstein, corresponds to the calendar year. See Elena Aizenshtein, *Iz moei trideviatoi strany: Stat'i o poezii* (Moscow: Izdatel'skie resheniia, 2015), 178. In his article "Semiotika istorii: B. A. Uspenskii i O. A. Sedakova," Aleksandr Markov draws parallels between the "Azarovka" cycle and Uspenskii's work on semiotics, "Historia sub specie semioticae," noting the synchronous appearance of these two works. Markov claims that in "Azarovka" Sedakova manages to realize the very "passage from everyday topology to history itself, in the form of a transition f rom folkloric and everyday notions about man and the world to Christian and scientific [. . .] ones." See http://syg.ma/@alieksandr-markov/siemiotika-istorii-b-a-uspienskii-i-o-a-siedakova, accessed March 17, 2018.

11. Out of the twelve sketches in the cycle, only the third poem, "V kustakh," differs in its metric structure.

12. In describing the semantic tenor of the amphibrach, Mikhail Gasparov mentions the theme of visions and sleep, which appears in secret in Sedakova's cycle. However, Gasparov mostly deals with examples of amphibrachic trimeter. See Mikhail Gasparov, *Metr i smysl: Ob odnom iz mekhanizmov kul'turnoi pamiati* (Moscow: RGGU, 1999), 135–36. Joseph Brodsky's characterization of the amphibrach is useful for our purposes. He stresses the neutrality of this meter and prefers it in his later nativity poems. See "Tochka otscheta: Beseda Iosifa Brodskogo s Petrom Vailem," in *Rozhdestvenskie stikhi*, by Iosif Brodskii, 4th ed. (Moscow: Nezavisimaia gazeta, 1998), 59.

13. Jens Herlth points out sub- and intertextual allusions in the poem "Vesna," and concludes that Sedakova achieves a representation of the concept of the indistinguishability of the systems of nature and art. The poet-heroine proficient in the language of nature does not perceive its system of signs as hermetic and incomprehensible. Disharmony in the relations between nature and reality is also understood as a fact of contemporary life. Jens Herlth, "Ol'ga Sedakova: Vesna," in *Die russische Lyrik*, ed. Bodo Zelinsky (Cologne: Böhlau Verlag, 2002), 394–401.

14. In his analysis of *Kitaiskoe puteshestvie*, he notes that "Sedakova creates a situation in which time is absent—she takes it out, spreading out different countries and epochs like cards in game of solitaire, all on one plane, along one line." Dmitrii Bavil'skii, "Malen'kaia vechnost'," *Postskriptum: Literaturnyi zhurnal* 5 (1996): 110, http://www.vavilon.ru/metatext/ps5/bavilsky2.html, accessed March 17, 2018.

15. "Transparency" and "purity" appear in Sedakova's poetics as ideal qualities of the absolute form and an embodiment of poetic freedom. Using an example from Pushkin—"In the scarlet [. . .] dawn / the snow dust sparkles like silver"—Sedakova develops the idea of the ideal purity of poetic speech: "For me, freedom consists, ultimately, in the possibility of privileging purity over all else. The possibility of not even including an epithet, if precisely the right one does not come to mind." "Razgovor o svobode," 4:52. On the subject of Sedakova's "poetic dialogue" with Pushkin, see Stephanie Sandler, "Pushkin among Contemporary Poets: Self and Song in Sedakova," in *Two Hundred Years of Pushkin*, ed. Joe Andrew and Robert Reid (Amsterdam: Rodopi, 2003), 175–95.

16. "This is not a visionary journey to heaven or hell, to pure or impure lands," Kseniia Golubovich notes in her introduction to *Dva puteshestviia*, "this is also not the usual exotic journey beyond the border. The border on and beyond which this journey takes place is at first imperceptible [. . .]." Kseniia Golubovich, "Puteshestvuia v puteshestviia," in *Dva puteshestviia*, by Ol'ga Sedakova (Moscow: Logos, 2005), 7.

17. Ibid.

18. Sedakova's descriptions of liturgical verse focus on aspects that can also be used to analyze her own poems. "I love the very form of liturgical poetry, its Byzantine interweaving of ideas and their shades of meaning. And also the way it develops a particular sensibility, one that is completely free of affectation and sentimentality and yet far from cold." Cited from Sedakova, "Veshchestvo chelovechnosti," 4:352. On the absence of rhyme in old Russian poetry and psalms, see Iurii Lotman, *O poetakh i poezii: Analiz poeticheskogo teksta* (St. Petersburg: Iskusstvo-SPB, 1996), 68.

19. Alongside the explicitly Christian connotations in the motif of "the memory of the other life that is hidden in the soul," Sedakova also sees echoes of Hellenic culture. "A

Hellenic feeling: a feeling of the soul unbound from flesh and blood, dwelling somewhere in the distance, far from the person to whom it belongs. The guest soul that has come from far away and that preserves the memory of its distant origin, of the Other, to the end of its earthly days" ("Iskusstvo kak dialog s dal'nim"; 4:327).

20. This idea can also take us in a different direction: since poetic language in Sedakova is by nature part of the prelinguistic silence, it carries within itself part of divine silence and does not strive toward description. "The silence within words is the fundamental principle of hesychasm, and for Sedakova, it is the source of poetry" (Polukhina, "Olga Sedakova," 1447).

21. Epstein defends the generation of the 1980s from criticism of their intentional use of complicated and hermetic forms by pointing out the reader's unwillingness to accept the unusual. Mikhail Epshtein, "Pokolenie, nashedshee sebia (O molodoi poezii nachala 80-kh godov)," *Voprosy literatury* 5 (1986): 44.

22. Using Lotman's terminology, we can talk about the presence of minus-devices in *Starye pesni*, that is, "systems of consistent and conscious negations that can be sensed by the reader." The notion of the "unmaterialized" part of the poetic text also points to Lotman, who emphasizes the entirely real character of these unmaterialized textual elements (minus-devices) in the structure of the text. See Lotman, *O poetakh i poezii*, 36, 39–40.

23. Bavil'skii, "Malen'kaia vechnost'," 110.

24. The poem "Veniamin" can serve as an example: "O, Tvorets, / v tvoikh ushchel'iakh, / v tishine Tvoikh pustyn', / na raskachannykh kacheliakh / zvezd, so sten Tvoikh tverdyn'" ("Oh, Creator, in your canyons, / in the silence of your wastelands, / in the swung swings of your stars, / from your firmament's high walls"; 1:368). In the essay "Tvorchestvo i vera: Vremia i iazyk; Avtor i chitatel'" (4:227), Sedakova writes about the difficulty of conveying prelinguistic meaning through language and gives poetic language a special role.

25. "What does he do where he is not? / Where being flows in endless torrents" ("Chto delaet on tam, gde net ego? / Gde vechnym livnem l'etsia sushchestvo"), Sedakova poses a rhetorical question in the poem "Stansy vtorye. Na smert' kotenka," 1:279. A reflection on the theme of meeting one's true self in the afterworld unfolds in the poem "Bolezn'," 1:108.

26. On interior spaces in Sedakova's poetry: "Access to interior worlds maps the pathway of many of Sedakova's poems, but the distances travelled grow vast, allowing the inner spaces of spirituality and subjectivity to mirror the cosmic enormity of a world divinely ordered." Sandler, "Mirrors and Metarealists," 5.

27. Sedakova, "In Praise of Poetry," 3:61.

28. Sedakova, "Puteshestvie v Briansk," in *Dva puteshestviia*, 53.

29. Ibid.

30. The loss, with age, of the childlike (heavenly) outlook and the ability to understand "the language of nature" is the subject of the poem "Portret khudozhnika v srednem vozraste," 1:407.

31. We should note the specificity and frequency of the so-called "metaphors-metamorphoses" in Sedakova's work, which, aside from referencing folklore (through similes using the instrumental case and parallelism), represent a new, special sense of the

world. The principle of "metamorphization" is "the leading principle of the poetic worldview" of the poets from the eighties, according to Epshtein. Epshtein, "Pokolenie, nashedshee sebia," 67, 70.

32. Sedakova, "Puteshestvie v Briansk," 54.

33. Osip Mandelstam, "For the Sake of the Future's Trumpeting Heroics," trans. Clarence Brown and W. S. Merwin, *The Selected Poems of Osip Mandelstam* (New York: New York Review of Books, 2004), 60.

34. Maria Khotimsky underscores the connection between sleep/visions and the description of the creative process and the "spiritual autobiography" in the work of the two poets. These motifs are also the frame for the intertextual dialogue between Sedakova and her colleagues in craft. See Maria Khotimsky, "Singing David, Dancing David: Olga Sedakova and Elena Shvarts Rewrite a Psalm," *Slavic and East European Journal* 51, no. 4 (2007): 739.

35. Sedakova, "Puteshestvie v Briansk," 53–54.

36. In his overview of the cultural history of water, Hartmut Böhme repeatedly turns to the question of the indistinguishability of the divine origin from the element of water in biblical cosmogony. Böhme discusses the utopian and absurd nature of the modern desire for autonomy from nature: when it comes to water, man is always both subject and object at the same time. See Hartmut Böhme, "Umriss einer Kulturgeschichte des Wassers," in *Kulturgeschichte des Wassers* (Frankfurt: Suhrkamp, 1988), 10, 16.

37. In her later work Sedakova moves away from the motif of the mirror. The possibility that this change suggests a renunciation of self-writing and of the self and a move toward openness to the world merits separate study. (I would like to thank Margarita Krimmel for this valuable observation.)

38. Stephanie Sandler stresses the self-reflexive nature of this image not only with relation to the subject writing but to writing itself and the creative process. See Sandler, "Mirrors and Metarealists," 4.

39. One of the leitmotifs of Sedakova's aesthetics of the other world is the paradoxical sense of one's own self in the moment of dying, or during the transitive states of sleep, visions, illness, and journeys. The change in the material order of being allows an immersion in the essence of things and of the self: thus, in the afterlife consciousness is resurrected by the true life.

40. The garden also carries a special semantic tenor in Sedakova's prose. When describing her childhood dacha Sedakova embellishes it, so that it becomes a heavenly garden: "A few cherry trees behind the house made up the huge garden, a heavenly garden" (3:48).

41. On the question of the aesthetic system of medieval monastery gardens, see Dmitrii Likhachev, *Poeziia sadov: K semantike sadovo-parkovykh stilei* (Leningrad: Nauka, 1982), 41.

42. Ibid., 17.

43. The epiphanic and intimate sense of one's own self when contemplating a garden is described in "Utro v sadu" ("Morning in the Garden"; 1:116). Real phenomena disappear; instead a sense of the true self arrives and is experienced as unity with divine matter and light.

44. Likhachev writes about the similarity between the layout of a garden, systems in general and poetic systems in particular, and the close correspondences between poetry and gardening, noting the "poet-gardeners" Petrarch, Joseph Addison, Alexander Pope, Johann Wolfgang von Goethe. He adds, "In the middle ages the work of the writer was compared to the work of the gardener planting flowers" (Likhachev, *Poeziia sadov*, 11, 41).

45. Aizenshtein reveals the intertextual allusions in "Sad," in which reside "the memory of dead poets, locked in the language, in conversations with them in verse." On a lexical level, we can trace the dialogue with Marina Tsvetaeva, Mikhail Kuzmin, Osip Mandelstam, and Anna Akhmatova. See Aizenshtein, *Iz moei tridevіatoi strany*, 180.

46. Sedakova, "Iskusstvo kak dialog s dal'nim," 3:326..

The Immanence of Transcendence

Poetic Reflections on the Mystical Aspects of Olga Sedakova's Lyric Poetry

HENRIEKE STAHL

For Vladimir Ivanov

Metabolic Poetry

Olga Sedakova situates her poetic work beyond literary groupings and at a distance from recent Russian poetry that can be described in sociological terms.[1] The frequent classification of her work as an example of metarealism goes back to the writing of Mikhail Epstein, who suggested a theoretical categorization of new Russian poetry as early as the 1980s.[2] Epstein defines metarealism in opposition to conceptualism, as a second stylistic tendency of special importance to the unofficial poetry of the period (*nepodtsenzurnaia poeziia*).[3] To characterize metarealism, Epstein relies on a poetic device whose definition he himself invented. He resorts to a stylistic element of the ancient rhetorical tradition, metabole, which he invests with new meaning.[4] The concept helps Epstein define the specific manner in which metarealist poetry uses images, as well as the philosophical and conceptual significance expressed by such imagery. Epstein views metabole as similar to metaphor in that both conjoin different realms of being and kinds of objects:[5] "Metabole is an image that cannot be separated into a literal and a figurative meaning, into a described object and a coopted likeness. It is the image of a self-dividing, yet unified reality."[6] In contrast to metaphor, however, metabole eliminates the divide between such realms by constructing chains and networks of images. The multiplicity of realms, dimensions, and worlds is thus interleaved and transformed, giving it the appearance of a world with many organically interwoven subsystems that recalls the postmodern theory of the rhizome.[7] To some extent, metaphors gain a metonymic significance in these texts and Epstein's metabole can also be seen as a synthesis of metaphor and metonymy.

Examples of such image interferences are also found in earlier poetry, particularly in various Modernist tendencies, and are therefore not an exclusive defining characteristic of metarealism, all the more so since this category unites a diverse set of poets. But the term nevertheless allows us to identify a key feature of Olga Sedakova's poetry. She is not concerned with a plurality of worlds that are interconnected, but typically only with two worlds: the realm of appearances that can be grasped through the senses, and a spiritual, non-sensory world, which still stands in a *certain* relationship to the former, and can enter into and express itself through it.[8]

Not coincidentally, Sedakova's cosmos of images is defined by places and states of transition. A key volume of her poems is entitled *Gates, Windows, Arches* (*Vrata, Okna, Arki*). Many of her poems feature thresholds, doors, windows, the contrast of inside and outside (in the image of house and garden, for instance), of the above and the below (in the image of heaven and water), of childhood and adulthood, as well as epiphanies of the deceased or of divine and spiritual beings (such as the angels and Christ). Psychological threshold states triggered by dreams, illness, or death are another central theme in her work.[9] One of her essential aims is to transcend the normal state of everyday consciousness. Poetry is a "trace" of the poet's experience of inspiration as an encounter with a different dimension that transcends our ordinary consciousness. Sedakova's poetics is situated at the crossing between different worlds and dimensions, and at those points where they enter into one another.

This theme of the interconnected sensory and spiritual worlds allows us to characterize Sedakova's poetry as "religious"[10] or as marked by "mystical experience."[11] Generally, however, her poems are not religious in a narrow confessional sense.[12] This has changed in Sedakova's poems of more recent years, which at times contain a message clearly related to Christianity. Thus, for instance, the poem "Everything at Once" ("Vse, i srazu") offers her poetic interpretation of a verse from John 14:27, which the poet also used as the programmatic title of her 2009 volume of poems (1:416).[13] This poem also concludes the volume of poetry (*Stikhi*) in Sedakova's four-volume collected works.

Although scholars have repeatedly noted the mystical element present in Sedakova's poetry from the very beginning, its fundamental poetic significance has not yet been grasped. Based on a representative selection of poems from different periods of her work, this essay will show the mystical orientation of her verse to be a recurring and significant element of her poetics. In contrast to the term "religious," which generally refers to a faith-based relationship with God or another divine spiritual being, the concept of the "mystical"[14] entails experiencing the presence of the divine. The various forms of this experience typically transcend the ordinary dimensions of being and consciousness.[15]

The poems analyzed below each contain an anthropological statement about the relationship between the human and the divine or spiritual, combined with an account of poetic creativity. At times, a mystical dimension is also performatively enacted by the very form of the poetic text. Four themes fundamentally determine the mystical element of Sedakova's work: the spirituality of humanity; the existence of a spiritual world; the human being and poetry as interfaces between the sensory and the spiritual world; and poetic creativity as anamnesis of the divine.

The Human as an Immortal Spiritual Being

The poetry volume of Sedakova's collected works opens with an early poem, "One day, when I die through and through" ("Odnazhdy, kogda ia umru do kontsa," 1967), which gains a programmatic meaning through its prominent placement:

Однажды, когда я умру до конца
и белый день опадет с лица,
услышу я, как спросонок:
по тонким дранкам заборов моих
бежит, спотыкаясь, веселый мотив:
их трогает палкой ребенок.

И каждая нота в мотиве таком
сама по себе и к тому же с ледком,
как буквы в Клину и Коломне . . .
И буду я думать: играй же, играй
про отчий мой край,
про чуждый мой край,
про то, что я знаю, а ты не узнай—
про то, что никак не припомню. (1:17)

One day, when I die through and through,
and white day falls from my face,
I'll hear, as it were, half-awake:
along my fences' frail boards
a happy motif that stumbles along:
a child knocking each with a stick as he goes.

And every note in this matchless motif,
each on its own, and add ice to that, too,
is like letters in Klin and Kolomna . . .

And I'll think: so play, then, play
of my father's home,
of my foreign home,
of what I know, but don't want you to know—
of what there's no way I'd recall.

The first line of the poem takes up a traditional theme of Russian poetry, the famous Horatian ode "To Melpomene" ("Exegi monumentum"), which remains alive and productive thanks to ever new poetic adaptations, responses, and allusions to this text and its reception. At first, Sedakova's poem distances itself from the line "No, I shall not wholly die" ("Net, ves' ia ne umru") in Pushkin's adaptation of Horace: her text allows the "I" to "die completely" ("ia umru do kontsa") and without erecting a monument in the traditional sense of this image: as an intellectual or poetic legacy. But the "I" survives here, too. On the one hand, it is isolated from the world and can only look back at the wooden remains of the "fences" of its former property: "along my fences' frail boards" ("po tonkim drankam zaborov moikh"). Figuratively speaking, the "I" looks back at its physical remains and at the earthly life associated with them. On the other hand, this review of life leads into the "happy motif," as the "child" playfully elicits sounds from the planks of the fence, and, by extension, from the poet's remains.

The lyrical "I" does not endure in the individual "notes," but in the combination of these sounds, in the composition of a tonal sequence or melody. The latter is meant to express everything connected with the "I" ("moi krai"), things that nobody else is supposed to know ("chto ia znaiu, a ty ne uznai")—its autobiographical knowledge—and that which it cannot even remember itself ("chto nikak ne pripomniu"). In a sense, the rhyme pattern conjoins those elements of the tune that are known to the "I" and that constitute the song's theme: "play-home-home-know" ("igrai-krai-krai-uznai"). At the same time, the rhymes associate that which the "I" remains unaware of with the poem's outer linguistic form and its interconnectedness, which creates words and motifs out of sounds ("Kolomne-pripomniu"). By extending the verse from six to eight lines, repeating the same rhyme and the anaphora *pro* (used four times in the poem), as well as other forms of parallelism, the poem creates a sense of expanse and continuation that contrasts with the words "to die completely" in the first line.

Sedakova thus extends the "Exegi monumentum" tradition in a novel way: her poet figure, too, continues to survive in her work. But this work is simultaneously detached from the poet—and more than he or she realizes. It is also not immortal: as music, poetry is fleeting and depends on a performance that continues to revive the melody and to instill the dead remains—the text—with new life.

The child playing with a stick is thus also a symbol of the reader, or the recipient, of poetry, whose touch alone can make the latter resound.

The motif of the musical stick is also found in a poem from the volume *The Wild Rose* (*Dikii shipovnik*), where it establishes contact between humanity and the earth: "We'll walk along slowly, listening carefully" ("Medlenno budem idti i vnimatel'no slushat'"; 1:98). The lyrical "we" uses the stick to auscultate the earth as if using a divining rod, in search of its deeper intrinsic being, which can answer the question: "who's there" ("kto tam"). But the two spheres of being remain unconnected: the poem ends with question and search, because the earth's answer, in the form of an echo, is itself a counter-question. Nevertheless, a relationship emerges between the "we" and the earth, as imagined by the lyrical "we" of the poem. The stick thus becomes an image for writing and interpreting poetry, both of which are ways of searching for hidden spiritual meaning.

This volume of verse also contains the poem "Not the angel that sounds out like a crevasse" ("Ni angela, zvuchashchego, kak shchel'"; 1:101). Here God's "experienced hand" elicits sounds from "strings" (the life of a saint) and he is "hearing itself," and "there," with God, "all" beings are said to resound. Life is music, that is, a tonal composition, which is echoed in the poem. Sedakova uses rhyming couplets, uncommon in modern poetry, to express the close relationship between the musician as creator and music as creature. Man's "thinking spirit" ("dumaiushchii dukh") is simultaneously music and thought; it is the human creative element that speaks to the lyrical "I" in the poem. It forms the bridge between the lyrical "I," which represents the human being with its everyday consciousness, and God, by explaining to the lyrical "I" and God in place of the lyrical "I": "there all sound out except for You, for You are hearing itself" ("tam vse zvuchat, no Ty ostalsia—slukh"). Here, "You" is capitalized, as in the phrase "Your fearsome encounters," signaling the divine.

In the poem "One day, when I die through and through," Sedakova's lyrical "I" contains several components: the reflecting "I," which imagines itself as an "I" looking on after death; the (dead) biographical self, restrained by its "fences," and finally the "child." The latter alludes to the "playing child" in Friedrich Nietzsche's *Thus Spoke Zarathustra*, which represents the third and final stage of man's transformation: his absolute freedom. In this respect, the "child" becomes an image for the immortal "I" that assembles life into a fate, a melody, while the reflecting "I" can only watch and listen to this connection "as though asleep." It is unable to creatively shape the "motif" itself.

Formally, the poem embodies both the reflecting self and the child: the first stanza transforms the underlying amphibrach into the same "running, stumbling" melody ("bezhit, spotykaias'") that the child elicits with a stick. The second stanza, which conveys the thoughts of the lyrical self, presents a vivid contrast with its regular amphibrach pattern. On the level of rhythm, the poem's two stanzas thus contain both the child as a creative entity, and the reflecting self. Together they form the unity and wholeness of both human being and poem. Accordingly, both stanzas end in a line with the same sequence of stressed vowel phonemes that symbolically express unity and closedness: O-A-O. Omega, the end, encompasses Alpha, the beginning.

The poem thus conveys the anthropological assumption that each human being contains an immortal instance that transcends his or her reflecting consciousness. Endowed with imagination, the consciousness of the poet, however, is capable of intuiting this deeper essence, and thus the essential being of man, and to express it in the form of poetry. The "I" of the poet, which is not explicitly introduced but corresponds to the narratological concept of the "abstract author," is analogous to the playing child in the contemplation of the reflecting lyrical "I," while the poem itself correlates to the "joyful motif."

Sedakova thus believes that poetry not only bears witness to the existence of a human spiritual essence, but also allows it to become present in the creative process itself. Poetry encompasses both the mortal and the immortal dimensions of human existence and therefore transcends the conscious reflections of the lyrical "I." Poems are thus not only written *about* human spirituality, but rather *out of* its experience, by revealing this spirituality in their very form and performatively bringing it alive. In a later poem from the volume *The Beginning of the Book* (*Nachalo knigi*), entitled "Nothing" ("Nichto"), the lyrical "I" even reflects this connection explicitly: where the soul has not been touched by resurrecting powers, such as those of Lazarus, it should remain silent: "my soul! hush / until *this* touches you" ("dusha moia! molchi, / poka tebia *eto* ne kosnulos'"; 1:400).

Human Epiphanies of the Divine

A number of Sedakova's poems depict man's higher spiritual essence as being close to the divine. It becomes sensible to the divine especially in threshold situations, such as during birth, in early childhood, and shortly before death. She associates this spiritual core with a series of recurring images that pervade her entire work and gain the status of symbols due to their constant semantic content.

For instance, Sedakova often associates the purity of the divine gift to humanity with the motif of the (paradisiacal) garden, which has appeared in her work since the earliest poems. Most recently, she dedicated a selection of earlier poems to the garden motif; only the final text, "Dedication" ("Posviashchenie"), was written more recently, in 2012. Published in 2014 and illustrated by the artist Tatiana Ian, the book is entitled *The Universal Garden* (*Sad mirozdan'ia*). In her preface, Sedakova notes that her "garden" has not been destroyed by time, using the old metaphor of the garden to refer primarily to her "poetic garden" (we may recall, for instance, Simeon Polotsky's *Garden of Many Flowers* [*Vertograd mnogotsvetnyi*]): "Still my garden has remained intact" ("Utselel poka moi sad").[16]

This volume also reproduces the poem "Surely, Maria, it's not just window frames creaking" ("Neuzheli, Maria, tol'ko ramy skripiat," 1973; 1:27).[17] Here, the lyrical "I" remains indeterminate, just like its addressee, Maria.[18] Because a Russian speaker would hardly use the formal "Maria" to address a close relative or even a nanny, we may even read this as a child addressing Mary, mother of Jesus. The poem's plot also suggests the image of a frightened sick child: its thoughts are reproduced by an adult alter ego, which vividly recalls childhood while retaining its adult manner of speaking and modes of the imagination.

As in many other poems by Sedakova, the garden reappears here as an image associated with childhood[19] and endowed with paradisiacal connotations: it is a "covenanted" garden ("zapovedannyi sad"). This garden is treated as the property of the lyrical "I" ("my garden"—"sad moi"), although the lyrical "I" perceives it as located "above" itself. This position recalls the head of a bed, an image also present in other poems by Sedakova and usually associated with the divine (in the form of guardian angels or Christ).

The imaginary "I" is clearly situated on the threshold—here denoted by the frame and the glass of a window—between the spiritual and the external world, and the latter is felt to be a threat:

Неужели, Мария, только рамы скрипят,
только стекла болят и трепещут?
Если это не сад—
разреши мне назад,
в тишину, где задуманы вещи.

Если это не сад, если рамы скрипят
оттого, что темней не бывает,
если это не тот заповеданный сад,
где голодные дети у яблонь сидят
и надкушенный плод забывают,

где не видно огней,
но дыханье темней
и надежней лекарство ночное . . .
Я не знаю, Мария, болезни моей.
Это сад мой стоит надо мною. (1:27)

Surely, Maria, it's not just window frames creaking,
not just windowpanes hurting and trembling?
If it isn't the garden—
then let me back in
to the silence where things are thought up.

If it isn't the garden, if the window frames creak
because it doesn't get darker than this,
if it isn't the garden we've been covenanted,
where hungry children sit under apple trees
and forget the fruit they once tasted,

where no branch can be seen,
but breathing is darker
and night's medicine more to be trusted . . .
I don't know, Maria, what is making me ill.
It's my garden that stands over me.

The lyrical "I" tells "Maria" that it wants to return to a prenatal realm—"to the silence where things are thought up" ("v tishinu, gde zadumany veshchi"). The poetic speaker's desire likens this place to the "garden" to which it also aspires. But in the end the "I" realizes that it does not need to return to the sought-after garden, because the garden exists parallel to the exterior world—albeit in another dimension: "over me" ("nado mnoiu"). The possessive and personal pronouns of the first-person singular are incorporated into those rhymes that refer to the garden: "temnei-nochnoe-moei-mnoiu" ("darker-night's-my-over me"). The poem thus suggests that the garden is part of the self and entangled with it.

The presence of a divine instance innate to human life is expressed even more clearly in "Childhood Guests" ("Gosti v detstve," 1973), a poem overtly related to a childhood experience. In "Surely, Maria" the difficulty consisted in constructing a referent for the lyrical "I" as speaker and as object of its own speech act, since its manner of thinking and speaking seemed to resemble that of an adult speaker, while the imagined situation more closely corresponded to the perception of a sick child. The poem "Childhood Guests" also relies on a lyrical "I" that both speaks and is spoken about, although the relationship between them is now clear: the adult lyrical "I" places itself back into the perspective of its childhood alter ego, whose imagination transforms the visit of a guest—which takes place behind a half-closed door, a symbol of the boundary between worlds—into an epiphany of angelic beings. The guests, who are "like angels," leave something behind in the house: a “word” that is not further defined, but that is located at the head of the child’s bed and “stands” above it just like the “garden” in the previous poem:

Гости в детстве

В двух шагах от притворенной
двери в детскую, за щель
шепчут стайкой оперенной
в крыльях высохших плащей.

Что ни скажут, позабудут.
Чем сулятся, не поймут.
Вместе выйдут, ливнем будут.
Только слова не возьмут.

И стоит оно слезами
изголовья моего:
словно ангелы сказали,
не запомнив, для чего. (1:32)

Childhood Guests

Just behind the pulled-to door
to the nursery, through the crack
they whisper in a feathered flock with
wings of raincoats hung to dry.

They say something, they’ll forget it.
What they swear by, they don’t get it.
They walk out, they shower like rain.
But the word they leave behind.

And it remains like tears I’ve shed
on my pillow in my bed:
like the angels speaking, then
not remembering why they did.

The poem avoids a precise definition of this epiphany: the terrestrial visit stands as a symbol for a spiritual occurrence, but just as likely it is only present to the child’s imagination. Using the future tense, the second stanza presents the fantastical thoughts of the child, as reconstructed by the adult “I,” and forms a strong rhythmic contrast to the first stanza: flowing enjambments in the first stanza versus a rigid structure with even syntactical breaks mid-line in the second stanza. Sedakova uses this form of rhythmic opposition in many of her texts to distinguish between experience and reflection, such as, for instance, in the poem "One day, when I die through and through." The third stanza synthesizes the two rhythmic movements and also adds a conclusion regarding the poem's content: the speaker's epiphany acquires fantastical traits ("as though the angels had spoken it") and thus elides any defining grasp.

Since it is not described further, various symbolic meanings can be assigned to the "word" that is left behind. Like the "garden," the "word" may point to the child's higher spiritual realm or to a facility for words related to it: to poetic talent. The word also evokes associations with Logos, the divine word of Christ. One reason for this interpretation is the word's origin among the angels: it seems "as though" ("slovno") they pronounced it and left it behind at the head of the bed. At the same time, the playful connection between *slovo* ("the word") and *slovno* ("as though") calls into question this explicit reading of the poem as a fantasy and suggests a realistic interpretation instead ("They will leave only the word"; "as though the angels had spoken it").

The reading according to which the angels, as God's messengers, left the power of Logos at the child's bed is supported by a parallel passage in the poem, "Were there master craftsmen on earth" ("Byli by mastera na svete"), from the "Third Notebook" of *Old Songs* (*Starye pesni*). Here an angel is supposed to supply the word, that is, to inspire: "An angel would whisper a word to me, / beloved as the evening stars, / dear to the mind and to the ear, / and everyone would repeat it" (1:212). And the final poem of the First Notebook of *Old Songs,* entitled "The Word" ("Slovo"; 1:189), reveals a connection between the word and Christ by alluding in the last two lines to John 8:32–36. The word thus appears as a person's divine essential core, which connects her with Christ and can also be the source of poetic talent.

In a much later poem, "In Memory of Father Alexander Men" ("Pamiati ottsa Aleksandra Menia," dated 1996–2005), Christ himself assumes the position at the head of a sick bed, which is a symbol for the *conditio humana* of a fallen humanity. Here Christ appears in the image of a doctor who has brought resurrecting powers into the world. At first, the two worlds are clearly separated into a "here" and "there": "Father Alexander, no one *here* / knows about what's there" ("nikto ne znaet / *zdes'* o tom, chto tam"), but Christ then bridges this divide. According to the poem, his resurrection is a gift to every human being and an indestructible presence in the world (see the third stanza below):

Памяти отца Александра Меня

Отче Александр, никто не знает
здесь о том, что там.
Вряд ли кто-то называет
то, что сердце забывает,
как назвать,
каким словам
сделаться без звука, без сказанья,
как открытая рука . . .
Вашей радости названье
выглянет, как солнце в облака:

это называется любовью,
для которой нет чужих.
Врач, стоящий в изголовье,
пламя нежного здоровья
он зажег уже в больных.

Ливень не зальет,
и ветер не задует,
не затопчет человек.
И не так он страшен, как малюют,
этот мир и этот век. (1:374)

In Memory of Father Alexander Men

Father Aleksandr, no one *here*
knows about what's there.
Could a person ever name
what the heart itself forgets
how to name,
what words should
give their sound and story up
like an open hand . . .
Your joy's name
will peek like the sun through clouds:

it's called love,
none's a stranger to it.
Standing bedside, a physician,
he's already lit a flame,
sparked in patients tender health.

Downpours won't extinguish it,
and winds won't blow it out,
no one's going to stamp it out.
And it's not as scary as they paint it,
this world and this age.

The power of Christ can also become effective through humans, in this case, as the poem demonstrates, through the priest Alexander Men. The speaker of the poem only arrives at this conviction through an internal dialogue with the departed Father Men. Initially the speaker rejects the presence of the divine in the world and knows neither name nor form (an open hand) for grasping that which lies beyond. But the sense of joy with which Father Men leaves the speaker then leads her to an expression: "love." Finally, the poem presents the image of Christ the "physician" who embodies the afterworld within this world and the "fire" whose resurrecting power is everlasting. Through an allusion to Christ and to Song of Songs 8:7 ("Many waters cannot quench love; rivers cannot sweep it away"—"Bol'shie vody ne mogut potushit' liubvi, i reki ne zal'iut ee"), the poem frames the priest's sun-like love for man as the transmission of resurrecting powers.

The first stanza has ten lines; the two following stanzas also contain a total of ten lines, which together form the second part of the poem. One line in each part uses visual line breaks that break up the rhyme scheme: "how to name, / what words should" ("kak nazvat', / kakim slovam") and "it's called love" ("eto nazyvaetsia liubov'iu), "downpours won't extinguish it / and winds won't blow it out" ("liven' ne zal'et / i veter ne zaduet"). The two parts have an analogous rhyme sequence (enclosed rhyme-alternating rhyme), as well as a corresponding structure of themes and motifs (heart/love; sun, clouds/rain, wind; question/answer). Another source of the poem's cohesion is the uninterrupted flow of trochees, which seems to derive from Father Alexander's first name, which in Russian is three syllables, A-le-ksandr (even the two broken lines mentioned above blend into the stream of trochees when read together). This coherence of the poem's parts indicates the presence of the divine. But to become conscious of it, the speaking voice must first remember Men and conduct an internal dialogue with him.

For Sedakova, the boundaries between worlds are thus permeable: Christ, angelic beings, as well as the deceased can actually cross over from the spiritual world, whereas human beings belong to both worlds and are rooted in the spiritual world with their deeper essence. Although humans are typically not conscious of this belonging, they can become aware of it under certain circumstances: the worlds can be bridged using inspiration, fantasy, and the imagination, as well as through its creative linguistic shaping, that is, through poetry. The poem to Father Alexander Men shows that certain individuals, too, can become a bridge leading to the divine—in this case, Father Alexander Men—and that the text is tasked with making readers conscious of this presence.

On the one hand, Sedakova's poems explicitly address this connection with the spiritual and the divine on the level of content, using dreams or dream-like states of consciousness, as well as fantastic ideas often associated with early childhood. On the other hand, many of her poems are directly presented as fantasy images rooted in dreams or the imagination, and thus embody in themselves the bridge between two worlds. Or they can serve to make readers conscious of the immanence of transcendence in the world through Christ.

Poetry and the Human as a Bridge between Worlds

The poem "A Fairy Tale" ("Skazka"), also from the volume *The Wild Rose*, shows how Sedakova's poetics represents the passage between worlds through human action and poetic means. Aside from the image of the garden it contains other motifs characteristic of her lyric poetry, such as the house and the candle, which serve as ciphers in her work and tie in to a long-standing literary tradition of the emblem, particularly that of the Baroque. These images also allude to the symbolism of Christianity and mysticism, as well as to folkloric material such as fairy tales:

Сказка

Так она лежит, и говорят,
что над ней горит, не убывая,
маленькая свечка восковая
и окно ее выходит в сад.

Странно, или сердце рождено,
чтобы так лежать? Веретено
на полу валяется и снится.
И она лежит, как тихий вход
в темный сад, откуда свет идет
и скрипит по древним половицам.

Глубоко, как сердце, глубоко,
как глубокий обморок, и глубже,
в глубине пропущенных веков
спи, голубка, долго, глубоко:
кто узнает, что идет снаружи?

Если это скрип и это свет,
понемногу восходящий кверху,—
сердце рождено, чтоб много лет
спать и не глядеть, как ходит свет
и за веткой отгибает ветку.

Никому не снится этот сон:
он себе и дом, и виноградник,
и дорога, по которой всадник
скачет к ней, и этот всадник—он.

—Много я прошу, но об одном
выслушай по милости огромной
и тогда разрушь меня, как дом,
непригодный для души бездомной:

это будет то, что я хочу.
Остальное бедно и обидно.
И задуй мне душу, как свечу,
при которой темноты не видно. (1:136–37)

A Fairy Tale

There she lies, and over her, they say,
there burns a little candle made of wax,
its light does not grow dim,
and her window looks out onto a garden.

Strange it is, or is the heart born
to lie there like that? The spindle knocks about
on the floor and comes to her in dreams.
And there she lies like a peaceful entrance
into a dark garden, from where light comes
and scrapes along the ancient floorboards.

Deeply as a heart, deeply now
as ever swoon was deep, and still more deeply,
in the depth of ages that have long passed
sleep, my dove, deeply and for ages:
after all, who knows what goes on from without?

If it is a scraping and a light
that make their way up slowly, bit by bit,—

then the heart is born to sleep for years,
and not to look and see how light goes walking,
how behind a branch it bends a branch.

None there is who dreams this dream:
it is a home unto itself, and a vineyard, too,
and a road down which a rider
gallops to her, and this rider, too, it is.

"I ask for much, but in your enormous mercy
hear out this one thing
and then demolish me like a house
that's unfit for a soul without a home:

that will be exactly what I want.
Everything else is miserable, offensive.
And blow my soul out like a candle
that hides the darkness from our sight."

Sedakova's poem begins with the image of an unnamed female figure who is only referred to by the open-ended personal pronoun "she." Here it is a "candle" that burns "over her"—in the same position as the "garden," "word," and Christ as "physician" in the poems read above. This position already indicates the spiritual significance of the motif. The candle makes the darkness inside the house visible and simultaneously corresponds to the light entering from the equally dark garden; it is a light gathered from the darkness. As such it resembles the spiritual light of mysticism, which is perceived as darkness compared to ordinary light. This reading is further suggested by the fact that the candle's light "does not grow dim," as natural light would.

The text thus invokes the context of Christian mysticism, which is intensified in the ensuing description of the sleeping lyrical persona. She is compared to a "peaceful entrance / into the dark garden," that is, she is the place where the two worlds are both separated and conjoined. "She" herself embodies the transition between worlds, although this persona is a "nobody": she sleeps, but her dream is without a subject: "the spindle [. . .] comes to her in dreams," but the poem does not mention to whom the spindle appears. Furthermore, the text explicitly states: "None there is who dreams this dream" and her sleep is deep and unconscious like a blackout, and thus without a subject. The dove as a symbol for the sleeping woman refers to her deeper spiritual essence (the dove as a Christian symbol for the Holy Spirit), which sonically is at one with the "depth" ("deep," "deeper," "depth"—"gluboko," "glubzhe," "glubina"). This "depth" is a traditional image of God in Christian mysticism and in the negative theology based on Pseudo-Dionysius the Areopagite and his *Mystical Theology*. According to its teachings, God has no earthly traits and is therefore not knowable and should be only referred to as "Nothing" or "Nobody."[20] In this context, the deep sleep of the lyrical persona refers to the "spiritual" or "mystical sleep" that Bonaventure, for instance, defined as the highest degree of contemplation. In such a sleep, the soul rests within God; sleep is here a symbol of the *unio mystica*.

In accordance with the mystical tradition, Sedakova's poem transforms the woman into a symbol of the soul, whose true being lies hidden in the unconscious, where it is at one with God. In her dream, which is "dreamt by nobody," the lyrical persona addresses the dream itself in a circular manner. This dream is at once "house," "vineyard" (an equivalent of the "garden"), "path," and "horseman." The horseman ("on"—"he") is contained in the word for sleep ("son") but the lyrical persona is only present proportionally: "ona" (she). She is more than her dream and this "more" is the "nobody," her inner essence that rests in God. The dream thus encompasses the entire situation, including the person dreaming of herself. Just as the child in "Surely, Maria" wishes to return "into silence," here the dreaming female speaker asks that the "house" be destroyed and the interior light—the "candle," or "soul"—be extinguished. This would remove the separation between light and dark, interior and exterior, and between the world of the senses and the spirit.

The divide is not visible to the woman in her deep, and unconscious, sleep. Life and fate are a dream that separates her from divine reality, with which she was united in her unconscious sleep, before the "heart was born." By the same token, the dream itself is what enables the individual to perceive not only this divide, but also its true home in a spiritual realm that cannot be grasped with the senses. By returning to the world of God and negating the dream, and thus consciousness, the separation of both worlds, which the dreaming figure itself embodies, would be cancelled.

This poem offers an understanding of human individuals as composed of several instances: first, the female figure that can be objectified and physically grasped ("she lies"). Second, her deeper, purely inner being, which elides any access through her unconscious sleep. It is thus treated as a "nobody," but nevertheless characterized by a God-given spiritual existence to which the motifs of the candle, the lower depth, and the pigeon allude. The third instance is the figure that speaks in the dream and voices the desire to abolish the self, so as to be reunited with the "darkness" of spiritual existence. And the poem itself is the site that connects the two dimensions of being, which are separated in and through the consciousness of the figure.

While poetry's exceptional status as a transition between worlds is only implied in "Fairy Tale," it becomes more explicit in the poem "Night Sewing" ("Nochnoe shit'e") in the volume *Gates, Windows, Arches*:

Ночное шитье

Тяпе

Уж звездное небо уносит на запад
и Кассиопеи бледнеет орлица—
вот-вот пропадет, но, как вышивки раппорт,
желает опять и опять повториться.
Ну что же, душа? что ты, спишь, как сурок?
Пора исполнять вдохновенья урок.

Бери свои иглы, бери свои рядна,
натягивай страсти на старые кросна—
гляди, как летает челнок Ариадны
в твоем лабиринте пред чудищем грозным.
Нам нужен, ты знаешь, рушник или холст—
скрипучий, прекрасный, сверкающий мост.

О, что бы там ни было, что ни случится,
я звездного неба люблю колесницы,
возниц и драконов, везущих по спице
все волосы света и ока зеницы,
блистание нитки, летящей в иглу,
и посвист мышиный в запечном углу.

Как древний герой, выполняя заданье,
из сада мы вынесем яблоки ночи
и вышьем, и выткем свое мирозданье—
чулан, лабиринт, мышеловку, короче—
и страшный, и душный его коридор,
колодезь, ведущий в сокровища гор.

Так что же я сделаю с перстью земною,
пока еще лучшее солнце не выйдет?
Мы выткем то небо, что ходит за мною,
откуда нас души любимые видят.
И сердце мое, как печные огни,
своей кочергой разгребают они. (1:241–42)

Night Sewing

to Tiapa

The stars in the sky move away to the west,
the eagle of Cassiopeia pales—
nearly gone, but like rapport needlework,
it wants to repeat itself over and over.
And you, soul? you're curled up asleep like a marmot?
It's time for the work inspiration has taught.

Take up your needles and take up your flax,
stretch your passions on an antique loom—
watch Ariadne's shuttle fly
through your labyrinth, the frightful fiend chasing behind.
What we need is a hand-woven linen, you know—
a creaking, a splendid, a glistening bridge.

No matter what's there and no matter what happens,
I love the chariots of stars in the sky,
the charioteers and dragons who bear on their spokes
all hairs of the light, all apples of the eye,
the gleam of the thread flying into the needle,
and the whistle of mice tucked away by the stove.

Like a hero of old fulfilling his quest
we'll bring back the apples of night from the garden,
we'll sew and we'll weave our own creation—
the pantry, the labyrinth, the mouse trap: that is—
its hallway that frightens and stifles us, too,
the well that will lead to the mountains' vast treasure.

So what shall I do with the dust of the earth
as we wait for a much better sun to come out?
We'll weave the sky that follows behind me,
from where souls we love look out and see us.
And just as though it were a fire in the stove,
they'll take up their poker and rake at my heart.

The title itself invokes the traditional metaphor of poetry as sewing or weaving, and of fabric or tissue, adding that this is a nocturnal activity and thus something that eludes any conscious grasp. The "starry sky," an image for the spiritual world, cannot be viewed during the day. In daytime consciousness, the soul can only establish a connection to its night side by repeating "the lesson of inspiration." The resulting creative fabric then becomes "a creaking, a splendid, a glistening bridge" to the nocturnal realm, which can be transported into the daytime world in the form of images. Correspondingly, the poet and artist is compared to two figures of ancient mythology, Theseus and Hercules. The latter retrieves the "apples of night" from the "Garden" of the Hesperides, that is, the "golden apples" that the myth treats as a means to rejuvenation and immortality. Poetry thus becomes a site, which, like the labyrinth of Daedalus, mysteriously preserves a part of the spiritual world in the form of art, simultaneously concealing and revealing it.

As the image of the starry sky—the spiritual world—poetry is at first beautiful and appealing, as the lyrical "I" attests ("I love"). Like the dream, poetry is a "corridor" and a "well," a transition into the dimension of the spirit and the night world. But unlike the image of the starry sky, neither the passage itself, nor the relics of the spirit world that become visible during the transition, are seen as beautiful by humans in daytime consciousness. From the point of view of ordinary consciousness, the poetic process and the act of poetic interpretation turns poetry's spiritual substance into "dragons" and the "corridor" that leads there now "frightens and stifles us."

When poetry is rooted in mystical experience, it can become a threat to our daytime consciousness, which is incommensurable with nocturnal consciousness. A brave hero is needed to enter into this zone of transition, that is, to engage with poetry. Sedakova thus ascribes to poetry an ancient mystical notion according to which the realm of mysteries holds many terrors for the uninitiated, which the initiate must train to overcome.

She transfers the basis of poetry to an actual relationship between the poet and the spiritual realm, and both the poet and the interpreting reader become mythological heroes who must find and conquer the Minotaur. Sedakova locates the passage toward the spiritual world in "inspiration." Without inspiration, the poet remains an ordinary human being, asleep to the netherworld. Sedakova thus does not view the poet as a mystic who spends his entire life training for initiation and a life in the spirit, and who actively strives toward a mystical experience. Rather, mystical experience is bestowed upon the poet as a gift of revelation.

In this poem, the spiritual world is thus actively involved with inspiration, but the poet remains unaware of its direct participation: the "heaven" of the spirit world "walks behind me" and the "souls" of the dead influence the poet's "heart," or the poet's semi- or unconscious realm of emotions and desires, but not the poet's head, the reflecting consciousness. Due to this concealed connection with the spirit world, which eludes the conscious mind yet remains active in inspiration, the poem becomes an image of precisely this world. It is a living image that holds the spiritual world deep within: "We'll weave the sky that follows behind me." Art, or rather poetry, creates symbols for the spiritual world, but it is the reality of this world that enables art to be its image. This deeper actuality lies concealed within art and can be reexperienced through its reception. For Sedakova, poetry is thus, by analogy to her definition of human beings, a bridge to the spirit, which can express itself in and through the poem. She views poetry as the most intrinsic human activity, in which our essence as a transition between world and God finds expression.

Poetry as a Memory of God

One defining feature of Sedakova's poetry is that it withdraws from any direct rational approach. Through its hermetic dimension, it gestures toward the night side of consciousness and the corresponding spiritual world. The poem "Coda" ("Koda"; 1:292), for instance, figuratively conveys how the style of the text forms a threshold for our normal consciousness and manifests indeterminacy and infinity. Poetry's spiritual origin withdraws from our focused, three-dimensionally oriented gaze and can only be envisioned by "squinting." But even so, one should not attempt to find a rational resolution: normal consciousness perceives the poem and its sound (its composition) as accidental, like the chirping sounds of a "grasshopper," an anacreontic image for the poet with a long tradition in Russian poetry. In some of Sedakova's texts, the spiritual dimension that remains intangible in poetry is reified as a mystical apparition that is perceived either as a figure or as a mere voice. Its primary characteristic is its openness.[21] In these cases, the intangibility of the spirit returns in the ambiguity of a voice or the figure of a "nobody" or an unknown "somebody," for instance. The poems "I raise up the radiance, like a fallen hand" ("Kak upavshuiu ruku, ia pripodnimaiu siiani'e"; 1:140) and "Postscript: The Old Poet" ("Postskriptum: Staryi poet"; 1:141–42), for example, describe an undetermined voice whose speaker can be associated with God, or with God's word in the form of Christ. At times, this voice is joined by the appearance of an unidentified person, which establishes a relationship to the lyrical "I" by looking, nodding, or smiling at it.

A short poem in Sedakova's cycle *Old Songs*, "Childhood" ("Detstvo"), hardly remarkable at first glance, treats the mystical encounter with God paradigmatically as the origin of all poetry. It is the only poem in Sedakova's collected works in which the lyrical "I" is explicitly identified using the poet's own name. This particularly rare autobiographical connection to the poet lends the poem an exceptional status. It also reveals the religious and mystical foundation of Sedakova's poetic work with particular clarity:

Детство

Помню я раннее детство
и сон в золотой постели.

Кажется или правда?—
кто-то меня увидел,
быстро вошел из сада
и стоит улыбаясь.

—Мир—говорит,—пустыня.
Сердце человека—камень.
Любят люди, чего не знают.

Ты не забудь меня, Ольга,
а я никого не забуду. (1:183)

Childhood

I remember early childhood
and my dream in the golden bed.

Was it truth, or just a dream?—
someone caught sight of me,
he rushed in from the garden
and he stands there, smiling.

"The world," he says, "is a wilderness.
The human heart is a stone.
People love what they don't know.

Don't you forget me, Olga;
there's no one I'll forget."

The versifying lyrical "I," Olga, here also uses memory to revert to her childhood alter ego, which has an experience similar to that described in "Childhood Guests." Here the event is suspended not between reality and imagination, but between dream and reality. The only rhyme in the poem, however, suggests that the dream should be treated as reality: the garden (in the genitive, "sada") from which someone emerges, and which usually carries religious connotations in Sedakova's work, rhymes with the word for truth or reality ("pravda").

As so often in Sedakova's poetry, she here conveys a threshold state using the spatial image of the house and the garden, which are united when a person steps inside. Interior and exterior, as a symbol of the terrestrial and the spiritual world, are conjoined in this vision. The poem further introduces the subject of theophany by alluding to Mary Magdalene's encounter with the resurrected Christ leaving the garden, whom she at first mistook for a gardener (John 20:11–18).[22] The unknown "someone" from the "garden" can be identified as Christ appearing to the child Olga.

Such a vision requires transforming ordinary consciousness, as the very manner of its depiction indicates: Sedakova suggests this transformation by reversing the viewer's perspective. The child does not catch sight of "someone"; instead "someone" catches sight of the child. Here Sedakova takes up the motif of an all-seeing God who gazes at man, with its rich iconographic heritage. In the form of Christ, God turns toward man. As a result, the adverbial participle "smiling" constitutes the arithmetical center of the poem (it is preceded and followed by twenty-one words): Christ is smiling at the child.

This stanza further continues the reversed perspective from "someone" onto the child: "someone" does not leave the garden to enter the house, as the child would perceive it from within the house, but enters from the garden into the house. The lyrical "I" thus describes the crossing of the threshold in reverse perspective: the moment of entering is seen not by the child, but by a "someone." The acts of catching sight and of entering are narrated in the perfective, and thus cannot be directly perceived by the child; it is as though the child had put itself into the perspective of the "someone."

Sedakova's reversal of perspective in connection with dreams and the perception of the divine may harken back to Pavel Florensky's remarks on the role of perspective in iconography. Florensky argued that the shift from the central perspective and three-dimensionality used in early iconography toward a direct reversal of perspective and polyperspectivity was due to the incommensurability of finite and infinite forms of consciousness. He noted that dreams also display such a reversal of perspective in relation to external reality and the actual flow of time.[23]

The message of an unnamed "someone" is an admonition: he reminds the child to be aware that there is more to life than the earthly "world," which humans love by mistake. Here Sedakova employs biblical imagery: the world as a desert and the heart of stone. The "someone" makes present and personifies the divine as an alternative world, which humans should love instead. If the child should ever lose the ability to intuit Christ, like the other adults in the "world," she should recall this encounter.

The adult lyrical "I" fulfills precisely this mission with the poem. The first word of the text establishes a link to the last word, which is spoken by the "someone": just as there is no one he will forget, so the lyrical "I" remembers the encounter. The poem thus implements its theme performatively; that is, the act of poetic creativity itself is the remembrance of a mystical experience: the encounter with the resurrected.

Sedakova's later poem "Nothing" ("Nichto"; 1:400) returns to this metapoetic idea and further intensifies it: the soul must "be silent" and refrain from all poetic creativity until it has been touched by "*this*" ("*eto*"). The poem identifies "this" with the "creative hands" that helped raise Lazarus from his grave, and thus with the touch of Christ's powers of resurrection.

In many of Sedakova's poems, mystical experience is depicted using hints that permit a Christian interpretation, but without clearly defining it as such. Central to these texts is an encounter or revelation experienced by the lyrical "I" or another lyrical persona. Christian allusions and motifs appear in such texts as an interpretive offer presented by the lyrical "I"; but the experience itself simultaneously withdraws from any description or reflection. This openness, or the presence of the not immediately graspable, guards Sedakova's verse from a denominational religious definition and enhances its poetic qualities.

The Mystical Foundations of Poetry

Over and over, Sedakova's essays ask what the nature of poetry is and what is its task. One point of departure for these reflections is the basic anthropological notion that a sense of religiosity is innate to all human beings. In contradistinction to Dietrich Bonhoeffer, who speaks of the "religionlessness of a humanity come of age,"[24] Sedakova suggests that a relationship to the divine is inherent to humanity: "'religiosity' pertains not to the 'childhood of humanity' but to humanity in general" ("Ditrikh Bonkheffer dlia nas"; 4:497). But she, too, admits that this innate awareness of a divine relationship is not always accessible. Her poems imply that it is especially present in early childhood, as well as in certain "threshold states." By contrast, her poems depict the everyday world of adulthood as marked by a loss of this consciousness, which results in cultural and moral impoverishment. Sedakova refers to the living relationship to God as "a memory of Eden"—and proper human happiness consists of precisely this. Her poems also often use the symbol of the (paradisiacal) "garden" in this sense. For Sedakova, one of poetry's key tasks is to reawaken this "memory of Eden," as she names it in "'In the Chaste Abyss of a Line of Verse': On Poetic Meaning and Doctrinal Meaning" ("'V tselomudrennoi bezdne stikha": O smysle poeticheskom i smysle doktrinal'nom," 2003; 3:139). She believes that a poetry that is itself rooted in our deeper spiritual dimension can appeal to an inner essence that lies unconsciously hidden in our "depth" (3:138). This belief in an immortal spiritual core is the basis of her view of innate human religiosity. However, this essence is not something that separates us into distinct individuals, but the source of everything that humans hold "in common": our spiritual core makes each human being at once an individual and a part of mankind (3:138).

In Sedakova's view, poetry evokes the memory of man's spiritual origin not by depicting religious content or mystical experience, but by making such experience present in the form of poetry itself. The poetic text does not serve to communicate something to the rational mind, but rather to exert a direct influence on the recipient. Poetry enables the reader to both witness and relive mystical experience by performatively enacting it, rather than communicating something about it: the poem carries out that which it describes. To be effective, the poetic text must make its reader part of this performative dimension and let it unfold within his or her experience of the poem.[25] This explains why such a poetics is not necessarily indebted to a particular religious tradition. Above all, Sedakova wants to afford an experience of a divine or spiritual dimension incompatible with our ordinary consciousness, something different and more elevated that both transcends and encompasses the earthly realm.[26]

This orientation toward a mystical encounter with God lends Sedakova's poems a sense of infinity that expresses itself in their semantic inconclusiveness and tendency toward silence. Like the reader, the poet cannot elude this openness: for Sedakova, the process of writing as well as interpreting poetry must exceed rational reflection and construction, and it must place the reader into a higher and more encompassing state of consciousness.[27]

Poetry's mystical foundation unfolds its effect when it defines the text as a whole; that is, when it is not the object of a description, but becomes the object itself and expresses itself in the context of all of its elements and levels. This context is something that cannot be grasped as a fact, but that appears only during the process of interpretation. Once the process has concluded, it disappears and eludes any clear identification and objectification. For Sedakova, poems become "units of force" due to the meaning present in their formal elements (in the composition or the semantic aura of a particular symbol or image), which lives exclusively in the reader's perception. The poem's effect, however, does not determine the reader, but sets him or her free, since it results from his or her own activity: "These 'big words' don't *mean* something: they simply *are something*. And the reality of their existence moves us. We recognize in the poet's 'big words' our own language, not as a unit of thought but as a unit of force" ("Komu my bol'she verim: Poetu ili prozaiku?"; 3:160). For Sedakova, the source of poetry—a place where the reader can be led as well—is a form of awareness that withdraws from our ordinary state of consciousness. It reaches deep into that which usually remains unknown to us and that Sedakova believes can be found in dreams or the expanded consciousness of mystics. This all-encompassing state of consciousness is the site from which the form and composition of poetry derives.[28]

Sedakova's recent essays reveal a strong religious orientation, similar to that expressed in her later poems. Instead of only ascribing the revival of religious consciousness to poetry, she now credits it to the Church and associates poetry with the Church and with her faith: "I think it will become patantly impossible to create art that is inimical to faith" ("Blagoslovenie tvorchestvu i parnasskii ateizm," 2000; 4:345). It remains to be seen whether and how this intensified confessional engagement will transform Sedakova's verse and her poetics; no new volumes of poems have appeared in recent years.

The Mystical Element in Sedakova's Poetry

Sedakova's poetry constitutes a cosmos of meaning that jointly encompasses all of the author's texts. Over the course of her work, she develops symbols with a particular semantic spectrum and transports them even into her later texts. In some respects, Sedakova's poems confirm her reflections about other writers, which illuminate a number of her symbols, as has been shown in the case of the "garden." In many poems, the "garden" is a symbol of divine provenance and of man's essence, which we ought to remember in the time of the "desert," as Sedakova describes our godforsaken contemporary civilization. Her poems themselves contribute to this process of remembering.

Sedakova's poetry is rooted in a personal experience of spiritual freedom from the world, in a mystical encounter with an "other" realm of existence that she identifies with the divine in a Christian sense, and that is not usually accessible to human consciousness. This dimension not only becomes a theme in its own right, but is expressed performatively by the fact of the poem itself. With their semantic openness, Sedakova's poems often initially appear hermetic and thus create an interpretive threshold that must be crossed, and that also enters the poetic text as a theme. Sedakova counteracts this hermeticism by inviting the reader into a conversation. This is achieved through the personal modes of address among various lyric voices and personas, which can also address the reader directly, as well as by the indeterminate nature of the poems' pronouns, which also invite the reader to identify with them. In terms of both content and form, Sedakova's poems are defined by their dialogic nature, which both enacts and demands creative production, attentive perception, as well as changing points of view and relationships to other speakers (and to the poets and thinkers implied by intertextual references). In short, her lyric texts are an invitation to cross thresholds in the medium of poetry.

Sedakova's poetic worldview is thus structured by analogy to Epstein's idea of the metabole: she divides the worlds of sensory impressions and of the spiritual or divine through a "high threshold." However, it is still possible to connect the two worlds by crossing the threshold, which enables the presence of one world within the other. In Sedakova's work, this transition is based on Christianity from the very beginning: Christ himself connects the two worlds and through him humans can also partake of it. Mystical experience—in fact, the very process of writing poetry—can reveal the coincidence of opposites (as Nicolas of Cusa called it) and help us find our inherent purpose. In contrast to Elena Shvarts,[29] Sedakova does not strive for a poetics of transcendence that lets readers actively cross borders and penetrate through the world of appearances into a divine realm. Instead, she subscribes to a poetics of the immanence of transcendence, which is ontologically grounded and a gift of God. Her view of the poetic act is based on accepting divine revelation as a gift to humanity, which awakens us toward an experience of God's presence in the beyond.

Translated from German by Philipp Penka

Notes

1. See Valentina Polukhina, "Conform Not to This Age: An Interview with Ol'ga Sedakova," in *Reconstructing the Canon: Russian Writing in the 1980s*, ed. Arnold McMillin (Amsterdam: Harwood Academic Publishers, 2000), 43 and 58. For more on the concept of the field and Russian contemporary poetry, see Henrieke Stahl and Marion Rutts, eds., *Imidzh, dialog, eksperiment: Polia sovremennoi russkoi poezii; Image, Dialog, Experiment—Felder der russischen Gegenwartsdichtung* (Munich: Otto Sagner, 2013).

2. See Mikhail Epshtein, "O metarealizme," in *Postmodern v russkoi literature* (Moscow: Vysshaia shkola, 2005), 147. For a critical approach to Epstein's concept, see Aleksandr Zhitenev, *Poeziia neomodernizma* (St. Petersburg: Inapress, 2012), 9. Sedakova herself indicates her proximity to metarealism in an article whose title might be translated as "Success with a human face" ("Uspekh s chelovecheskim litsom," 1998; 3:154–55). In contrast to Epstein, however, she uses the term to describe the religious and mystical art and poetry characteristic of unofficial Russian culture since the 1970s. Sedakova describes such art forms as "priest-like" and "Pythian" ("zhrecheskoe," "pificheskoe"). She further associates them with a "new metaphysics" and a "new mysticism," citing the example of Mikhail Shvartsman.

3. Sergei Biriukov emphasizes that various forms of the "neo-avant-garde" must be seen as a third major stylistic tendency. See Sergei Biriukov, "Grani neoavangarda: Deistvuiushchie litsa, institutsii, izdaniia, prezentatsii, i t.d.," in Stahl and Rutts, *Imidzh, dialog, eksperiment*, 65–76. Robert Hodel, who examines how these and similar terms have been used to categorize the poetic landscape of the last thirty years, aptly suggests that the proposed terminology is neither clear enough for a classification nor has it succeeded in reflecting the growing diversity of poetic forms. It must thus be used only tentatively and

with caution. See Robert Hodel, "Russische Lyrik nach dem Moskauer Konzeptualismus," in *Gedichte schreiben in Zeiten der Umbrüche. Tendenzen der Lyrik seit 1989 in Russland und Deutschland*, ed. Henrieke Stahl and Hermann Korte, Neuere Lyrik: Interkulturelle und interdisziplinäre Studien (Leipzig: Biblion Media, 2016), 115–28.

4. In the rhetorical tradition, the term *metabole* (Greek, meaning dislocation, conversion, or transition) describes a reversed sequence of subclauses or terms. In versification, it indicates a transition to a different meter; in music, to a different key.

5. See Mikhail Epshtein, "Ot metafory k metabole," in *Postmodern v russkoi literature*, 152–55.

6. Ibid., 154.

7. The rhizome as a metaphor for labyrinthine forms of thinking and writing is described in Gilles Deleuze and Félix Guattari, *Rhizome: Introduction* (Paris: Éditions de Minuit, 1976).

8. Stephanie Sandler aptly notes that Sedakova's lyric poetry often connects different levels of meaning metonymically, in "Thinking Self in the Poetry of Ol'ga Sedakova," in *Gender and Russian Literature: New Perspectives*, ed. Rosalind J. Marsh (Cambridge: Cambridge University Press, 1996), 310.

9. Regarding the dream motif, Sedakova herself notes: "Dreams, the state of dreaming, have, from childhood on, meant more to me, perhaps, than reality" (in Polukhina, "Conform Not to This Age," 42).

10. Polukhina views Sedakova as "one of the best confessional Christian poets writing in Russian today" (Polukhina, "Conform Not to This Age," 33), whereas Hodel stresses that her "metaphysical search is often dressed in religious garb, but without being tied to a particular confession." Sedakova's outlook is indeed Christian, but her lyric poetry (with few exceptions) does not adhere to any firm ecclesiastical or strict confessional rules. See Hodel, "Russische Lyrik nach dem Moskauer Konzeptualismus," 120. Ona Renner-Fahey's attempt to cast Sedakova as a committed Orthodox poet is not convincing, at least in the context of her work overall. See Ona Renner-Fahey, "Mythologies of Poetic Creation in Twentieth-Century Russian Verse" (PhD diss., Ohio State University, 2002), 138–83.

11. Benjamin Paloff uses the term "expressive mysticism" in "The God Function in Joseph Brodsky and Olga Sedakova," *Slavic and East European Journal* 51, no. 4 (2007): 716.

12. The description of Sedakova's verse as "metaphysical poetry" is based on Sergei Averintsev. On this point and on the religiosity of Sedakova's poetry more generally, see N. G. Medvedeva, *"Tainye stikhi" Ol'gi Sedakovoi* (Izhevsk: Udmurtskii gosudarstvennyi universitet, 2013), 7. Medvedeva argues that Sedakova's poetry is "illuminated by the light of Orthodoxy" even though Sedakova views herself as a secular poet (208). See also Polukhina, "Conform Not to This Age," 234.

13. Ol'ga Sedakova, *Vse, i srazu* (St. Petersburg: Pushkinskii fond, 2009).

14. My definition of mysticism is based on Bernhard McGinn's study *The Presence of God: A History of Western Christian Mysticism* (New York: Crossroad, 1991–). McGinn views the "mystical element in Christianity" as "the preparation for, the consciousness of, and the reaction to what can be described as the immediate or direct presence of God." See McGinn, *The Growth of Mysticism* (New York: Crossroad, 1994), xvii.

15. Sedakova reports seeing an apparition (*iavlenie*) as a child, an event (*proisshestvie*) that significantly influenced her. She sensed the existence of a different dimension of being, without finding herself capable of understanding or interpreting this experience. See Sedakova, "Zametki i vospominaniia o raznykh stikhotvoreniiakh, a takzhe Pokhvala poezii," 3:13–95.

16. Ol'ga Sedakova, *Sad mirozdan'ia* (Moscow: Art-Volkhonka, 2014), 7.

17. See also ibid., 16.

18. Maria was the name of Sedakova's mother and Marusia that of her nanny, who is the subject of the short story "Marusia Smagina." See Anna Gal'perina, "Ol'ga Sedakova: Ne khochu uspekha i ne boius' provala," interview published in Pravmir.ru, December 26, 2014, http://www.pravmir.ru/olga-sedakova-ne-xochu-uspexa-i-ne-boyus-provala/, accessed March 15, 2018.

19. In her interview with Polukhina, Sedakova describes childhood as a "private Eden." See Polukhina, "Conform Not to This Age," 37 and 67, as well as Gal'perina, "Ol'ga Sedakova."

20. See Alois M. Haas's chapter "Das Nichts Gottes und seine Sprengmetaphorik," in *Mystik im Kontext* (Munich: Fink, 2004), 89–104.

21. See Paloff, "The God Function," 729.

22. Polukhina explains that the title and the motif of the "wild rose" ("dikii shipovnik") are also related to this passage in the Gospels. Polukhina, "Conform Not to This Age," 233.

23. Pavel A. Florenskii, *Ikonostas*, in *Sochineniia v 4-kh tomakh* (Moscow: Mysl', 1994–2000), 2:419–527.

24. Dietrich Bonhoeffer, *Widerstand und Ergebung: Briefe und Aufzeichnungen aus der Haft*, ed. Eberhard Bethge (Munich: Kaiser, 1985), 191.

25. See Sedakova, "Poeziia i antropologiia," 1999; 3:112.

26. Sedakova's reflections on the mystical substrate of Aronzon and Celan's lyric poetry can also be applied to her own poetry. See Sedakova, "Leonid Aronzon: Poet kul'minatsii," 2007; 3:527.

27. See Sedakova, "Iskusstvo kak dialog s dal'nim," 2003–4; 4:332.

28. See Sedakova, "Stikhotvornyi iazyk: Semanticheskaia vertikal' slova," 1989; 3:175.

29. For more on Shvarts, see Henrieke Stahl, "'Pominal'naia svecha' Eleny Shvarts—poetika transtsendentirovaniia," in *Imidzh, dialog, eksperiment*, 435–449.

PART 3

Contextual Readings

Languages, Cultures, and Sources

Stylized Folklore as a Recollection of Europe

Olga Sedakova's Old Songs *and Alexander Pushkin's* Songs of the Western Slavs

ILYA KUKULIN

In memory of M. L. Gasparov

This essay sets out the terms of the dialogue initiated by Olga Sedakova's *Old Songs* (*Starye pesni*) with Alexander Pushkin's *Songs of the Western Slavs* (*Pesni zapadnykh slavian*, 1831–35).[1] One of the distinguishing qualities of Sedakova's work of the 1970s–80s is a firm rejection of any obvious reference to contemporary contexts, excepting a very few works from the early 1980s such as "Marching Song" ("Pokhodnaia pesnia"), with its direct political invective, and particularly the "Elegy That Turns into a Requiem" ("Elegiia, perekhodiashchaia v rekviem," 1984). This rejection is characteristic for many writers in the 1970s, official and unofficial alike, but in Sedakova's case it is particularly marked. In the late 1970s and early 1980s, she turned to the themes of medieval Europe (the long poem *Tristan and Isolde* [*Tristan i Izol'da*]; 1978–82) and the ancient world (the cycle *Stelae and Inscriptions* [*Stely i nadpisi*]; 1982), as well as Chinese art (*Chinese Journey* [*Kitaiskoe puteshestvie*]; 1986—although this topic necessarily gestures toward the "Chinese" poems of Ezra Pound and Paul Claudel as well). This is the period in which *Old Songs* was written: Sedakova began work on them in 1980 and finished the cycle in 1992.

Sedakova's work can be characterized as *uchronic*, with reference to *uchronia*, a term analogous to "utopia" coined by the French writer Charles Renouvier in 1876. One of the reasons behind this uchronic quality is the peculiar perception of time in late Soviet unofficial culture. Within this community, time had come to be understood as a marginal category, one that questioned the prevailing concept of the present-day as too politicized, too "colonized" by Soviet propaganda. During these decades, the concept of "great time" (*bol'shoe vremia*), introduced by Mikhail Bakhtin in his "Response to the Editors of *Novyi mir*" (1970), became very popular among Russian intellectuals. As Bakhtin writes:

> if the significance of any work is reduced, for example, to its role in the struggle against serfdom (as is done in our secondary schools), this work will lose all of its significance when serfdom and its remnants no longer exist in life. It is frequently the case, however, that a work gains in significance, that is, it enters *great time*. But the work cannot live in future centuries without having somehow absorbed past centuries as well. If it had belonged *entirely* to today (that is, were a product only of its own time), and not a continuation of the past or essentially related to the past, it could not live in the future. Everything that belongs only to the present dies along with the present.[2]

Sedakova herself subsequently defined this "great time" as a time of crisis:

> When we really and truly "return to culture," we find ourselves not in some timeless preserve, some kind of Limbo, where Homer converses with Virgil and Dante with Eliot, but in the concrete, historical situation of culture—what has long been described as "the crisis of art," "the collapse of humanism," "the crisis of language" and so on. The embrace (conscious or not) of this situation as a point of departure strikes me as the key innovation of this body of lyric poetry [uncensored poetry of the 1970s] in the context of the Russian tradition.[3]

I maintain that at least some of Sedakova's most significant work was called upon to address cultural and social questions as well as poetic ones, questions that were important in the concrete historical moment when they were written. The task of answering these questions remains inseparable from the innovative nature of Sedakova's poetry and its unique meanings.

I argue that *Old Songs* is a cycle of poems that creates an image of Russian culture as European. The cycle was begun in 1980, a time when the concepts of "Russia" (and "Russia's special path") and "Europe" were growing ever further apart in Soviet societal consciousness (even in its unofficial part). The cycle takes a polemical stance with regard to these stereotypes. In seeking to find a synthesis of the Russian and European, Sedakova turned to a dialogue with Pushkin's *Songs of the Western Slavs,* which had grappled with a relatively similar task in 1835: to create an image of shared national identity, or nationhood (*narodnost'*) that would render "Russian" part of a universal whole including both the European and the Slavic. As it turned out, the only form this kind of nationhood could take in Pushkin's work was the inseparable coexistence of "us" and "them" (*svoe/chuzhoe*).

In its current form, *Old Songs* consists of five parts: The First, Second and Third Notebooks, with their poems given in numerical order, and two appendices, respectively entitled "Poems with No Place in the Second Notebook" and "Poems Added to *Old Songs*." The poems in the appendices are not numbered. For the purposes of this essay, I will give only a brief, necessarily sketchy overview of the overall meaning of the cycle, which is made up of many different motifs and deserves a detailed study in its own right. The main ideas, which appear variously in different poems, are (1) a super-rational grasp of the paradox of ethical values and moral gifts (like bravery and mercy) inaccessible to everyday consciousness, gifts that in their absolute depth require renunciation rather than acquisition; and (2) the paradox of the very existence of ethical values and moral gifts in a world built upon death, loss, and destruction.

In her discussion of Sedakova's *Tristan and Isolde*, Ksenia Golubovich sets up an ethical conception that applies equally well to *Old Songs*, which Sedakova was writing at the same time. Golubovich suggests this conception as a framework for the style initiated in *Tristan and Isolde*—a style that would subsequently underlie the entire plot of *Old Songs*. As Golubovich notes:

> [Sedakova's] poetry . . . does not say that Love, Mercy, Beauty, Justice, Meekness, Strength are things that we can own. In the heart of these things there is darkness, there is absence. Every Great Thing denies itself—the phrase "I am just" provokes ethical revulsion (also recall the "ethics of politeness" that Derrida suggests as an ethics of the impossible condition). As demonstrated by the entire post–Second World War experience, the heart of Great Things contains renunciation, because these things assume distance, deferment, expectation, parting, separation and mortality.[4]

The First Notebook is a key part of *Old Songs*. Its poems rely heavily on the motif of unclean conscience. This is not the conscience of a concrete individual, and neither is it the abstract human sinfulness of theological works; rather, Sedakova creates a generalized image of the kind of conscience that can make a person unhappy. The sixth poem begins:

Человек он злой и недобрый,
скверный человек и несчастный.
И кажется, мне его жалко,
а сама я еще недобрее.

И когда мы с ним говорили,
давно и не помню сколько,

ночь была и дождь не кончался,
будто бы что задумал,
будто кто-то спускался
и шел в слезах и сам как слезы (1:185)

There's a man who is spiteful and mean,
a bad man and unhappy, too.
Somehow I think I feel sorry for him,
though I'm even more unkind.

And when we talked, the two of us,
so long ago I don't know how long,
it was night and the rain wouldn't stop,
as though it was thinking of something,
as though someone was descending
in tears, someone who was very like tears

Demonstrations of the world's variability play a crucial role in Sedakova's poetic investigation of unclean conscience: the events described (or more often implied) are presented as one of many possible outcomes. They exist against the background of that impossible happiness often encountered in dreams that reveal the untried variations of human life, as in the fourth poem from the Third Notebook, which ends:[5]

И мне снилось, как меня любили
и ни в чем мне не было отказа,
гребнем золотым чесали косы,
на серебряных санках возили
и читали из таинственной книги
слова, какие я забыла. (1:210)

And I dreamed that I was loved,
no request of mine was refused,
they combed my braids with a golden comb,
they bore me on a golden sleigh
and read to me from a mysterious book
words that I've forgotten.

There are concrete historic, aesthetic, and religious meanings behind the persistent return to the unclean conscience motif in *Old Songs*. In historical terms, people with a strong moral sensibility (or even just those given to reflection) experienced everyday life during the final years of Soviet power as bleak and demeaning, something that forced them to make compromises both small and large (both equally fruitless). Given these circumstances, an unclean conscience was seen as a problem without a solution. From the religious point of view, both the gift and the miracle take on particular significance in the context of the unclean conscience. And viewed from the aesthetic angle, the confusion of the cycle's protagonist provides a necessary contrast with its paradoxical images and claims.

The Second Notebook is dedicated to the author's grandmother, Darya Semyonovna Sedakova, and the third, completed after her death, to her memory. The grandmother figures only briefly in the Second Notebook, and in passing, as in the reference to "my grandmother's lapis ring" ("lazurnyi babushkin persten'") in "Beads" ("Busy"; 1:205). But her image becomes one of the most important in the Third Notebook:

Как из глубокого колодца
или со звезды далекой
смотрит бабушка из каждой вещи: (1:211)

From a deep well
as from a distant star,
my grandmother looks out from each thing:

Even if we know nothing about the real Darya Sedakova, the poet's address to her grandmother tells us that the speaker-narrator values biographical time and the time of memory, established through confiding and personal relationships, far more than historical time.[6] Both this address and the grandmother's "quoted" responses in the poems become the motivation (in Viktor Shklovsky's sense of this word) for the markedly simple language of *Old Songs*, which exists somewhat in contrast to their complicated metaphors. Finally, memories of time spent together with her grandmother in childhood allow Sedakova to interpret the references to folklore in *Old Songs* as both a dialogue with Pushkin and a set of intimate experiences: folklore, fixed sayings, and rhythmic speech make up a "grandmotherly" language. Or a language that flickers between the meanings of "cultural" and "grandmotherly."

A number of contexts are pertinent to understanding *Old Songs*. For instance, the "Marching Song" paraphrases a poem by Mikhail Mikhailov, "Grenadiers" ("Grenadery"), itself a liberal translation of Heinrich Heine's "Die Grenadiere" (1827), later put to music by Robert Schumann. In twentieth-century Russia,

Mikhailov's poem became well-known as a song performed to Schumann's music. "The Return: A Poem about Alexei" ("Vozvrashchenie: Stikh ob Aleksee"; 1:195) is a variation on a Russian folk poem, "Poem about Alexei, Man of God," which originates in a late fourth- or early fifth-century legend.[7] As a whole, *Old Songs* are also in conversation with a cycle of poems by Elena Shvarts, "Simple Poems for Myself and for God" (1976, published in the samizdat journal *Chasy* in 1977). In this cycle, the poems make up a prayerful address to God, and they also emphasize the paradoxical rift and contrast between the poverty of man, his enslavement to everyday vanities, and the incomprehensibility of God. In this connection, both Shvarts and Sedakova recall the "dialectical theology" or "theology of paradox" developed in Germany in the 1920s–30s by the writers behind the journal *Zwischen den Zeiten*. However, our primary interest here is the interaction between Sedakova's cycle and *Songs of the Western Slavs*. Why did Sedakova turn to Pushkin when writing a cycle with this particular content?

Sedakova's dialogue with Pushkin had a different meaning from her interpretation of classical tombstones in *Stelae and Inscriptions*[8] and the Chinese landscape paintings and poetry in *Chinese Journey*.[9] The classically themed poems in the former cycle are written in a free verse that varies and disrupts the Russian equivalents of hexameter or elegiac distich (a meter that distantly recalls the hexameter-like verse of some of Rilke's *Duino Elegies* and his poem "Elegie," 1926, addressed to Marina Tsvetaeva: "O die Verluste ins All, Marina, die stürzenden Sterne!").[10] *Chinese Journey*, although also written in free verse, evokes instead the rhythms of Russian translations of classical Chinese poetry: mixed-meter lines that lean trochaic, freely alternating with dactylic, with all feminine endings and generally shorter lines than in *Stelae and Inscriptions*.[11]

Old Songs do not refer to any concrete historical or cultural realia. They are extra-temporal in their "decor," with repetitions of images that are probably connected to Jungian archetypes: fire, a cradle, water/a river, a garden, and so on. As Olga Muravyova noted of Pushkin, "[he] freed the *Songs of the Western Slavs* from any exotic flavor, and the folk consciousness—here expressed outside of any correlation with other types of consciousness—appears adequate unto itself and self-sufficient."[12] Muravyova also observes that "Pushkin makes no real effort to adhere to a specifically Serbian coloring; it is more like generalized Slavic folklore."[13] Sedakova's cycle barely hints at even the small amount of Serbian exotica that can be found in Pushkin's poems (unless you count details like the speaking horse).

In this way, the connection among the images, the system of motifs, and the meter is less obvious than in *Chinese Journey* and *Stelae and Inscriptions*. In the USSR of 1980, Pushkin was not an exotic writer demanding special erudition; Sedakova's other historical/cultural cycles do refer to realia that require specialized knowledge. Thus, there must have been other reasons for her turning to *Songs of the Western Slavs,* which today we can attempt to reconstruct.

E. A. Kniazeva has discussed the interrelation between *Old Songs* and *Songs of the Western Slavs.*[14] She shows that Sedakova's cycle refers to Pushkin's in its meter and epigraph (although the latter did not in fact come from the cycle as published, but rather from the poem "What gleams white there on the green hill? . . ." ["Chto beleet na gore zelenoi? . . ."], which Pushkin intended to include in *Songs of the Western Slavs* but left unfinished; it was unpublished during Pushkin's lifetime). The rhetorical structure of some of Sedakova's poems also refers to Pushkin's cycle, particularly those that include chains of negation. Dialogue emerges at the visual level as well: Kniazeva suggests that the central image of Sedakova's cycle is the "green hill" ("zelenaia gora") mentioned in the Pushkin epigraph. A character in the poem "The Steed" ("Kon'") refers to a corresponding image from Pushkin's well-known poem of the same name. As another scholar has noted, "The speaking horse in Serbian and Russian songs is an archaic vestige that attests to the long-standing kinship of both peoples."[15] The situation Sedakova describes, however—in which the horse, instead of becoming an oracle in a crisis, simply carries on a long and unhurried conversation with his rider—recalls C. S. Lewis's *The Horse and His Boy* (1954) rather more than it does Pushkin.

The meter of *Songs of the Western Slavs* was studied intensively for several decades, beginning with S. G. Bobrov's first works in 1915 and ending in the late 1960s; however, some scholars still believe that the question of their meter remains an open one.[16] The *Songs of the Western Slavs* are written in blank (unrhymed) three-ictus *taktovik*[17] with feminine endings, a tendency toward anapestic openings, and a "strong overall tendency to decasyllabism of the whole line"[18] ascribed to Pushkin's interest in the *deseterac,* the decasyllabic line of Serbo-Croatian folk poetry. Viacheslav V. Ivanov writes that Pushkin's rhythmic experimentation unintentionally reconstructs the archaic forms of ancient Slavic verse, as well as its strong visual component: "Pushkin's poem (like Vostokov's [earlier] adaptation 'The Plaintive Song of Asan-Aginica'), particularly in 'What gleams white there on the green hill?' precisely recreates that Serbian epic text with its comparison of various white objects (snow, a swan), which can very likely be traced back to the ancient Slavic."[19] We should recall that Sedakova was educated as a scholar of Slavic folklore and surely knew of Ivanov's 1967 article;[20] by the time she was writing *Old Songs* in 1980, she may well have taken his thesis about the reconstructive poetics of Pushkin's *Songs of the Western Slavs* into account.

In *Old Songs,* Sedakova holds to the basic elements of Pushkin's line (a primarily three-ictus *taktovik,* no rhyme, all feminine endings), but slightly destabilizes them. Some three-ictus lines are eleven or twelve syllables long.[21] The heterogeneous structure of Sedakova's whole cycle is also distinctly aligned with the structure of Pushkin's cycle. In addition to the poems written in innovative "folk" verse, Pushkin included several written in the standard syllabo-tonic meters known to readers of his time: the "Funeral Song of Hyacinth Maglanovich" ("Pokhoronnaia pesnia Iakinfa Maglanovicha") and "Bonaparte and the Montenegrins" ("Bonapart i chernogortsy") are written in rhymed trochaic tetrameter, and "The Nightingale" ("Solovei") in the unrhymed trochaic tetrameter typically used for early nineteenth-century poetic translations of anacreontic verse. Sedakova similarly includes the "Marching Song" in the Second Notebook, a poem written in rhyming amphibrachic hexameter (slightly loose) with all masculine endings and a caesura after the third foot.[22]

In terms of plot, *Songs of the Western Slavs* often recall grim Romantic ballads. This holds for both the poems Pushkin translated from Prosper Mérimée and the ones he wrote himself, like "Yanysh Korolevich."[23] In comparison, Sedakova's plots are heavily psychological and outwardly subdued. The characters in her poems more often find themselves facing the line between "gravity and grace" (to borrow Simone Weil's phrase), despair and epiphany, than the one dividing life and death. The poem "The Unfaithful Wife" ("Nevernaia zhena") is an exception, but it differs in other ways from Pushkin's poems: in its paradoxical plot, the heroine is exposed in a way that denies all the genre conventions of the traditional ballad about the denigrated wife (cf. Pushkin's "Feodor and Elena"):

Покажи ему, Боже, правду,
покажи мое оправданье!—

Тут собака, бедное созданье,
быстро головой тряхнула,
весело к ней подбежала,
ласково лизнула руку—
и упала мертвая на землю.

Знает Бог о человеке,
чего человек не знает. (1:192)

Show him the truth, oh, God,
show him my innocence!—

Here the dog, poor creature,
shook its head briskly,

ran up to her cheerfully,
licked her hand affectionately—
and fell dead on the ground.

God knows about a person
what a person does not know.

Old Songs comes closer to Pushkin's cycle through the shared motif of unfounded, extra-experiential knowledge that links the worlds of the living and the dead. This is how Janko Marnavich learns of his impending death, and how Feodor finds out who is truly responsible for the death of his child. Compare a similar motif in the Third Notebook of Sedakova's *Old Songs*:

Ничего, что я лежу в могиле,—
чего человек не забудет!
Из сада видно мелкую реку.
В реке видно каждую рыбу. (1:207)

No matter that I'm lying in my grave,—
a person forgets all kinds of things!
From the garden you can see the shallow river.
In the river you can see each fish.

Sedakova's method of interpreting Pushkin in *Old Songs* can be seen in her cycle's one direct dialogue with his texts. In "Consolation" ("Uteshen'e"), the female speaker addresses a character who is fantasizing about everyone pitying him after his death:

Лучше скажи и подумай:
что белеет на горе зеленой?

На горе зеленой сады играют
и до самой воды доходят,
как ягнята с золотыми бубенцами.
Белые ягнята на горе зеленой.

А смерть придет, никого не спросит. (1:186)

Better to say and to think to yourself:
what gleams white there on the green hill?

On the green hill gardens are playing,
they go right up to the water's edge
like lambs with golden bells.
White lambs on a green hill.

But death will come, will ask no one.

This fragment refers to both the Pushkin poem cited earlier and to lines from a poem by Osip Mandelstam: "Where the bath-houses are, the cotton-mills / And the widest green gardens, / By the Moscow River there's a house where light can speak" ("Tam, gde kupal'ni, bumagopriadil'ni / I shirochaishie zelenye sady, / Na Moskve-reke est' svetogovoril'nia," 1932).[24] But what is crucial here is that Sedakova transforms the folklore images of nature into images of dancing gardens and lambs, not opposing one another, not canceling one another out, but flowing into one another. Death is depicted here as part of an endless game.

The language of *Old Songs* appears to be consciously simplified in comparison to the complex metaphorical constructions found in Sedakova's work of the 1970s. The poems in *Old Songs* often use rhetorical constructions that seem folkloric, including parallelisms, anaphora, and anadiplosis: "You can fool the deep, deep earth— / the deep, deep earth is asleep and can't hear" ("Mozhno obmanut' glubokuiu zemliu— / glubokaia zemlia spit i ne slyshit"; 1:184), and so on. But this quasi-folkloric language obscures complex, philosophically dense metaphorical constructions: "You, word, are the robes of Kings, / a dress of patience, both long and short" ("Ty zhe, slovo, tsarskaia odezhda, / dolgogo, korotkogo terpen'ia plat'e"; 1:189). Sedakova thus takes the methods used in *Songs of the Western Slavs* to a new level—their folkloric stylizations combine with Romantic ballad plots and the intentionally shocking brutality of key episodes: "He will use your skin to cover / My sweat-drenched flanks" ("Kozhei on tvoei pokroet / Mne vspotevshie boka"); these are the final lines that close the entire cycle. She also makes use of Pushkin's (and Alexander Vostokov's) rhythmic innovation: the meter developed from bylina verse and the Serbian *deseterac* may have looked like folk verse, but was completely unprecedented in its time.

The literary context of the *Songs of the Western Slavs* has been well established. In addition to Mérimée's *Guzla* and Vuk Karadžić's collection of Serbian folksongs, Pushkin relied on the folkloric stylizations of Alexander Sumarokov and Alexander Vostokov and a number of other texts, including European operas.[25] The social and cultural context, however, has drawn less attention. P. V. Alekseev connected the impulse behind the cycle with contemporary events in the Balkans:

the London Protocol of 1830, Russia's struggle with Great Britain for influence in the Balkans, and the broadening of Serbia's borders in 1831–33 (Alekseev does not mention this last factor). All of these events meant that complicated political games were being played around the weakening Ottoman Empire (at least in its western holdings) and, in Pushkin's view, that European influence was gaining—including the influence represented by Russia. Alekseev writes, "The ring composition [of the cycle] takes shape through the image of skin flayed from the Illyrian Christian by the Muslim Turk. [...] The central theme of the 'Songs ...' [...] is the problem of an individualist comprehension of freedom and national independence."[26] Of course, it's not clear how to connect this with Pushkin's intention of including his "Tale of the Fisherman and the Fish" in the *Songs* (the manuscript has the tale labeled "18th Serbian Song").[27] The tale is also written in blank three-ictus *dol'nik*,[28] but has nothing to do with national independence and is thought to have been drawn from German rather than Serbian sources.

The early 1830s in Russia saw intensive efforts toward the development of a notion of national identity or nationhood (*narodnost'*) as a cultural and political category expressive of the unity of society above and beyond class boundaries. As Muravyova notes, "Imitations of folk art became [... at this time] a literary fashion. The methods of poetic transformation of folklore material were hotly discussed and debated. [...] Critics of Pushkin's time interpreted the concept of *narodnost'* as primarily psychological: the revelation of the people's spirit, a sort of national essence."[29] In 1833, Sergei Uvarov gave a report to Emperor Nicholas I "On certain general elements that can serve as a guide in directing the Ministry of National Education"; it articulated the famous triad of "Orthodoxy, Autocracy, Nationality" for the first time.[30]

This project of cultural nation-building, however, encountered an apparently unprecedented obstacle. Russian society was divided by strict class barriers and significant cultural differences. As Andrei Zorin explains, "The Romantic version of nationhood could not be applied [to representatives of other nations and creeds, as well as] to the 'great Russian' part of the population. [...] It was admittedly impossible to find any common practices of any kind shared by the nobility and the serfs. The prospect of a [shared] language was no better—suffice it to say that the very document that confirmed *narodnost'* as the cornerstone of Russian statehood had been written [by Uvarov] in French."[31] The emperor and state officials saw themselves as the primary "architects of the state." In accordance with this position, Uvarov worked to construct nationhood as a variable entity, subjectively dependent on "Orthodoxy" and "autocracy": "a Russian is someone who believes in his church and his sovereign."[32] Zorin continues: "An ideological system had to be created that would provide Russia with the possibility of both belonging to European civilization (outside of which Uvarov could not imagine either himself or his work as minister of national education) and simultaneously putting up an impassible barrier between itself and that civilization."[33]

I conjecture that Pushkin was genuinely interested in the events unfolding in the Balkans and in the possibility of recreating a kind of exotic Serbian "local color" in Russian (which earned the poet increasingly passionate accolades from Vissarion Belinsky).[34] But Pushkin's wish to include his "Tale of the Fisherman and the Fish" in the *Songs of the Western Slavs* probably indicates yet another intention. Pushkin understood—or sensed intuitively—the same problems around defining "Russianness" that troubled his longtime acquaintance Uvarov. But his work was engaged with other problems, and he avoided the conceptual obstacle described by Zorin by taking a completely different, and much more productive, path. In *Songs of the Western Slavs*, Pushkin actually introduces a project for depicting nationhood as a fundamentally heterogeneous category, one that necessarily includes both "us" and "them," bringing them into dialogue and placing multiple nationhoods into a shared universal space.

Pushkin's preface to the *Songs of the Western Slavs* makes it clear that the verse identified as "Russian folk verse" had been created by translating contemporary European poetry. Russian literature had already seen this sort of Russification, for instance, in the adaptations of "Ossian" by Vasily Kapnist and Nikolai Gnedich (written in Russian folk meters).[35] Taking things to a new level, Pushkin transformed this Russification into a conscious and overt device that worked toward universalizing nationhood and establishing an understanding of it as heterogeneous.

In an interview with Olga Timofeeva in March 2015, Sedakova commented on recent social and political changes in Russia, particularly the rise in anti-Western and anti-European sentiment:

> For me Russia—even pre-Petrine Russia—has always been culturally a part of Europe. An Eastern-Christian branch, and certainly unique—but then every European culture is unique: Italians and Swedes, Germans and Spaniards are not especially similar to one another. And to set Byzantium in opposition to Europe is absurd. It's the other half, the "other lung," as the poet Viacheslav Ivanov once said, and this is a phrase John Paul II loved to quote. One same Christian civilization breathing with two lungs. [. . .] A break with the West means very simply, a decisive break with Christian humanism, the rejection of universally accepted norms of justice, custom and common life.[36]

There is no way to check whether Sedakova "always" thought this way: her early essays that have been published, such as the preface to the 1983 samizdat collection *Gates, Windows, Arches* (*Vrata, Okna, Arki*)[37] do not include any ruminations on this or related topics. But her post-Soviet writings do reveal some thoughts about writers whose 1970s work, in Sedakova's estimation, was a testament to the "Europeanness" of Russian culture: Yuri Lotman and Sergei Averintsev.

The cultural avant-garde in the 1970s was aligned with Western Europe, at least partially (a shift from the America-focused 1960s). This tendency could be seen in the boom in structuralism and the school of cultural studies centered in Tartu, Moscow, and Leningrad, which constituted the avant-garde of Soviet humanities in the 1960s–70s. The work of Sergei Averintsev, who called himself a man of the Mediterranean soil ("sredizemnomorskii pochvennik"), opened horizons still broader. As Sedakova explains, "For us the 'world culture' of European humanism opposed only and exclusively Soviet culture, not the Russian tradition (which in the prerevolutionary period existed in that same otherworldly space). Unlike the 'classic' period of Westernizers and Slavophiles, for us the opposite of this 'West' was not Russia, but the 'brave new world.' 'Russia' was meanwhile in the same camp as the 'West': a space where the soul was possible, where freedom and genius were possible."[38] In another essay dedicated entirely to Averintsev, Sedakova highlights the "European" element in Russian culture overlooked by those whose analysis relies on existing stereotypes:

> Equilibrium and balance are qualities hardly ever associated with the Russian tradition, both here and in the "myth of Russia" worldwide. As we all know, the Russian soul is expansive and knows no moderation; in fact, it takes pride in being expansive and unruly. I sincerely regret that our national myth took this particular form. It excludes what is perhaps most dear to me in our national heritage: early architecture, Epiphanius the Wise, Vladimir-Suzdal icons, the human temperament reflected in the lives of the Russian saints. A flexible, agile equilibrium—that is probably what most defines this kind of mentality. In the more or less Dostoevskian (or even merchant-class) "myth of Russia," there is, of course, no place for any of this, just as there is no place for *The Captain's Daughter*, or a Venetsianov landscape, or Glinka. I recall all of this, everything that has been eclipsed by those notorious "paroxysms" and "abysses," by the gypsy choir at "Yar.'"[39]

At this point we should take a moment to recall the historical and political context of *Old Songs*, which was not one that favored the rapprochement of the "Russian" and "European." In December 1979, Soviet forces invaded Afghanistan and brought about violent regime change. In January 1980, the academician

Andrei Sakharov was exiled from Moscow for his protests against the war. He was sent to Gorky (now restored to its earlier name, Nizhny Novgorod, but then a city closed to foreigners), which made contact between the dissident scholar and the outside world extremely difficult. In anticipation of the Moscow Olympic games, the authorities began to purge the city of undesirable residents. Throughout the 1970s, the Soviet regime had been hypocritical, cruel, and not particularly observant of international norms. Still, its aggression and isolationism became noticeably worse in 1979–80 (despite the Olympics), and this was felt throughout the country. Sociologists who emigrated from the USSR and thus observed it from afar asserted that the basic structure and values of Soviet and Western society were fundamentally different and incommensurate, and that the situation was unlikely to change anytime soon.[40]

At the same time, changes were afoot in the position of Orthodoxy in the world. On November 30, 1979, Pope John Paul II and Ecumenical Patriarch Dimitrios I announced the creation of a Joint International Commission for Theological Dialogue between the Catholic Church and the Orthodox Church, which confirmed the non-isolationist status of Orthodoxy and the possibility for its equal participation in an overall Christian dialogue. Recall that Sedakova has frequently mentioned the importance she places on being an Orthodox Christian.

This is the context in which she began *Old Songs*, an extremely intimate and introspective cycle. Despite these qualities, Sedakova's dialogue with Pushkin reveals the political, cultural, and aesthetic project simultaneously undertaken in the cycle. Its poems combine the Russianness of the verse line and the motifs of miracle, risk, and death with a nuanced, reserved, and extremely reflexive style. I would go so far as to say that Sedakova sought to develop a model of Russian poetic writing that was—broadly speaking—European, that is, connected with European, Western cultural traditions and founded on an aesthetics of "flexible, agile equilibrium." She was not suggesting a new style: as she demonstrates in the cycle itself (as well as in the 2015 interview and her post-Soviet essays), Russian poetry had always been (at the very least, from Pushkin onward) European; it had always and unavoidably contained European and universalist stylistics. And moreover, this was still the case at the time, that is, in the early 1980s.

In the *Songs of the Western Slavs*, Pushkin presented the "folk" element as something archaic and even frightening, but inevitably present in the "modern" world of the 1810s–30s. Despite the fact that it contains the prideful "Bonaparte and the Montenegrins," the cycle generally refrains from expressing any enthusiasm for any sort of "national spirit." Like Pushkin, Sedakova sought to create a "Russian-European" style at a time of societal crisis, a symbolic dead-end; but hers was an entirely different kind of society. In comparison to Pushkin's cycle,

Old Songs demonstrate a radical turn to psychology. In their combination of the motifs of unclean conscience and miracle, they allow for no pride to be taken in either "Russianness" or "Europeanness." Any value, including cultural tradition itself, is presented as more of a gift from above than a human accomplishment.

Sedakova's attempt to describe Russian culture as European in *Old Songs* includes the implication that Russian religiosity can also be European. This interpretation of European roots links *Old Songs* with the politically charged research undertaken by Sergei Averintsev in the 1970s, particularly his monograph *The Poetics of Early Byzantine Literature* (*Poetika rannevizantiiskoi literatury*, 1977). Published in an officially atheist country, Averintsev's monograph became a sensation among the critically inclined intelligentsia. Essentially, Averintsev presented Byzantine Orthodox hymnography and hagiography as a legitimate object for historical and philological study. He cited liturgical hymns that, in Old Church Slavonic translation, were still used in Russian Orthodox church services (such as the Akathistos of the Holy Virgin Theotokos). In analyzing these texts, instead of "exposing religious prejudices," Averintsev described Eastern Christianity as cultural innovation. In the eyes of his readers, this made his book a scholarly justification of religion. This ultimately contributed to Averintsev's book being somewhat forgotten after the Russian Orthodox Church acquired greater freedom in the perestroika era: its academic significance was overshadowed by its political and religious elements. Sedakova, meanwhile, remembers this book well and continues Averintsev's work to this day: her website features studies of the poetics and metaphors of Orthodox liturgical hymns.[41]

The cultural and political problems Averintsev wrestles with in his book were more complicated than the description given above indicates. The late 1960s and early 1970s were a time of crisis in Soviet ideology and a moment when the intelligentsia was turning to religion, mostly Orthodoxy. Ideas of Russian ethnic nationalism were also starting to spread at this time.[42] Russian Orthodoxy was understood as first and foremost a "national," "native," "traditional" faith, one that testified to the uniqueness of Russia and her place in the world. For many people, the shift away from the progressive Soviet worldview to Orthodoxy understood in this way marked a sort of new arrangement or transposition (in the musical sense)[43] of the anti-Western, isolationist motifs typical of Soviet propaganda.

This was the context in which Averintsev's book appeared, with its hidden polemics with both official Soviet atheism and the new quasi-Orthodox nationalist xenophobia.[44] *The Poetics of Early Byzantine Literature* was meant to show that before the division of Christianity into Orthodoxy and Catholicism, Eastern Christianity was a European religion founded on super-rational Christian revelation and the Greco-Roman cultural heritage. In his later works, Averintsev presented Christian universalism more explicitly as the result of a Mediterranean cultural synthesis including both European and Middle Eastern cultures, such as the Syrian, Egyptian, and Jewish. This is evidently what Sedakova has in mind when she writes that Averintsev's thought "opened up still broader perspectives."[45]

The handful of poems that Averintsev published over the years are written for the most part in the same meter as *Old Songs*—unrhymed three-ictus *dol'nik*. This is probably connected to the fact that Averintsev saw Sedakova's cycle as the realization of a cultural and political program congenial to his own efforts: to present "Russian" and "Orthodox" as "European" and "universal." Here are some passages from his poems:

Стих о святой Варваре

—Я вижу в рубище славу
и свет—в темнице непроглядной.

рабы ликуют в оковах,
и дитя смеется под розгой.

До крови, до кости, до боли,
до конца и без конца—радость.

и земля, и море проходит,
но любовь пребывает вовеки. (1983)[46]

Poem about Saint Barbara
I see glory in rags
and light in a dark prison.

slaves rejoice in fetters,
and the child laughs beneath the whip.

To the point of blood, bone, pain,
to the end and without end—joy.

earth and sea shall both pass,
but love will be for all time.

Роль

    такого Мирового Театра
ни Шекспиру ни Кальдерону
ни Третьего Ордена брату

ни во сне ни в яви не мнилось
разве на малое мгновенье
когда Сам Ты неслышно был рядом
рукописи их правил. (1993)[47]

Role

  such a world theater
neither in dream nor waking could appear
neither to Shakespeare nor Calderon
nor to brothers of the third order
not for the tiniest instant
when You Yourself were there in silence
correcting their manuscripts

Another important point of orientation for Averintsev in his efforts to create this image of Orthodoxy was the mature work of the poet Viacheslav Ivanov, to whom Averintsev devoted a number of studies.[48] He and Sedakova both quote Ivanov's statement that for him, Orthodoxy and Catholicism are two lungs, which only in tandem allow for full breathing; they understood this to be an expression of European religious and cultural commonality.[49]

The poems in *Old Songs* are not only uchronic; they intentionally omit marks of time and place. The few exceptions are non-systematic and refer to works far from the twentieth century: Heine's (and Mikhailov's) "Die Grenadiere" or "Poem of Alexei, Man of God." In its structure, the cycle suggests an enumeration of various peripeteia (in the Aristotelian sense) in the internal life of the modern individual. I am avoiding saying "the internal life of the Soviet non-conformist intellectual" because Sedakova's cycle—thanks both to its references to Pushkin's well-known work and his understanding of *narodnost'*, and to the stylized simplicity of her writing with its "folkloric" phrases—implicitly destroys stereotypical ideas about the opposition of "the people" and "the intelligentsia." The style of *Old Songs* strives to be neither "folk" nor "intellectual." In the context of this list of peripeteia, the direct quotations acquire new meaning. Thus, "The Return: A Poem about Alexei" simultaneously varies an old theme (rather like Mandelstam's lines "And once again the skald will write another person's song, / And sing it like his own" ["I snova skal'd chuzhuiu pesniu slozhit, / I kak svoiu ee proizneset"])[50] and expresses a dream of the new vision that can bless a person who has rejected stable social status. For such an ascetic, "the objects of the world shine, / like tiny distant stars" ("veshchi krugom siiaiut, / kak dalekie melkie zvezdy"; 1:195).

The cycle resembles a set of emotionally impressive images and their transformations. One can even suppose that the paradigmatic organization is no less important for *Old Songs* than the syntagmatic structure. Of course, like any cycle of poems, the syntagmatic and paradigmatic principles of *Old Songs* exist in complicated interaction. And each of the three notebooks has its own internal syntagmatic relationships, in addition to those that exist in the cycle as a whole. *Old Songs* end with the poem "Bring warmth, O Lord, to your Beloved" ("Obogrei, Gospod', Tvoikh liubimykh"; 1:215), which contains the cycle's only direct address to God from the position of human poverty. The "Added Poems," meanwhile, end with the poem "The cold of the world" ("Kholod mira"), which hints at apocatastasis, the universal restoration at the end of time:

Этих чудищ
кто-нибудь возьмет за руку,
как ошалевшего ребенка:

—Пойдем, я покажу тебе такое
чего ты никогда не видел! (1:218)

Someone will take these beasts
by the hand,
like an unruly child:

"Let's go, I'll show you something
the likes of which you've never seen!"

However, because of the cycle's overall meter and complicated construction, the paradigmatic, enumerative qualities of its poetics are more evident than the syntagmatic.

In connection with this enumerative poetics and deconstruction of the notion of *narodnost'*, Sedakova's cycle unexpectedly recalls the work of the Moscow conceptualists. In his poems of the late 1970s to early 1980s, Dmitry Prigov began to dispute the demagogical Soviet understanding of "the people," expelling "turncoats" from its midst (this was the contemporary media's preferred designation for dissidents). Consider, for instance, Prigov's well-known 1976 poem:

Народ он делится на не народ
И на народ в буквальном смысле
Кто не народ—не то чтобы урод
Но он ублюдок в высшем смысле

А кто народ—не то чтобы народ
Но он народа выраженье
Что не укажешь точно—вот народ
Но скажешь точно—есть народ. И точка.[51]

The people can be divided into
not the people and literally the people
Being not the people doesn't make you a monster exactly
But definitely a kind of mongrel

And then the people isn't exactly people
It's the expression of the people
So you can't say exactly, look, there's the people
But you say for sure there is the people! Period.

Sedakova's comments on the conceptualists at this time were critical, but interested. Consider her programmatic preface to *Gates, Windows, Arches*: "No more of those 'autumn twilights' from Chekhov, no more private, everyday life; all that psychological verisimilitude is merely a literary construct. What we find in its place is in fact the 'nothing' described by Dmitry Prigov in his topical poems and by Ilya Kabakov on his empty pages. They are consistent and therefore truthful in their own way; they leave nothing unsaid. I would like to leave nothing unsaid in a different way, one completely opposite from that of the conceptualists."[52] Sedakova's few readers (at that time) evidently got the sense that for her the conceptualists were opponents; there was no possibility for a rapprochement between them, but their argument promised to be productive. Meanwhile, in unofficial Moscow art circles, the conceptualists were seen as radically innovative. For this reason, despite Sedakova's polemical comments, she immediately made an effort to articulate the aesthetic problem that she shared with the conceptualists, a key aesthetic problem at that time. As early as 1984 Mikhail Epstein wrote an essay comparing Sedakova and Lev Rubinstein, suggesting that both poets' work (in different ways) demonstrated the possibility of an otherness (*inobytie*) that transcended everyday reality while being simultaneously rooted in that reality—in contrast to the duality of the Romantics.[53]

In my view, a more productive approach than reconstructing the worldview behind the work of Sedakova and Rubinstein (or the other conceptualists) would be to contrast their uses of the catalogue or list as a literary device. As Sedakova herself wrote, unofficial writers understood ongoing existence in crisis as a basic premise of their writing. But—and here I disagree with Sedakova—this was not the same "crisis of culture" that had been described by early twentieth-century Modernists.[54] Instead, this was a radical psychological crisis specific to the USSR, which was articulated by the critically inclined intelligentsia of the 1970s and affected these intellectuals and other social groups.[55]

An understanding of the contemporary crisis as psychological is what substantially differentiates the 1970s generation of unofficial writers from Joseph Brodsky, who came of age in the 1960s and perceived the crisis as primarily a question of civilization. Consider these excerpts from his poetry:

И от чего мы больше далеки:
от православья или эллинизма?
К чему близки мы? Что там, впереди?
Не ждет ли нас теперь другая эра? (1966)[56]

And which is further from us now:
Fair Orthodoxy or the ancient Hellenes?
What's near to us? And what lies up ahead?
Do we await the dawn of a new era?

Вокруг—громады новых корпусов.
У Корбюзье то общее с Люфтваффе,
что оба потрудились от души
над переменой облика Европы. (1973)[57]

Heaps of new buildings all around.
Corbusier and the Luftwaffe have in common
prolonged and earnest efforts
to change the face of Europe.

Although they were both born in 1940, Brodsky and Prigov belonged to different generations in their understanding of the crisis.[58]

Note that in her essays of the 1990s–2010s, Sedakova often mentions the crisis of contemporary civilization, but interprets the crisis primarily in moral and psychological terms.[59] One way of aesthetically dealing with the crisis of consciousness in the 1970s was to map it, to grasp its specific features and possibilities: what it was made of and how it might change. This method called for the depiction of the contemporary crisis-consciousness as a semantic space of complicated structure that existed in an extremely generalized "great time."

The conceptualists interpreted this space as an anti-logical collection of estranged and frozen ideological signs no longer capable of legitimizing anything, but connected deep down with violence. Although it is possible to go beyond the borders of this collection, this transcendence would be non-symbolic, trans-semiotic, and always require critical examination. A nearly programmatic example of this union of the sign and the extra-symbolic can be found in Erik Bulatov's paintings of the 1970s, which depict Soviet symbols (like the "Sign of Quality" or the "Glory to the CPSU" slogan) that are unable to completely block out the sky. This kind of consciousness can also be found in Venedikt Erofeev's characters, especially in his play "Walpurgis Night, or The Commander's Steps" ("Val'purgieva noch', ili Shagi komandora").

Sedakova conceptualized this space cataphatically, rather than apophatically—as a selection of possible vectors for movement beyond the limits of the crisis state. Defending her method in the 1983 essay, she polemicizes with her opponents the conceptualists, calling them the "nihilist avant-garde"—evidently, in order to emphasize their differences (when these were in fact not so radical): "The nihilistic avant-garde takes as its primary subject the 'normal' world of Ivan Ilyich. The kind of work I prefer takes as its subject what Ivan Ilyich sees when his impending death pulls him right out of this normality, what he sees in the end and in actual fact. (To be sure, Tolstoy says very little about this.) [. . .] What could he possibly be seeing [. . .]? [. . .] I think, quite simply, he sees reality, the very reality that is entirely at home even in our world."[60]

Pushkin's *Songs of the Western Slavs* were useful to Sedakova because she was proceeding from the notion that the peripeteia/vectors pointing beyond the limits of the crisis consciousness could be created aesthetically out of the language of a reconsidered literary tradition. This tradition no longer legitimized anything, but it could be revived through attention to its critical strength and its resistance to existing social clichés and the stereotypes of ordinary consciousness that prevent the human "I" from opening up to the outside world. Sedakova heard a similar resistance in *Songs of the Western Slavs*, which had otherwise seemed hopelessly mummified in school reading lists and the cultural canon. This ability to discern a critical method in long-since-established works of Russian literature and song is once again becoming highly relevant for Russian culture today.

Translated from Russian by Ainsley Morse

Notes

I would like to thank Igor Kotiukh, the editors of this volume, and the peer reviewers for their valuable comments, and Ainsley Morse for her wonderful translation.

1. The poems in *Old Songs* are cited from the four-volume set used throughout this volume. *Songs of the Western Slavs* are cited from A. S. Pushkin, *Polnoe sobranie sochinenii*, 17 vols. (Moscow: Voskresen'e, 1995), 3:334–63, 377.

2. Published in *Novyi mir* 11 (1970): 237–40. M. M. Bakhtin, *Estetika slovesnogo tvorchestva*, ed. S. S. Averintsev and S. G. Bocharov (Moscow: Iskusstvo, 1979), 328. Judging from the comments in his notebooks, it appears that Bakhtin developed the term "great time" and the ideas surrounding it in the late 1960s. See Bakhtin, *Sobranie sochinenii*, 7 vols. (Moscow: Russkie slovari, 2002), 6:433. For an English translation by Vern W. McGee, see M. M. Bakhtin, *Speech Genres and Other Late Essays* (Austin: University of Texas Press, 1986), 4.

3. Sedakova, "Muzyka glukhogo vremeni (russkaia poeziia 1970-kh godov)," http://www.olgasedakova.com/Poetica/175, accessed March 15, 2018. Translation by Martha Kelly and Ainsley Morse.

4. K. Golubovich, "'Tristan i Izol'da' v ispolnenii Ol'gi Sedakovoi," *Volga* 9 (2011), http://magazines.russ.ru/volga/2011/9/g014.html, accessed March 15, 2018.

5. It would seem that this kind of description—of events that happened one way but could have taken another course—can be traced genetically to Anna Akhmatova's "Northern Elegies" ("Severnye elegii"), particularly ". . . Like a River, I" (". . . Menia, kak reku") and "There Are Three Ages to Reminiscences" ("Est' tri epokhi u vospominanii"). For the cycle, see Anna Akhmatova, *Ia—golos vash . . .* , ed. V. A. Chernykh (Moscow: Izdatel'stvo Knizhnaia palata, 1989), 214–19.

6. A more radical interpretation of the cycle might see in it the production of a deliberately "female," anti-chronological time of the sort described by Julia Kristeva in "Women's Time," trans. Alice Jardine and Harry Blake, in *Signs* 7, no. 1 (Autumn 1981): 13–35.

7. V. P. Adrianova-Peretts, *Zhitie Alekseia cheloveka Bozhiia v drevnerusskoi literature i narodnoi slovesnosti* (Petrograd: Ia. Bashmakov i ko., 1917). See also the Old Believers' variations on this poem collected in the 1970s by Serafima Nikitina, a folklore scholar and old friend of Sedakova (Sedakova mentions Nikitina in the 1998 essay "Journey to Tartu and Back" ["Puteshestvie v Tartu i obratno"]): http://philologos.narod.ru/nikitina/Spiritual_Verses.htm, accessed March 15, 2018.

8. For more on this interpretation, see S. Stepantsov, "Posleslovie," in *Stely i nadpisi*, by Ol'ga Sedakova (St. Petersburg: Izdatel'stvo Ivana Limbakha, 2014), 21–40.

9. On this cycle, see E. A. Kniazeva, "Vliianie kitaiskoi peizazhnoi liriki na poeziiu O. Sedakovoi," in *Problemy mezhkul'turnoi kommunikatsii: Mezhvuzovskii sbornik nauchnykh trudov* (Perm: n.p., 1999), 66–73.

10. "Oh, the losses into All, Marina, the plummeting stars!" Stepantsov has made a detailed study of the classical—and "Russo-classical"—reminiscences in the rhythmic structures of *Stely i nadpisi*. See Stepantsov, "Posleslovie," 28–33.

11. Sedakova herself traces the lines and stanzas in *Tristan and Isolde* to those of *Das Nibelungenlied* (oral commentary during the author's public recital of this long poem, 1990), but in my view, they go back to Mandelstam's translations of Old French epic poetry and to Arseny Tarkovsky's poem "I Was Born So Long Ago" ("Ia tak davno rodilsia"), which features the first appearance of the system of regular internal rhymes subsequently developed by Sedakova; for the poem, see Arsenii Tarkovskii, *Stikhotvoreniia i*

poemy (Moscow: Profizmat, 2000), 40. Dmitry Kuz'min was the first to compare Tarkovsky's and Sedakova's stanzaic form (personal communication, 2000). However, we can assume that Tarkovsky's poem also shows the influence of Mandelstam's "Old French" meters.

12. O. S. Murav'eva, "Iz nabliudenii nad 'Pesniami zapadnykh slavian,'" in *Pushkin: Issledovaniia i materialy* (Leningrad: Nauka, 1983), 11:155.

13. Murav'eva, "Iz nabliudenii," 153.

14. E. A. Kniazeva, "Epigraf k tsiklu v poezii Ol'gi Sedakovoi," *Vestnik Permskogo universiteta: Rossiiskaia i zarubezhnaia filologiia* 4 (2009): 88–92.

15. V. Chernyshev, "A. S. Pushkin i serbskie i russkie narodnye pesni," *Izvestiia AN SSSR: Otdelenie literatury i iazyka* 7 (1948): 162.

16. Primary works: B. I. Iarkho, "Svobodnye zvukovye formy u Pushkina," *Ars poetica* 2 (1928): 169–82 (esp. 170); N. S. Trubetskoi, "K voprosu o stikhe 'Pesen zapadnykh slavian' Pushkina" (1937), in *Three Philological Studies*, Michigan Slavic Materials 3 (Ann Arbor: Department of Slavic Languages and Literatures, University of Michigan, 1963); K. Taranovskii, "O vzaimootnoshenii stikhotvornogo ritma i tematiki," *American Contributions to the Fifth International Congress of Slavists* (The Hague: Mouton, 1963), 1:293–95; A. N. Kolmogorov, "O metre pushkinskikh 'Pesen zapadnykh slavian,'" *Russkaia literatura* 1 (1966): 98–111; V. E. Kholshevnikov, "Stikhoslozhenie," in *Pushkin: Itogi i problemy izucheniia* (Moscow: Nauka, 1966), 542–44; S. Bobrov, "K voprosu o podlinnom stikhotvornom razmere pushkinskikh 'Pesen zapadnykh slavian,'" *Russkaia literatura* 3 (1964): 119–37; V. V. Ivanov, "Zametki po sravnitel'no-istoricheskoi indoevropeiskoi poetike" (1967), in Ivanov, *Izbrannye trudy po semiotike i istorii kul'tury* (Moscow: Iazyki slavianskoi kul'tury, 2004), 593–96, 599–600. Also see S. M. Bondi, "Narodnyi stikh u Pushkina" (1945), in *O Pushkine: Stat'i i issledovaniia* (Moscow: Khudozhestvennaia literatura, 1978), 372–441.

17. A form of verse allowing one, two, or three unstressed syllables between the stressed ones, as defined by Mikhail Gasparov in M. L. Gasparov, *Russkii stikh nachala XX veka v kommentariiakh* (Moscow: Fortuna Limited, 2001), 153.

18. Kolmogorov, "O metre pushkinskikh," 100.

19. Ivanov, "Zametki," 596. Ivanov gives a reference for this phrase in the Bulgarian, Moravian, and Slovakian parallels indicated in P. G. Bogatyrev, "Nekotorye zadachi sravnitel'nogo izucheniia eposa slavianskikh narodov," in *IV Mezhdunarodnyi s''ezd slavistov* (Moscow, 1958), 15–16, as well as other sources in his own scholarship.

20. In 1983 Sedakova defended her doctoral dissertation on "Ceremonial Terminology and the Structure of the Ceremonial Text (Burial Ceremonies of the Eastern and Southern Slavs)" ("Obriadovaia terminologiia i struktura obriadovogo teksta [pogrebal'nyi obriad vostochnykh i iuzhnykh slavian]"). Evidently, she was working on her dissertation and *Old Songs* at the same time. In 2004 Sedakova published *Poetika obriada: Pogrebal'naia obriadnost' vostochnykh i iuzhnykh slavian* (Moscow: Indrik, 2004).

21. In Russian: "Mozh-no ob-ma-nut' vy-so-ko-e ne-bo— /Vy-so-ko-e ne-bo vse-go ne u-vi-dit," "Vspom-niu mno-go, za-bu-du—eshch-e bol'-she," while the "Additions" even include two-ictus lines of only four to seven syllables ("Kho-lod mi-ra / Ko-go-ni-bud' so-gre-et") as well as dactylic (and not anapestic or iambic) anacruses ("Bed-ny-e, bed-ny-e liu-di!").

22. In this poem, Sedakova transforms the meter of Mikhailov's "The Grenadiers" ("Grenadery"), which was written in amphibrachic trimeter with alternating masculine and feminine endings and AbCb rhyme; Sedakova essentially makes each of Mikhailov's couplets (paired lines) into a single line. Sedakova knew the romance well (based on the Heine poem): she knew the famous operatic bass Mark Reizen (1895–1995), who regularly performed Mikhailov's translation at his concerts. They were acquainted through Sedakova's close friend, the pianist Vladimir Khvostin (1937–82), Reizen's concertmaster. There is a video recording of Reizen singing "Grenadery," accompanied by Khvostin: https://www.youtube.com/watch?v=7nqGM_cpSl4&list=PLnjoy3Y1nwtSUATdM98UJCoAdasncMap4h&index=2, accessed March 15, 2018. In changing the meter, however, Sedakova enters into dialogue with more than just Heine, Mikhailov, and Reizen: she probably was also thinking of a poem by the Estonian folklorist, theologian, poet, and dissident Uku Masing (1909–85), "Song of the Soldiers, Retreating from the Onslaught of Evil" ("Tontide eest taganejate sõdurite laul"), which had been translated into Russian (by Svetlan Semenenko) using the same meter Sedakova would later use in her "Marching Song"; the poem was published in the *tamizdat* journal *Kovcheg* 1 (1978): 49. The possible influence of Mazing is suggested by several features: the similar meter, the shared motif of the necessity of moral fortitude despite defeat, the genre of the ballad-parable, a little bit unusual for the late twentieth century, and the organization of both poems around the pronoun "we."

23. Murav'eva, "Iz nabliudenii," 155.

24. Cited from Osip Mandel'shtam, *Polnoe sobranie stikhotvorenii* (St. Petersburg: Gumanitarnoe agenstvo "Akademicheskii proekt," 1995), 217.

25. Murav'eva, "Iz nabliudenii"; Ivanov, "Zametki."

26. P. V. Alekseev, "Otrazhenie vostochnogo voprosa v tvorchestve A. S. Pushkina 1830-kh godov," *Filologicheskie nauki: Voprosy teorii i praktiki* 4, no. 34, part 3 (2014): 19–23.

27. P. V. Annenkov, *A. S. Pushkin: Materialy dlia ego biografii i otsenki proizvedenii* (St. Petersburg: Obshchestvennaia pol'za, 1873), 366–67.

28. The *dol'nik* is a poetic meter with a fixed number of stressed syllables and a variable number of unstressed syllables between them.

29. Murav'eva, "Iz nabliudenii," 154.

30. A. L. Zorin, *Kormia dvuglavogo orla: Literatura i gosudarstvennaia ideologiia v Rossii v poslednei treti XVIII–pervoi treti XIX veka* (Moscow: Novoe literaturnoe obozrenie, 2001), 33–374.

31. Ibid., 364.

32. Ibid., 366.

33. Ibid., 367.

34. In his review of *The Poems of Alexander Pushkin* (*Stikhotvoreniia Aleksandra Pushkina*, published in 1836), Belinsky wrote: "And so, for instance, everyone knows that Pushkin translated sixteen [*sic*] Serbian songs from the French, and that these songs were counterfeit, invented by two French charlatans—and so what? [. . .] Pushkin was able to lend these songs a Slavic coloring such that if the mistake had not come to light, no one would ever have thought that these were counterfeit songs." V. G. Belinskii, *Polnoe sobranie sochinenii*, 13 vols. (Moscow: Izd-vo Akademii Nauk SSSR, 1953), 2:82. In his fifth article on Pushkin

(1844), Belinsky was still more enthusiastic: "The 'Songs of the Western Slavs' are the greatest-ever demonstration of Pushkin's inconceivable poetic tact and the flexibility of his talent. [. . .] We don't know how these counterfeit songs sound in French [. . .] but in Pushkin's rendering they breathe with all the sumptuousness of local color, and many of them are excellent" (7:352).

35. Iu. D. Levin, *Ossian v russkoi literature: Konets XVIII–pervaia tret' XIX veka* (Leningrad: Nauka, 1980), 58–63.

36. O. Timofeeva, "Ol'ga Sedakova: 'Aktivisty'—gore nashei strany," *Novaia gazeta,* March 13, 2015, http://www.novayagazeta.ru/arts/67586.html, accessed March 15, 2018.

37. Republished on Sedakova's website: http://www.olgasedakova.com/Poetica/1534, accessed March 15, 2018. Note that the title of this volume, when Sedakova republished it, became *Vorota, okna, arki.*

38. Ol'ga Sedakova, "Evropeiskaia ideia v russkoi kul'ture: Ee istoriia i sovremennost'" (a reworking of a 2010 lecture), http://www.olgasedakova.com/Moralia/1547, accessed March 15, 2018. Translation by Martha Kelly and Ainsley Morse.

39. Sedakova, "Rassuzhdenie o metode: Sergei Sergeevich Averintsev i ego kniga *Poety* (1997)," http://www.olgasedakova.com/Moralia/296, accessed March 15, 2018. Translator's note: the gypsy choir at Yar' refers both to the Sokolovsky choir that used to sing at the well-known Yar' restaurant in Moscow, and also to a popular song ("romance") entitled "The Sokolovsky Choir at Yar.'" Translation by Martha Kelly and Ainsley Morse.

40. David Zilberman, "Orthodox Ethics and the Matter of Communism," *Studies in Soviet Thought* 17, no. 4 (1977): 341–419; Zilberman, "The Post-Sociological Society," *Studies in Soviet Thought* 18, no. 4 (1978): 261–328; A. Zinov'ev, *Kommunizm kak real'nost* (Lausanne: L'Âge d'homme, 1981). To some extent, this point of view reactualizes the ideas expressed by Nikolai Berdiaev in *The Origin of Russian Communism* (London: G. Bles, Centenary Press, 1937).

41. Sedakova's fourteen essays on liturgical poetry appeared on the website. For example, see http://www.olgasedakova.com/Poetica/1128, accessed March 15, 2017. Her work has now appeared in print as well: *Mariiny slezy. Poetika liturgicheskikh pesnopenii; Kommentarii k pravoslavnomu bogosluzheniiu* (Moscow: Blagochestie, 2017).

42. See N. A. Mitrokhin, *Russkaia partiia: Dvizhenie russkikh natsionalistov v SSSR 1953–1985* (Moscow: Novoe literaturnoe obozrenie, 2003).

43. Transposition refers to the performance of a work of music in a different tonality.

44. Averintsev openly refused to characterize early Christianity in terms of class relations, which violated the formal "Marxist" conventions of Soviet scholarship.

45. Sedakova, "Rassuzhdenie o metode."

46. Sergei Averintsev, *Stikhotvoreniia i perevody* (St. Petersburg: Izd-vo Ivana Limbakha, 2003), 69–70. English translations by Ainsley Morse.

47. Ibid., 89.

48. Averinstev, "Poeziia Viacheslava Ivanova," *Voprosy literatury* 8 (1975): 145–92; *"Skvoreshnits vol'nykh grazhdanin . . ." Viacheslav Ivanov: Put' poeta mezhdu mirami* (St. Petersburg: Aleteiia, 2001).

49. In a reference to Ivanov's statements made in the early 1980s, Pope John Paul II called Western and Eastern Christianity "two lungs" and later, in his encyclical "Ut Unum

Sint" (1995), he repeated this quotation and said that "the Church must breathe with her two lungs!" See S. S. Averintsev, "Khristianskie temy u Viacheslava Ivanova," *Khristianos* 5 (1996): 161–65. Interview translation by Martha Kelly and Ainsley Morse. An English translation of the encyclical is available online at http://w2.vatican.va/content/john-paul-ii/en/encyclicals/documents/hf_jp-ii_enc_25051995_ut-unum-sint.html, accessed June 11, 2018.

50. Mandel'shtam, "Ia ne slykhal rasskazov Ossiana . . . ," in *Polnoe sobranie stikhotvorenii*, 120.

51. Dmitrii Prigov, "Narod on delitsia ne na narod . . . ," in *Sobranie stikhov*, vol. 2, *1975–76* (Vienna: Wiener Slawistischer Almanach, 1997), 163. English translation by Ainsley Morse.

52. Ol'ga Sedakova, "Ob"iasnitel'naia zapiska: Predislovie k samizdatskoi knige stikhov *Vorota, Okna, Arki* (1979–1983)," http://www.olgasedakova.com/Poetica/1534, accessed March 15, 2018. Translation by Martha Kelly and Ainsley Morse.

53. The only publication of this essay I know of is the English translation, which was published in Mikhail Epstein, Alexander Genis, and Slobodanka Vladiv-Glover, eds., *Russian Postmodernism: New Perspectives on Post-Soviet Culture* (New York: Berghahn Books, 1999). Epstein's comparison of Sedakova and Rubinstein as extremely different poets of the same generation who turn out to be working on similar poetic problems distinctly recalls Kornei Chukovsky's comparison of Akhmatova and Mayakovsky: K. Chukovskii, "Akhmatova i Maiakovskii," *Dom iskusstv* 1 (1921): 23–42 (the article was subsequently published as a brochure and reprinted many times).

54. N. Berdiaev, *Krizis iskusstva* (Petrograd: Leman i Sakharov, 1918); A. Belyi, *Na perevale*, vol. 3, *Krizis kul'tury* (Petrograd: Alkonost, 1920).

55. See, for details, I. Kukulin, "Novaia logika: O perelome v razvitii russkoi kul'tury i obshchestvennoi mysli 1969–73 godov," *Toronto Slavic Quarterly* 61 (2017), http://sites.utoronto.ca/tsq/61/Kukulin61.pdf, accessed March 17, 2018.

56. Iosif Brodskii, "Ostanovka v pustyne," in *Stikhotvoreniia i poemy*, 2 vols. (St. Petersburg: Izdatel'stvo Pushkinskogo Doma, Izdatel'stvo "Vita Nova," 2011), 1:212. English translation by Ainsley Morse.

57. Iosif Brodskii, "Rotterdamskii dnevnik," in *Stikhotvoreniia i poemy*, 2:21. English translation by Ainsley Morse.

58. Brodsky and Prigov have been compared before: see B. Grois, "Poeziia, kul'tura i smert' v gorode Moskva," *Kovcheg* 5 (1980): 73–83; A. L. Zorin, "Pamiati Dmitriia Aleksandrovicha Prigova," Polit.ru, July 17, 2007, http://polit.ru/article/2007/07/17/zorin_o_prigove/, accessed March 15, 2018.

59. Ol'ga Sedakova, "Postmodernizm: Usvoenie otchuzhdeniia," in *Dvukhtomnoe sobranie sochinenii* (Moscow: En Ef K'iu/Tu Print, 2001), 2:334–43; Sedakova, "Posle postmodernizma," 2001, http://www.olgasedakova.com/Moralia/277, accessed March 15, 2018; Sedakova, "Posredstvennost' kak sotsial'naia opasnost'," public lecture at the Arkhangel'sk Dobroliubov Library, November 28, 2005, http://www.olgasedakova.com/Moralia/280, accessed March 15, 2018.

60. Sedakova, "Ob"iasnitel'naia zapiska." Translation by Martha Kelly and Ainsley Morse.

The Poetic Anthropology of Olga Sedakova

In Dialogue with Sergei Averintsev and Boris Pasternak

VERA POZZI

In him was life, and that life was the light of mankind

—John 1:4

Свете тихий [. . .] Сыне Божий, живот даяй
O Gentle Light [. . .] O Son of God and Giver of Life

—Orthodox Prayer

The four-volume edition of Olga Sedakova's collected works shows the author's creative and intellectual engagement with numerous areas of inquiry and expertise; the titles of each volume alone—*Poems, Translations, Poetica, Moralia*—reveal the breadth of her interests. In her work, poetry and essay writing are two strands of a larger project addressing the central themes of humanistic culture.

At the root of *Poetica* is the verb *poiein*,[1] which is a reference to the practical side of poetic creation, and of creation more generally. The essays in this volume are primarily devoted to poetry as it relates to many other fields, including philosophy, history, ideological dissent, as well as the poetic craft itself. Several essays also discuss individual poets, including Alexander Pushkin, Velimir Khlebnikov, Boris Pasternak, Ivan Bunin, Anna Akhmatova, Joseph Brodsky, and Elena Shvarts, among others. Taken as a whole, these essays are also a kind of poetic activity in themselves, and a creative act.

The title *Moralia*, meanwhile, takes as its subject the present day, vividly describing the mores of our historical period. And yet the volume also points readers beyond the borders of their time, toward a more complex *mos maiorum*, a system of values and problems that pertain not only to recent history, but to all human culture. Thus Sedakova writes about freedom, friendship, the will, tradition, symbols, humanism, myths, happiness, death, and hope. We notice immediately a series of polarities: past/present, tradition/novelty, listening/creating, which make it impossible to define Sedakova's "anthropology" within the categorical binary of conservative versus progressive.

Frequent references to literary and humanistic works provide further clues to Sedakova's anthropological thought. An important aspect of it is the presence of an *other*—as artist, as thinker, or, most essentially, as human being—who is not some unknowable monad, some creator of a private, inaccessible world. For Sedakova, the other deserves our attention and respect because his experience is the common experience of all human beings. Sedakova understands that this notion of a shared belonging is anything but commonly accepted: "unlike their primordial predecessors, these more recent myths and metaphors are personal, 'made for one.' But they, too, are in their own way complete, they, too, comprise part of a systemic whole that we call the 'world of the poet.' [. . .] And yet in all this we fail to ask a simple question: how does each of these personal 'worlds' relate to the world we all hold in common?" ("Poeziia i antropologiia"; 3:101).

Sedakova's poetic universe builds on direct and indirect encounters with texts, authors, and other artistic sources that influenced her worldview. Any consideration of her work has to account for those influences, and for the ways in which her poetics is both unquestionably personal and a continuation of the Russian and European traditions. As the poet attests: "I had realized fairly early on that the state of poetry in the second half of the twentieth century needed greater consideration, and that the innovation—the new linguistic freedom and depth brought by both European and Russian moderns (Mandelstam, Khlebnikov, Rilke, Eliot, the French symbolists [. . .])—had not yet been thought through."[2] The search for this "linguistic freedom" does not imply a departure from the historical reality in which Sedakova lives. It strives toward "a simplicity that has passed through the school of the difficult and a clarity that is aware of the dramatic tension of the modern."[3]

At the thematic level, Sedakova's poetics is more intensive than extensive, we might say. Unlike the prevailing tendencies in postmodern art, her poetics displays a unique and all-encompassing quality that permits a descent into lower stylistic registers. But she imbues this stylistically lower register with kenotic tension. Sedakova notes:

> Perhaps that is precisely why I find myself in such a lonely position in the contemporary scene. [. . .] The inertia of downward movement is very apparent to me. That has been the vector which art has been pursuing for centuries now, "speculations on degradation." [. . .] But that movement in one direction alone has become

> senseless inertia. [. . .] When Baudelaire discovered the beauty of the trivial, of evil even, that grabbed his reader's attention as a widening of experience, in its own peculiar way an act of kenosis. It is no accident that in Rilke, the poète maudit is confronted by the image of St. Julian, who bestows a kiss upon a leper.[4]

This position might not be shared by many contemporary poets, but it is more common in the broader cultural field. An example is the collection entitled *Our Situation: The Image of the Present* (*Nashe polozhenie: Obraz nastoiashchego*), which appeared in Moscow in 2000.[5] It includes essays and other writings by Sedakova, Vladimir Bibikhin, Anna Shmaina-Velikanova, Anatoly Akhutin, Alexander Vustin, and Sergei Khoruzhy. Despite differences in their points of view and disciplinary orientations, the authors express a shared position in discussing the present. I am speaking about a group of philologists, philosophers, poets, and musicians whom Sedakova has known from the late 1960s onward (the names of Evgeny B. Pasternak and Sergei Averintsev should be recalled as well), and with whom, in her own words, she shares a feeling of "spiritual community."[6] The work of each author is important in its own right, but their belonging to this community suggests that the relationships between them are as worthy of consideration as their individual positions.[7]

In this essay, I examine the relationship between Sedakova and the two "fixed stars" in her poetic firmament. First, I consider her relationship with Sergei Averintsev, whom Sedakova has spoken of as her teacher on her journey toward understanding ancient and modern culture. Averintsev occupies a central role in what I have called Sedakova's anthropology. Second, I analyze Sedakova's relationship with Boris Pasternak—which is not a personal relationship, but one of spiritual affinity. Pasternak's international reputation as a poet, novelist, and translator is established, but far too little is known of the influence that his worldview had on the Russian generation of the 1960s and 1970s and, more specifically, on the members of the spiritual community discussed in this essay.

I believe that the influence of Sergei Averintsev and Boris Pasternak has been a decisive factor in the development of Sedakova's cultural, religious, and anthropological views. From Averintsev, Sedakova learned a method of reading history and culture that has influenced her understanding of the current state of humanity and given her a hopeful outlook on its future. The poet herself has remarked in an interview that a considerable portion of her work is "dedicated to Averintsev."[8] As for Pasternak, Sedakova has drawn from his work, in particular *Doctor Zhivago*, a sense that the poetic word should be understood as a gift and as a message of redemption.

Poetry as Anthropodicy: Sergei Averintsev's Legacy in Olga Sedakova's Poetics

Sergei Averintsev's work—as a classical philologist, philosopher, translator, religious scholar, and poet—is unfortunately little known to readers and researchers outside of Russia. His father, a biologist and the son of serfs, belonged to the old Russian intelligentsia, and he conveyed to his son a sense of historical continuity with the nineteenth century and with the art and literature of a period that in those years must have seemed distant and closed off. Between 1969 and 1971, Averintsev taught courses on Byzantine aesthetics at Moscow State University. His lectures on subjects ranging from Greek and Latin patristics to liturgical hymnography and mysticism became very popular; the subjects were innocent enough but touched on themes rarely discussed at the time, and his lecturing style was markedly unconventional. He was later removed from this position and accused of "religious propaganda," but was still allowed to publish and was frequently consulted by other scholars for his vast erudition.

Sedakova recalls: "for many, many years now—in the Soviet Union and then in Russia—the memory of his presence has had a tremendously important place in our life. I say 'our,' leaving the reader the right to decide whether or not to join this 'we'" ("Dva otklika na konchinu Sergeia Sergeevicha Averintseva"; 4:795). It was during one of his courses in 1969 on Byzantine aesthetics, which Averintsev was able to teach thanks to the support of Viktor Lazarev, where Sedakova first heard the man who would soon become her teacher. A previously unknown world opened up for her. She encountered Greek and Latin culture, the writings of Dionysus the Areopagite, and the European poetic tradition, including the work of Paul Celan and Paul Claudel.

For Sedakova's generation, these lectures would have been unlike anything they had ever experienced, and the spirit of the times made them approach many of the central ideas of the course with suspicion. She writes: "When I first encountered Averintsev's thought as a student, my approach (though I couldn't have articulated it then) to things of the mind and to the 'extra-rational,' so to speak, was more or less what one might expect, given the social environment in that particular time and place. The bright, rational intellectual was in a most unenviable position" ("Apologiia ratsional'nogo: Sergei Sergeevich Averintsev"; 4:526). Intelligence (*um*) and reason (*razum*) seemed inextricably linked to a narrow, miserable, and violent model of thinking. So much so that "everything wonderful and profound, everything real and intimate disappears" (4:526). Her meeting with Averintsev, by contrast, astounded her "above all, for this: a different way of describing the mind" (4:526).

For Sedakova, this kind of intelligence is radically inclusive. It does not exclude the experience of suffering, and does not consider it a disagreeable, accidental, and senseless aspect of human life. Averintsev saw the Enlightenment as the culmination of an "exclusive" mode of thought that denied any possibility of finding meaning in the act of suffering.[9] However, he observed that the Enlightenment's exclusion of suffering was born of a desire to improve the lot of mankind; for him, the error of the Enlightenment stemmed not from "harshness of heart," but from intellectual shortcoming. Sedakova goes even further: "It is important to note that even in the post-Enlightenment period art has never forgotten the old wisdom, it has continued to know and love the loftiness and meaningfulness of suffering: 'And the life-giving light of suffering / Above them slowly burned' (Zabolotsky)" (4:527).

Averintsev's definition of reason did not deprive suffering of meaning, nor did it dismiss the possibility of comprehending the reality of poetry and of the miraculous. Reason, so odious to Sedakova and her generation, excluded from its line of inquiry anything related to art, the unquantifiable, and the non-prosaic. In other words, it excluded the more complex forms of reality. Averintsev goes beyond the rational/irrational binary, and rediscovers reason as an instrument that allows us to closely examine every aspect of human experience without reducing it or changing its meaning.

This absence of violence reveals the second characteristic of Averintsev's reason: its dialogism (*sobesedovanie*). For Sedakova, Averintsev's key term is understanding: "As he sought to name the basic subject undergirding his various projects, he landed on understanding" (4:533). This understanding preserves the object's right to speak for itself and does not dominate it: "It is not the kind of knowledge that masters its subject, locking it up for later use in a prison of foregone conclusions, not Bacon's 'knowledge is power'" (4:534).

Another essay, which takes as its subject not Averintsev but Goethe and Pasternak, epitomizes this concept of reason. In it, Sedakova follows in Averintsev's footsteps and introduces the two terms *attention* (*v-nimanie*) and *perception* (*vospriiatie*): "I am tempted to write these words as Heidegger would, in a form that would highlight their moment of 'reception,' 'absorption'" ("Simvol i sila: Getevskaia mysl' v *Doktore Zhivago* Borisa Pasternaka"; 4:551). Sedakova further adds, quoting Pasternak, that "what sight does with the visible world has nothing to do with its 'estrangement'—quite the opposite: it constitutes 'recognition' of the world, reception or perception of it, a 'receptivity of the utmost inspiration'" (4:553).

According to Sedakova, Averintsev's concept of reason is connected to the "extreme receptivity of inspiration," which is crucial to the relationship between man and the world. In her cycle *Chinese Journey* (*Kitaiskoe puteshestvie,* 1986), we read:

> несчастен,
> кто делает дело и думает, что он его делает,
> а не воздух и луч им водят,
> как кисточкой, бабочкой, пчелой;
> [...]
> И еще несчастней,
> кто не прощает:
> он, безумный, не знает,
> как аист ручной из кустов выступает,
> как шар золотой
> сам собой взлетает
> в милое небо над милой землей. (1:335)

> unhappy,
> is he who does what he does and thinks he does it
> and not that air and light guide him,
> like a paint-brush or butterfly or bee;
> [...]
> But even more unhappy
> is he who won't forgive:
> this insane one does not know
> how the tame stork steps out of the bushes,
> how the golden sphere
> flies up by itself
> into the sweet heaven over the sweet earth.

Happiness is bound up with intelligence, specifically the form of reason that is open to the world and its wonders: "We could call this peculiar perception-attention-creation the art of thought, meaning not objective or speculative thought, but rather Goethean 'contemplative thought' or 'thinking contemplation'" (4:554).

Another element that Sedakova's anthropology borrows from Averintsev is her understanding of the *other*. Sedakova's openness toward the other, the interlocutor, owes much to the openness and respectfulness that characterize Averintsev's intelligence. This quality always struck his listeners. Sedakova recalls how, during Soviet times, the main concern of official culture was to avoid spreading ideas that "the simple man" would have trouble understanding (4:804). Averintsev, however, addressed himself to everyone: "Averintsev's speech was addressed to friends, to people about whom he never said in advance, 'they don't need this,' 'they won't understand this'" (4:804). Averintsev's openness to his interlocutors and his efforts to introduce them to unfamiliar concepts were not seen as the imposition of a "superior" form of knowledge, inaccessible and therefore frustrating. On the contrary, Sedakova writes, "everything about this discourse was the opposite of what might be expected: most of all, his trust in and respect for the listener, his trust in and respect for the object of his thought" (4:804). For Averintsev, the foundation of dialogue was paying attention to one's interlocutor and taking care not to let speech become a monologue.

This dialogic nature of discourse and attention to the interlocutor are echoed in Sedakova's poetics. We can see Sedakova's application of Averintsev's ideas to poetic experience in one of her programmatic texts on the subject—her speech on the occasion of receiving an honorary degree in theology from the University of Minsk. Here, she describes poetic experience as a gift that, once received, can be given by the poet to the other: "and, most strikingly, this most solitary of experiences can be voiced and shared! The very same event transpires in the reader, if he is a true reader" ("'V tselomudrennoi bezdne stikha': O smysle poeticheskom i smysle doktrinal'nom"; 3:137).

The many interconnected facets of Averintsev's rationality point to the human nature of communication: its "com-prehension" (*pri-nimanie*), "attention" (*v-nimanie*), its openness toward meanings not produced by the subject, the "consciously public nature of his way of speaking."[10] As Sedakova claims: "I spoke of how obvious it is that modern art has lost its choral source. [...] Now, not a choral communion but a mysterious muster, a response from the depths of one human to the depths of another. The 'verse's chaste abyss,' as with any other form of art, is the *domain of communion*. [...] We could put it this way: it is the common human in the human being, the very substance of humanity in the human, in his heart" (3:137). The third important characteristic of Sedakova's anthropology is, consequently, this "substance of humanity," the nature of the "I" in Averintsev's thought. Sedakova describes it as follows: "what was in question for him—and quite consciously—was the subject of discourse, the statement-making subject. This *I* was not a perfect entity, this *I* could be mistaken; but this situation still did not preclude the existence of certain invariables, certain a priori propositions" (4:542).

In her essay "Mediocrity as a Social Danger" ("Posredstvennost' kak sotsial'naia opasnost'," 2003–5), Sedakova tells the story of a German artist who admitted to her that she hated great art. For the artist "anything that contradicted the average evoked in her a hatred she herself could not understand. This shouldn't exist, it's skewing all the maps, it's destroying my world!" (4:383). According to Averintsev, this kind of reaction to "great art" speaks to the condition of modernity. Sedakova clarifies Averintsev's position: "One feature of modernity he categorically refused to accept: its mood of adolescent rebellion. Expressions of such rebellion against elders, against orders, against the bourgeois struck him as insufficiently serious for big things, for 'the business of life,' for a defined worldview" (4:529). For Averintsev, reason is not an oppositional principle, and neither is the "I." The "I" is instead tied to "a new depth of forbearance that expands what we consider to be 'our own' life, beyond the boundaries of our bodily, psychic, biographical borders" (4:530).

Sedakova locates the boundaries of ordinary life inside the "everyday, ordinary consciousness" of man: "Above all, it is the acceptance of everyday experience as the one possibility—and because of this it cannot accept what is never or extraordinarily rarely experienced in the everyday: the miraculous" (4:530). The hatred of great art in Sedakova's previous example fades away only by moving beyond the "ordinary" ("obydennyi"), beyond consciousness habituated to half-truths: "Only after great inner upheaval did she realize to what extent she had been shackled by a kind of dedication to half-truth. It was not an outright lie, no: merely a half-truth" (4:383). What makes this kind of consciousness ordinary is its tendency to narrow the horizons of the "I," reducing everything to mere survival. This happens when the bonds with the outside world and with others are broken. For Sedakova, the "I," like the "center" and the "heart," is a point that was originally open. She writes that "'heart' ('serdtse') in Russian is of the same root as the words 'middle,' and 'core' ('seredina,' 'serdtsevina'). It is the paradoxical center, center of personality which is, at the same time, its border, and the broken one" (4:683). Thus, "internal change" ("vnutrennii perevorot") is a kind of *metanoia* that breaks down barriers around "ordinary" ("obydennyi") consciousness. Sedakova writes: "the critical point of this change is called 'metanoia' in Greek (literally; change of mind), repentance or conversion; in Russian, it is 'umilenie,' a great revealing shock of tenderness; or 'breaking of heart' ('sokrushen'e serdtsa'). It is the collapse of some inner walls which help the individual remain in an isolated position and which 'defend' him from the look of Truth" ("The Light of Life"; 4:682). The "depth of patience" that Averintsev describes is precisely this "change" ("perevorot"), when what once seemed impossible becomes possible: the ability to experience the "immutable," the marvelous, unexpected, yet strangely familiar, without having created them yourself.

Let us look at Sedakova's poem "Fifth Stanzas" ("Piatye Stansy"):

Большая вещь—сама себе приют.
[...]
Как в раковине ходит океан—
сердечный клапан времени, капкан
на мягких лапах, чудище в мешке,
сокровище в снотворном порошке—
так в разум мой, в его скрипучий дом
она идет с волшебным фонарем . . . (1:305)

A great thing is a haven for herself.
[...]
As the ocean swims inside a shell—
the heart-valve of time, a trap
on soft paws, a marvel in a sack,
a treasure in a sleeping potion,—
so into my reason, into its creaking house,
she goes into with her magic lantern . . .[11]

That which is dark, which lives in a creaking house—“my reason” (“razum moi”)—is illuminated by a new miraculous light. The magnitude of this visit makes it impossible to establish its proportions according to known terms, “as the ocean swims inside a shell.” Nevertheless, we do not perceive this phenomenon as violent or excessive. The immutable, the miracle that illuminates the “creaking house” of the “I,” “destroys” (to use the words Sedakova quotes from the unnamed German artist) only its own “powerlessness.” This remarkable act of destruction is a source of hope, as shown in the beginning of the poem “Nothing” (“Nichto”):

Немощная,
совершенно немощная,
как ничто,
которого не касались творящие руки,
руки надежды (1:400)

Feeble,
perfectly feeble,
like nothing
untouched by creator hands,
hands of hope

Hope is a constant in Averintsev's thought. It relates to the concepts of time and man in contemporary culture. We have previously noted how sectarian radicalism was foreign to his thinking. As Sedakova recalls, "two polarised positions (for Averintsev) are not polarised after all, inasmuch as they are equally distant from something else."[12] In the opening remarks for a conference on the future of Christianity in Europe (1993), Averintsev expressed this in the following manner: "In truth, 'I am not a prophet nor the son of a prophet' (Amos 7:14), and my task is difficult for me. More than anything, I want to save myself from two diametrically opposed kinds of foolishness. From the Scylla of optimism and the Charybdis of pessimism."[13] Man cannot know his own future, and in fact he has a hard time seeing what Averintsev calls "God's tactics"; therefore, "without a doubt, pessimism is nonsense, [. . .] and optimism is a lie."[14] The dichotomy of optimism and pessimism begins on the outer margins of hope. Pessimism radically negates hope, while optimism mystifies it, taking it to mean a broad belief in the good, and a blind irresponsibility in the face of complex events.

In an essay on Averintsev's method, Sedakova considers his ideas about the Silver Age, which he approaches as an interlocutor and not merely a scholar: "His thought constituted a sobering corrective to the enthusiasm of the beginning of the century, and without it, any discourse after Auschwitz and the Gulag would simply have been *false*."[15] In spite of this "sobering corrective," without which only the lie of optimism would remain, Averintsev is eager to share a hopeful thought with his audience: "Do not despair! *Homo sapiens, homo loquens, homo humanus* has not vanished altogether, however implausible this might sound after all that has taken place here!"[16] Sedakova takes up this call and addresses it to poetry. She writes: "how to speak of 'another,' 'new' *person* in oneself. That would be the very embodiment of 'art after Auschwitz and the Gulag'" ("Veshchestvo chelovechnosti"; 4:357).

The sense of reality with which Averintsev viewed contemporary life comes across in one of his articles from 2002, where hope is viewed as an alternative to the culture of death. Averintsev discusses the latter in biblical terms—as the antagonist of Wisdom (Proverbs 9:13–17).[17] He identifies this false wisdom with the contemporary culture of death and finds it within our television screens. It reserves "the right to determine what its students and protégés ought to consider pleasurable."[18] The principal trait of contemporary mass culture is a new totalitarian attitude, tolerant only in word. "My main issue with neoliberalism is precisely that it is not liberal, that *it is not inherently tolerant*; in fact, quite the opposite."[19] As Averintsev underscores, "those who wish to reeducate all of mankind are hardly interested in being permissive and tolerant."[20]

These quotations underscore the spiritual kinship of the two thinkers. We see a similar attitude in Sedakova's writing in 2000, when she observes: "It seems to me that the problem lies not in power's disappearance from the scene, but rather in its taking on a new, little-recognized form—and this particular form enables it to infiltrate places previously inaccessible to classical and ideological despotism" ("Vlast' schast'ia"; 4:279–80). Sedakova will also take up this theme in later essays, and in a piece written between 2003 and 2005, she gives a name to this new form of power: "I have called this danger, this tyrannical force threatening the contemporary world, *mediocrity*" (4:397). By employing the term "mediocrity," Sedakova builds on the work of Dietrich Bonhoeffer and Georges Bernanos. This kind of mediocrity should not be confused with the golden mean (*zolotaia seredina*) or *aurea mediocritas* of Aristotle's *Ethics*, which was so dear to Averintsev. On the contrary, as I have shown, the latter kind of mediocrity can be equated with non-sectarian thought, which observes things in order to grasp their truth.

One final point of commonality in their work concerns the traits of false wisdom and foolishness as discussed by Averintsev, and mediocrity as described by Sedakova. Because these terms could be seen as an indictment of an entire swath of humanity as foolish or mediocre, both writers clarify their intention in the opening lines of their respective essays.

Averintsev reminds us that "it is essential to remember that the words we associate with foolishness mean something different in the Bible—not merely a weakness of intellect but more importantly its mendacious stance. Nonsense freely *chosen* over sense. In other words, a fortitude not exactly dianoetic but ethical and pneumatological."[21] Sedakova also writes that "mediocrity is not an innate human characteristic, it is a *choice*. It is of this choice that I wish to speak" (4:378). Averintsev's clear-eyed view of human history led him to declare that "history does not end. It has already ended several times" (4:809). He was also sure that "this end too shall pass" (4:811). Sedakova explains that she uses these quotes not to prove "his sagacity" ("ne o prozorlivosti"), but rather to show his "hermeneutical method" (4:810). In Sedakova's own words, this is "the method of *wisdom*—of the biblical figure of Sophia the Wisdom of God" and "at one and the same time, [of] deep, heartfelt engagement with the present moment—and sober detachment from it" (4:810).

Much of Averintsev's work is dedicated to wisdom, the "man-loving spirit" ("dukh chelovekoliubivyi)" (4:810). In conclusion, I offer an excerpt from his lengthy article written in 1964 on the theme of the inscription inside the dome of the apse in the St. Sophia Cathedral in Kyiv, alongside an excerpt from Sedakova's poem "The Angel of Reims":

This inscription reproduces Psalm 46:5 ("God is in the midst of her; she shall not be moved: God shall help her, and that right early"). The psalm is built on the contrast between two images: the chaos of the world and the unshakeable blessed city. Wars and natural disasters rage around its walls [...] but for the city and house of God this play of cosmic forces transforms into joy because it is safeguarded by God's presence.[22]

Ангел Реймса
Посвящается Франсуа Федье

Ты готов?—
улыбается этот ангел—
[...]
ты готов?
к мору, гладу, трусу, пожару,
нашествию иноплеменных, движимому на ны гневу?
Все это, несомненно, важно, но я не об этом.
Нет, я не об этом обязан напомнить.
Не за этим меня посылали.
Я говорю:
ты
готов
к невероятному счастью? (1:414–15)

The Angel of Reims
Dedicated to François Fédier

"Are you ready?"
this angel smiles.
[...]
are you ready?
For plague, hunger, cowardice, fire,
attack by other tribes, wrath that closes in on us?
This is all very important, no doubt, but that's not what I mean.
No, I'm not here to remind you about that.
That's not why I was sent.
I'm saying:
are you
ready
for unbelievable happiness?

Both texts may be read as messages, and we should ask to whom they are addressed and what tidings they bring. Sedakova marked the passing of John Paul II, whom both she and Averintsev knew personally and respected, with the following tribute: "The first words that the newly elected Pope John Paul II pronounced to the people in Rome in 1978 were: 'Be not afraid!' [. . .] To stand up straight, to free oneself, to reassert one's innate dignity, the dignity of God's beloved creature—this was what could be accomplished by the evangelistic news that he proclaimed to the world with all his might" ("Dva otklika na konchinu Papy Ioanna Pavla II"; 4:826). It follows that Averintsev's and Sedakova's message is essentially anthropological; it is addressed to *Homo humanus* and is an exhortation to keep hope alive. Both Psalm 46 and the words of the angel serve as a reminder that fear and despair prey on humanity. And yet, in both texts there is a glimmer of light from the word joy (*vesel'e, schast'e*). In the spirit of the new Christian humanism (which opens its message to all, just like the sacrifice of Christ), Sedakova and Averintsev turn the language of tradition into a testimony communicating a promise of life.

"The Light of Life": The Influence of Boris Pasternak in Olga Sedakova's Poetics

Sedakova first encountered Boris Pasternak and his novel *Doctor Zhivago* in her early youth. At the time, she was particularly taken with his poems. Later, she would also come to appreciate him as a thinker, specifically a Christian thinker. Sedakova credits Anna Shmaina-Velikanova with rediscovering Pasternak as a Christian author.[23] Shmaina-Velikanova has also published a number of studies on Pasternak's thought and, together with Evgeny Pasternak, belongs to Sedakova's spiritual community.

In her article "Symbol and Power: Goethean Thought in *Doctor Zhivago*" ("Simvol i sila: Getevskaia mysl' v *Doktore Zhivago*"; 2005–8),[24] Sedakova observes that "thus far the thinking and the peculiarly doctrinal side of Pasternak's work has been little theorized; he remains unrecognized as an unphilosophizing philosopher, an untheologizing theologian" (4:549). Quoting from a draft of *Doctor Zhivago*, she uses "The Novelty of Life" ("I zhizni novizna") as the title for one of her essays on Pasternak.[25] Elsewhere, in talking about poetry, she uses the expression "the awakening of the other" ("probuzhdenie drugogo"; 3:136). Life, novelty, "awakening": we can reconstruct the significance of these terms, so central to Pasternak's poetics, if we trace their progressive—and interrelated—levels of meaning.

For Pasternak, "novelty" ("novizna") is primarily the possibility of a new outlook on reality. In a letter to Stephen Spender from 1959, he writes, "I have always understood totality—reality as such—as a message, or an unexpected arrival, and have always strived to recreate this sense of a message intended for me, which, it seemed, revealed itself to me in the nature of phenomena" (4:624). And another quotation invoked by Sedakova: "I would picture nature and the universe (metaphorically speaking) not as a painting hanging motionlessly on the wall, but as a painted canvas awning or a curtain in the air, ceaselessly swaying and inflated by some immaterial, unknown and unknowable wind" (4:571–72).

The meaning of this message is anything but "concealment." Pasternak does not believe that the phenomenological world needs "decoding." Sedakova cites these lines from Goethe: "What is the hardest of all? That which seems most simple: / to see with your eyes what is before your eyes" ("Was ist das Schwerste von allem? Was dir das Leichteste dünket: / Mit den Augen zu sehen, was vor den Augen dir liegt"; 4:552). Subsequently, she notes that "the investigative gaze looks but does not look out, does not peek ('what is actually there?'). It knows that what is 'actually' there is what is visible, not what is hidden; what affects feelings, not the extrasensory" (4:623). "The nature of phenomena" ("priroda iavlenii") is, therefore, a message as in the Church Slavonic meaning of the word *iavliatisia* (ꙗвлѧтисѧ)—"to open, to become manifest" ("otkryt'sia, stat' iavnym").[26] The term is a calque from the Greek *epiphainō, phaneeromai,* which connotes "manifestation."[27]

Sedakova reflects on the manifestation of the world in yet another important work, "The Light of Life: Some Remarks on the Russian Orthodox Perception" (2005).[28] Here, the term "perception" (*vospriiatie*) has a double meaning. On the one hand, it means the Orthodox Weltanschauung. On the other, "perception" is a specific property of what Sedakova calls "Orthodox sensibility," which is not always explicitly confessional (4:702–5). In the ninth paragraph, entitled "*Think or see?*" she writes that "this type of mentality definitely prefers *image* to *concept,* as the most (if not the only) proper form of representing the perceived meaning. All the vital truths are supposed here to be represented in images" (4:690). The main vehicle for knowledge is not the concept, but the image. Indeed, "one can't contemplate a concept, nor *have a personal contact with* it, as one usually does with the open, dynamic and inexhaustible presence of an image" (4:690). Everything in the world, and particularly in nature, which is so important to the poetic sensibilities of both Pasternak and Sedakova, takes part in the life of man and carries a message for him.[29] The novelty of which we speak is revealed to man, whose subjectivity is fundamentally receptive. One could even say, using Pasternak's expression, that it functions "in the passive form" (4:597), or, in other words: "you didn't have to think of anything: the rocks cried out, things thought for you" (4:690).

This understanding of subjectivity is characteristic of Sedakova's anthropology, which explains passivity in terms of the receptivity of contemplation. She writes that "we have to keep in mind that 'contemplation' in Russian means not 'thinking,' but 'seeing with the greatest attention,' and being 'plunged' into what one sees" (4:690). This sort of contemplation does not in any way suggest hostility to reason. On the contrary, it constitutes an experience of knowledge. The Church Slavonic term that corresponds to the Russian "contemplation" (*sozertsanie*) is *zrěnie* (зрѣние), which in turn originates from the Greek *theōria*.[30] We should therefore bear this in mind when we read Sedakova's assertion that "to see well means to theorize" (4:627).

Sedakova goes even further. She makes her way back to the sources of that Orthodox sensibility that is also the fertile soil that nourishes Pasternak's world.[31] She reads subjectivity as a heart (*serdtse*), as a center (*serdtsevina*) projected ecstatically outward. She writes that "the 'heart' means here the very center of the human person, it is not only emotional, but cognitive and physical at once. [. . .] It is the paradoxical center, center of personality, which is, at the same time, *its border, and the broken one.* In its heart (or even 'in the heart of heart,' as the Orthodox mystics say) the human being comes to its limit and to its 'being-with' or 'being-between,' i.e., to its participation in The Other" (4:682–83). As is evidenced by the preceding passage, one finds a shared belonging, a mutual implication between the first and the second levels of meaning I have described, which are the levels of the world as a message and of the ecstatic addressee of its revelation. Sedakova writes that "organic knowledge of the organic, the thought of Goethe and Pasternak, calls for unifying things that mechanistic thinking would view as irresolvable antinomies. These things include theory and phenomenon, outer and inner, vision and reflection, sensible and intelligible, subject and object" (4:632). Sedakova describes this shared belonging, a trait of Yuri Zhivago, as "influence" ("vliianie") and "affinity" ("srodstvo"; 4:626), terms borrowed from Pasternak. We read, for instance, that "Yuri Andreievich woke up shortly after midnight brimming with a vague feeling of happiness, which was, however, strong enough to have aroused him. [. . .] But there was a waterfall nearby. It widened the expanse of the white night by a breath of freshness and freedom; that was what had filled him with happiness in his sleep."[32]

In the conclusion to "The Light of Life," Sedakova quotes the ending to one of Ivan Bunin's poems:

The summer wind is swinging
The leaves of the long branches
And I know what reaches me:

The light of your smile.
Not a gravestone, not a cross—
I see, as I saw once
The dress of a boarding schoolgirl
And the shining eyes. (4:704)

One of her comments on this text reads: "In the image of this smile we comprehend the impressions of flight, light and of something sonorous at once: *a hint of visitation*. The smile is not there, it seems to remain in its distance; it is but *its light* that comes. [...] But what we immediately feel (as the hero does) is that death *does not matter*" (4:704). This "hint" brings us very close to what Pasternak calls a symbol (*simvol*), and the "visitation" amounts to what he calls power or force (*sila*). In *Safe Conduct* (1958), Pasternak notes: "If [...] I decided now to write an aesthetic of creativity I would build it on two conceptions, the conception of power and the conception of the symbol. I would point out that [...] art concerns itself with life as the ray of power passes *through* it."[33]

An important aspect of what Pasternak calls "symbol" and Sedakova "hint" is its lack of fixity. This pertains not to specific objects, or those objects that are usually considered worthy and elevated. Rather, they are the most ordinary objects, they could be anything. This is what Pasternak means by "the realistic."[34] It is an art that is "focused on a reality which feeling has displaced, [...] a record of this displacement. It copies nature."[35]

Sedakova emphasizes this idea and cites an example from Origen, who claims that "other kinds of seeds, plants, birds, etc. can serve as such symbols of the whole" (4:647). She continues by noting that "things that serve interchangeably as symbols point us to what can, by nature, be expressed by practically anything—by something singular, accidental and random, or by everything all at once" (4:647).

The second key element in Pasternak's conception of the symbol has to do with perception of power or force. In *Doctor Zhivago*, we read that Yuri Zhivago "saw the two sleeping heads [of Lara and Katen'ka] on their snow-white pillows. The purity of their features, and of the clean linen and the clean rooms, and of the night, the snow, the stars, the moon, surged through his heart in a single wave of meaning [*propushchennuiu volnu*], moving him to a joyful sense of triumphant being."[36] Sedakova takes up Pasternak's idea of power or force and emphasizes its relation to beauty and distance from violence; she reminds us that power can also relate to happiness. She writes that "it would be really strange to revolt against the power of Beauty—just like to revolt against the power of Happiness. It is the soft power: it does not command, it endows. A human heart meets Beauty (like Happiness) as the fulfillment of its own wish and the meeting has the taste of Plato's *anamnesis*" (4:689).

There is a third element as well. Sedakova describes Pasternak's symbol as "an event of recognition" ("sobytie opoznovaniia") that takes place "always suddenly" ("vsegda vdrug"; 4:644). This conception of the symbol is clearly active in Sedakova's poetics. The poem "Sant'Alessio. Roma" is a good example:

Sant Alessio. Roma

Римские ласточки,
ласточки Авентина,
когда вы летите,
крепко зажмурившись

(о как давно я знаю,
что все, что летит, ослепло—
и поэтому птицы говорят: Господи!
как человек не может),

когда вы летите
неизвестно куда неизвестно откуда
мимо апельсиновых веток и пиний . . .

беглец возвращается в родительский дом,
в старый и глубокий, как вода в колодце.

Нет, не все пропадет,
не все исчезнет.
Эта никчемность,
эта никому-не-нужность,
это,
чего не узнают родная мать и невеста,
это не исчезает.
Как хорошо наконец.
Как хорошо, что всё,
чего так хотят, так просят
за что отдают
самое дорогое,—

что всё это, оказывается, совсем не нужно.

Не узнали—да и кто узнает?
Что осталось-то?
язвы да кости,

Кости сухие, как в долине Иосафата. (1:401–2)

Sant'Alessio. Roma

Roman swallows,
swallows of the Aventine,
when you fly
with your eyes squeezed shut

(oh, how long I've known

that everything that flies has gone blind—
and that's why birds say, "Lord!,"
like a person can't),

when you fly
who knows where from who knows where
past orange tree branches and pines . . .

the refugee returns to his parents' home,
which is old and deep like water in a well.

No, not everything will pass away,
not everything will disappear.
This for-nothingness,
this needed-by-no-one-ness,
this,
what mother and bride do not recognize,
this does not disappear.

How good at last.
How good that everything
they want so much, ask for so much,
for which they'd give away
what they love most,—

that all of this, it turns out, is absolutely needless.

So you didn't recognize it—well, who would?
What's left, then?
sores and bones,

Dry bones, like the Valley of Jehoshaphat.

The symbol coincides with both individual elements of this poetic text—the swallows, the orange trees, the pines, the image of the fugitive returning home—

and the totality of these elements, since "each symbol and all symbols together unite us not with any concrete 'meaning' (albeit richer and more complex than in the modern technique of symbols as found in the Symbolists), but with the 'unsearchable whole,' with the 'legend,' with the meaning that exists not as a 'thing,' but as an environment" (4:644–45). For a brief instant, these elements, taken in their totality, acquire meanings that fill them and exceed their borders. The resulting atmosphere is described in the fifth stanza: "No, not everything is lost, / Not everything vanishes." The innocence of the swallows, the light in Rome, the return to the father's home—these images recall episodes in the life of St. Alexis. At the same time, they awaken in the reader a sense of recognition that does not come from a perceived similarity between one's own daily existence and that of the saint. It derives, instead, from the sudden, in some sense inexplicable perception of joyous light, the light of a new life.

"I zhizni novizna." What, then, is that very "novelty" ("novizna") that we have been describing so far from the point of view of its manifestations—message, symbol, power, and to use Sedakova's language, hint and visitation? What is its content? Pasternak's and Sedakova's texts offer some guidelines. We find clues that help us answer these questions in the piteousness (*zhalost'*) and weeping (*plach'*) of the wind; the tenderness (*nezhnost'*) and healing (*vyzdorovlen'e*) of the pond; and, finally, Zhivago's exultation (*likovanie*) and the swallows' pointlessness (*nikchemnost'*).

To answer these questions, I would now like to devote a few words to the poetic nature of Sedakova's anthropology in light of the connection between Pasternak's "novelty of life" and the nature of poetry (and of inspiration) as described by Sedakova in the essay "Poetry and Anthropology" ("Poeziia i antropologiia," 1999). Here, poetry is "the realization of the human being at the very limit of his 'measure'" (3:111). Sedakova then claims that "we could speak of this measure as mortality; we could speak of it as *humanity* in the sense with which we began (*mere* humanity, so to speak). But no matter how we interpret it, *measure* becomes *moribund* when it is struck by the spark of form. Form is not an object: it is a force" (3:111–12).

The experience of poetry is at once death and birth, or rebirth. It is the death of life as *bios*, "finite, determinate life, life that contains its own death" ("Simvol i sila"; 4:558), and the birth of life as *zoē*, "infinite, nondeterminate life, completely opposed to death, the very element or power of life, 'the sort of thing that does not let death approach it'" (4:558). *Bios* is the dead life seen from above in the poem "Sant'Alessio. Roma" (1:401). We recognize it, but no longer recognize ourselves in it, in its pile of dry bones.[37] In the words of Yuri Zhivago, "art has two constant, two unending concerns: it always meditates on death and thus always creates life."[38] The novelty of life, therefore, is the novelty of *life as zoē*, which expresses itself symbolically in the elements we have listed above and particularly in the power of compassion, freedom, and happiness.

For Sedakova, the novelty of life as *zoē* pertains to human experience as such and it is linked with poetry described as "anthropological experience, experience of the improbable human, *Homo impossibilis* [. . .] on the threshold, at the source, as a *promise* of something entirely other that he will at once recognize as what is most *native* to him" ("Poeziia i antropologiia"; 3:112). In my opinion, the most important aspect of Sedakova's poetic anthropology is precisely the fact that poetic experience (as the climactic moment of human experience) belongs in equal measure to both the artist and the reader: "most essentially, this experience [. . .] can be shared and declared. [. . .] It takes place in both the author and his reader—in which of these more fully, it is hard to say" (3:112).

Sedakova has repeatedly emphasized that the person of the twenty-first century, responding to the trauma of totalitarianism and the death camps, has had to learn anew that evil is present within and to remember the truth of original sin (4:407). It is in this context that the most important message for Sedakova—the message of memory—emerges: "There is something else even more thoroughly forgotten, and perhaps it is worth saying: '*Remember that there is something innately good about you.*'"[39]

This memory lives, first and foremost, in the experience of received compassion. In Church Slavonic, the term *zhalost'* (жалость) has the same meaning as the Greek *zēlos*: fervent transport, love.[40] The same term is described by Pasternak as a gift, who declares: "You hand me the gift of compassion, the most important of Your gifts, the one that comes from the Holy Spirit, from which flow all others."[41] Sedakova echoes this sentiment in a footnote: "it is pity that keeps people alive and keeps worlds in motion, pity as a gift of the Holy Spirit—the Russian version of Love, a word that is a little unclear in the Russian language, a little abstract" (4:559n1). For instance, in the poem "In Hospital," Pasternak writes:

"Кончаясь в больничной постели,
Я чувствую рук Твоих жар.
Ты держишь меня, как изделье,
И прячешь, как перстень, в футляр."[42]

"Though I'll die on this sick-bed of mine
Your warm hand I feel guide my way,
For you've made me and hold me and now
Like a gem you encase me away!"[43]

The object of compassion is Mary Magdalene, a central figure in Zhivago's poems. She expresses paradoxically the frailty of humanity and its resurrection through the gift of compassion. Mary Magdalene, in turn, offers as a gift her most precious possession, her life, in the image and likeness of him who has healed her. She declares:

Я жизнь свою, дойдя до края,
Как алавастровый сосуд,
Перед Тобою разбиваю.[44]

Me, here upon the final brink,
My life before you I would break,
An alabaster vase of doom.[45]

In Mary Magdalene, Sedakova also sees the highest expression of Christian freedom as a willingness to offer oneself up "to the brink" ("do kraia") in response to the liberation from death that Christ bestowed onto men ("Svoboda kak eskhatologicheskaia real'nost'"; 4:13–30). Mary Magdalene's compassion broadens in the contemplation of his sacrifice:

Слишком многим руки для объятья
Ты раскинешь по концам креста.

Для кого на свете столько шири,
Столько муки и такая мощь?
Есть ли столько душ и жизней в мире?
Столько поселений, рек и рощ?[46]

While your arms outstretched on the cross
Spread too wide with your vast embrace;

For who in all the world needs this
Embrace, such torment and such power?
Has earth so many lives and souls,
Woods, rivers, villages, to shew?[47]

The reflection of such breadth comes to the fore in Sedakova's *Chinese Journey*:

А потому что не хочется, не хочется своего согрешенья,
потому что пора идти

просить за всё прощенья,
ведь никто не проживет
без этого хлеба сиянья.
Пора идти туда,
где всё из состраданья.[48] (1:341)

It's because we don't want, don't want our sins,
because it's time to go
ask everyone's forgiveness,
after all, no one will survive
without this bread of radiance.
It's time to go
where everything's made of compassion.

Finally, *zoē*, and the memory it carries, brings about an utterly miraculous sense of happiness. When we look at the swallows of the Aventine, which, in their essential pointlessness, fly toward mercy and compassion with their eyes shut, we perceive what Sedakova calls "the gift of poetry" ("dar poezii"). She explains: "a person would call this moment of rightness—this miraculous forgetfulness of the very possibility of mistake and blunder, and of our painful imperfection—pure happiness. [. . .] The gift of suddenly remembering our native land, of being struck by our friendly and familiar ways of relating to what normally, ordinarily we face with dread and guilt. The gift of the memory of Eden" (3:139).

"Remember that there is something innately good about you."[49] This is the culmination of Sedakova's poetic anthropology. In it we find the voices of Averintsev, his message of hope in the *Homo humanus*, and of Pasternak, of *zoē* as life resurrected: "You are anxious about whether you will rise from the dead or not, but you rose from the dead when you were born and you didn't even notice it. [. . .] 'There will be no death,' says St. John. There will be no death because the past is over; that's almost like saying there will be no death because it is already done with, it's old and we are bored with it. What we need is something new, and that new thing is life eternal."[50] In short, in Sedakova's poetic anthropology we hear the voice of Christianity. However, as she stresses, this is a new voice. "Death, Judgment, the Afterlife as eternal life—these three 'ultimate questions' comprised the nerve center of classic Christian art. [. . .] But in Pasternak new Christian art has introduced another theme."[51]

Evgeny Pasternak quotes a few lines of a letter from Boris Pasternak to his parents: "There is something faith-like, if not faith itself, that suggests to me that fate cannot but linger with love on that which is vitally beautiful and vitally meaningful. [. . .] I am wary of these words. [. . .] But in essence I am not speaking about fate, but about a certain angel of fate. [. . .] And, ultimately, of God."[52] Evgeny Pasternak then remarks that Boris Pasternak "understood that by bringing love to life through the word he performed a divine mission and in this he saw his calling."[53] This is the kind of love that Dante, one of Sedakova's favorite poets, calls the "prime mover" of the universe.

"Creation, Healing (these are the words associated with Salvation, in Pasternak's *Doctor Zhivago*), Life"—these words constitute Pasternak's new Christian art.[54] For Sedakova, the corresponding terms are pity, power, and happiness. These are the features of her anthropology, which finds in poetry not metaphorical expression but its own voice, as in these lines from *Tristan and Isolde* (*Tristan i Izol'da,* 1978–82):

—Да сохранит тебя Господь,
Который всех хранит.
В пустой и грубой жизни,
как в поле, клад зарыт.
И дерево над кладом
о счастье говорит.
[. . .]

Да сохранит тебя Господь,
читающий сердца,
в унынье, в безобразье
и в пропасти конца—
в недосягаемом стекле
закрытого ларца.

Где, как ребенок, плачет
простое бытие,
да сохранит тебя Господь
как золото Свое! (1:175–76)

"May the Lord protect you,
He who protects each one.
In this rude and empty life,
this field, there's buried treasure.
And a tree leans over it
and tells of happiness.
[. . .]

May the Lord protect you,
He who reads every heart,
when you despair or go astray,
when you reach the final precipice—
may he keep you safe from harm
in a secret box of glass.

Where being, plain and simple,
is weeping like a child,
may the Lord guard and keep you,
as though you were His gold."

In September 2014, in a presentation that also bore the title "Poetry and Anthropology," Sedakova described the poetic voice as the discovery of "another self" within the self ("opyt cheloveka neveroiatnogo—*Homo impossibilis*").[55] Sedakova uses her own poetic voice to work out the meaning of "anthropodicy," which takes the form of an "eschatology."[56] This happy tension echoes Rilke's appeal in the *Duino Elegies* to show the Angel the things of this world.

Translated from Italian by Gabriella A. Ferrari

Notes

1. Ol'ga Sedakova, *Tserkovnoslaviano-russkie paronimy: Materialy k slovariu* (Moscow: Greko-latinskii kabinet Iu. A. Shichalina, 2005), 353–54. The Church Slavonic term **творити** holds the same meaning as the Greek *poiein*. The Creator is **Творецъ** (*Poiētēs*).

2. "An Interview with Olga Sedakova," in *In Praise of Poetry*, ed. Caroline Clark, Ksenia Golubovich, and Stephanie Sandler (Rochester, NY: Open Letter Press, 2014), 193.

3. Ibid., 194.

4. Valentina Polukhina, "Conform Not to This Age: An Interview with Olga Sedakova," in *Reconstructing the Canon: Russian Writing in the 1980s*, ed. Arnold McMillin (Amsterdam: Harwood Academic Publishers, 2000), 43–44.

5. Ol'ga Sedakova et al., *Nashe polozhenie: Obraz nastoiashchego* (Moscow: Izdatel'stvo gumanitarnoi literatury, 2000).

6. Sedakova underscored the importance of these relationships for the development her anthropological and cultural views in "'Zalog velichiia Ego': K istorii svobody v Rossii," http://www.olgasedakova.com/Moralia/1612, accessed March 17, 2018.

7. The shift in this direction is apparent in the historiographical studies of the twenty-first century. See Olga Sedakova, "Reflections on Averintsev's Method," *Studies in East European Thought* 58, no. 2 (2006): 73–84. This issue contains several other essays pertinent to late Soviet Christianity and Orthodoxy, including Jonathan Sutton's "'Minimal Religion' and Mikhail Epstein's Interpretation of Religion in Late-Soviet and Post-Soviet Russia," 107–35.

8. Sedakova, *In Praise of Poetry*, 206.

9. Averintsev's reflection on the narrowness of Enlightenment thought is not unique. Sedakova notes that Georges Bernanos took a similar position: "L'intelligence, réduite à ses propres forces, ne croit trouver dans la nature qu'indifférence et cruauté, mais c'est sa propre cruauté qu'elle y découvre. . . . En réalité l'intelligence ne s'indigne pas contre la souffrance, elle la refuse, comme elle refuse un syllogisme mal construit." Georges Bernanos, *La Liberté, Pour Quoi Faire?* (Paris: Gallimard, 1953), 223, quoted in Ol'ga Sedakova, "Apologiia ratsional'nogo: Sergei Sergeevich Averintsev," 4:519–49. The year 1947 saw the publication of a crucial text on this matter, Theodor Adorno and Max Horkheimer's *Dialectic of Enlightenment*, in which Enlightenment is characterized as "the amputation of the incommensurable." Max Horkheimer and Theodor Adorno, *Dialectic of Enlightenment*, trans. Edmund Jephcott (Stanford, CA: Stanford University Press, 2002), 9.

10. Sedakova, "Reflections on Averintsev's Method," 79.

11. See Andrew Kahn's chapter for his full translation of "Fifth Stanzas."

12. Sedakova, "Reflections on Averintsev's Method," 81.

13. Sergei Averintsev, "Budushchee khristianstva v Evrope," in *Sofiia-Logos* (Kyiv: Dukh i Litera, 2006), 763.

14. Ibid.

15. Sedakova, "Reflections on Averintsev's Method," 76.

16. Ibid., 79–80.

17. Sergei Averintsev, "Bibleiskii obraz mudrosti kak al'ternativa kul'ture smerti," in *Rimskie rechi. Slovo Bozhie i slovo chelovecheskoe* (Moscow: Izdatel'stvo Moskovskoi Patriarkhii; Rome: Sofia. Idea russa, idea d'Europa, 2013), 447.

18. Ibid., 459.

19. Ibid., 463. The italics are mine.

20. Ibid., 459.

21. Ibid., 437.

22. Averintsev, "K uiasneniiu smysla nadpisi nad konkhoi tsentral'noi apsidy Sofii Kievskoi," in *Sofiia-Logos*, 573.

23. See, for example, Anna Shmaina-Velikanova's essay "Poeziia kak vykhod iz bogoslovskogo tupika: *Doktor Zhivago* i ego posledstviia," in Sedakova et al., *Nashe polozhenie*, 280–91. Sedakova also mentions the work that Jacqueline de Proyart devoted to Pasternak's Christianity.

24. Sedakova's first draft of this long essay coincided with the publication of Boris Pasternak's complete works: Boris Pasternak, *Polnoe sobranie sochinenii s prilozheniiami v odinnadtsati tomakh* (Moscow: Slovo, 2003–5). Sedakova makes special mention of volumes 7–10, which contain Pasternak's letters; she values them no less highly than the poetry or prose.

25. Ol'ga Sedakova, "'I zhizni novizna': O khristianstve Borisa Pasternaka," http://www.olgasedakova.com/Moralia/1032, accessed March 17, 2018.

26. Sedakova, *Tserkovnoslaviano-russkie paronimy*, 401.

27. Ibid.

28. Recall that 2005 is also the year Sedakova started drafting her essay on Pasternak, "Simvol i sila," 4:548–655.

29. For example, see the poem "The pond speaks . . ." ("Prud govorit . . .") in Sedakova's *Chinese Journey* (1:328) and the lyrical poem "Wind" in Boris Pasternak's *Doctor Zhivago*, trans. Max Hayward and Manya Harari (New York: Pantheon, 1958), 532.

30. Sedakova, *Tserkovnoslaviano-russkie paronimy*, 136.

31. Sedakova notes that "what most clearly connects Pasternak's Christian thought with Orthodox tradition is its relation to the image, to poetry (liturgical poetry) as the most profound medium of thought. (The novel lays out its most important ideas about the precise nature of Christianity's novelty in the world through a selection of liturgical poetry, the canons of Holy Week)." Sedakova, "'I zhizni novizna.'"

32. Pasternak, *Doctor Zhivago*, 234.

33. Boris Pasternak, *Safe Conduct: An Autobiography, and Other Writings* (New York: New Directions, 1958), 71.

34. Ibid., 70.

35. Ibid., 72.

36. Pasternak, *Doctor Zhivago*, 437.

37. We could go further in identifying elements typical of Orthodox sensibility by quoting another word central to "The Light of Life" regarding the experience of the death of life as *bios* and its rebirth as *zoē*. This word is *umilenie* ("a great revealing shock of tenderness"), which produces something like *sokrusheniie serdtsa* ("breaking of the heart").

38. Pasternak, *Doctor Zhivago*, 90.

39. Olga Sedakova, "Vopros o cheloveke v sovremennoi sekuliarnoi kul'ture," http://www.olgasedakova.com/Moralia/872, accessed March 17, 2018.

40. Sedakova, *Tserkovnoslaviano-russkie paronimy*, 121.

41. Pasternak, *Polnoe sobranie sochinenii*, 4:712.

42. The passage is quoted in Sedakova, "'I zhizni novizna,'" and cited here from Pasternak, *Polnoe sobranie sochinenii*, 2:144. This is the end of an internal quotation within the poem.

43. The translation is from Pasternak, *In the Interlude: Poems, 1945–1960*, trans. Henry Kamen (London: Oxford University Press, 1962), 85.

44. Pasternak, "Magdalina I," in *Polnoe sobranie sochinenii*, 4:545.

45. Pasternak, *In the Interlude*, 46.

46. Pasternak, "Magdalina II," in *Polnoe sobranie sochinenii*, 4:546.

47. Pasternak, *In the Interlude*, 48.

48. The term *sostradanie* corresponds to the Church Slavonic *sostrastie* (сострастїе) a calque from the Greek *sumpatheia*.

49. Sedakova, "Vopros o cheloveke."

50. Pasternak, *Doctor Zhivago*, 68.

51. Sedakova defined the principles of "new Christian art" in her speech at the Vatican, delivered on July 1, 1998: "Shchastlivaia trevoga glubiny," http://www.olgasedakova.com/Moralia/266, accessed March 17, 2018.

52. Boris Pasternak, *Pis'ma k roditeliam i sestram* (Moscow: Novoe literaturnoe obozrenie, 2004), 109.

53. See Olga Sedakova, keynote address to the exhibition "Mia sorella la vita. Boris Pasternak" (My sister, life. Boris Pasternak), October 11, 2011, http://www.youtube.com/watch?v=MU31RScwa5A, accessed July 4, 2018.

54. Sedakova, "Schastlivaia trevoga glubiny: Rech' pri vruchenii premii 'Khristianskie korni Evropy' imeni Vladimira Solov'eva," http://www.olgasedakova.com/Moralia/266, accessed March 17, 2018.

55. Ol'ga Sedakova, "Poeziia i antropologiia," https://sfi.ru/sfi-today/article/i-chto-chelovek-chto-ego-beregut-gnezdo-razorenya-i-stona.html, accessed March 17, 2018.

56. In the same speech, Sedakova defines poetry as an "eschathological image" ("eskhatologicheskii obraz") and as "anthropodicy" ("antropoditseia").

The Semantic Vertical

Church Slavonic Heritage and Olga Sedakova's Poetics of Translation

MARIA KHOTIMSKY

The real danger in poetic translation is the absence of courage.

—Olga Sedakova, "The Art of Translation"

Over the course of her artistic career, Olga Sedakova has translated a remarkable range of poets: from Horace, Petrarch, and Dante, to Emily Dickinson, T. S. Eliot, Paul Claudel, Paul Celan, and others.[1] As Sedakova recalls, her first translations date back to her secondary school years. Remembering these early attempts, she describes a feeling of wonder "as if crossing a sea of nonexistence that separated the English original and its Russian version," where the foreign text disappears and "reemerges on the other shore, with its rhythms and sounds, and with great losses, of course."[2] In this tender and ironic look back at her first forays into poetic translation, Sedakova highlights the miraculous feeling that accompanies the transformation of a poem into another language. This sense of poetic quest is essential for her work: translation is a challenge to be overcome, ripe with difficulties but also discoveries. It offers the poet new ways to broaden her own poetics, or to use one of her metaphors, "a gift of meaning to grow into" ("dar smysla na vyrost").[3]

This artistic approach to translation played a pivotal role in the development of the Russian literary tradition. Sedakova follows in the footsteps of generations of poets who found inspiration in their work as translators. However, at the time of her literary debut, not only Sedakova's poems, but also her translations were denied publication on the grounds that they were "too strange." The poet recalls a conversation with an editor who scathingly dismissed her translations of Emily Dickinson's poetry: "'This doesn't sound Russian! No one says it like this in Russian! Unintelligible! Wrong!'—I constantly heard such reviews of my translations during Soviet times. [. . .] If I objected that even the originals of my translations had neither 'correctness' nor 'coherence' (as, for example, with Emily Dickinson's poems), it didn't impress anybody."[4] This critique is representative both of Sedakova's independent poetic stance, and of the era when she began her literary career; in the Soviet period, translation editors tended to avoid innovative and experimental poetics. As I would like to suggest, both contexts—the vision of translation as a creative dialogue with rich transformative potential, and the restrictive context of the Soviet translation tradition—are important for understanding Sedakova's philosophy of translation. As the poet's reflections show, her views on translation developed in opposition to mainstream stylistic expectations. And while other poets of the Thaw era shared with Sedakova the experience of discovering new styles through translating, her own vision of translation is unique in its emphasis on semantic growth, for which she finds a model in the history of the Church Slavonic language.

Sedakova's translations have already attracted some critical attention. Ketevan Megrelishvili and Henrieke Stahl have explored Sedakova's versions of Paul Celan's poetry.[5] The poet's dialogue with Rilke has been addressed by Sergei Averintsev and Elena Aizenshtein.[6] Other chapters in this volume touch on Sedakova's dialogue with Rilke (Andrew Kahn), Modernist poetry (Sarah Pratt, Benjamin Paloff, Emily Grosholz), and Celan (Ksenia Golubovich). My goal is to focus specifically on Sedakova's philosophy of translation and to explore its role in her poetic development. In the first part of this chapter, I will discuss Sedakova's views of translation in their contemporary context (the Soviet school of translation) and compare them to some Western theories of translation. The second part is devoted to Sedakova's perception of Church Slavonic as a model for thinking about translation. In the third part, I turn to several textual examples, looking at translations from Dickinson, Rilke, and Celan in connection with Sedakova's own evolving poetics.

Sedakova's Concept of Translation

Olga Sedakova entered the literary scene in the late 1960s, when opportunities for publication were restricted, and translation offered one of the few viable ways of earning a living for a writer. Although the question of the Soviet school of literary translation and its influence on the poetic tradition is beyond the purview of this chapter,[7] I would like to highlight some of its key traits that have a bearing on Sedakova's stance as a translator. On the one hand, the Soviet era witnessed large-scale investment in translation, including the creation of new publishing houses, the establishment of a union of translators within the Writer's Union, and the development of a sophisticated system of translation editing and censorship.[8] Whether building the socialist literary canon of the postrevolutionary years, translating the literature of the Soviet Republics, or reshaping the concept of world literature, the field of translation was a site of ideological investment by the state. These political and social circumstances also led to the use of translation as a cultural "niche," a possible realm of dissent and covert communication with readers.[9] Official and grassroots translation seminars and workshops led by translators such as Efim Etkind, Elga Linetskaia, Tatiana Gnedich, Vilgelm Levik, and others, created possibilities for artistic communication and the preservation of poetic tradition.

At this paradoxical juncture of control and freedom, the position of poet-translators was particularly fraught. For some authors, translation offered a means of self-expression when their original work could not be published (for example, Maria Petrovykh's translations of Armenian poetry, or Nikolai Zabolotsky's deeply personal investment in translating *The Igor Tale*). However, many authors who turned to translation as a way to earn a living drew a sharp line between translation and their own writing. Thus, Arseny Tarkovsky once remarked: "Translations are our daily work, our own poems are our rare holidays."[10] Restrictive ideological demands were not the only reason for such alienation. Poets often felt estranged from the texts they were translating due to the short terms of translation contracts and the need to work on little-known authors; moreover, they often did not know the language of the original and would use crudely prepared interlinear prose trots (*podstrochniki*).[11] In addition, dominant stylistic trends in translation were based on a conservative idea of "the poetic," which favored rhymed syllabo-tonic verse and was distrustful of innovative imagery. This phenomenon resulted in a set of "ideological filters"—to use Ilya Kukulin's term—that affected not only the choice of authors and subject matter, but also the stylistic expectations of poetic translations.[12]

The point of all this context is to highlight Sedakova's unique and somewhat rebellious position. In many of her statements, the poet defines her understanding of translation in contrast to the mainstream practices of the Soviet school of translation. For example, she often questions one of its key concepts—the idea of "translatability" (that is, the possibility of producing a poetically viable rendition of a foreign text in any language):

> For me, each text presents a problem: will it submit itself to translation? First of all, can it be translated into the Russian language, carried over to the Russian [poetic] tradition in the broadest sense of this word, including our versification and repertoire of rhymes. Furthermore, can it be translated by me; that is, are my own poetic resources suited to the task? And if I feel that this is not the case, I do not even try. Although I love Rilke, and was steeped in his poetry in my youth, I have only

> translated a few of his poems. It would never even occur to me to translate an entire book of Rilke's poetry.[13]

This statement packs many critiques into one concise paragraph. Sedakova is suspicious of the Soviet tradition of anthological translation: detailed and exhaustive editions representative of a particular author or literary group. In her view, each poem is a unique challenge both to the author-translator's poetic self, and to his or her vision of the Russian poetic tradition. For Sedakova, translation is first and foremost a matter of learning, and she calls for a thorough knowledge of the foreign languages and literary traditions on which one works. As she observes: "In order to translate one poem, I must read as many texts by the author as possible, and, where applicable, I also read the author's theoretical prose; in other words, I must get to know his artistic persona extremely well."[14]

Many of Sedakova's contemporaries, especially those who debuted during the Thaw era, when a wider range of European and American authors was available for translation, treated their translations as learning experiences. This was true of Asar Eppel and Natalya Gorbanevskaya's translations from Polish, and the young Joseph Brodsky's translations of British and American poets. Incidentally, Sedakova has observed that poets of her generation revived the prerevolutionary tradition of dialogic translation. She describes "a decisive change that happened with Joseph Brodsky, who was searching for similar things in English, Latin, and Polish poetry, as Pushkin had in French, British, and Italian; that is, a path to a new world of meaning and forms."[15]

Another significant feature of the translation process, in Sedakova's view, is its difficulty. She is distrustful of easy stylistic solutions. As she writes: "What the art of translation demands is a highly developed sense of the unique and inimitable (precisely because translation is the art of imitation), i.e., the sense of the whole. [. . .] And the only instrument we can use to grasp the *whole* is, unfortunately, intuition, not theoretical premises and statements."[16] Sedakova's understanding of translation as an intuitive and deeply personal creative activity has many parallels in Western translation theory. Thus, Gayatri Spivak calls translation "a most intimate kind of reading."[17] Echoing this view, Sedakova characterizes translation as "work as intimate as one's own composition," and adds that she always translates very selectively, turning to particular authors at specific stages in her poetic career.[18]

Sedakova shares this hermeneutic understanding of translation as exploration with other scholars and philosophers. Like Walter Benjamin, for whom absolute language (*reine Sprache*) was the ultimate basis of translation, Sedakova speaks of "trusting poetry as such": "The most important condition of poetic translation is to trust poetry as such, poetry as a message and its addressee."[19] Such trust depends on the poet-translator's capacity to change. Sedakova is moved to explore what Maurice Blanchot described as "an identity on the basis of alterity,"[20] and she is drawn to authors whose poetics have few analogs in the Russian tradition. As she explains, the most difficult part of translation is to recognize the other, to open up to it: "When you clearly see that the Russian language, Russian poetry, the Russian concept of 'the poetic' lacks the discursive structures to convey how ruthlessly T. S. Eliot's writing treats itself. That Russian lyrical poetry does not have the structures, the vocabulary, or the rhythms to convey Paul Celan. All these things are created along with the translation. And this is the most difficult part. After that, things get easier."[21] Rendering a different poetics does not result in a "smooth" translation. As Sedakova recalls, "the most valuable (and most innovative) elements in translation were often crossed out by the editors."[22] These were poetic elements "that conveyed irregular, strange, difficult speech," "the very presence of language trying to cope with yet-unknown turns of meaning."[23] This reaching for the previously impossible is what she aspires to in her translations. The ultimate goal of translation and of poetry in general, according to Sedakova, is to create "new semantic verticals of meaning" ("novye semanticheskie vertikali znacheniia").[24] In her view, daring poetic innovation allows author-translators to achieve new possibilities akin to the spiritual breakthrough of early Church Slavonic translations of Greek texts into Slavic dialects. This is one of the cornerstones of Sedakova's thinking about translation that is reflected in her poetry, essays, and scholarship, and I will turn briefly to this topic before discussing her translations of European and American poetry.

Church Slavonic as a Model of Translation

Let me begin with a longer quotation, in which Sedakova links her understanding of translation with the history of Old Church Slavonic (a language based on South Slavic dialects and created for the purpose of translating liturgical texts from the Greek).[25] She describes the work of the first translators the following way:

> It is interesting to trace how they worked with language. For example, to render the Greek *pneuma* (spirit) they took the Slavonic *dukh* ("spirit" in modern standard Russian). But in Slavic dialects *dukh* did not mean "spirit" (nor does it nowadays). It meant just "breath" or "smell" or "vital force" ("he breathed his last"). In Greek, the word *pneuma* also bore such tangible meaning, at, one might say, the lowest end of its spectrum of meanings, the most concrete. The Teachers of the Slavs

> (as St. Cyril and St. Methodius are called) linked Greek and Slavonic words via their material, tangible meanings; they thereby endowed the Slavonic word with the semantic vertical that Greek culture had achieved through centuries of work. They built the semantic vertical dimension that the Slavonic words lacked. In this way, the brothers created a whole field of abstract and spiritual notions that the Slavonic language did not yet possess.[26]

As a poet-translator, Sedakova dwells on this transformative moment. In her view, the invention of Old Church Slavonic by the legendary brothers St. Cyril and St. Methodius was an act of translation par excellence, introducing religious connotations into the cultural and linguistic contexts of local dialects, and thereby imbuing existing words with new spiritual meanings. The subsequent history of Church Slavonic and its impact on spiritual culture bears the imprint of this miraculous moment.[27]

In her creative writing and scholarship, Sedakova often refers to linguistic and historical studies of Church Slavonic, but her take on this history is idiosyncratic. For example, Riccardo Picchio has described the importance of Church Slavonic heritage for the formation of local literary languages and for the establishment of "supranational" unity among the countries of "Slavia Orthodoxa."[28] As Picchio explains, the stability of Church Slavonic, which functioned as the language of religious services and church literacy, contributed greatly to the sense of shared cultural legacy.[29] Citing Picchio, Sedakova emphasizes this unifying role of Church Slavonic, describing it in poetic terms as a text in which each quotation is imbued with the richness of the spiritual tradition: "Even the shortest quotation suffices to recall the entire image of a church service: its smells, its fabrics, the flicker of lights in the semidarkness, its melodic turns, its withdrawal from linear time [. . .] everything bound to the materiality of the church service. Not only a quotation, but even a minimal sign of this language, some grammatical form, even an irregular one, suffices to convey this image."[30] The poet often uses Church Slavonic words in their original historical meaning, and these words function as signs of the Christian Orthodox tradition.

In her translations and scholarship, Sedakova also explores connections between Church Slavonic and Russian linguistic elements. She often invokes Boris Uspensky's concept of *diglossia*—the coexistence of Church Slavonic and Russian as sacral and vernacular domains within one language.[31] But while Uspensky stresses the impossibility of translation between two languages in *diglossia*, since these two languages "are perceived as one, and their contexts of usage have a complementary distribution,"[32] Sedakova is interested in translating from Church Slavonic into Russian. She spent many years working on a dictionary of Church

Slavonic-Russian paronyms (words that appear the same, but vary in their meaning and usage in the two languages), and she explores these fine distinctions in her reflections on translation: "This heritage of *diglossia* can be agonizing for translators. When we work with serious, spiritually exalted texts, with European poetry—Dante or Rilke—where an angel might appear, we tend to use Church Slavonic forms involuntarily and automatically. But this two-tiered approach to language is nowhere to be found in the original. It is one and the same word; for example, 'Augen' encompasses both the Slavonic, archaic word for eyes (*ochi*) and the modern word (*glaza*)."[33] As a poet whose work often addresses spiritual themes, Sedakova is particularly careful when navigating so-called lofty poetry, which has historically relied on Church Slavonicisms. She tries to avoid fixed expressions associated with an elevated style, but at the same time she defines Church Slavonic as a prototype of poetry: "In my view, the very concept of poetry as a 'special language,' sacred or prophetic, which differs essentially from prosaic speech, consciously or unconsciously goes back to St. Cyril's heritage."[34] In her translations of Church Slavonic texts, including liturgical poetry, excerpts from *The Sinai Patericon*, and other texts, Sedakova aspires to the "simple and living word" ("prostoe i zhivoe slovo")—qualities she praised in Anri Volokhonsky's translations from Church Slavonic into Russian.[35] Her work on European poets of different epochs follows a similar principle: finding a lyrically compelling expression for personal spiritual themes. Sedakova models translation as an exploration of new semantic possibilities, and Church Slavonic becomes an emblem of poetry as a gift of sacred speech. Sedakova reflects on this heritage not only in her essays, but also in her poems.

A fine example is "Mountain Ode" ("Gornaia Oda"), which shows the interconnected sides of Sedakova's artistic persona as a scholar, poet, translator, and Christian thinker. As Andrew Wachtel suggests, the genre and structure of this poem allude to the eighteenth-century solemn ode (*torzhestvennaia oda*). The key themes of "Mountain Ode," according to Wachtel, are "metaphysical despair in the face of death and the possibility of posthumous survival in works of art."[36] Sedakova's sources for this poem include the odes of Mikhail Lomonosov and Gavrila Derzhavin, as well as Mandelstam's "Slate Ode" ("Grifel'naia oda," 1923/1937). Yet despite clear allusions, its rhythmical structure and rhyme scheme are different (Sedakova uses only feminine rhymes with the rhyme scheme ABABCDCDEE). "Mountain Ode" signals a strong connection with tradition, but also departs from it in search of a simple, concrete language for the poet's spiritual concerns. Sedakova purposefully avoids elements associated with the high style: some Church Slavonic words do appear in the poem, but are used in their original meanings, creating a hidden "code" that runs through the text. The culminating moment of "Mountain Ode"—the bestowal of poetic gifts—is linked to the Cyril-Methodian heritage:

Скажи, скажи на языке Кирилла
или на том, какого не бывало,
как снисхожденье с нами говорило
и небо прятало, как покрывало. (1:232)

Tell, oh, tell us in the tongue of Cyril,
or even in a tongue that never was,
how descent spoke with us where we were,
how the heavens hid us like a blanket.

The speaker in "Mountain Ode" experiences a momentary epiphany and partakes in sublime language. "Sniskhozhdenie" ("condescension" or "leniency" in contemporary Russian) is used here in its Church Slavonic meaning—"descent from Heaven"—and has strong archaic and religious connotations.[37] The poem's visual and linguistic richness come together as the speaker describes her journey and the mountain landscape she beholds. As Stephanie Sandler observes, the spatial dynamics of the poem embrace the vast landscape in an intent and thoughtful lyrical gaze: "By the poem's end, ascent has turned horizontal, vertical movement has gone round."[38] The poem culminates with the enigmatic image of a "rounded vertical":

Не на такой ли круглой вертикали
мне дар передавали безвозмездный,
и золотом, как взглядом, отыскали
и разрешили от надежды тесной? (1:234)

Was it not on such a rounded vertical
that I once received the costless gift,
that I was, like gold, divined by searching gaze,
and I was released from stifling hope?

In this excerpt, Sedakova uses the word "tesnyi" in its original, Church Slavonic meaning. The English translation doesn't quite convey the interplay of this word's Russian and Church Slavonic definitions: *těsnyi* (тѣсныи) means tight or stifling, but also "mournful" or "solemn"—the latter meaning stems from the Church Slavonic word *těsnota* (тѣснота), meaning "sorrow, worry."[39] The word "razreshit'" is also used in its historical meaning—"to relieve, to let go" (in contemporary Russian it means "to permit, to allow").[40] As the poetic speaker travels through the mountain landscape, she experiences relief and empowerment. The letting go of sorrow and the acquisition of poetic voice are played out on multiple levels of the text simultaneously: visual, phonetic, and semantic. The ascent to poetry's heights (the vertical of meaning) becomes round, embracing the arch of the sky and the flow of the mountain river through the valley. In this way, Sedakova transforms the style and sound of the "high ode" by using Church Slavonic words in their original meaning.

The image of the "rounded vertical" brings us back to Sedakova's theories of translation, in particular, her idea that the heritage of Church Slavonic created a "vertical of meaning" within the Russian language. Sedakova has even described her approach to translation as "Cyril-Methodian": "As you can easily guess, I wholeheartedly subscribe to the translation method you might call 'Cyrillian' and try to follow it in my own practice. This means, first and foremost, that to follow tradition is in no way to dread the tradition (as if it were a set of rigid rules and norms). Tradition itself begins with the creation of unprecedented things and demands that we recognize what we now lack."[41] Sedakova's idiosyncratic development as a translator, which was shaped by her educational and spiritual roots, stood in contrast with the prevalent Soviet-era views on translation, but it found many surprising parallels with Western thinkers and scholars, who explored the artistic aspects of translation and its impact on the translator's self. Like Walter Benjamin, Maurice Blanchot, Paul de Man, and Gayatri Spivak, Sedakova defines translation as an open hermeneutic act. Translation exposes the difficulties of writing and forces the translator to experience the limitations of language. Pushing back against the domesticating stylistic trends of the Soviet era, Sedakova uses translation to explore different poetic modes. She creates her own aesthetic lineage, and for her the history of Church Slavonic exemplifies an act of translation that opens new semantic possibilities. She has also compared this foundational moment to later developments in the Russian poetic tradition: "In both its Greek and Western European adventures, the Russian language behaved in an amazing manner: modestly and boldly at once. Modestly, because it demonstrated readiness and even pleasure to follow its new guide without anxiety over losing its own identity. And boldly, because it (I mean, the language as expressed by its authors) did not worry too much about what was possible or impossible, permissible or not permissible. They did what had seemed impossible until they did it."[42] In this statement, Sedakova defines translation as an act, not a result. The adverbs "modestly and boldly" can serve as her translator's credo. In her opinion, translation demands both modest compliance in following the voice of the other and boldness in exploring new poetic possibilities in Russian. Let us turn to some specific examples that demonstrate these principles at work in her translations and in her own poetry.

Translations of Emily Dickinson

Sedakova's translations of Emily Dickinson's poetry are an important part of her early work. Sedakova remembers the first time she read Dickinson on Vladimir Muravyov's advice: "These poems have impressed me in the most profound way. I began translating them right away."[43] Sedakova notes that Muravyov liked her translations, especially "the rhythm, and the power in the breaks between words,"[44] although these were precisely the features that would make her translations hard to publish.

As Dickinson's poetry became more widely available in the late 1960s and 1970s, many poet-translators were mesmerized by her artistic persona as an outsider poet. Several of Sedakova's contemporaries, including Vera Markova, Arkady Gavrilov, and Alexander Velichansky, translated multiple poems by Dickinson, and even devoted essays, diary entries, and original poems to her memory. While Sedakova shared these authors' enthusiasm for Dickinson, she translated only a few texts (in her essay on Dickinson, Sedakova mentions translating thirty poems, but many drafts did not survive; at present, translations of eleven poems are included in Sedakova's collected works). One of the poems she chose to translate is the famous "I dwell in Possibility" (fragment 466, dated 1862), where poetry is compared to a house for the poet:

I dwell in Possibility—
A fairer House than Prose—
More numerous of Windows—
Superior—for Doors—

Of Chambers as the Cedars—
Impregnable of eye—
And for an everlasting Roof
The Gambrels of the Sky—

Of Visitors—the fairest—
For Occupation—This—
The spreading wide my narrow Hands
To gather Paradise—[45]

Here is Sedakova's translation, with a close English rendition of the Russian text:

Возможное—мой Дом—
Прекрасней Были сей—
И множеством Окон—
И вырубом Дверей—

Тверд—как ливанский Кедр—
Моих Покоев Рост—
И Кров—доска к доске—
Покрыл Небесный Тес—

И тысячи Гостей—
Из дали—принимай—
Стремятся в тесное кольцо—
К рукам—собравшим—Рай— (2:306–7)

The Possible—is my House—
More beautiful than this Tale—
By its many Windows—
And the cut of its Doors—

Firm—as the Cedar of Lebanon—
Is the Growth of my Chambers—
And the Roof—from plank to plank—
Is covered by the Heavenly Boards—

And thousands of Guests—
From afar—please receive—
Hurry to the narrow circle—
To the hands—that gathered—Paradise—

The creation of poetic space in "I dwell in Possibility" relies on a peculiar combination of internal and external characteristics: the space of the house and the metaphorical space of creativity, denoted by the contrast of "Prose" and "Possibility." As Helen Vendler observes, "The normal opposite of Prose is Poetry. Dickinson renames poetry 'possibility,' a witty gesture that requires her to describe her 'dwelling' place."[46] Furthermore, the English verb "to dwell" often appears in a biblical context; thus, Dickinson's description of poetry becomes a description of one's spiritual home, an idea that Sedakova develops in her translation. The philosophical and spiritual dimensions of the text are also foregrounded by

Sedakova's translation of the key word "Possibility." While other Russian translators have opted for direct renditions, translating it as "vozmozhnost'" ("possibility") or "veroiatnost'" ("probability"), Sedakova chooses the unusual and abstract term "Vozmozhnoe" ("the possible").[47] Furthermore, to capture Dickinson's contrast, in place of "Prose" Sedakova chooses the archaic word "Byl'" ("tale," also, real tale; it is worth noting that the line where this word appears actually sounds like the English word "possibility"), which is capitalized, along with other key images of the poem. Sedakova relies on unusual word choices throughout the text, as she tries to avoid poeticisms and the clichés of traditional high style poetry. The inverted syntax in the poem's first two lines, where Sedakova uses the archaic adjective "sei" ("this") in postposition, also contributes to the sense of strange or unusual speech.

In both this line and the following quatrain, Sedakova deviates from the original text. For example, in rendering "And for the everlasting Roof / the Gambrels of the Sky," she chooses another archaic expression: "I Krov—doska k doske— / pokryl Nebesnyi Tes—" ("And the Roof—from plank to plank— / Is covered by the Heavenly Boards—"). Other Russian translators choose "krysha" or "krovlia" for "roof," whereas Sedakova conveys "everlasting Roof" with the word "krov"—an archaic root that also appears in such words as *pokrov* ("shroud"). These interpretations bring her own deep knowledge of the Russian Orthodox tradition to her translation. Her early translations are stylistically uneven, as the poet tries to avoid poeticisms and fixed expressions, and frequently makes religious allusions or uses Church Slavonic words in their original meaning. As Sedakova recalls, reading and translating Dickinson gave her a new perspective on poetry: "Perhaps, thanks to Emily Dickinson I clearly felt for the first time that the most important thing is not the 'language,' [. . .] but the experience of thought and passion, the personal experience. The linguistic form required to express it is also very important, of course, but not as much."[48]

The theme of experience is treated in another early translation—Dickinson's "I stepped from Plank to Plank" (poem 875, dated 1864):

I stepped from Plank to Plank
A slow and cautious way
The Stars about my Head I felt
About my Feet the Sea.—

I knew not but the next
Would be my final inch—
This gave me that precarious Gait
Some call Experience.—[49]

Sedakova's translation, followed by a back-translation into English:

Так шла я от Черты к Черте
Вприкидку, как слепой,
Я звезды слышала у лба—
И хляби под стопой.

Я понимала—новый Шаг
Последний мой и тут
Далась мне поступь—пусть ее
Познаньем назовут. (2:309)

So I walked from Line to Line
By feel, as if a blind man,
I heard the stars at my forehead—
And the heavenly oceans under my foot.

I understood—this new Step
Is my last one and here
I achieved the countenance—let it
Be called Learning.

In translating this poem, Sedakova preserves the fractured, difficult syntax, and the connections between thought and imagery. Compared to other Russian translators, she conveys Dickinson's use of the dash in the most consistent way, especially in this poem, where dashes visually echo both the type of movement ("stepping") and the division of space into "planks." In her opinion, preserving this strange and fractured structure is necessary if one is to convey the lyrical self of Dickinson's poetry: "the speed of Dickinson's writing amazed me," she wrote, adding that the poetry conveys "a special state of the soul, a very special experience" (2:312). In her translation, Sedakova retains not only the syntax, but also the capitalization of key nouns in the poem, something other Russian translators do very rarely. Her translation captures the key themes that drew her to Dickinson's poetry in the first place: spiritual search and the expression of lyrical thought. These early translations are an influential and important part of Sedakova's own poetics, where, according to Stephanie Sandler, "thinking always includes the self-conscious moment when the thought, as it were, looks back at itself."[50]

The liberties Sedakova takes in translating Dickinson reflect her interest in the poetry of thought (*poeziia mysli*); her interpretation of this poem emphasizes cognition and exploration. In the very first line, Sedakova uses "ot Cherty k

Cherte" ("from Line to Line") to convey Dickinson's "from Plank to Plank." As if enacting this very image, Sedakova performs an act of boundary crossing by mixing words from different stylistic registers, such as "khliabi," a rare, archaic biblical word for "heavenly waters" or "abyss," which she uses to translate "oceans." In Sedakova's translation, the movement across different styles—from plank to plank, or, in her interpretation, form boundary to boundary—describes the poet's own "steps." Unlike other Russian translations that use "opyt" ("experience") to convey the poem's final term, Sedakova favors "poznanie" ("learning" or "knowledge"). Sedakova views her early translations of Dickinson as one of her first encounters with the poetry of thought: "Later on, other poets—above all Rilke—made her verse less immediate for me. But the power of encountering her poetry is beyond question. An encounter with a soul immersed in thought, a thinking self."[51] In choosing other poets to translate, Sedakova is drawn to the power of lyrical encounter that guides and inspires her own poetics. One such profound and lasting influence is the poetry of Rainer Maria Rilke.

Sedakova's Translations of Rilke

In an interview with Elena Kalashnikova, Sedakova recalls: "Rilke was the most important poet of my youth, and translating his poetry provided a certain test: do I really understand his poetry well enough to be able to render it into Russian? For me, as well as for many Russian poets of the twentieth century, Rilke was a teacher of poetry, *a poet par excellence*."[52] Sedakova's collected works include translations of ten poems by Rilke, as well as the 1979 essay "New Lyrics of Rainer Maria Rilke: Seven Reflections." However, Rilke's presence in her work is ubiquitous. Sedakova often refers to Rilke when writing about poetry or the tasks of Christian art. Many of her own poems respond to his texts, especially her poems on biblical themes that explore similar motifs: "The Flight of the Prodigal Son" ("Pobeg bludnogo syna"), "The Garden of Gethsemane" ("Gefsimanskii sad"); "Resurrection of Lazarus" ("Voskreshenie Lazaria"); "David Sings for Saul" ("David poet Saulu"). Sedakova's encounters with Rilke's poetry inform not just specific poems, but the entire trajectory of her poetic development. For this reason, Sergei Averintsev has described her poetry as "the realization of Rilke's paradigm in Russian."[53]

Building on her interest in Dickinson's "poetry of thought," Sedakova is inspired by the idea of poetic cognition in Rilke. For her, Rilke's lyrical world epitomizes poetry's mission to find new heights of spiritual meaning, a new poetic vision. As Sedakova sees it, his ideal is "the perceiving 'I' as identity in its profoundest sense, linked with the general task of new poetry—to learn or, in Rilke's terms, to understand."[54] Translating his poetry was the first step to understanding the poet; Sedakova also modeled her own poetics on his example. She is demanding in her work as a translator, and she is critical of existing Russian versions of Rilke's poetry: "Rilke became popular in Russia in translations that were, for the most part, clumsy retellings, decorated with poetic fluff that would be unthinkable in his poetics, which are so carefully measured, intense in compositional structure, and purified of any external props of versification and poeticisms."[55] In this critique, Sedakova names the features she tries to avoid in her own work. She argues against stylization and excessive detail, and she calls for heightened attention to poetic structures. Translating Rilke allows her to explore new ways of structuring poetic discourse, and her translations reflect this ongoing process of negotiation. At times, she remains close to the structure and syntax of the original, even going against grammatical norms in Russian. She also takes liberties with other elements of translation, creating her own metaphors to interpret Rilke's imagery.

Let us turn to her translation of the second poem in the *Sonnets to Orpheus* cycle. The original text and Sedakova's translation are quoted below:

> Und fast ein Mädchen wars und ging hervor
> aus diesem einigen Glück von Sang und Leier
> und glänzte klar durch ihre Frühlingsschleier
> und machte sich ein Bett in meinem Ohr.
>
> Und schlief in mir. Und alles war ihr Schlaf.
> Die Bäume, die ich je bewundert, diese
> fühlbare Ferne, die gefühlte Wiese
> und jedes Staunen, da mich selbst betraf.
>
> Sie schlief die Welt. Singender Gott, wie hast
> du sie vollendet, daß sie nicht begehrte,
> erst wach zu sein? Sieh, sie erstand und schlief.
>
> Wo ist ihr Tod? O, wirst du dies Motiv
> erfinden noch, eh sich dein Lied verzehrte?—
> Wo sinkt sie hin aus mir? . . . Ein Mädchen fast . . .[56]

Sedakova's translation:

> И, девочка почти, она вошла
> из общей славы голоса и лиры
> и просияла в ткани прихотливой
> и слух мой, как постель, разобрала

и спит во мне. И это сон ее:
деревья торжества и восхищенья,
луг ощутимый, дали ощущенья
и всё, чем сердце тронуто мое.

И спит о мире. Боже, научи,
как ты свершил ее, не пробуждая?
и спит, и возникая восстает . . .

Где смерть ее? куда мотив ведет?
куда исчезнет песня, поглощая
себя во мне? о, девочка почти . . . (2:362)

And, nearly a girl, she entered
from the common glory of voice and lyre
and she shone in a whimsical fabric
and laid out my hearing like a bed

and sleeps in me. And this is her dream:
the trees of triumph and amazement,
a tangible meadow, the distances of feeling,
and everything that my heart has felt.

And she sleeps about the world. O God, explain
how you created her, without waking her?
she sleeps, and rises up emerging . . .

Where is her death? Where does the motif lead?
where will the song disappear to, swallowing
itself in me? o, nearly a girl . . .

Sedakova starts her translation with the anaphoric conjunction "and," just as in the original, as if continuing the theme of the first sonnet. Bringing her own voice to the translation, she renders "aus diesem einigen Glück von Sang und Leier" as "iz obshchei slavy golosa i liry," where a Church Slavonic word, *slava* (a celebratory prayer, song, or church hymn), stands out in the context of a Western European poem. *Slava* is an important term in Sedakova's poetics and thought; it represents an incarnation of the living, powerful, spiritual Word, deeply linked to Orthodox liturgical traditions, and at the same time one of the key motifs of Rilke's *Sonnets to Orpheus*.

Another telling deviation from the original is Sedakova's choice of "golos" ("voice") to translate German "Sang" ("song"). By contrast, in Alexei Purin's and

Vladimir Mikushevich's translations we find "pesnia" or "penie"—"song" and "singing"—which are closer to the original text. With her word choice, Sedakova emphasizes the capabilities of the poetic subject; she takes the analogy further by rendering "und machte sich ein Bett in meinem Ohr" ("she made herself a bed in my ear") as "i slukh moi kak postel' razobrala" ("she laid out my hearing as a bed"). Typically, Russian translators preserve Rilke's unusual image in this line. Sedakova's translation shifts the emphasis to the capabilities of the poetic subject, to the voice and the faculty of hearing (or "the musical ear," echoing the German idiom "Ohr für Musik").

Sedakova responds not only to the themes, but also the formal peculiarities of Rilke's poems, such as his transitive use of intransitive verbs. In this translation, she reproduces the parallelism in the original text—"Und schlief in mir" ("And sleeps in me") and "Sie schlief die Welt" ("she sleeps the world")—as "I spit vo mne" ("And sleeps in me") and "I spit o mire" ("she sleeps about the world"). Her translation captures the bizarre expression "she sleeps the world," yet allows for a possible grammatical "explanation" by using a Russian prepositional construction that denotes an object of thought and feeling, or prayer. In the third stanza, Sedakova uses another atypical construction—"Kak ty svershil ee" ("How you accomplished her")—to translate "wie hast du sie vollendet." The verb chosen by Sedakova implies an act of creation and a sense of fulfillment; it also connotes the performance of a miracle. Even though Sedakova's translation may seem ungrammatical, it captures the paradoxes of the original poem. While other Russian translations of this sonnet tend to avoid these two grammatical constructions or make them seem more logical, Sedakova purposefully breaches the conventions of grammar in order to convey the strangeness of the original text. Thus she responds to one of the central features of Rilke's poetry: the way it points to the limitations of conventional linguistic expression, and at the same time continues reaching for the ineffable, the "ultimate supremacy of silence."[57] Many of these themes and devices appear in Sedakova's own poetry; for example, in both "Fifth Stanzas" ("Piatye stansy," 1984–85) and a poem in memory of Velimir Khlebnikov, "A Butterfly or Two of Them" ("Babochka ili dve ikh," 1990–2000), she uses intransitive verbs transitively.

Rilke's poetics inform not only Sedakova's approach to translation, but also her understanding of poetry as a profound spiritual quest: "a poetry of limits; poetry that has the power to descend to Hades, like Orpheus, and to return with a new word more silent than silence itself."[58] To achieve this model of poetic discourse, Sedakova follows the credo "modestly and boldly," modestly following the voice of the poet she translates, and boldly trying out new poetic possibilities. Sedakova singles out her work on Paul Celan as one of her most transformative translation experiences: "My most recent poetic experience was Paul Celan. A great post-catastrophic poet. Perhaps the only great poet of this non-poetic epoch."[59] In the concluding part of the chapter, I turn to several examples of Sedakova's translations of Celan's poetry.

Sedakova's Translations of Paul Celan

Sedakova's collected works include translations of thirty-four poems by Celan—more than by any other author. She has also devoted several interviews and essays to his poetics, as well as to her experience of translating his verse. As with her earlier translations of Dickinson and Rilke, Sedakova recalls her first encounter with Celan and the profound impact that it had on her: "The first poem by Celan that I read in German was 'Psalm' [. . .] How it impressed me! All the more so because I didn't know the biographical and historical circumstances of Celan's life, anything that could explain the intensity of this form. I felt only pure amazement at a spiritual forcefulness and directness one would expect from medieval authors [. . .] or poets confronting 'great times,' like Rilke in his *Book of Hours*."[60] While in such early recollections Sedakova compares Celan and Rilke, she later emphasizes the contrast between the two poets: "I remembered Rilke's contemplative nature as the polar opposite of Celan."[61] As Sedakova recalls, her first encounter with Celan's poetry had the intensity of an imperative, "an impression that it was absolutely necessary to learn all that I could about the author of this 'Psalm' and, secondly, to try to translate it into Russian."[62] For Sedakova, translating Celan was a test of poetic possibilities, an attempt to recreate his intense, highly charged lyrical discourse in an epoch distrustful of lyric poetry.

In her analysis of Sedakova's translation of Celan's "Psalm," Ketevan Megrelishvili describes Sedakova's translation as both "literal and sensitive to the original" ("bukval'nyi i chutkii perevod").[63] Without stylizing or simplifying the original text, Sedakova's translation brings its foreignness into the structure of Russian poetic speech. For example, in places where other Russian translations employ double negation, Sedakova uses impersonal constructions with a dative subject to render Celan's powerful negative pronoun: "Niemand knietet uns aus wieder aus Erde und Lehm"—"Nekomu zamesit' nas opiat' iz zemli i gliny" ("There is no one to knead us again from earth and clay").[64]

In order to convey Celan's austere poetics, particularly the sense of fracture in his poems and his complicated new verbal constructions, Sedakova relies on her own cultural heritage. Drawing on her own religious perspective, she chooses words of Church Slavonic origin to render Celan's neologisms, and adds religious connotations, often based on Orthodox tradition. For example, in her translation of "Psalm" one finds the following expressions, which amplify the biblical connotations of the poem: "purpurnoe slovo" ("maroon/purple word"), "krasnyi venets" ("red wreath of thorns"), "poverkh ternii" ("over the thorns"; 2:483). Other Russian translators tend to parse, explain, or substitute Celan's neologisms and rebuild the semantic components of his words; Sedakova tries to recreate his compound words in Russian. The experience of translating Celan, in turn, made its way into Sedakova's poetic dialogue with his poetry: her later poems often use his intonations and even turns of phrase. While scholars have compared her early poetry (especially her collections *Gates, Windows, Arches* [*Vrata, Okna, Arki*] and *The Wild Rose* [*Dikii shipovnik*]) to Rilke, many of her later poems, from the collections *Evening Song* (*Vecherniaia pesnia*) and *Beginning of the Book* (*Nachalo knigi*), are reminiscent of Celan's poetics. For example, her poem "Nothing" ("Nichto") uses negative pronouns in the subject position of the sentence, much like Celan's "Psalm."

The experience of translating Celan resonates with one of the main themes of Sedakova's literary and theoretical writing: the possibility of powerful lyrical discourse in a post-catastrophic era. To describe this feature of Celan's poetics, Sedakova brings together imagery from art and poetry. "That which old masters possessed with ease—the air, the harmony of images—has become heavy and impenetrable, like earth. In Celan's world, the air itself resembles earth: one must dig in it," remarks Sedakova, as if quoting her translation of Celan's poem "Es war Erde in ihnen":[65]

Земля была в них и они рыли.

Они рыли и рыли. На это ушел
их день, их ночь. И они не славили Бога,
который, как они слышали, все это замыслил,
который, как они слышали, все это провидел.

Они рыли дальше не слушали; и они не стали мудрей, не сложили песен,
Не придумали для себя никаких языков.
Они рыли.

И штиль навещал их, и вал штормовой,
и—все—их моря навестили.
Я рою, ты роешь, вон червь дождевой
тоже роет. Вот песнь: они рыли.

О Некий, о Всякий, о ты, Никакой!
Где теперь то, что шло на нигдейность?

О, ты роешь, я рою; я рою к тебе, за тобой
и наш перстень на пальце не спит, как младенец. (2:479)

Here is a close English rendition of Sedakova's translation:

Earth was in them and they dug.

They dug and they dug. This took up
their day, their night. They did not praise God,
who, they'd heard, had
conceived all of this,
who, they'd heard, had
foreseen all of this.

They dug further and did not listen; and
they did not become wiser, did not compose songs,
Did not invent any languages for themselves.
They dug.

And the still came upon them, and the storm wave,
and—all—the seas visited them.
I dig, you dig, the earthworm there
digs too. Here is the chant: they dug.

Oh Some, oh Any, oh you
None!
Where is it now, that which went for
Nowhereness?
Oh, you dig, I dig; I dig toward you, after you
and our ring on the finger sleeps not, like an infant.

In one of her essays, Sedakova discusses the incantation-like repetition of verbs in Celan's poems, which gives them a ritual quality: "It sounds like a paradox, but the constant change expressed by action adds a certain monumental, static, immutable quality to the verb's meaning—a super-real scale of things—so that we behold a kind of alternative metaphysics."[66] The poem "Earth was in them" is built around repeated verb forms, and Sedakova is careful to preserve this aspect of the original text. She employs a refrain-like conjugation pattern in translating the lines "Ich grabe, du gräbst, und es gräbt auch der Wurm" ("ia roiu, ty roesh', von cherv' dozhdevoi / tozhe roet"). Sedakova aims to recreate the rhythm of the original, as well as the rhymes that become more pronounced in the final lines of the poem, especially in the address to a higher being, where she adds capitalization in translating Celan's line "o, einer, o keiner, o Niemand, or du."

John Felstiner points to the importance of psalmic references in this poem, noting that the poetics of the Psalms also reinforce the Holocaust theme in this poem, whose key word, *graben* ("to dig") shares a root with *Grab* ("grave").[67] Axel Englund comments on the musical elements in the text, its use of folk song motifs and compositional devices.[68] Sedakova's translation incorporates both the biblical connotations and musical elements of the poem. She is careful to preserve Celan's repetitions, and she chooses verbs that emphasize the text's religious and metaphysical dimensions:

der, so hörten sie, alles dies wollte,
der, so hörten sie, alles dies wusste.

который, как они слышали, все это замыслил,
который, как они слышали, все это провидел.

The images in the original, and the word choices in her translation recall Sedakova's reflections on Celan's poetry. The sensation of submerging oneself in "blind earth" in order to capture the very essence of existence is a leitmotif of his poetry, according to Sedakova: "This impression of blind matter [. . .] is perhaps one of the most important in Celan."[69] The post-catastrophic nature of his poetry—as indicated by its difficulty and its depth, but also its hidden hope and imperative—is expressed in her version of the poem's final line: "und am Finger erwacht uns der Ring," which she translates "i nash persten' na pal'tse ne spit, kak mladenets" ("and our ring is awake on the finger, like an infant"). This is certainly a deviation from the original text, and it provides Sedakova with a rhyme ("nigdeinost'—mladenets") but it also introduces an important image from her poetics into the translation; in her own poetry, the infant signifies "preverbal existence, first encounters between reality and language."[70]

By adding this new image, Sedakova writes her interpretation of Celan's poetry into her translation. And by exploring his dense imagery, she arrives at new poetic methods in her own writing: "The difficulty and inaccessibility of his sky is the experience all new art has come up against, all the bravest art of our century."[71] And although Sedakova juxtaposes Rilke's and Celan's poetic worlds, the qualities she values in their respective poetries, and her approach to translating them, follow similar principles. If, according to Sedakova, the first translators of the Bible into Slavic dialects introduced a "vertical of meaning" (that is, the possibility of "high/lofty" spiritual expression) into simple words, Sedakova's goal in translating Celan's poetry is to bring language back to earth, to make the sky "inaccessible" again. This, in turn, would make a new semantic vertical (or a new semantic thrust) possible.

The idea of a demanding poetic and ethical thrust is a recurring theme in her reflections on Celan's poetics: "He needs so much of what art has long stopped demanding: he needs everything."[72] Similar ideas can be found in many of Sedakova's interviews and articles of the past two decades, as well as in her most recent poetry:

Всё, и сразу

«Не так даю, как мир дает»,
не так:
всё, и сразу, и без размышлений,
без требований благодарности или отчета:
всё, и сразу.

Быстрей, чем падает молния,
поразительней,
чем всё, что вы видели и слышали и можете вообразить,
прекрасней шума морского,
голоса многих вод,
сильней, чем смерть,
крепче, чем ад.

Всё, и сразу.
И не кончится.
И никто не отнимет. (1:416)

Everything at Once

"I give not as the world gives,"
not that way:
everything at once, with no deliberation,
with no demand for gratitude or reckoning:
everything at once.

Faster than lightning falls,
more strikingly
than everything you've seen and heard and can imagine,
more splendidly than the noise of the sea,

than the voice of many waters,
more powerfully than death,
more strongly than hell.

Everything at once.
And it won't end.
And no one will take it away.

The formal aspects of this poem, such as the repetition of verb forms, syntactic parallelism echoing the austerity of biblical speech, and even a quotation from the Gospels (John 14:27), give this poem a dialogic impulse. Her voice is at once austere, impersonal, omniscient, and humble, and this gives her lyrical poetry its unique quality.

In the decades spent translating poetry from many different historical periods, Olga Sedakova has always followed her own path. Her thinking about translation has evolved, but she has always based her views on the dialogic approaches to translation shared by many nineteenth- and twentieth-century Russian poets, and aspired to the example set by the Old Church Slavonic tradition. Starting with her early work on Dickinson, her search for simple and concrete language in translations of Rilke, and her more recent translations of Paul Celan's poetry, Sedakova has treated translation as part of a demanding aesthetic quest. "Everything at Once" is the inner imperative of her work, in which artistic and ethical reflection is fused with lyrical dialogue across centuries, following the ever-demanding thrust of the vertical of meaning.

Notes

1. Most of Sedakova's translations are published in the second volume of her collected works, along with essays devoted to the translated poets. Those essays include the 1997 lecture from which the epigraph to this chapter is taken: Ol'ga Sedakova, "Iskusstvo perevoda. Neskol'ko zamechanii. Lektsiia, prochitannaia v Britanskom Muzee," 2:20. For the text in English, see http://www.olgasedakova.com/eng/Moralia/272, accessed March 17, 2018.

2. Ol'ga Sedakova, "Beseda o perevode stikhov na russkii iazyk i s russkogo," interview with Elena Kalashnikova, http://www.olgasedakova.com/interview/131, accessed March 17, 2018.

3. Ol'ga Sedakova, "Dusha izgnana iz publichnogo . . . ," interview with Alexander Kyrlezhev, http://www.olgasedakova.com/interview/1100, accessed March 17, 2018.

4. Sedakova, "Iskusstvo perevoda," 2:21–22.

5. Ketevan Megrelishvili, "Ol'ga Sedakova: Chuvstvo nasushchnoi neobkhodimosti russkogo Tselana," in *Imidzh, Dialog, Eksperiment—polia sovremennoi russkoi poezii*, ed. Henrieke Stahl and Marion Rutz (Munich: Verlag Otto Sagner, 2013), 451–62; Henrieke

Stahl, "Stikhotvorenie Paulia Tselana 'Mandorla' v pol'skikh i russkikh perevodakh," in *Found in Translation: Transformation, Adaptation and Cross-Cultural Transfer*, ed. Kumi Tateoka et al. (Belgrade: Logos, 2016), 146–71.

6. Sergei Averintsev, "'Uzhe nebo, a ne ozero': Risk i vyzov metafizicheskoi poezii," in Ol'ga Sedakova, *Dvukhtomnoe sobranie sochinenii*, vol. 1, *Stikhi* (Moscow: En Ef Kiu/Tu Print, 2001), 5–13; Elena Aizenshtein, "'David poet Saulu' Sedakovoi," in *Iz moei trideviatoi strany: Stat'i o poezii* (Moscow: Izdatel'skie resheniia, 2015), 229–34.

7. For more on the Soviet school of translation, see Susanna Witt, "Byron's *Don Juan* in Russian and the 'Soviet school of translation,'" *Translation and Interpreting Studies* 11, no. 1 (2016): 23–43; for a general overview of the development of the Soviet translation field, see chapter 5 of Brian Baer's *Translation and the Making of Modern Russian Literature* (New York: Bloomsbury Academic, 2016), 60–91.

8. See Samantha Sherry's recent study of this last topic, *Discourses of Regulation and Resistance: Censoring Translation in the Stalin and Khrushchev Era Soviet Union* (Edinburgh: Edinburgh University Press, 2015).

9. Brian Baer, "Literary Translation and the Construction of a Soviet Intelligentsia," in *Translation, Resistance, Activism*, ed. Maria Tymoczko (Amherst: University of Massachusetts Press, 2010), 149–67.

10. Arsenii Tarkovskii, "Vozmozhnosti perevoda," in *Khudozhestvennyi perevod: Vzaimodeistvie i vzaimoobogashchenie literatur*, ed. V. Ganiev (Erevan: Izdatel'stvo Erevanskogo Universiteta, 1973), 263.

11. Susanna Witt discusses this phenomenon in "The Shorthand of Empire: Podstrochnik Practices and the Making of Soviet Literature," *Ab Imperio* 14, no. 3 (2013): 155–90.

12. Il'ia Kukulin, "Rol' stikhotvornogo perevoda v tvorchestve russkikh poetov 1990–2000 godov," in *Poesia Russa da Puškin a Brodskij: E ora? Atti del Convegno Internazionale di Studi Roma, 29–30 settembre 2011* (Rome: Nuova Cultura, 2012), 156.

13. Sedakova, "Beseda o perevode."

14. Ibid.

15. Ol'ga Sedakova, "M. L. Gasparov i inertsiia sovetskogo perevoda," http://www.olgasedakova.com/127/1820, accessed March 17, 2018.

16. Sedakova, "Iskusstvo perevoda," 2:17.

17. Gayatri Spivak, "The Politics of Translation," in *Outside in the Teaching Machine* (New York: Routledge, 1993), 181.

18. Ol'ga Sedakova, "Urok Tselana," interview with Anton Nesterov, http://olgasedakova.com/interview/1058, accessed March 17, 2018.

19. Sedakova, "Iskusstvo perevoda," 2:20.

20. Maurice Blanchot, "Translating," in *Friendship*, trans. Elizabeth Rottenberg (Stanford, CA: Stanford University Press, 1997), 59.

21. Ol'ga Sedakova, "Poeziia—protivostoianie khaosu," interview with Ol'ga Balla, http://olgasedakova.com/interview/178, accessed March 17, 2018.

22. Sedakova, "M. L. Gasparov."

23. Ibid.

24. Ol'ga Sedakova, "Stikhotvornyi iazyk: Semanticheskaia vertikal' slova," 3:173.

25. I use "Old Church Slavonic" in reference to the first translations from the Greek (which is a symbolic event in Sedakova's interpretation of translation), and "Church Slavonic" in reference to later redactions of this language.

26. Sedakova, "Iskusstvo perevoda," 2:23–24.

27. Martha Kelly's and Sarah Pratt's chapters in this volume explore Sedakova's ties with the Christian Orthodox tradition, its thought, and its visual culture.

28. Riccardo Picchio, "Church Slavonic," in *The Slavic Literary Languages: Formation and Development*, ed. Alexander M. Schenker, Edward Standkiewicz, and Micaela S. Iovine (New Haven, CT: Yale Concilium on International and Area Studies, 1980), 22.

29. Picchio, "Church Slavonic," 23.

30. Ol'ga Sedakova, "Tserkovnoslavianskii iazyk v russkoi kul'ture: Aktovaia lektsiia, prochitannaia v Sviato-Filaretovskom Institute 2 dekabria 2004 goda," http://olgasedakova.com/dictionary/136, accessed March 17, 2018.

31. Boris Uspenskii, *Istoriia russkogo literaturnogo iazyka (XI–XVII vv.)* (Munich: Otto Sagner, 1987), 15.

32. Ibid., 17.

33. Sedakova, "Tserkovnoslavianskii iazyk v russkoi kul'ture."

34. Sedakova, "Iskusstvo perevoda," 2:24.

35. Sedakova, "Bogosluzhebnyi tekst na russkom vozmozhen: Ol'ga Sedakova o perevodakh Anri Volokhonskogo," http://www.colta.ru/articles/literature/9901, accessed March 17, 2018.

36. Andrew Wachtel, "The Youngest Archaists: Kutik, Sedakova, Parshchikov," in *Rereading Russian Poetry*, ed. Stephanie Sandler (New Haven, CT: Yale University Press, 1999), 278.

37. Ol'ga Sedakova, *Slovar' trudnykh slov iz bogosluzheniia: Tserkovnoslaviano-russkie paronimy* (Moscow: Greko-latinskii kabinet Iu. A. Shichalina, 2008), 366.

38. Stephanie Sandler, "Thinking Self in the Poetry of Olga Sedakova," in *Gender and Russian Literature*, ed. Rosalind Marsh (Cambridge: Cambridge University Press, 1996), 309.

39. Sedakova, *Slovar' trudnykh slov*, 306.

40. Ibid., 296.

41. Sedakova, "Iskusstvo perevoda," 2:27.

42. Ibid., 2:26.

43. Sedakova, "Ob Emili Dikinson," 2:310.

44. Ibid.

45. Emily Dickinson, *The Poems of Emily Dickinson: Variorum Edition*, ed. Ralph W. Franklin, 3 vols. (Cambridge, MA: Belknap Press of Harvard University Press, 1998), 1:483–84.

46. Helen Vendler, *Dickinson: Selected Poems and Commentaries* (Cambridge, MA: Belknap Press of Harvard University Press, 2010), 222.

47. The Russian version of this chapter compares Sedakova's translations with other Russian texts by Arkady Gavrilov, Alexander Velichansky, and Vera Markova in more detail.

48. Sedakova, "Beseda o perevode."

49. Dickinson, *The Poems of Emily Dickinson*, 2:853.

50. Sandler, "Thinking Self," 312.

51. Sedakova, "Beseda o perevode."

52. Ibid.

53. Averintsev, "Uzhe nebo, a ne ozero," 9.

54. Sedakova, "Novaia lirika Rainera Maria Rilke," 2:388.

55. Ibid., 2:391.

56. Rainer Maria Rilke, *Die Sonette an Orpheus*, http://gutenberg.net.au/ebooks10/1000531h.html, accessed April 8, 2018.

57. See Linda S. Pickle, "The Balance of Sound and Silence in the 'Duineser Elegien' and 'Sonnette an Orpheus,'" *The Journal of English and Germanic Philology* 70, no. 4 (1971): 583–99.

58. Ol'ga Sedakova, "Chtoby rech' stala tvoei rech'iu," a conversation with Valentina Polukhina, in *Dvukhtomnoe sobranie sochinenii*, vol. 2, *Proza* (Moscow: En Ef K'iu/Tu Print, 2001), 878.

59. Sedakova, "Chtoby rech' stala tvoei rech'iu," 878.

60. Sedakova, "Paul' Tselan," 2:506.

61. Sedakova, "Urok Tselana," interview with Anton Nesterov, http://www.olgasedakova.com/interview/1058, accessed March 17, 2018.

62. Sedakova, "Paul' Tselan," 2:507.

63. Megrelishvili, "Ol'ga Sedakova," 461.

64. Paul Celan, "Psalm," in *Poems of Paul Celan*, trans. Michael Hamburger (New York: Persea Books, 1988), 125.

65. Sedakova, "Paul' Tselan," 2:508. For the full German original of "Es war Erde in ihnen," see Paul Celan, *Die Niemandsrose* (Frankfurt am Main: S. Fischer Verlag GmbH, 1963), 9.

66. Sedakova, "Paul' Tselan," 2:526.

67. John Felstiner, *Paul Celan: Poet, Survivor, Jew* (New Haven, CT: Yale University Press, 1995), 151–52.

68. Axel Englund, *Still Song: Music in and around the Poetry of Paul Celan* (Burlington, VT: Ashgate Publishers, 2012), 81.

69. Sedakova, "Urok Tselana."

70. Sedakova, "Ne khochu uspekha i ne boius' provala," interview with Anna Gal'perina, http://www.olgasedakova.com/interview/1135, accessed March 17, 2018.

71. Sedakova, "Urok Tselana."

72. Sedakova, "Paul' Tselan," 2:231.

Olga Sedakova's Journey through *The Book of Changes*

NATALIA CHERNYSH

The goals of this essay are to offer an interpretive reading of Olga Sedakova's *Chinese Journey* and to uncover the conceptual links connecting it with *The Book of Changes*. Sedakova uses ancient Chinese culture as a sort of holy book, which guides the poet and her readers on a fascinating journey to the classical East. My interpretation of *Chinese Journey* differs from previous studies of this cycle's Chinese leitmotifs, imagery, and symbols.[1] In this essay, I will perform a step-by-step analysis of the meanings that unfold over the course of the eighteen poems of *Chinese Journey*, using the ancient text of *The Book of Changes* as a guide. But first, I will begin with a few preliminary observations.

The first poem in *Chinese Journey* sets the tone for the entire collection. The landscape that stretches out before us is not the stereotypically exotic land of junks, pagodas, and curved roofs (though such images do appear later on). The first, and therefore strongest, impression of this poetic journey to China is given by a meeting with a tree that reminds us of home:

> Родина! вскрикнуло сердце при виде ивы:
> такие ивы в Китае,
> смывающие свой овал с великой охотой (1:327)

> Motherland! cried the heart at the sight of the willow:
> there are such willows in China,
> they wash off their oval with great eagerness

So begins Olga Sedakova's journey to the East. Having already inspired her admiration, Eastern culture becomes her cherished teacher and friend. Sedakova's careful poetic treatment of China's cultural gifts allows their original meanings to shine through. Eventually, it is as if the objects begin to speak for themselves. In fact, this impression is a perfect microcosm of the loving and careful way in which

Classical Eastern thought is presented throughout *Chinese Journey*. The reader's gaze relaxes, as though they were standing in front of a Chinese painting, one whose goal is not to arouse strong emotions, but to engender a sense of peace, calm, and enlightenment. This is precisely the quality of ancient Eastern culture that has made such an indelible impression on Olga Sedakova. In one of her lectures, the poet observed: "Eastern culture represents a rich and quiet world: not an exotic realm, but an alternate, universal path towards growth. In this context, nature is appreciated rather than processed; the most important thing is to pay attention, not to act. This world is constructed according to delicate and humble principles, and violence has no place here."[2]

In Sedakova's *Chinese Journey*, readers can discover the hidden mythological images of Pangu and the Jian-mu tree, come into contact with the ideas of Laozi and the wisdom of Confucius, and find resonances with the *Shijing*, the oldest surviving anthology of Chinese poetry. However, the most unexpected discovery concerns the internal connections that link this collection with the ancient Chinese secrets of the Yi Jing as revealed through *The Book of Changes*.[3] Classical thought makes up the primary landscape of *Chinese Journey*. Here, it is represented in the form of an enormous old tree:

задыхается, бегом бежит сердце
с совершенно пустой котомкой
по стволу, по холмам и оврагам веток (1:329)

a gasp, and the heart runs off
with a perfectly empty knapsack
along the trunk, along the hills and ravines of the branches

Time holds no sway in such a context, and thus "Falling, they do not fall, / they dip into the water and don't get wet, / the long sleeves of the trees" ("padaia, ne padaiut, / okunaiutsia v vodu i ne moknut / dlinnye rukava derev'ev"; 1:329). The wisdom of ancient China appears in condensed form over the course of the eighteen poems that make up *Chinese Journey*.[4]

The epigraph to *Chinese Journey* comes from the fourth chapter of the *Dao de jing* as translated by Yang Xingshun.[5] It reads like a riddle addressed to readers "in the know." Sedakova echoes this epigraph in her fourth poem, which also takes the form of a riddle:

Величиной с око ласточки,
  с крошку сухого хлеба,

с лестницу на крыльях бабочки,
  с лестницу, кинутую с неба,
с лестницу, по которой
  никому не хочется лезть;
мельче, чем видят пчелы
  и чем слово есть. (1:330)

The size of a swallow's eye,
  a crumb of dry bread,
a ladder on the wings of a butterfly,
  a ladder thrown down from the sky,
a ladder that
  nobody wants to climb;
tinier than bees see
  and than a word is.

What could this be? If we pause to consider the juxtaposition of these two poems, the results might prove to be very interesting.

Ancient Chinese tradition revolves around the idea of the person of great culture and knowledge (*junzi*, the gentleman), to whom Confucius opposes small, or petty people (*xiao ren*). Many of Confucius's arguments stem from this juxtaposition. *The Chinese Journey* does not mention Confucius by name, but the outlines of the Confucian person of culture are present. Sedakova often writes in a confidential tone, describing the kind of trust that comes from sharing extremely private information, the sort that can only be shared with those closest to us. The thirteenth poem in this cycle represents the culmination of this friendly bond between those "in the know." This idea of "knowing" takes on greater significance as it is repeated four times. The key to understanding this sequence lies in its use of the semantically loaded word *loving* and, more specifically, of the phrase "two people who love being together" ("liubiashchie byt' vmeste"). This moment places the words *knowing* and *loving* into a single, common order. Here, the happiness of people who know and love is contrasted with "real cheapskates and jerks"—Confucius's petty people. This opposition brings to mind the warning contained within the cycle's ninth poem: "Unhappy is he who is fretful and stingy" (1:335).

The overall composition of *Chinese Journey* reflects Confucius's thoughts about the mission of poetry. Confucius is credited with having compiled the oldest existing anthology of Chinese poetry, the *Shijing*, also known as *The Book of*

Songs. Its structure can be described as a falling and rising pattern that follows its own strict developmental logic. In ancient China, poetry was considered to be a path of ascension (*xing* 兴) from coarse material forms to the world of spiritual renewal: "having risen from the depths of a crowd of hearts, it [the spirit] becomes concentrated in the unified breathing of a unified mouth."[6] Sedakova's *Chinese Journey* begins with images of joyful appreciation and discovery: "how calm the waters" ("kak spokoiny vody"), "how slowly the junk floats between the stone banks" ("kak medlenno plyvet dzhonka v kamennykh beregakh"; 1:327). The seventh poem, however, presents a different view, introducing an image of a darkening sky: "the sky swiftly darkens / and looks down with eyes of another sapphire" ("nebo bystro temneet / i glazami drugogo sapfira gliadit"; 1:333).

The ninth and tenth poems of *Chinese Journey* constitute what appears to be the work's compositional low point. From this moment onward, from the initial word/action, "let us praise" ("pokhvalim"), to the final word/state, "praise" ("khvala"), the movement trends upward, culminating in the sense of gratitude expressed by "the unified breathing of a unified mouth" in the cycle's final poem. Later on, I will show how the eighteenth poem combines the images and themes that appear in the texts that precede it. This is entirely in keeping with the symbolism of the eighteenth hexagram of *The Book of Changes*, which instructs us to "reestablish relations with our ancestors" through a "sacrifice to the western mountain."[7] This sacrifice comes in the form of praise for those who wield "positive forces" and the "achievements of previous positions."[8]

The Book of Changes is the primary text of ancient Chinese literature. It has accumulated a great deal of commentary over the millennia. Today, its authoritative translation into Russian is by Iulian Konstantinovich Shchutsky, a distinguished student of the well-known sinologist Vasily Mikhailovich Alekseev. It is Shchutsky's insights that I rely upon in my own analysis. *The Book of Changes* is also known as the *Yi jing*—*yi* meaning "changes" and *jing* meaning "canonical book" or "seminal treatise." In its primary dictionary definition, the character *jing* (经) signifies "warp, warp yarn, principal channel, primary vein, blood vessel." *The Book of Changes* functions similarly to each of these objects over the course of *Chinese Journey*.

Sedakova does not give her poems names. In this way, her book is reminiscent of the *Dao de jing*, in which each poem is a stand-alone work bearing no obvious connection to the others. In *Chinese Journey*, though, the situation is somewhat different. I argue that these eighteen poems *do* have names, and that these names are actually those of the first eighteen hexagrams of *The Book of Changes*. This ancient Chinese book serves as the warp for the cloth of Sedakova's text, which has been embroidered with the words of the contemporary Russian poet. It is important to note that the links between the names of the hexagrams and the topics of the poems become more obvious starting with the ninth poem of *Chinese Journey*. In the first half of the book, these links remain hidden. Sedakova herself has acknowledged that she has some familiarity with *The Book of Changes*: in one letter, she writes that she has leafed through the book, but that she is not closely acquainted with its hexagrams.[9] This comment makes it all the more interesting to examine the direct and indirect coincidences of themes and images that occur between *Chinese Journey* and the first hexagrams of this ancient book.

The overall principle governing the succession of hexagrams in the King Wen sequence remains a mystery to this day.[10] However, the hexagrams are clearly presented in pairs. In each pair, the first (even) element exhibits *yang* characteristics (active, solar, dynamic), while the second (odd) element displays *yin* characteristics (passive, lunar, accepting). The same principle is at play in Sedakova's book. Pairs of poems enter into a peculiar dialogical relationship with each other: like *yin* and *yang*, they complement each other and give rise to a shared conceptual whole. *Chinese Journey* is similar to the ancient books in the coded nature of its text; it may be read attentively and at length, yet never divulge all of its secrets.

The Book of Changes is not just an ancient divinatory tool, but also a serious philosophical text. It represents an enormous vein of verbal artistry that has inspired numerous commentaries; it lies at the root of Chinese and, more broadly, Eastern culture. *The Book of Changes* is a work comprising multiple levels. Its unusual structure is based on abstract symbols made up of broken and unbroken lines. The combination of these lines into bigrams, trigrams, and hexagrams describes various situations and meanings. *The Book of Changes* lies at the heart of Chinese medicine, technology, and urban planning—among many other disciplines. It teaches its readers to think harmoniously in images and symbols. Understanding this text requires a sympathetic effort on the part of the reader, who must be prepared to think in figurative and symbolic ways. When read properly, this text reveals eternal sources of creativity, awakens one's spiritual (and mental) powers, and uncovers fresh avenues for exploration.

Shchutsky notes that the physical agents at work in *The Book of Changes* are the agents of imagery. For example, one of its characteristic formulations, which acts as a sort of stock phrase in the book, is "crossing the great river is auspicious," a phrase that describes a situation in which the stage has been set for a major undertaking.[11] The images that appear in *The Book of Changes* affect the reader's ability to perceive the work's underlying premise, which is one of changeability and movement. Therefore, the images in *The Book of Changes* can be understood as *foretastes of something that is, as yet, unknown.* Each hexagram is a symbolic description of a real-life situation that has a beginning, a middle, and an end. According to Shchutsky, "the theory underlying *The Book of Changes* examines the processes of emergence, existence, and disappearance."[12] To a greater or lesser extent, this is true of all poems. As Shchutsky notes, *The Book of Changes* is a text about the changeability of everything that exists (变), about the movement of everything that exists (动). Therefore, the ordering of its hexagrams tells a story about the rules that govern this movement. In his most famous work, Shchutsky analyzes the King Wen sequence. This is the version with which Olga Sedakova is familiar, and so I will use Shchutsky's interpretations as a starting point for my analysis.

Let us attempt to follow the path of Olga Sedakova's journey, using *The Book of Changes* as our guide.

1. ䷀ 乾 Gan. *Creation.*

The name of the first hexagram derives from the symbolic meaning of its six unbroken (*yang*) lines: the lower and upper trigrams come together to signify "creation." The most ancient interpretation of this hexagram is: "Sublime success. Perseverance is auspicious," and the hexagram tacitly implies that everything that exists has arisen from creative origins: "the *accidentia* of the heavens as a manifestation of the creative force that lies at the *beginning* of everything that exists."[13] This sort of creation is auspicious for everything around it. A "meeting with a great person" is particularly auspicious.

At the beginning of the first poem in Sedakova's *Chinese Journey*, there is a meeting. And later, wholly unexpectedly, we find: "for only our generosity / will meet us beyond the grave" ("ibo tol'ko nasha shchedrost' / vstretit nas za grobom"; 1:327). Apparently, *perseverance* should be read as *generosity*. In the beginning, generosity is auspicious to creation: "There are such willows in China, / they wash off their oval with great eagerness" ("Takie ivy v Kitae, / smyvaiushchie svoi oval s velikoi okhotoi"; 1:327).

2. ䷁ 坤 Kun. *Implementation.*

The second hexagram is related to the first through the unchanging principle of opposition. All six of its lines are *yin*. The lower and upper trigrams both signify "implementation."[14] The secondary level of *The Book of Changes* proclaims: "Sublime success. The perseverance of the mare is auspicious." Shchutsky explains this in the following manner: "Even the most intense urge toward creation cannot be realized without the sort of environment that makes it possible. And in order for absolute creation to be able to manifest itself, its environment must be absolutely amenable and yielding. [...] This completely self-negated force expresses itself in the image of the *mare,* which, though lacking the stallion's obstinacy, is no less capable of action."[15] Sedakova's second poem features an environment that is similarly favorable to the manifestation of creative beginnings: the *pond.* The image of the *mare* in the ancient text corresponds to the image of the "house pet" in Sedakova's: "I would put my hands on your knees, / like a house pet" ("polozhil by ia tebe ruki na koleni, / kak komnatnaia zverushka"; 1:328). This is also an image of an environment amenable and yielding enough for a creative beginning to take place.

The middle of this poem echoes the commentary to the fifth line of the hexagram: "Though it is the principal line in this symbol, because it occupies the most advantageous position in the upper trigram (which represents the external), the fifth line nevertheless symbolizes the possibility of outward manifestation. In a sense, outward manifestations act as a sort of clothing."[16] The following appears in Sedakova's second poem:

Люди, знаешь, жадны и всегда болеют
и рвут чужую одежду
себе на повязки. (1:328)

People, you know, are greedy and always hurting
and rip others' clothes
into bandages for themselves.

But the next poem includes the lines: "The magical invisibility hat, / clothing of the gods, clothing made from eyes" ("Shapka-nevidimka, / odezhda bozhestva, odezhda iz glaz"; 1:329). What we see on the surface and what goes on inside the "clothing made of eyes" are not one and the same.

This poem can tell us something about the nature of creation, which occurs not through violence, but, as the name of this hexagram suggests, through *implementation.* The following correspondences may be established between the hexagram and the poem:

1. Perseverance is *generosity*
2. The mare is the *house pet*
3. Clothing as an outward manifestation is *others' clothes*
4. Implementation is *healing.*

3. ䷂ 屯 Tun. *Difficulty at the Beginning.*

The third hexagram consists of the lower trigram "thunder" (lightning, movement) and the upper trigram "water" (clouds, danger). The secondary level of *The Book of Changes* states: "Difficulty at the beginning. Sublime success. Perseverance is auspicious." Shchutsky explains that "the *beginning* of any action consists in the *overcoming* of some previous state. Hence the *difficulty* expressed in the name of this hexagram."[17] He notes that "the same thing is true of the *conscious* life of an individual: from the very moment of its inception, conscious thought moves under cover of unfamiliarity, cloaking itself in various guises. This idea finds expression in the symbolism of the hexagram: inside, there is thunder and lightning, while outside, there are clouds. The lightning of conscious thought cloaks itself in clouds of representation, and in turn, these representations facilitate thought."[18] These words are particularly useful in the interpretation of Sedakova's third poem, where instead of the "clouds of representation," there are *trees, pagodas,* and *roads,* while the *heart* takes the place of the lightning of thought:

задыхается, бегом бежит сердце
с совершенно пустой котомкой
по стволу, по холмам и оврагам веток
в длинные, в широкие глаза храмов,
к зеркалу в алтаре,
на зеленый пол. (1:329)

a gasp, and the heart runs off
with a perfectly empty knapsack
along the trunk, along the hills and ravines of the branches
to the long, to the broad eyes of the temples,
toward the mirror in the altar,
to the green floor.

The images of the *tree trunk, the hills, the ravines of branches, the temple,* and *the mirror in the altar* can be read as the collection of texts that a single person has inherited from a culture with a more than thousand-year history. The assimilation of such a history presents this individual with *difficulty at the beginning.* Also, difficulty at the beginning is often accompanied by indecision, and the images of the main text of *The Book of Changes* declare three times that "the cart and the horses are pulling in opposite directions."[19] Sedakova writes:

Не довольно ли мы бродили,
чтобы наконец свернуть
на единственно милый
    никому не обидный
        не видный
            путь? (1:329)

Have we not wandered enough now
that we can turn off at long last
onto the uniquely dear,
    uniquely inoffensive,
        invisible
            path?

—at which point the poem revisits its opening lines, repeating: "falling, they do not fall" ("padaia, ne padaiut"). This section also reveals how the number three, which acts as this poem's name, draws its strength from its symbolic self-sufficiency.

4. ䷃ 蒙 Meng. *Immaturity*.

Acting in accordance with the principle of *fan* (opposition), the lines of this hexagram are a mirror image of those found in the previous hexagram: this time, the trigram "water" (danger, immersion) is on the bottom, while the trigram "mountain" (abidance, stability) is on top. In the secondary level of *The Book of Changes* reads "Immaturity. Success. It is not I who seek the youths, it is the youths who seek me."[20] Sedakova's fourth poem begins with the image of a *mountain*, which, in the context of this poem, can be read as the image of a teacher. This particular teacher, however, is not entirely comprehensible to a person who is still "immature"—in other words, a student:

Там, на горе,
у которой в коленях последняя хижина,
а выше никто не хаживал;
лба которой не видывали из-за туч
и не скажут, хмур ли он, весел,—
кто-то бывает и не бывает,
        есть и не есть (1:330)

There, on the hill
with the last hut at its knees,

above which no one's ever gone;
whose brow you can't see through the clouds
to say if he's gloomy or cheerful,—
someone appears and does not appear,
    is there and is not there

Shchutsky writes: "The title of this hexagram signifies immaturity and ignorance. [. . .] Thus, this hexagram illustrates the process that takes place between teacher and student, the way in which previously assimilated knowledge comes into contact with fresh cognitive acts."[21] It is as if Sedakova is responding to this idea in the following lines:

  с лестницу, кинутую с неба,
с лестницу, по которой
никому не хочется лезть (1:330)

  a ladder thrown down from the sky,
a ladder that
nobody wants to climb[22]

The other images found in the second half of this poem can be read, in the given context, as the knowledge that exists "there, on the hill." In isolation, it is "tiny"; the most that we can say about it is that it exists: it is "tinier than a word." Over the course of this poem, we come to a new understanding of the teacher-student relationship, which is referenced by the title of the hexagram, "Immaturity."

5. ䷄ 需 Xu. *The Need to Wait.*

The fifth line of this hexagram is accompanied by the following commentary: "Sublime success to the bearer of truth. Perseverance is auspicious. Crossing the great river is auspicious."[23] The lower trigram signifies "creation" (fortitude, the heavens), while the upper trigram signifies "water" (danger, immersion). The figure of the "truth-bearer" also appears to be the overall theme of Sedakova's fifth poem. This theme might also be defined as the overcoming of worldly attachments, which is one of the deepest kinds of knowledge there is. These ideas are conveyed through the images of the *unmoored boat* and the *broken-off branch*:

Отвязанная лодка
плывет не размышляя,

обломанная ветка
прирастет, да не под этим небом. (1:331)

The unmoored boat
floats without thought,
the broken off branch
will grow back, just not under this heaven.

Subtle connections also begin to emerge between this poem and another "dark spot" in the hexagram: "A weak line on top. / You will enter a cave. / Three unhurried guests will arrive. / You will honor them, and, in the end, there will be good fortune." For Shchutsky, these "three unhurried guests" are the forces of youth "that have accumulated over the first *three* preparatory *stages of waiting*."[24] In Sedakova's work, these three forces of youth are represented in the figures of Joy, Compassion, and Reason. It is, however, crucial that these figures are joined together by the word "neither": "neither joy [. . .], neither regret [. . .], neither sense" ("i ni radost' [. . .], i ni zhalost' [. . .], i ni razum"; 1:331). In this way, the forces appear to diminish, to subside: "The unmoored boat / won't knock long against the shore" ("otviazannaia lodka / ne dolgo tychetsia v bereg"). There is something at work here that is capable of transcending these moral virtues: "nothing can stop / simple delight, / simple delight / that sets like the sun" ("prostogo voskhishchen'ia / nichto ne ostanovit, / prostogo voskhishchen'ia, / zakhodiashchego, kak solntse"). This something, which Sedakova calls "simple delight," is that very same "truth-bearing" power that serves as the creative impulse indicated by the lower trigram ("creation").

Another possible interpretation of the "three unhurried guests" is that Joy, Compassion, and Reason correspond to the three stages of human life: childhood (Joy), maturity (Compassion), and old age (Reason). In that case, the "delight" that resembles the setting sun would be associated with the West, which is to say, with the image of *another world*. Other images in the poem and in this hexagram support such an explanation: the unmoored boat, the broken-off branch, and crossing the great river. It is important to note that the original meaning of the Russian word *voskhishchat'* ("to delight") is "to carry upward," and, according to the scriptures, the Rapture (*Voskhishchenie*) will occur when God takes his believers up to heaven from the earth.

6. ䷅ 讼 Song. *The Trial (Legal Dispute).*

The commentary to this hexagram points to the fact that it has been structured according to the principle of *fan* (opposition): it is the mirror image of the fifth hexagram. "The bearer of truth meets with obstacles. Observing the middle with trepidation leads to good fortune. Taking things to extremes leads to misfortune. A meeting with a great person is auspicious. Crossing the great river is inauspicious."[25] It appears that the trigrams have switched places: "water" is now on the bottom and "creation" is on top. Between them stands "the trial." According to Shchutsky's interpretation, "if one does not give in to its [the water's] pull, but gazes upon the heavens as on the highest human ideal of creation, if one *goes to see a great person*, it will lead to prosperity, and, vice versa: *if one plunges into the stream of life of his own accord*, it will not lead to prosperity."[26]

The entire sixth poem of *Chinese Journey* describes precisely such a meeting with a *great person*, one who possesses the same lofty qualities of fortitude and perseverance that are expressed by the trigram of "creation" (the heavens), in which no action should be undertaken: "crossing the great river is inauspicious."[27] There is a difference between actions undertaken on one's own authority and those undertaken on the authority of a king. The time will come when the truth-bearer must decide how he will act: will he go his own way or will he follow the *great person*? This is the greatest trial that can occur within a person. In Sedakova's poem, we find:

шла бы я за ним, плача:
сколько он идет, и я бы шла, шагала
таким же не спорящим шагом. (1:332)

I'd walk behind him, crying:
I'd go as far as he goes, I'd tread
with a step undisputing as his.

7. ䷆ 师 Shi. *The Army.*

The seventh hexagram differs from the sixth in that its upper trigram represents "implementation" rather than "creation." The secondary level of the main text explains: "The Army. Perseverance. Good fortune for the mature man. There will be no slander."[28] Shchutsky reads this hexagram as the action undertaken after a potentially unfair trial (as represented by the sixth hexagram) in a gloomy and dangerous place (the inner hexagram is water).[29] This idea provides a key to understanding Sedakova's poem. Danger rears its head in the first four lines of this poem:

Лодка летит
по нижней влажной лазури,

небо быстро темнеет
и глазами другого сапфира глядит. (1:333)

The boat flies
along the watery azure,
the sky swiftly darkens
and looks down with eyes of another sapphire.

Here, the boat represents the army and time. The watery azure and the dark sky represent *another world*. There is a danger inherent in the secrets told by children, who are models of purity and unsullied conscience. A secret that "no one has ever believed" is passed along to someone else, who might not believe it either. The flying boat represents the moment in which knowledge passes from one heart to another, "as child to child" ("kak rebenok rebenku"), as Sedakova puts it in her seventh poem. It is important to note that, despite the tone of its opening lines, this poem ends on a bright note:

пока лодка летит, солнце светит
и в сапфире играет
небесная радость. (1:333)

while the boat flies along, the sun shines
and in the sapphire
heavenly joy plays.

8. ䷇ 比 Bi. *Confluence.*

In accordance with the principle of *fan*, this hexagram stands in direct opposition to the one preceding it: "earth," which was the seventh hexagram's external trigram, becomes the eighth hexagram's internal principle, while "water" comes to govern its external order. The secondary level of *The Book of Changes* declares: "Good fortune. Consider the divination carefully. Sublime, eternal perseverance. There will be no slander. Is it not better to arrive right away? Misfortune to the one who is too late."[30] This hexagram starts off with good fortune. In the context of the previous hexagram, this good fortune can be interpreted as the kind that is associated with approaching a gift that has already been accepted, coming closer to knowledge. In Sedakova's poem, this takes the form of the surprise and joy of learning: "Are you kidding? Really? Absolutely delighted!" ("Chto vy? neuzheli? rad serdechno!" 1:334). The secondary level of *The Book of Changes* goes on to describe the next stage in the process of confluence: "Consider the divination carefully." This line from the *eighth* hexagram shines through in the imagery associated with the *terrace* that appears in the *eighth* poem:

Террасы, с которых вечно
видно всё, что мило видеть человеку:
сухие берега, серебряные желтоватые реки,
кустов неровное письмо—любовная записка,
двое прохожих низко
кланяются друг другу на понтонном мосту
и ласточка на чайной ложке
подносит высоту: (1:334)

Terraces from which you can eternally
see everything a person cherishes seeing:
dry banks, yellowish silver rivers,
the uneven writing of bushes—a love letter,
two passersby bow
low to each other on the pontoon bridge
and a swallow in a teaspoon
holds up the high places:

Is this a description of another world? The kind of world that contains a canonical book (such as *The Book of Changes*) in which a person can find everything they need, up to and including healing knowledge? The poem exhibits the following correspondences:

1. The *swallow* ("lastochka") is the herald of good fortune;
2. The *dry banks* ("sukhie berega") represent the pages of a book;
3. The *yellowish silver rivers* ("serebrianye zheltovatye reki") represent curving lines;
4. The *uneven writing of the bushes* ("kustov nerovnoe pis'mo") represents hexagrams and characters;
5. The *two passersby* ("dvoe prokhozhikh") represent the people who have written commentaries on the book.

In various cultures, the *pontoon bridge* (which is invoked in the ninth line of this poem) has acted as a metaphor for the connection between possible and impossible achievements. At the end of this poem, the phrase "but then" ("vprochem") signals a twist: "But then, no one in China is ever ill" ("Vprochem, v

Kitae nikto ne boleet"; 1:334). There is a world where no one is ever sick (*Chinese Journey*) or "too late" (*The Book of Changes*).

9. ䷈ 小畜 Xiao Xu. *The Taming Power of the Small.*

The interpretation offered in the secondary level of *The Book of Changes* states: "Success. Dense clouds—and yet no rain; [the clouds] come from our Western borderlands."[31] This hexagram consists of the lower, internal trigram "heaven" (creation) and the upper, external trigram "wind" or "tree" (penetration). The central theme of Sedakova's ninth poem is creation that meets with obstacles along its path: in other words, the theme is *weakness*. It is not entirely clear why Shchutsky would translate the character *xu* (畜) as "taming" in this context, using it as a foil for "obstacles."[32] The literal dictionary meaning of this character is "household animal, livestock." For this reason, V. M. Iakovlev translates the title of this hexagram as "petty livestock."[33] Bearing in mind this translation, O-yi's observation (which is mentioned by Shchutsky) becomes clearer: "The all-wise one who rules over the world does not despise people in their limitations. In saving all things, Buddha does not scorn even the demons. [...] When the swine come to the golden mountain, they magnify the mountain's splendor; when the hoarfrost and the snow accumulate, the pines and cedars become more magnificent."[34] Our concern for "petty livestock" becomes an obstacle along the path to growth. Only *taming* (Shchutsky) and *forgiving* (Sedakova) make it possible for the "rain to pour down," giving water to those who are thirsty. Only then does it become possible to learn:

как шар золотой
сам собой взлетает
в милое небо над милой землей. (1:335)

how the golden sphere
flies up by itself
into the sweet heaven over the sweet earth.

10. ䷉ 履 Lu. *Approach. (Tread.)*

This hexagram is the mirror image of the one preceding it: "heaven" (creation), which had been the inner trigram, moves into the outer position, while "lake" (assent) now functions as the lower trigram. The secondary level of *The Book of Changes* declares: "Step on a tiger's tail. If the tiger does not bite you, you will achieve success."[35] Here, it is important to note that, though the central image of this hexagram remains an animal, it is no longer a tame creature like the "petty livestock" of the previous hexagram. Rather, it is a wild beast, one that Chinese mythology lifts up as the sovereign of all terrestrial animals, the king of beasts, with all of the dignity, courage, and ferocity that such a rank entails.

The tenth poem of *Chinese Journey* continues with the theme of creative inspiration, but with an entirely different angle: this poem glorifies the state of inspiration. The lack of inspiration, the situation in which "the spirit abandons [us]," provides the necessary "muscle" that is described in the previous hexagram: "who for the tenth time in the same murky place / seeks a pure spring" ("kto desiatyi raz na mutnom meste / ishchet chistyi kliuch"; 1:336). But this is not a case of someone "spinning their wheels." Rather, it reflects precisely the sort of goal-oriented approach that is indicated by the title of the tenth hexagram. Shchutsky writes: "everything that such an approach entails has already been accomplished, and, proceeding from the knowledge and know-how we have gained, we must *act over and over again*, bearing in mind our previous experiences and attending to what has yielded the best possible results in the past" (emphasis mine).[36] Recurring action is indicated by the title character itself, *lu* (履), where the grapheme 复 signifies recurring repetition. This kind of approach is justified by the thought that true creative action must begin precisely through repetition. After all, inspiration means believing in a miracle. As Sedakova concludes:

кто выпал из руки чудес, но не скажет:
  пусты чудеса!—
перед ним с почтением
  склоняются небеса. (1:336)

who has fallen out of wonders' hands, but will not say:
  wonders are empty!—
before him with reverence
  the heavens will bow down.

11. ䷊ 泰 Tai. *Blossoming.*

The secondary level of *The Book of Changes* states: "The small one departs, the great one arrives. Good fortune. Growth."[37] This hexagram[38] represents the most harmonious possible combination of light and dark, which are, after all, the fundamental categories that underlie *The Book of Changes*. In such a context, the images of *tenderness* and *depth* that appear in the tenth poem of *The Chinese Journey* can be interpreted as light/tenderness and darkness/depth spilling over into one another. This interaction is clearly reflected in the first lines of the poem:

ибо только нежность глубока,
только глубина обладает нежностью,— (1:337)

for only tenderness is deep,
only depth bears tenderness,—

In his commentary to the fifth line of this hexagram, Shchutsky highlights two things: first, its flexibility and resistance to inertia and, secondly, the mutual understanding that exists between the hexagram's higher and lower elements (expressed here by the word "concordance" ["sootvetsvie"]).[39] This second quality features in the second half of the poem, where the images of the sun and the lantern (the moon) act in "concordance" as symbols of divine love ("the first, last Sun")[40] and human love ("the lantern," "the moth trap"). The eleventh poem also contains a message about the total interaction that takes place between the forces of light and dark and the divine power of love, about their harmonious merging and mutual understanding: "the sun of tenderness and depth" can be found in the name of this hexagram, "Blossoming."

12. ䷋ 否. Fou. *Stagnation.*

This hexagram is the mirror image of the previous one: "earth" (implementation) is on the bottom, while "heaven" (creation) is on top. They do not come into contact with each other in any way. The interaction observed in the previous hexagram is entirely absent here. Such a context makes it necessary for people to overcome enormous limitations. The secondary level of *The Book of Changes* reads: "The great one departs, the small one arrives. The perseverance of the noble person is inauspicious."[41] This hexagram expresses the total isolation and dissonance that exist between light and dark, heaven and earth: "Light—the great one—departs, while Dark—the small one—arrives."[42] These inhibitive and reactionary forces are embodied in the form of the "petty person." In order to overcome his nature, the "petty person" must join forces with someone else who is moving forward, who is himself experiencing enormous obstacles along his path. Sedakova writes:

но что же с плачем мчится
крылатая колесница,
ветер, песок, побережье,
океан пустой—
и нельзя проститься,
негде проститься с тобой.

О, человек простой—
как соль в воде морской (1:338)

so why does the winged chariot
rush on, weeping,
the wind, the sand, the shore,
the empty ocean—
no time to bid farewell,
nowhere to bid farewell to you.
Oh, a person, plain and simple,
is like salt in sea water

Like the ladder, the boat, and the bridge, the cart appears in various cultures as a means of crossing over into the celestial world. In Christianity, for example, the cart (in the form of the wagon, the ark, the dray, etc.) symbolizes the way in which the church allows believers to "cross over" into heaven. According to Dante, its two wheels represent *desire* and the *will, good works* and *good sense.* It is important to note that, as a symbol, the cart always appears together with its constituent parts. Taken as a whole, this twelfth poem is like a lament for the simple person who "with no one to turn to, / keens by himself" ("ne imeia k komu obratit'sia, / prichitaet sam s soboi"; 1:338).

13. ䷌ 同人 Tong Ren. *Kindred Spirits (Kin).*

The lower trigram of this hexagram is "fire" (coupling) and its upper trigram is "heaven" (creation). The secondary level of *The Book of Changes* declares: "[Kin are] in the fields. Success. Crossing the great river is auspicious. The noble person's perseverance is auspicious."[43] Shchutsky interprets this (and, in particular, the phrase "crossing the great river is auspicious") as a representation of the great and dangerous events that will come to pass in the future through people's collective efforts. Here, the most important thing is to act "in rhythmic harmony with others." The theme of "kindred spirits" facing separation also appears in Sedakova's work: "We won't part like all the rest, / like all the rest, / will we?" ("Neuzheli i my, kak vse, / kak vse / rasstanemsia?" 1:339). The commentary to the first line contained in the tertiary level of *The Book of Changes* states, "kindred spirits stand at the gate," which, according to Shchutsky, means that "at this moment, the process is just beginning."[44] In Sedakova's poem, a similar theme comes into play when two kindred spirits recognize their identical natures. This theme is highlighted by the repeated use of the participial form "znaiushchie" ("those who know"). Despite their perfectly synchronized natures, these kindred spirits still find themselves on the same level as the ignorant, miserly, and coarse when faced with the inevitable: they are "like all the rest." This opposition of the knowing to the ignorant is a reference to the well-known Confucian distinction between the gentleman (*junzi*) and the petty person (*xiao ren*). It is important to note that in this poem the inevitability of separation is expressed by a three-part question, which prepares the ground for a particular answer and thus creates hope for a potential future meeting. Similarly, the tertiary level of commentary to the fifth line of this hexagram states: "the great armies are defeated, [and there will be] a meeting."[45]

14. ䷍ 大有 Da You. *Possession in Great Measure (Possession of Many).*

This hexagram mirrors the preceding one, with "heaven" (creation) on the bottom, acting as its internal principle, and "fire" (clarity, light) on top, serving as its external principle. The secondary level of *The Book of Changes* keeps its commentary brief: "Sublime success."[46] The title of this hexagram, *Possession of Many*, is symbolically reflected in the way that its five *yang*, light-oriented lines bend toward the solitary *yin* line occupying the fifth position: "They work together in concert, which is why, as in the previous hexagram, coordinated action plays a particularly prominent role here."[47] In Sedakova's fourteenth poem, this kind of coordinated action may be seen in the "sociability" of all things:

Флейте отвечает флейта,
не костяная, не деревянная,
а та, которую держат горы
в своих пещерах и щелях,
струнам отвечают такие же струны
и слову слово отвечает.

И вечерней звезде, быстро восходящей
отвечает просьба моего сердца (1:340)

Flute answers to flute,
not of bone, not of wood,
but the one mountains hold
in their caves and crevices,
strings answer to strings like them
and word answers to word.

And my heart's plea answers
The swiftly rising evening star

The parallel between "star" and "heart," which forms the backbone of this work, calls to mind another text: a letter from Pavel Florensky to Vasily Rozanov. In this letter, Florensky shares his impressions of Venus: his view that, in its dual capacity as both morning and evening star, its image shows remarkable depth. He refers to this duality using the phrase, "two secrets, two lights" ("dve tainy, dva sveta").[48] In Sedakova's poem, we read:

Ты выведешь тысячи звезд
вечерняя звезда,
и тысячами просьб
зажжется мое сердце,
мириадами просьб об одном и том же:
просыпайся,
погляди на меня, друг мой вдохновенный,
посмотри, как ночь сверкает . . . (1:340)

You'll lead out stars by the thousands,
evening star,
and my heart will catch fire
with thousands of pleas,
myriad pleas for the self-same thing:
wake up,
look at me, my inspired friend,
see how the night flashes . . .

15. ䷎ 谦 Qian. *Modesty.*

The secondary level of *The Book of Changes* states: "The noble man carries things through."[49] This hexagram consists of the lower trigram "mountain" (abidance, stability) and the upper trigram "earth" (selflessness, implementation). This crucial denial of personal achievement is labeled as "modesty" and is reflected in the very image of the hexagram: the sign of the mountain (*gen*) appears underneath the sign of the earth (*kun*). Usually, the mountain rises up over the earth. The mountain taking its place under the earth elegantly conveys an image of modesty.[50] Sedakova's fifteenth poem (1:341) correlates surprisingly closely to the tertiary level of the main text of *The Book of Changes*:

Modesty. Growth. Achievement awaits the noble person.

По белому пути, по холодному звездному облаку,
говорят, они ушли и мы уйдем когда-то:

By the white way, by the cold, starry cloud
they've gone, it's said, and we'll leave, too, someday:

A weak line at the beginning. The noble person is the meekest of the meek. [They] must wade across the great river.

с камня на камень перебредая воду,
с планеты на планету перебредая разлуку,

making our way stone by stone through water,
making our way planet by planet through separation,

A weak line in the second position. Harmonious modesty. Perseverance is auspicious.

как поющий голос с ноты на ноту.

as a voice note by note.

A strong line in the third [position]. The noble person made modest by [his] labors will complete his works. Good fortune.

Там все, говорят, и встретятся, убеленные млечной дорогой.

There, it's said, everyone meets, turned white by the milky way.

A weak line in the fourth [position]. Nothing inauspicious. Modesty beckons.

Сколько раз—покаюсь—к запрещенному порогу подходило сердце, сколько стучало,
обещая неведомо кому:

So many times—I'll confess—my heart's approached
the forbidden threshold, knocked so many times,
assuring who knows whom:

A weak line in the fifth [position].
You will not become rich off the backs of your neighbors.
The need to enact vindictive aggression leads to prosperity.

Никто меня не ищет, никто не огорчится,
не попросит: останься со мною! . . .
О, не от горя земного так чудно за дверью земною.

Nothing inauspicious.

А потому что не хочется, не хочется
своего согрешенья,

No one looks for me, no one gets upset
or pleads: "Stay with me! . . ."
Oh, the wonder behind earth's door is not
from earth's grief.
It's because we don't want, don't want our
sins,

A weak line on top. Resounding modesty. The need to move armies and march on cities and kingdoms is favorable.[51]

потому что пора идти
просить за всё прощенья,
ведь никто не проживет
без этого хлеба сиянья.
Пора идти туда,
где всё из состраданья.

after all, no one will survive
without this bread of radiance.
It's time to go
where everything's made of compassion.

It is crucial to note that the Chinese images of *vindictive aggression* and *armies* are expressed through the symbolism of action that manifests itself "as the need to master that which has emerged as a result of obedience."[52] These images can be read in precisely the same way in Sedakova's poem; however, the sort of action that she favors takes the form of modesty, compassion, and forgiveness.

16. ䷏ 豫 Yu. *Freedom.*

The secondary level of the main text includes the following statement: "The installation of princes and the movement of armies is auspicious."[53] This hexagram[54] is clearly a mirror image of the one preceding it: now "earth" (selflessness) is on the bottom, while "thunder"/"lightning" (movement) is on top. From the condition of modesty represented by the previous hexagram, a period of selflessness (the "earth" trigram) passes into a state of activity ("thunder"/"lightning"). It is precisely this sort of activity that makes it possible to be completely open to a world that is ready and waiting to hear what one has to say:

Ты знаешь, я так тебя люблю,
что если час придет

и поведет меня от тебя,
то он не уведет—(1:342)

You know, I love you so much
    that if the hour comes
and takes me from you,
it won't take me away—

The theme of death/immortality, which recurs several times over the course of the earlier poems, reappears here, albeit in a different form. The development of this theme can be traced from the thrice-repeated question ("We won't part like all the rest, / like all the rest, will we?" in the thirteenth poem), through a site of abstracted knowledge ("There, it's said, everyone meets, turned white by the milky way" in the fifteenth poem) to a state of total confidence, a knowledge of the heart ("if the hour comes / and takes me from you, / it won't take me away"). This is just as one might expect: after all, this hexagram is accompanied by the admonition "[not to] doubt."

17. ䷐ 随 Sui. *Succession.*

The secondary level of the main text of *The Book of Changes* provides the following analysis: "Sublime success: perseverance is auspicious. There will be no slander."[55] The lower hexagram is "thunder"/"lightning" (movement) and the upper hexagram is "lake" (assent, joyousness). The idea of perseverance runs throughout *The Book of Changes*, acting as its central theme and serving as the deciding factor between fortune and misfortune at various points throughout the text. In some instances, perseverance acts as a sort of bolster against chaos taking over; in others, it represents a kind of stagnation that makes it difficult to accept that which is new and vital. This is, in fact, the theme of this hexagram: *succession*. Sedakova writes:

Когда мы решаемся ступить
    не зная, что нас ждет,
на вдохновенья пустой корабль,
    на плохо связанный плот,
на чешуйчатое крыло, на лодку без гребцов,
воображая и самый лучший
    и худший из концов
и ничего не ища внутри:
    там всему взамен
выбрасывают гадальные кости на книгу перемен. (1:343)

When we decide to step,
  not knowing what awaits us,
onto the empty boat of inspiration,
  onto the poorly bound raft,
onto the scaly wing, onto the boat with no one to row it,
imagining the very best
  and worst of endings
and seeking nothing within:
  there in exchange for everything
they cast the bones of fortunetelling onto the book of changes.

The imagery in this excerpt points toward instability, while these images function individually as metaphorical allusions to *The Book of Changes*:

1. The *empty boat* and the *boat with no one to row it* represent *The Book of Changes,* which has no guide other than itself;
2. The *poorly bound raft* represents *The Book of Changes,* which has inspired a great deal of conflicting commentary and consists of multiple layers;
3. The *scaly wing* represents the hexagram or turtle shell that is used in divination.

This sequence culminates in a direct reference to the *Book* itself. This reference is not set off by parentheses, suggesting that this book is not just any divinatory tool, accessible to any would-be fortune-teller who is sufficiently sensitive to the changeable nature of life. I would argue that the entire seventeenth poem uses the Christian worldview as its leitmotif. After all, in the Christian tradition, a divine beginning stands behind the moving forces of darkness and light. It is for this reason that the poem ends with the following lines:

если бы знал он, смертный вихрь,
  и ты, пустая гладь,
как я хочу прощенья просить и ноги целовать. (1:344)

if only the deadly vortex had known,
  and you, too, smooth, blank surface,
how much I want to beg forgiveness and kiss your feet.

Moreover, the "deadly vortex" and the "smooth, blank surface" happen to match the primary symbols of the seventeenth hexagram: "thunder" and "water." The following admonition is given in the commentary to the sixth line of this hexagram: "make connections with what has already been gained, join forces with those whom you are following. The king must make a sacrifice to the western mountain."[56] This idea sets the stage for the next and final poem of *The Chinese Journey*.

18. ䷑ 蠱 Gu. *[Restoration of] decay.*

The secondary level of the main text of *The Book of Changes* states: "Sublime success. Crossing the great river is auspicious. [Be vigilant] three days before and three days after the beginning."[57] The tertiary level of the main text, in its commentary to the final line of the previous hexagram, says: "The king must make a sacrifice to the western mountain"; Shchutsky further explains that "a sacrifice to the western mountain is tantamount to the restoration of relations with one's ancestors. In other words, it represents a link to the growth that has already taken place." He goes on to observe that the ideogram 蠱 depicts a cup or vessel (*min* 皿) in which, "because it has not been used for a long time," worms (虫) have begun to breed.[58] This points toward the main theme of this hexagram, which is "the restoration of decay": "the peace and quiet that have kept the country bound in stagnant slumber far too long will result in its decomposition and decay [. . .] the restoration of what our fathers have allowed to decay" is crucial.[59] Similarly, in the tertiary level of the main text, in the commentary to the eighteenth hexagram, it says: "A weak line in the fifth [position]. The restoration of what the father has ruined. *Praise is crucial*" (emphasis mine).[60] Shchutsky offers the following commentary: "The fifth position represents the maximum external manifestation of internal forces and capacities. [. . .] It is precisely in this moment that they are capable of giving praise."[61] "The restoration of relations with our ancestors" through a "sacrifice to the western mountain" must manifest itself through the *praising* of all those who represent "positive forces" and the "achievements of previous positions." This idea manifests itself poetically in the eighteenth poem, which fits nicely into the category of "praise." In addition, "the achievement of previous positions" embedded in the images that appear throughout the various poems of *Chinese Journey* also resounds in its final poem. The other poems from the cycle echoed here are indicated by the numbers to the right:

Похвалим нашу землю, 13
    похвалим луну на воде,
то, что ни с кем и со всеми,
    что нигде и везде—
величиной с око ласточки,
    с крошку сухого хлеба 4

с лестницу на крыльях бабочки
с лестницу, кинутую с неба.
Не только беда и жалость—
сердцу моему узда, 2
но то, что улыбалась
чудесная вода.
Похвалим веток бесценных, темных 3
купанье в живом стекле
и духов всех, бессонных 5
над каждым зерном в земле.
И то, что есть награда,
что есть преграда для зла, 18
что, как садовник у сада,—
у земли хвала. (1:345)

Let us praise our earth,
the moon on the water,
that which is with no one and with all,
that is nowhere and everywhere—
the size of a swallow's eye,
of a crumb of dry bread,
of a ladder on the wings of a butterfly,
of a ladder thrown down from the sky.
Trouble and pity do not alone
bridle my heart,
but also the smile
of the wondrous water.
Let us praise the swimming of the priceless, dark
branches in living glass
and of all spirits, sleepless
over each grain in the earth.
And that there is reward,
that there is a limit to evil,
that, as the gardener has his garden,
the earth has its praise.

In the moments highlighted above, the eighteenth poem reminds the reader of the hexagram with six *yang* strokes: *creation*.

Olga Sedakova's *Chinese Journey* is not a poetic commentary on the symbolic lines of *The Book of Changes* or a poetic setting of the hexagrams contained within it. Each poem in *Chinese Journey* represents a completed, self-sufficient whole. This discovery should motivate us to read each individual word and image just as we would read a poem, as "the composition serves each of its constituent words."[62]

It is as if the compositional principles of *The Book of Changes* have been superimposed over the images that unfold throughout *Chinese Journey*. Such layering brings to light new semantic elements and connections that lie deep inside the Russian text. Both the obvious and hidden resonances between *Chinese Journey* and *The Book of Changes* give us reason to suppose that the author wrote *Chinese Journey* with the composition and imagery of *The Book of Changes* in mind. But there is something else at work here. The essence of this ancient book lies in action—the kind of action that creates change. This action is not chaotic: it is subject to a certain order, certain rules. Its essence shines through in *Chinese Journey*, where it traces a path downward and up again over the course of the eighteen poems that represent the first eighteen chapters of the other book. If *The Book of Changes* deals in infinite transformations, then its sixty-fourth and final chapter describes the beginning of a new cycle of changes. Everything begins again. This hexagram is called "Not Yet the End." Like *Chinese Journey, The Book of Changes* ends with the "restoration of decay": praise for everything that is alive. The act expressed by the phrase "let us praise our earth" crosses over into a condition of "praise" ("khvala"): "as the gardener has his garden, / the earth has its praise" ("kak sadovnik u sada,— / u zemli khvala"). Praise be to all changes. This, perhaps, is the primary message contained in Sedakova's *Chinese Journey*.

Translated from Russian by Sarah Vitali

Notes

1. See, for example, Ekaterina Kudriavtseva, "Analiz i interpretatsiia poeticheskogo teksta: Sedakova, Ol'ga Aleksandrovna 'Kitaiskoe puteshestvie,'" in *Der russische Gedichtzyklus: Ein Handbuch*, ed. V. R. Ibler (Heidelberg: Universitätsverlag Winter, 2006), 531–36; Aleksandr Zholkovskii, "'Neuzheli?' (Ol'ga Sedakova, 'Kitaiskoe puteshestvie', 13)," *Zvezda* 11 (2007), http://magazines.russ.ru/zvezda/2007/11/zhz12.html, accessed March 17, 2018; Natal'ia Medvedeva, "Obraz Kitaia v russkoi poeticheskoi traditsii (Gumilev, Brodskii, Sedakova)," *Vestnik Udmurtskogo Universiteta: Istoriia, Filologiia* 1 (2008), http://cyberleninka.ru/article/n/obraz-kitaya-v-russkoy-poeticheskoy-traditsii-n-gumilyov-o-sedakova-i-brodskiy-1, accessed March 17, 2018.

2. Ol'ga Sedakova, "Besedy ob Organike 0/2," https://www.youtube.com/watch?v=xaJtcQxOFqU&list=PL_eijTvwb-o_vdDtaaiBqASWwZO12NiMo&index=3, accessed March 17, 2018.

3. The Yi Jing is more commonly known in the West as the I Ching.

4. Pangu, a hero of an ancient Chinese myth whose name literally translates to "coiled antiquity," required *eighteen* millennia to disentangle the heavens and the earth from the chaos that reigned in the beginning, and he needed another eighteen millennia to make the heavens high enough and the earth low enough for human activity to be possible. The *Dao de jing* reflects Pangu's cycle of *eighteen* thousand years: Laozi describes how to return the human heart to its proper state over the course of *eighty-one* chapters.

5. "If you dull its keenness, liberate it from its chaos, temper its brilliance, and compare it to a speck of dust, then it will seem clear to the people living now." Laozi, *Dao de jing*, trans. Yang Xingshun, in *Drevnekitaiskaia filosofiia: Sobranie tekstov*, 2 vols. (Moscow: Mysl', 1972), 1:116.

6. I. S. Lisevich, *Literaturnaia mysl' Kitaia na rubezhe drevnosti i srednikh vekov* (Moscow: Nauka, 1979), 130.

7. Iu. K. Shchutskii, *Kitaiskaia klassicheskaia "Kniga Peremen"* (Moscow: Nauka, 1993), 333. During the preparation of this translation, the following English-language translation of the German-language Wilhelm translation of the Yi Jing was consulted: *I Ching or, The Book of Changes*, trans. Cary F. Baynes and Richard Wilhelm, 3rd edition (Princeton, NJ: Princeton University Press, 1977).

8. Shchutskii, *Kitaiskaia klassicheskaia "Kniga Peremen,"* 333.

9. Ol'ga Sedakova, personal communication with Natalia Chernysh, February 8, 2011.

10. In the study of the Yi Jing, there are three sequences according to which the hexagrams can be arranged: the Fu Xi sequence, the King Wen sequence, and the Mawangdui sequence, which was discovered during a 1973 archaeological dig.

11. Shchutskii, *Kitaiskaia klassicheskaia "Kniga Peremen,"* 234.

12. Ibid., 86.

13. Ibid., 246, 282.

14. Translated into English as "The Receptive" in *I Ching*, 1:9.

15. Shchutskii, *Kitaiskaia klassicheskaia "Kniga Peremen,"* 246, 285.

16. Ibid., 287.

17. Ibid., 247, 287–88.

18. Ibid., 282.

19. Ibid., 289–90.

20. Ibid., 248.

21. Ibid., 291.

22. It is interesting to note that, in Chinese mythology, the Jian-mu tree acts as a celestial ladder: "It grew in the Douguang valley, which was believed to be the center of the heavens and the earth. In ancient times, the unimaginably tall trunk of the Jian-mu tree served as a celestial ladder: spirits from various locations used it to climb up into the heavens and down to earth. Jian-mu cast no shadow and created no echo" (V. V. Ezhov, *Mify drevnego Kitaia* [Moscow: Astrel', 2003], 92). Meanwhile, in Genesis 28:12 we find the following: "And he dreamed, and behold a ladder set up on the earth, and the top of it reached to heaven: and behold the angels of God ascending and descending on it."

23. Shchutskii, *Kitaiskaia klassicheskaia "Kniga Peremen,"* 248.

24. Ibid., 297, also the source for the previous sentence's quotation.

25. Ibid., 249.

26. Ibid., 301.
27. Ibid., 249.
28. Ibid.
29. Ibid., 297.
30. Ibid., 250.
31. Ibid., 250.
32. Ibid., 380.
33. *I tszin: "Kniga Peremen" i ee kanonicheskie kommentarii*, trans. V. M. Iakovlev (Moscow: Ianus-K, 1998), 56.
34. Shchutskii, *Kitaiskaia klassicheskaia "Kniga Peremen,"* 308.
35. Ibid., 251.
36. Ibid., 313.
37. Ibid., 252.
38. Translated into English as "Peace" in *I Ching*, 1:49.
39. Shchutskii, *Kitaiskaia klassicheskaia "Kniga Peremen,"* 316.
40. See Revelation 1:8.
41. Shchutskii, *Kitaiskaia klassicheskaia "Kniga Peremen,"* 252.
42. Ibid., 317.
43. Ibid., 253.
44. Ibid., 323.
45. Ibid.
46. Ibid., 253.
47. Ibid., 324.
48. P. A. Florenskii, "Mysl' i iazyk," in *Sochineniia v dvukh tomakh*, 2 vols. (Leningrad: Pravda, 1990), 2:316.
49. Shchutskii, *Kitaiskaia klassicheskaia "Kniga Peremen,"* 253.
50. Ibid., 327.
51. Ibid., 327–38.
52. Ibid., 329.
53. Ibid., 254.
54. Translated into English as "Enthusiasm" in *I Ching*, 1:70.
55. Shchutskii, *Kitaiskaia klassicheskaia "Kniga Peremen,"* 255.
56. Ibid., 333.
57. Ibid., 255.
58. Ibid., 333.
59. Ibid., 333–34.
60. Ibid., 334.
61. Ibid., 335.
62. Sedakova, "Zametki i vospominaniia o raznykh stikhotvoreniiakh, a takzhe Pokhvala poezii," 3:94

Afterword

On Olga Sedakova and Poetic Thinking

DAVID BETHEA

For those of us interested in the ongoing story of Russian poetic culture as that culture reinvents itself in a post-Soviet, postmodern world, Olga Sedakova represents the very best of her tradition, that which survives, as Vladimir Solovyov might say, because it is worthy of surviving. In a volume such as this it is always useful to examine its subject by first identifying her personal lodestars—Pushkin, Mandelstam, Khlebnikov, Dante, Rilke, St. Francis, her grandmother, Averintsev, and so on—that is, those who could be said to "explain" her by parallel study and association. She mentions what these *lichnosti* (a word more semantically loaded than "personality" in English) mean to her, how she came to love them, and how as a poet herself she has tried to absorb their lessons, and *that* is normally how we construct our current understanding of her place in the cultural firmament. Crudely speaking, she is what she has read and thought deeply about, her so-called poetic biography, the potential drama of her personal status vis-à-vis the power structures of the state and its institutions being very much, and consciously so in this case, in the background.

I would like in these closing remarks to flip somewhat the explanation from origins and suggest that the way Sedakova thinks is not only supremely healthy and, as it were, "growth-worthy" in its own right, but also may hold the secret to how poetry as a written phenomenon survives in a world that seems—and I say this without nostalgia or invidious inflection—more and more post-literate.

To situate my comments, I add to the discussion two thinkers who could not be more opposite but who both tried in their time to push the argument about *what should survive culturally* into the future. They felt keenly in their contexts the trend lines for what would eventuate, in the language of today's neo-Darwinian scientists, as biochemical equivalence, or the coevolution of culture and biology through the interlacing messaging of gene, cell, organism, kin, and group. Thus a more sophisticated Lamarckism is being quietly resurrected as a counterbalance to strict Darwinism, the thrust of what is learned and how that learning process takes place ("culture") ramifying outward from the individual (the DNA imprint in the phenotype) to her kin, group, and beyond. The randomness and passivity of the Darwinian algorithm (*nature* does the selecting) are increasingly viewed as mediated, to what extent we cannot yet say, by the cultural choices we make over time. It is in this space between Lamarck and Darwin that the poetic thinking of Sedakova and her tradition—her cultural "kin group"—becomes crucial.

Our first interlocutor is Dmitry Pisarev, bête noire of the 1860s cultural establishment, who wrote the following after the appearance of Nikolai Chernyshevsky's *What Is to Be Done?* (*Chto delat'?*, 1863) and Dostoevsky's *Notes from Underground* (*Zapiski iz podpol'ia*, 1864) and before the serial publication of *Crime and Punishment* (*Prestuplenie i nakazanie*, 1866):

> When readers acquaint themselves with Darwin's ideas, even as the latter are presented in my weak and pale essay, then I will ask them whether we acted well or poorly when we rejected metaphysics, scorned our poetry, and expressed utter contempt for our official aesthetics. Darwin, Lyell and other like thinkers—these are the philosophers, these are the poets, these are the aestheticians of our time.[1]

The second is Solovyov, in his own way equally a gadfly, who argued in his astonishing essay on Darwin, "Beauty in Nature" ("Krasota v prirode," 1889), that the explanation of culture from biology is insufficient and that the function of beauty in the living world is not reducible to and cannot sufficiently be explained by the survival instincts of procreation and sustenance:

> The question "*what is* a known subject?" never corresponds to the question "*from what* or whence *came* that subject?" The question of the origin of aesthetic feelings belongs to the field of biology and psycho-physiology; this, however, in no way resolves or even touches upon the question of what is beauty. [. . .] The breaking down of aesthetic phenomena into originating elements possessing the quality of usefulness or pleasantness is, perhaps, very interesting. But a genuine theory of the beautiful is that which focuses on the actual essence of beauty in all its expressions, both simple and complex.[2]

These two perspectives, I would submit, present the two boundaries between which Sedakova oscillates, sometimes in a wave pattern and other times in a particle pattern, as she writes and thinks about the past, present, and future of the poetic, broadly speaking.

Pisarev is pushing in one direction, Solovyov in the other. Pisarev's direction is, when transposed to aesthetic considerations and expressed in Sedakova's own words, the following:

> The inertia of downward movement is very apparent to me. That has been the vector which art has been pursuing for centuries now, "speculation about degradation." It seems that even in Renaissance times, art attempted to extend the realm of the aesthetic into the nonaesthetic, transmutation into a new, more complex, more spicy harmony which can barely be harmonized . . . But that movement in one direction alone has become senselessly inert . . . When Baudelaire discovered the beauty of the trivial, of evil even, it grabbed his reader's attention as a widening of experience, in its own peculiar way an act of kenosis. It is no accident that in Rilke, the poète maudit is confronted by the image of St Julian, bestowing a kiss upon a leper.
>
> You must understand that when I say that art is free not to find its subject matter in chaos, the gutter and so forth, I do not mean that it should exclude them completely and that we should return to writing idylls about Chloe and anthology pieces about roses. That would be simply dishonest. No, I think that, bearing all that in mind, knowing about it, you can express new experience through the very intensity of language. What does excite me is the intensity of a word, its semantic, phonetic, grammatical force, and it is there that I see new possibilities. [. . .] Ugliness, evil, chaos lack a well-defined image and for that reason our consciousness is incapable of dealing with them. "I looked and went on," as Virgil advised Dante in the Inferno.[3]

Pisarev says that his generation "reject[s] metaphysics, scorn[s] poetry, and expresse[s] utter contempt for official aesthetics" because apparently such categories belong to a cognitive "superstructure" that is somehow less real than the scientific, the empirical, the measurable. He essentializes the aesthetic as something superfluous, merely decorative. The aesthetic should be (his wish at the time) subsumed under the banner of heroic science. Sedakova answers that this betting on "downward movement," this undermining of the aesthetic in the name of a more grainy and degraded reality can, if pushed too far, become the realm of the "senselessly inert." By that she means that the aesthetic has come close to being attenuated out of existence and that "the intensity of the word" is under threat of losing its unique power to signify. And this is where we need minds like Solovyov's pushing in the other direction.

Solovyov, the quirky Neoplatonist, unites poetry and thought with an appreciation of modern scientific discovery, all the while operating unpinioned from rigid dogma and fundamentalist church authority. "Truth," "Beauty," and "Goodness" are not, for Solovyov, abstract essences distinct from the language expressing them or the actions embodying them; rather, they are life-affirming energy flows that emanate outward from a common source (what he would call the three hypostases of "God" if forced to express matters in theological terms) into the changing, adapting, material world ("Sophia"). The problem for Solovyov, and for Sedakova after him, is that these energy flows, like Werner Heisenberg's wave, cannot be captured in words, because, like Heisenberg's particles, they are always already in motion, hence not susceptible to snapshots. But to understand culture we need both the wave and the particles, and in this respect we cannot do without poetic language and poetic thought, which embodies the motion with stationary symbols on the page.

This is also where the beautiful (*prekrasnoe*) comes in. Solovyov introduces the concept back into the discussion of Darwin's discoveries by pointing to the inherent "ugliness" (*bezobrazie* = absence of *obraz*, or of an order trying to be born) of a worm, an organism defined primarily by procreation (its "massive sexual organs")[4] and feeding (endosmosis, or the sucking in of nutrients all across its surface). Ugliness then is what happens in the natural world when the beautiful (*prekrasnoe*), as expressed in a parts-to-whole arrangement of the species, has not yet emerged sufficiently from primitive survival instincts. Likewise, the intricate design on a crustacean's shell covering over the unsightly and vulnerable creature underneath. The poet in Solovyov sees that the nightingale's song is not the same as the rooftop caterwauling of a sexually aroused tomcat. "The question '*what is* a known subject?' never corresponds to the question '*from what* or whence *came* that subject?'" The scientist dismisses the nightingale-tomcat contrast as intelligent design wishful thinking; the poet embraces the difference as reason for being.

Thus, if not explicitly then implicitly, poetic language and poetic thought have always understood where modern-day astrophysics is going with its logic: the universe began with an immense jolt of energy, which over countless millennia is dispersing and gradually losing its heat and light. And since culture mirrors the natural world, and all living things by definition die, its heat and light are also dispersing over time. The "downward movement" of which Sedakova speaks—culture's reaction to the progressive satisfaction of survival needs by dispensing with religious myth and absorbing more and more of the "spicy harmony" of the everyday and the trivial—has eventuated in an opposite and equal reaction: her heroes—Dante, Pushkin, Mandelstam, Khlebnikov, Rilke—having to lift up this ever heavier burden with poetic words of commensurate power. Looked at this way, Dante *anticipates* Stephen Hawking, only the energy dispersed by the Big Bang and proving there is no God is restored to the black hole ("white hole"?) of the Empyrean, the poet's words as astrophysics fueled by love in *Paradiso*. "What does excite me is the intensity of a word, its semantic, phonetic, grammatical force, and it is there that I see new possibilities." The question is, can poetic words of equal force still be found?

Which brings us to the issue of *lichnost'*, poetic personhood, the coexistence of form and content, the individual and her style. Nikolai Gogol famously identified Pushkin as Russian man in his ideal composition, as he would appear in two hundred years. What he meant by this, among other things, is that between Pushkin the person and Pushkin the artist/writer there was a seamless fit. Mandelstam, perhaps Sedakova's favorite hero after Pushkin, was equally filled with the poetic, and her comments about the concordance between person and style in Mandelstam's case go to the core of her own value system with regard to poetry's role as a counterweight to the downward movement of culture writ large. "Yesterday has not yet been born. [. . .] I want Ovid, Pushkin, and Catullus to live once more"—these are also precisely Sedakova's sentiments as she talks about her hero.[5] Once again, however, as critics struggling with the notion of poetic identity we can tend to repeat ourselves; we explain Mandelstam and his creations by referring to the "womb world" of his Riga grandparents that he "fled, always fled."[6] Here then we make the mistake of merging the tomcat's noise with the nightingale's song. Thankfully, Sedakova gets it exactly right: "Style is not 'man' as 'originality' [*samobytnost'*], but man as a restricting and opening of self, which extends beyond the limits of his unique given reality by narrowing and adapting that self to something else, something clearly understood as both external imperative and internal desire all at once" (3:75).[7] The personhood described here is self-contradictory ("restricting and opening") because it is moving toward a fit that is never finished and because it feels a force and a need to adapt to that force at the same time. In this world everything is included, nothing ignored—once again, the all-encompassing "downward movement." Aesthetics defined broadly enough that they become ethics, pathos, and cheap sentimentality for effect are, as in Pushkin, bad taste.[8] There is a chasteness in this personhood, a hesitancy to expose the vulnerable, throbbing plasm underneath the exquisitely designed shell—indeed the chasteness has to do with the fact that shell and creature, poem and person, form and content are attached to each other, *are* each other. This is the parts-to-whole and whole-to-parts feedback loop, or, in Aristotelian terms, entelechy, that is essential to Lamarckism on the one hand and poetic thinking on the other. The giraffe—Lamarck's most famous example—survives in each generation of *Homo sapiens* by growing its neck *culturally*, which is to say, by joining the poet's person, the poet's language, and the poet's place in time through a sacrificial act of love.

Now, if we look for a moment at Mandelstam's haunting Lamarck poem ("Lamark," 1932) within the context of Sedakova's comments about the poet's chasteness, we catch a glimpse of how "beauty in [human] nature" emerges:

Был старик, застенчивый как мальчик,
Неуклюжий, робкий патриарх . . .
Кто за честь природы фехтовальщик?
Ну, конечно, пламенный Ламарк.

Если всё живое лишь помарка
За короткий выморочный день,
На подвижной лестнице Ламарка
Я займу последнюю ступень.[9]

There lived a man, shy like a young boy,
A very awkward, timid patriarch . . .
Whom to defend its honor did Nature employ?
What fiery fencer? But of course, Lamarck.

If living things are tiny ink blot marks
Frail evidence of a short, heirless day,
Then on this mobile ladder of Lamarck's
The final rung I'll gladly take.[10]

Here we see the impossible contrasts that go into a poetic nature: old, bashful, childlike, awkward, patriarchal. They do not "explain" anything. Put them all together, however, create sound and sense out of them, and we get the fiery scientist who fences for the honor and glory of nature. By virtue of a metempsychosis, a spiritual wave pattern, that makes Mandelstam both the fencer himself and the world he imaginatively names, the poet gladly takes his position on the lowest rung (which is also the highest rung, but out of modesty he does not say this) of the evolutionary ladder.

К кольчецам спущусь и к усоногим,
Прошуршав средь ящериц и змей,
По упругим сходням, по излогам
Сокращусь, исчезну, как Протей.

The annelids and cirripeds I'll visit,
With snakes and lizards rustle in the grass,

Down stiffened gangways, shapeless bridges
I'll shrink and disappear, like Proteus.

In this Lamarckian realm the poet will follow the inroads and declivities of lower order phyla and genera all the way back to the origins of life, where he will disappear into the plasm like Proteus, a.k.a. Pushkin himself. However, because Lamarck, not Darwin, is also Joseph Stalin's choice, the changes that will be wrought in him by his historical moment will be painful, even torturous. Indeed, the physical transformations the poet *willingly* takes on in the following stanzas (donning horn-shaped capes, foreswearing warm blood, growing suction cups) sound nothing so much as the Isaiah-inspired seraph's brutal refashioning of the speaker's body in Pushkin's "Prophet" ("Prorok," 1826):

Он сказал: довольно полнозвучья,—
Ты напрасно Моцарта любил:
Наступает глухота паучья,
Здесь провал сильнее наших сил.

И от нас природа отступила
Так, как будто мы ей не нужны,
И продольный мозг она вложила,
Словно шпагу, в темные ножны.

И подъемный мост она забыла,
Опоздала опустить для тех,
У кого зеленая могила,
Красное дыханье, гибкий смех . . .

He said: enough of harmony, sonority,—
You loved that Mozart piece in vain:
A spidery deafness now comes over me,
This force is stronger than our strength.

And from us Nature stepped aside
Not caring if we breathed,
A longitudinal brain she slipped inside
Like a sword in its dark sheath.

An elevated bridge she didn't provide,
She was too late to lower it for those,

Whose graves are green and not as bright,
Whose breath is red, whose laughter supply grows.

In the Stalinist age that the poet inhabits, God/the natural order is dead. Mozart's music has no place, a line that anticipates Adorno's famous apothegm about the fate of poetry after Auschwitz. Nature is leaving the scene because there is nothing natural about what is happening. Man's cruelty to man is much more than is necessary to survive; it is the apocalypse. The longitudinal brain that supposedly defines humans has been wedged in the skull like a sword in its dark sheath; placed where that sword is no longer available to be drawn and wielded by the fiery fencing master. Drawbridge raised and escape blocked, all that remains of the Lamarckian magic are the verbal traces of the living sacrifice: the grave that is green (life growing out of death?), the breath that is red (the flaming swordsman's movements through the air?), the laughter that is resilient (the poet's subversive humor?). To oscillate between the particle and the wave, to be in history but also to ride it, is usually tragic.

Sedakova's thinking is heir to Mandelstam's and Pushkin's. Her time is different and so her response to that time is different. When we look at the particles that fix her momentarily—the thorny rose of her ecumenical Christianity; the biblical motifs that do not seem to translate into plot or personal myth; the sensitive readings of important fellow poets; the quiet facility with the complex disciplines of philosophy, philology, and folklore—we lose sight of the wave and where it is moving. Yes, it is important that we collect the "bits" of the poetic *oblik* (person, linguistic context) that is Sedakova, whether the Dante and Rilke references, the youthful association with "Venichka" and his prodigal son, "life creation" (*zhiznetvorchestvo*), the cultural "potlatch" with Pope John Paul II, the generational links with Elena Shvarts and Viktor Krivulin in the "deaf time" (*glukhoe vremia*) following the departure of Brodsky to the West, and so on.[11] They are real. And yet, where is the *wave* moving and where is the *oblik* in the wave? I would say it is moving away from the celebration of heroic personality, a theme suggested often by Brodsky, toward a heroism that is maximally modest and invisible, one that embodies the sacrifice and pain of contemporary existence and does not reflect the suffering back upon itself: "*it is no longer about me.*" Sedakova's definition of "lyric material"? It sounds very much like the order trying to be born out of ugliness which Solovyov described. It is, literally, the organic form in which a consciousness worthy of survival begins. It is not "about" life; it is life.[12]

Notes

1. Cited from Dmitrii Pisarev, "Progress v mire zhivotnykh i rastenii," *Russkoe slovo* 4 (April 1864): 9. Translations here and subsequently by the author, unless otherwise noted.

2. V. Solov'ev, *Sobranie sochinenii,* 10 vols. (St. Petersburg: Prosveshchenie, 1911–14), 6:37.

3. Ol'ga Sedakova, "Excerpts from an Interview with Valentina Polukhina," 1994, http://www.olgasedakova.com/eng/interview/1058, accessed March 17, 2018.

4. Vladimir Solov'ev, "Krasota v prirode," in *Sobranie sochinenii,* 6:62–63.

5. Citation from Osip Mandelstam, "The Word and Culture," in *The Collected Critical Prose and Letters,* ed. Jane Gary Harris, trans. Jane Gary Harris and Constance Link (London: Collins Harvill, 1991), 113.

6. Cited phrases from Osip Mandelstam, *The Noise of Time: The Prose of Osip Mandelstam,* trans. Clarence Brown (San Francisco, CA: North Point Press, 1986), 77.

7. English translation by the author. For a different translation, see Olga Sedakova, *In Praise of Poetry,* trans. Caroline Clark, Ksenia Golubovich, and Stephanie Sandler (Rochester, NY: Open Letter Press, 2014), 168.

8. See the comments in Sedakova's essay "Pokhvala poezii," 3:73.

9. Osip Mandel'shtam, *Polnoe sobranie stikhotvorenii* (St. Petersburg: Akademicheskii proekt, 1995), 213–14. Subsequent citations from the poem in Russian from this source.

10. Here and below, translation by Misha Semenov, from http://www.mishasemenov.com/writings/lamarck, accessed March 17, 2018.

11. The named poets can be easily traced, but it is worth explaining that "Venichka" is Venedikt Erofeev (1938–90) and the prodigal son refers to the hero of his novel *Moscow to the End of the Line* (*Moskva-Petushki,* first published 1973).

12. "It [*liricheskaia materiia*] exists only under the condition that some meaning radiates outward while within the personality of the poet there shows forth that necessary 'monumental personality' whose entire essence is directed toward the unobstructed apprehension of that meaning" (3:90).

Chronology

Books by Olga Sedakova, including Translations

Vrata, Okna, Arki. Paris: YMCA-Press, 1986.

Kitaiskoe puteshestvie; Stely i nadpisi; Starye pesni. Moscow: Carte Blanche, 1990.

Stikhi. Moscow: Gnozis, Carte Blanche, 1994.

Paul Claudel. *Izveshchenie Marii.* Translated by Ol'ga Sedakova. Moscow: Casa di Matriona, 1999.

Nashe polozhenie: Obraz nastoiashchego. Coauthored with V. Bibikhin, S. Khoruzhii, A. Akhutin, A. Vustin, and A. Smaina-Velikanova. Moscow: Izdatel'stvo gumanitarnoi literatury, 2000.

Dvukhtomnoe sobranie sochinenii. 2 vols. Vol. 1: *Stikhi*; Vol. 2: *Proza.* Moscow: En Ef K'iu/Tu Print, 2001.

Kitaiskoe puteshestvie. Moscow: Graal', 2001.

Puteshestvie volkhvov: Izbrannoe. Moscow: Itaka, Logos, 2001.

Poems and Elegies. Edited by Slava I. Yastremski. Lewisburg, PA: Bucknell University Press, 2003.

Starye pesni. Moscow: Lokus-Press, 2003.

Poetika obriada: Pogrebal'naia obriadnost' vostochnykh i iuzhnykh slavian. Moscow: Indrik, 2004.

Tserkovnoslaviano-russkie paronimy: Materialy k slovariu. Moscow: Greko-latinskii kabinet Iu. A. Shichalina, 2005.

Puteshestvie volkhvov: Izbrannoe. Moscow: Russkii put', 2005.

Dva puteshestviia. Moscow: Logos, 2005.

Muzyka: Stikhi i proza. Moscow: Russkii mir, 2006.

Posredstvennost' kak sotsial'naia opasnost'. Arkhangelsk: Pravda Severa, 2006.

Kak ia prevrashchalas'. Moscow: Tim Partners, 2006.

Dve knigi: Starye pesni; Tristan i Izol'da. St. Petersburg: Izdatel'stvo Sergeia Khodova, 2008.

Slovar' trudnykh slov iz bogosluzheniia: Tserkovnoslaviano-russkie paronimy. Moscow: Greko-latinskii cabinet Iu. A. Shichalina, 2008.

Khriuntik Mamuntik. Moscow: Tim Partners, 2009.

Apologia razuma. Moscow: MGIU, 2009.

Vse, i srazu: Kniga stikhotvorenii. St. Petersburg: Izdatel'stvo Pushkinskogo fonda, 2009.

François Fédier. *Golos druga*. Translated by Ol'ga Sedakova. St. Petersburg: Izdatel'stvo Ivana Limbakha, 2010; second edition 2018.

Chetyre toma. Vol. 1: *Stikhi*; Vol. 2: *Perevody*; Vol. 3: *Poetica*; Vol. 4: *Moralia*. Moscow: Universitet Dmitriia Pozharskogo/Russkii fond sodeistviia obrazovaniiu i nauke, 2010.

Posredstvennost' kak sotsial'naia opasnost'. Moscow: Magistr, 2011.

John Donne. *Po kom zvonit kolokol*... Translated by Ol'ga Sedakova. Moscow: Enigma, 2012.

Apologiia razuma. Moscow: Russkii put', 2013.

Tri puteshestviia. Moscow: Novoe literaturnoe obozrenie, 2013.

Paul Tillich. *Muzhestvo byt'*. Translated by Ol'ga Sedakova. Kyiv: Dukh i Litera, 2013.

Philippe Jaccottet. *V komnatakh sadov: Dans les chambres des vergers*. Translated by Ol'ga Sedakova. Moscow: Art-Volkhonka, 2014.

Sad mirozdan'ia. Moscow: Art-Volkhonka, 2014.

Stely i nadpisi. St. Petersburg: Izdatel'stvo Ivana Limbakha, 2014.

Zametki i vospominaniia o raznykh stikhotvoreniiakh, a takzhe Pokhvala poezii. St. Petersburg: Izdatel'stvo Akademiia issledovanii kul'tury, 2015.

Stikhotvoreniia shagi. Moscow: Art-Volkhonka, 2017.

Mariiny slezy: K poetike liturgicheskikh pesnopenii. Kyiv: Dukh i Litera, 2017.

Mariiny slezy: Poetika liturgicheskikh pesnopenii; Kommentarii k pravoslavnomu bogosluzheniiu. Moscow: Blagochestie, 2017.

Puteshestvie s otkrytymi glazami: Pis'ma o Rembrandte. St. Petersburg: Izdatel'stvo Ivana Limbakha, 2017.

Lewis Carroll. *Alisa v strane chudes: Skazochnaia povest'*. St. Petersburg: Vita Nova, 2017.

Izbrannoe. St. Petersburg: Azbuka-Attikus, 2018.

Translations of Olga Sedakova's Writings into Other Languages

The Silk of Time: Bilingual Selected Poems. Edited by Valentina Polukhina. Keele: Ryburn Publishing, Keele University Press, 1994.

The Wild Rose. Translated into English by Richard McKane. London: Approach Publishers, 1997.

Mizmorim yeshanim. Translated into Hebrew by Hamutal Bar Josef. Jerusalem: Karmel Publishing House, 1997.

Die Reise nach Brjansk: Zwei Erzählungen. Translated into German by Erich Klein and Valeria Jager. Vienna: Folio Verlag, 2000.

Éloge de la poésie. Translated into French by Ghislaine Capogna Bardet. Lausanne: Âge d'Homme, 2001.

Le voyage en Chine et autres poèmes. Translated into French by Léon Robel and Marie-Noëlle Pane. Paris: Caractères, 2001.

Kinesisk Rejse og andre digte. Translated into Danish by Mette Dalsgaard. Copenhagen: Borgens, 2004.

Voyage à Tartu & Retour: Poésie & antropologie; Quelques remarques sur l'art de la traduction. Translated into French by Philippe Arjakovsky. Paris: Clémence Hiver, 2005.

Lëkurës rrjedh shikimi: Poezi. Translated into Albanian by Argon Tufa. Tirana: Bodimet ideart, 2006.

Voyage à Briansk: Le don de la liberté; Quelques mots sur la poésie sur sa fin, son commencement et sa continuation. Translated into French by Marie Noëlle Pane. Paris: Clémence Hiver, 2008.

Solo nel fuoco si semina il fuoco. Translated into Italian and edited by A. Mainardi. Bose: Edizioni Quiqajon, 2008.

Apologia della ragione. Translated into Italian by Giovanna Parravicini. Milan: Edizioni La Casa di Matriona, 2009.

Freedom to Believe: Philosophical and Cultural Essays. Translated into English and edited by Slava I. Yastremski and Michael Naydan. Lewisburg, PA: Bucknell University Press, 2010.

Naikrashchyi universytet: Epokha, osoba, tradytsiia. Translated into Ukrainian. Kyiv: Dukh i Litera, 2011.

Portar, Fönster, Valv. Translated into Swedish by Mikael Nydahl. Stockholm: Wahlström & Widstrand, 2012.

Elogio della poesia: Versi e saggi di Olga Sedakova. Translated into Italian by Francesca Chessa. Rome: Aracne, 2013.

Les Métamorphoses d'Olia. Translated into French by Gabriella Giandelli. Paris: Actes Sud, 2014.

Zavzhdy ie krok. Translated into Ukrainian by Valeriia Bohuslavs'ka. Kyiv: Vydavnychyi dim Dmytra Buraho, 2014.

Sami mogzauroba. Translated into Georgian. Tbilisi: Kavkazskii dom, 2014.

In Praise of Poetry. Translated into English and edited by Caroline Clark, Ksenia Golubovich, and Stephanie Sandler. Rochester, NY: Open Letter, 2014.

Chinese reis en andere gedichten. Edited and translated into Dutch by Alexandre Popowycz and Hubert Du Vogelaere. Amsterdam: Pegasus en Stichting Slavische Literatur, 2015.

Anioł Reims i inne wiersze. Edited and translated into Polish by Adam Pomorski. Wrocław and Wojnowice: Kolegium Europy Wschodniej, 2016.

Notes on Contributors

DAVID BETHEA is the Vilas Research Professor Emeritus of Slavic Languages and Literatures at the University of Wisconsin–Madison. Among his books about Russian literature are *Joseph Brodsky and the Creation of Exile* (1994), *Realizing Metaphors: Alexander Pushkin and the Life of the Poet* (1998), and *The Superstitious Muse: Thinking Russian Literature Mythopoetically* (2009). He edited *The Pushkin Handbook* (2005), and he is the lead editor for the collected works of Alexander Pushkin, in progress in Russian. Most recently he has coedited, with Siggy Frank, a volume entitled *Nabokov in Context* (2018).

BETHANY BRALEY received her PhD from Indiana University in 2015. Her scholarly translations include A. M. Panchenko's "Laughter as Spectacle" (translated with Priscilla Hunt and Svitlana Kobets) and E. Iwaniec's *History of the Old Believers in Poland* (forthcoming, ed. Jeff Holdeman). A chapter of her dissertation—"Extroverting the Cultural Interior: Symbolic Renovations in Recent Polish and Russian Verse"—is dedicated to the ideas of spiritual freedom and ecumenicity in the poetry and thought of Olga Sedakova.

NATALIA CHERNYSH is a *dotsent* in the Department of Comparative Philology at Dnipro National University in Ukraine. She defended her dissertation on Olga Sedakova's *Chinese Journey* in 2011. Her interests include contemporary and classical Chinese poetry, questions in poetics, and theories and practice of translation.

GABRIELLA A. FERRARI is a PhD candidate in the Department of Slavic Languages and Literatures at Princeton University, where she is writing a dissertation on the material language of Soviet propaganda. She holds a BA in classics and Slavic studies from Brown University and is fluent in Italian, English, and

Russian. Her wider research interests focus on the intersection of language and image in Soviet culture.

KSENIA GOLUBOVICH is a Russian writer, philologist, editor, and translator living in Moscow. She holds a graduate degree in English literature from Moscow State University. An organizer of the *Dictionary of War* project, she is an editor at the Logos publishing house and has translated works of philosophy, cultural theory, and literature into Russian, from Bruce Chatwin to Charles Sanders Pierce and Ezra Pound. Her translation into English of the poem *Tristan and Isolde* appears in Olga Sedakova's *In Praise of Poetry* (2014). Her publications in Russian include three books of fiction as well as an annotated translation of William Butler Yeats's *A Vision* (2000). In English, she has published in *Seven Poets, Four Days, One Book* (2009).

EMILY R. GROSHOLZ is Edwin Erle Sparks Professor of Philosophy, African American Studies, and English at the Pennsylvania State University. She has served as an advisory editor for the *Hudson Review* for thirty years. She edited *The Legacy of Simone de Beauvoir* (2004) and has published books and essays on early modern philosophy and philosophy of mathematics and science; her book *Starry Reckoning: Reference and Analysis in Mathematics and Cosmology* (2016) was awarded the 2017 Fernando Gil International Prize for Philosophy of Science. Her eighth book of poetry is *The Stars of Earth: New and Selected Poems* (2017), which follows *Proportions of the Heart: Poems That Play with Mathematics* (2014) and *Childhood* (2014), a book that has raised $3500 for UNICEF and been translated into Japanese, Italian, French, and German. Her book *Great Circles: The Transits of Mathematics and Poetry* appeared in 2018.

ANDREW KAHN is a professor of Russian at Oxford University and a fellow at St. Edmund Hall. He has written widely about the Russian Enlightenment in its European context and published several books on Alexander Pushkin, including *Pushkin's Lyric Intelligence* (2008). He is a coauthor with Mark Lipovetsky, Irina Reyfman, and Stephanie Sandler of *A History of Russian Literature* (2018).

MARTHA M. F. KELLY is an associate professor of Russian studies at the University of Missouri and the author of *Unorthodox Beauty: Russian Modernism and Its New Religious Aesthetic* (2016). She coedited, with Sibelan Forrester, the anthology *Russian Silver Age Poetry: Texts and Contexts* (2015). She is currently working on a book-length project tentatively entitled "How to Be a Russian Poet: The Public Life of Olga Sedakova."

MARIA KHOTIMSKY is a senior lecturer and coordinator of the Russian language program at MIT, where she is on the faculty of the Global Studies and Languages Department. She has published widely on nineteenth- and twentieth-century Russian poetry, the history and theory of poetic translation in the Soviet Union, and literary translingualism.

MARGARITA KRIMMEL studied philology at Novosibirsk State Technical University and has worked as principal editor for the website www.olgasedakova.com and for numerous books by Olga Sedakova, including the authoritative four-volume edition cited throughout this volume. She lives in Moscow.

ILYA KUKULIN received his PhD in literary theory at the Russian State University for the Humanities, Moscow, and is an associate professor (*dotsent*) at the Higher School of Economics in Moscow. He is the author of a Russian-language monograph on montage and aesthetics (*Mashiny zashumevshego vremeni: Kak sovetskii montazh stal metodom neofitsial'noi kul'tury*, 2015), which won the Andrei Bely Prize. He has written about the history of education and the cultural practices of the internal colonization in Russia, unofficial social thought, new media, and modern and contemporary poetry. His poetry has appeared in numerous journals and in book form (*Beidevind*, 2009). The Russian-language version of his essay in this volume won the Russian-Italian Literary Award Bella in 2017.

ALEKSANDR KUTYRKIN holds a candidate's degree in philosophy and writes on theology, philosophy, and theories of culture. This is his first essay to appear in English.

KETEVAN MEGRELISHVILI is a lecturer and academic researcher at the Institute of Slavic Studies, Ruprecht-Karls University in Heidelberg, Germany. She has published essays on Paul Celan and Olga Sedakova and is generally interested in problems in the translation of poetry, Russian-German literary relations, and the history of twentieth-century Russian poetry. This is her first essay to appear in English.

AINSLEY MORSE is a scholar, teacher, and translator of Russian and former Yugoslav literatures. Recent translations include *Kholin 66: Diaries and Poems by Igor Kholin* (2017) and Vsevolod Nekrasov's *I Live I See* (2013), both with Bela Shayevich, as well as Andrei Sen-Senkov's *Anatomical Theater* (2014), with Peter Golub. Along with Maria Vassileva and Maya Vinokour, she has edited and contributed her translations to Linor Goralik, *Found Life* (2018). Also published in

2018 were translations of the farcical Soviet pastoral production novel *Beyond Tula,* by Andrei Egunov, and *Permanent Evolution,* a collection of theoretical essays by the Formalist critic Yuri Tynianov, cotranslated with Philip Redko.

OLEG NOVIKOV is a cofounder of the Foundation for Research in Logic and Philosophy (Fond Logiko-filosofskikh issledovanii) in Moscow, which has supported several major research projects in the humanities, including an English-Russian dictionary of logic (*Anglo-russkii slovar' po logike,* in progress). His degree is from the Philosophy Faculty of Moscow State University.

BENJAMIN PALOFF is an associate professor of Slavic languages and literatures and of comparative literature at the University of Michigan, Ann Arbor. He is the author of *Lost in the Shadow of the Word: Space, Time, and Freedom in Interwar Eastern Europe* (2016) and of the poetry collections *And His Orchestra* (2015) and *The Politics* (2011). His many translations include Richard Weiner's *The Game for Real* (2015) and Marek Bieńczyk's *Transparency* (2012).

PHILIPP PENKA received his PhD in Slavic languages and literatures from Harvard University in 2016. He lives and works in Berlin, Germany.

VERA POZZI holds a PhD in philosophy from the University of Milan. In 2017–18 she was a postdoctoral research fellow at the National Research University Higher School of Economics (Moscow). She has published a translation into Italian of Olga Sedakova's essay "The Light of Life." Her scholarly interests include Russian intellectual culture and contemporary Orthodox lay thinkers.

SARAH PRATT is a professor of Slavic languages and literatures and vice provost for graduate programs at the University of Southern California. Her published work includes *Nikolai Zabolotsky: Enigma and Cultural Paradigm* (2000) as well as studies of Tiutchev, Baratynsky, Russian women's autobiography, the writings of Lydia Ginzburg, and the interconnections between poetry and icons in twentieth-century Russian culture.

PHILIP REDKO is a translator and editor. A collection of Yuri Tynianov's essays on literature and film, *Permanent Evolution,* cotranslated with Ainsley Morse, appeared in 2018. He lives in Cambridge, Massachusetts.

STEPHANIE SANDLER is the Ernest E. Monrad Professor and Chair of the Slavic Department at Harvard University. She writes about and translates contemporary Russian poetry and has also written about Pushkin, including *Commemorating Pushkin: Russia's Myth of a National Poet* (2004). She has been involved in a number of collaborative scholarly projects; the most recent is *A History of Russian Literature,* coauthored with Andrew Kahn, Mark Lipovetsky, and Irina Reyfman (2018). With Caroline Clark and Ksenia Golubovich, she edited and translated Olga Sedakova's *In Praise of Poetry* (2014).

HENRIEKE STAHL is a professor in the Slavic Department at the University of Trier, Germany. Her research focuses on Russian Symbolism, Russian religious philosophy and poetry, and contemporary poetry. She is a coeditor of a Russian-language volume of essays on contemporary Russian experimental poetry (*Imidzh—dialog—eksperiment: Polia sovremennoi russkoi poezii,* 2013) and the author of a German-language monograph about Andrei Bely's novels (2002). She is the director of the DFG Center for Advanced Studies "Russian-Language Poetry in Transition."

MARIA P. VASSILEVA is a poet, translator, and graduate student in Slavic at Harvard University. Her work has appeared in *The Virginia Quarterly Review, Modern Poetry in Translation,* and *Ploughshares.* Along with Ainsley Morse and Maya Vinokour, she has edited and contributed her translations to Linor Goralik's *Found Life* (2018).

SARAH VITALI is a PhD candidate in Slavic languages and literatures at Harvard University. Her published translations from Russian include Linor Goralik's short story "Agatha Goes Home" in the collection *Found Life* (2017) and Vladislav Khodasevich's memoir *Necropolis* (2019). She also translates poetry from Russian, Bosnian-Croatian-Serbian, and French.

Index

Individual works are indexed under their original title as well as their English-language title. Under the entry "Sedakova, Olga (works by)," titles are given in English and in Russian; for works with more than one English-language title, all versions appear.